Earthmoving Equipment Operations

Richard Skiba

Copyright © 2024 by Richard Skiba

All rights reserved.

No portion of this book may be reproduced in any form without written permission from the publisher or author, except as permitted by copyright law.

This publication is designed to provide accurate and authoritative information in regard to the subject matter covered. While the publisher and author have used their best efforts in preparing this book, they make no representations or warranties with respect to the accuracy or completeness of the contents of this book and specifically disclaim any implied warranties of merchantability or fitness for a particular purpose. No warranty may be created or extended by sales representatives or written sales materials. The advice and strategies contained herein may not be suitable for your situation. You should consult with a professional when appropriate. Neither the publisher nor the author shall be liable for any loss of profit or any other commercial damages, including but not limited to special, incidental, consequential, personal, or other damages.

Skiba, Richard (author)

Earthmoving Equipment Operations

ISBN 978-1-76350-134-8 (paperback) 978-1-76350-135-5 (eBook) 978-1-76350-136-2 (Hardcover)

Non-fiction

Contents

Preface	1
1. Introduction	3
2. Skid Steer Operations	18
3. Loader Operations	85
4. Backhoe/Loader Operations	148
5. Excavator Operations	202
6. Dozer Operations	270
7. Water Truck Operations	321
8. Haul Truck Operations	355
9. Surfacing Operations	430
10. Earthmoving in Mining and Civil Construction Work Environments	478
11. Operator Calculations	503
References	527
Index	529

Preface

This book covers a selective range of earthmoving equipment, specifically skid steers, front end loaders, backhoes, excavators, dozers, water trucks, haul and tip trucks, stabilizers and roller compactors. For each of these, the uses, key components, operating principles, preparation for operations, operational practices, safe operation and finalising operations is covered.

The earthmoving equipment information provided within this book is intended to be general in nature and may not encompass all aspects of its operation. It is important to note that each item of plant or equipment has its own specific characteristics and operational requirements that may vary. Earthmoving equipment operators are strongly advised to consult the manufacturer's guides and manuals prior to the operation of any equipment to ensure compliance with safety standards and operational procedures.

Furthermore, it is crucial to acknowledge that operations and terminology can differ across jurisdictions. Earthmoving equipment operators should be aware that regulations and guidelines pertaining to equipment usage may vary depending on the location. Therefore, it is essential for equipment operators to familiarize themselves with the applicable laws, regulations, and standards in their respective jurisdictions.

Additionally, earthmoving equipment operators are urged to review workplace policies and procedures before operating any equipment. Workplace-specific protocols may exist to address unique hazards and safety considerations, which must be adhered to for safe operations.

Moreover, it is important to recognize that in many jurisdictions, operational licensing requirements apply. Earthmoving equipment operators are responsible for ensuring that they meet all jurisdictional legislative requirements relevant to their sites of practice. This may include obtaining appropriate licenses, certifications, or permits to operate cranes legally and safely within their jurisdiction.

Sample load charts, specifications, interpretations and calculations are used throughout this book for demonstration purposes only and should not be taken to be used in any other manner. Every equipment model is accompanied by its own distinct operational charts and characteristics, which may vary depending on the equipment's configurations and rated capacity and is supplied by the equipment's manufacturer. They are not portable from one model to another, and operators must always ensure they are referring to documentation relevant to the plant they are operating.

While efforts have been made to provide accurate and informative equipment operation information, users are reminded of the need for due diligence and compliance with applicable regulations, manufacturer guidelines, workplace policies, and licensing requirements to ensure safe and lawful crane operations.

Chapter One

Introduction

Earthmoving equipment refers to a broad category of heavy machinery designed for various tasks related to moving earth, soil, rocks, and other materials during construction, excavation, mining, landscaping, and agricultural activities. These machines are used to manipulate the earth's surface for purposes such as grading, leveling, excavating, digging, and transporting materials. Some common types of earthmoving equipment include bulldozers, excavators, backhoes, wheel loaders, dump trucks, graders, trenchers, and skid steer loaders. Each type of equipment serves specific functions and is essential in different stages of construction and earthmoving projects.

Earthmoving encompasses the process of relocating large volumes of soil using heavy machinery, typically employed for excavating building foundations and transporting materials to and from construction sites.

Additionally, earthmoving equipment plays a crucial role in clearing debris, vegetation, and obstacles from designated areas. Its applications extend to excavating trenches, facilitating mining operations, and ensuring proper grading.

Furthermore, this equipment is indispensable for prepping land for various projects, including residential developments, civil engineering endeavours such as road construction, drainage systems, bridges, and parking facilities, among others. Essentially, earthmoving serves as the backbone of infrastructure and construction initiatives.

A diverse array of earthmoving machinery exists, ranging from compact units tailored for confined spaces to industrial-grade behemoths found in extensive mining and quarry operations. These machines may utilize steel or rubber tracks or heavy-duty tyres, depending on their intended use.

Each piece of earthmoving machinery is purpose-built, with some models designed for excavation and soil relocation, others for material transport, and yet others for compaction tasks. Specialized equipment is available for grading, creating inclines, trenching, and various ground-cutting operations. Moreover, versatile machinery is capable of multifunctionality, catering to a wide range of earthmoving requirements.

While the range of earth-moving equipment is extensive, encompassing everyday vehicles to specialized machinery, let's focus on the primary types commonly used today:

Excavator: Among the most prevalent and indispensable pieces of equipment on construction sites, the excavator is designed for excavation tasks. Comprising components like tracks/wheels, a cab, boom, stick, hydraulic arm, and attachment (usually a metal bucket or scoop), it efficiently removes soil and rocks from one location and deposits them elsewhere. Besides excavation, it performs diverse tasks such as material mixing, site cleaning, pipe laying, demolition, landscaping, trench digging, and more.

Figure 1: A Caterpillar 330 excavator scooping up dirt. Matthew T Rader, CC BY-SA 4.0, via Wikimedia Commons.

Wheel Loader: Crucial for moving heavy materials within construction sites, the wheel loader features a large front bucket or scoop for transporting dirt, rocks, or other materials. Equipped with four large wheels, a cab, booms, hydraulic arm, and a sizable metal bucket, it facilitates tasks like material transportation, loading into other vehicles, backfilling, site cleaning, and lifting.

Figure 2: Komatsu WA150 front end loader. Bob Adams from Amanzimtoti, South Africa, CC BY-SA 2.0, via Wikimedia Commons.

Backhoe Loader: Combining excavation and loading capabilities, the backhoe loader is versatile, featuring a front bucket for loading and a rear-mounted bucket for excavation. Its adaptability is enhanced by the option to replace buckets and loaders with various attachments. Apart from loading and excavation, it can be used for landscaping, material mixing, benching, lifting, trenching, and more.

Figure 3: Case 580 Super N backhoe loader. Daderot, CC0, via Wikimedia Commons.lly generated

Dozer: A heavy-duty machine capable of pushing vast amounts of dirt and rock with its front-mounted blade, the dozer is essential for leveling, drain cutting, and other tasks requiring significant pushing force. It often features a rear-mounted ripper for breaking harder materials. Modern advancements include programmable controls for precision grading.

Figure 4: Komatsu bulldozer pushing coal. Petar Milošević, CC BY-SA 4.0, via Wikimedia Commons.

Skid Steer Loader / Track Loader: Compact, agile, and highly versatile, the skid steer loader is ideal for manoeuvring in tight spaces. Its front attachment can be swapped for various options like a bucket, rotary hoe, dozer blade, hammer, or auger, making it adaptable for tasks such as rock breaking, site cleanup, loading, excavating, and more.

Figure 5: Mustang 2054 skid-steer loader. Orderinchaos, CC BY-SA 4.0 , via Wikimedia Commons.

Dump Trucks: Essential for transporting large quantities of materials within construction sites, dump trucks efficiently move material from one location to another before depositing it at the final destination.

Figure 6: Dump truck. Noorse, CC BY 2.0, via Wikimedia Commons.

Trenchers: Primarily used for digging trenches, trenchers employ a conveyor system to excavate and deposit dirt alongside the trench.

Figure 7: Eagle 6500 wheel trencher. Trencher Expert, CC BY-SA 3.0, via Wikimedia Commons.

Scrapers: Designed for swift movement of dirt across large areas, scrapers excel in digging and leveling tasks on expansive construction sites.

Figure 8: Caterpillar 613C Scraper. Bill Jacobus from Houston, USA, CC BY 2.0, via Wikimedia Commons.

The operational principles of earthmoving equipment vary depending on the type of equipment but generally include the following key aspects:

1. Power Source: Earthmoving equipment is powered by various sources such as diesel engines, electric motors, or hydraulic systems. The power source provides the energy required to operate the equipment's components.

2. Control Systems: Earthmoving equipment is equipped with control systems that enable operators to manage the movement and functions of the machinery. These control systems may include joysticks, levers, pedals, or electronic interfaces.

3. Hydraulic Systems: Many types of earthmoving equipment utilize hydraulic systems to generate power and control move-

ments. Hydraulic fluid is pressurized by a pump and then directed to hydraulic cylinders, motors, or other actuators to move components like booms, buckets, or blades.

4. Mechanical Components: Earthmoving equipment comprises various mechanical components such as tracks, wheels, gears, and bearings. These components facilitate movement, stability, and functionality of the machinery.

5. Attachments: Most earthmoving equipment can be equipped with different attachments to perform specific tasks. For example, excavators may use buckets, augers, or hammers, while bulldozers may use blades or rippers. The attachment is often interchangeable to suit different job requirements.

6. Safety Features: Safety is a paramount concern in the operation of earthmoving equipment. Equipment is designed with safety features such as rollover protection structures (ROPS), falling object protection systems (FOPS), backup alarms, and emergency stop mechanisms to protect operators and bystanders.

7. Maintenance Requirements: Regular maintenance is essential to ensure the proper functioning and longevity of earthmoving equipment. Maintenance tasks may include lubrication, inspection of components, replacement of worn parts, and troubleshooting of mechanical or hydraulic issues.

8. Operator Training: Proper training is necessary for operators to understand the operational principles, safety procedures, and maintenance requirements of earthmoving equipment. Training programs educate operators on equipment controls, techniques for efficient operation, and protocols for safe working practices.

Overall, the operational principles of earthmoving equipment involve the effective utilization of power sources, control systems, hydraulic mechanisms, mechanical components, attachments, safety features, maintenance practices, and operator training to accomplish various construction and excavation tasks efficiently and safely.

Earthmoving equipment operators need to possess a range of knowledge and skills to operate machinery safely and effectively. These include:

1. Equipment Familiarity: Operators should have a thorough understanding of the specific earthmoving equipment they will be operating, including its controls, functions, capabilities, and limitations. This includes knowing how to start and shut down the equipment properly.

2. Safety Procedures: Safety is paramount in the operation of earthmoving equipment. Operators need to be aware of safety protocols and procedures, including the proper use of personal protective equipment (PPE), adherence to site safety regulations, and precautions to prevent accidents, such as rollovers, collisions, or equipment malfunctions.

3. Site Conditions: Operators should assess site conditions before starting work, including terrain, ground stability, obstacles, and overhead hazards. Understanding the site environment helps operators anticipate potential risks and adapt their operating techniques accordingly.

4. Operating Techniques: Effective operation of earthmoving equipment requires skill and precision. Operators need to learn proper operating techniques for tasks such as digging, lifting, grading, pushing, and loading. This includes controlling equipment speed, direction, and attachments to achieve desired results efficiently.

5. Maintenance Awareness: Operators should be aware of basic equipment maintenance practices to ensure machinery remains in optimal working condition. This includes conducting pre-operation inspections, checking fluid levels, greasing moving parts, and reporting any mechanical issues or abnormalities.

6. Communication Skills: Clear communication is essential for safe and efficient operation, especially when working in teams or with ground personnel. Operators should be able to communicate effectively using hand signals, two-way radios, or other communication devices to coordinate movements, signal warnings, and convey instructions.

7. Emergency Procedures: Operators should be familiar with emergency procedures and know how to respond quickly and appropriately in case of accidents, equipment malfunctions, or other emergencies. This includes knowing how to shut down equipment, evacuate the area safely, and administer first aid if necessary.

8. Environmental Considerations: Operators should be mindful of environmental factors such as weather conditions, environmental regulations, and potential impacts on surrounding ecosystems. Minimizing environmental damage and ensuring compliance with regulations are important aspects of responsible equipment operation.

9. Regulatory Compliance: Operators should be aware of relevant regulations and standards governing equipment operation, including licensing requirements, load limits, noise restrictions, and emissions standards. Compliance with these regulations helps ensure safe and legal operation of earthmoving equipment.

By acquiring knowledge and skills in these areas, earthmoving equipment operators can perform their duties safely, efficiently, and responsibly, contributing to successful construction and excavation projects while minimizing risks to personnel and the environment.

Frequently, earthmoving machinery finds application in projects centred around land preparation and laying foundations, typically marking the outset of larger-scale endeavours.

Nevertheless, earthmoving equipment proves invaluable across a spectrum of projects, encompassing mining operations, aggregate quarries, bridge and tunnel construction, site clearance, reservoir and dam development, road and railway infrastructure, municipal constructions, as well as the installation of sewers and underground pipe networks.

The remaining chapters of this book cover the safe operating principles and applications of the following earthmoving equipment:

- Skid Steer Operations

- Loader Operations

- Backhoe/Loader Operations

- Excavator Operations

- Dozer Operations

- Water Truck Operations

- Haul Truck Operations

- Surfacing Operations

There are various reasons why individuals may be drawn to a career as an earthmoving equipment operator. Operating heavy machinery offers a hands-on and dynamic work environment. For those who thrive on physical engagement and enjoy working with their hands, the role of an earthmoving equipment operator can be highly appealing.

Earthmoving equipment operators have the opportunity to work with a diverse range of machinery, including excavators, bulldozers, loaders, graders, and more. This diversity keeps the job stimulating and allows operators to cultivate skills across various types of equipment.

The construction and mining industries, where earthmoving equipment is integral, often provide stable employment prospects. With ongoing demand for infrastructure projects and mining operations, there remains a consistent need for skilled equipment operators.

Earthmoving equipment operators typically receive competitive compensation, particularly as they accrue experience and proficiency in operating different types of machinery. Additionally, opportunities for overtime pay and benefits may be available, depending on the employer.

As at March 2024, in the United States, excavator operators earn an average hourly wage of $24.85 (USD), equivalent to $57,950 annually, with salaries ranging from $41,193 to $81,525. In Australia, the average annual salary for excavator operator positions falls between $130,000 and $150,000 (AUD). Meanwhile, in the United Kingdom, the typical wage for excavator operators is £19.35 per hour or £36,369 annually (GBP), and in Canada, it averages $62,098 per year (CAD) (Indeed, 2024b; Seek, 2024; Seek UK, 2024b; talent.com, 2024).

In Australia, the average annual salary for Dump Truck Operator positions spans from $115,000 to $135,000, with a median salary of $95,693 per year and a salary range of $92,000 to $124,000 for haul truck drivers. Meanwhile, in the United Kingdom, dumper drivers receive an annual median salary of £31,200 or £16 per hour, averaging £17.69 (Glassdoor, 2024; Indeed, 2024b; Seek UK, 2024b).

Backhoe operator salary in United States is $23.81 hourly, or $55,593 annually, with a range from $37,743 to $81,885. In UK, on average backhoe operators are paid £32,886 annually (Indeed, 2024a; Seek UK, 2024a).

Through accumulated experience and additional training, earthmoving equipment operators can progress in their careers and assume roles with greater responsibilities. These roles may include equipment supervisor, site manager, or safety coordinator, offering avenues for professional growth and development.

Many earthmoving equipment operators appreciate the opportunity to work outdoors, often in diverse settings such as construction sites, mining operations, and infrastructure projects. This outdoor work environment provides a refreshing change of scenery and allows individuals to connect with nature while working.

Earthmoving equipment operators play a pivotal role in construction and development endeavours, contributing to the creation of roads, bridges, buildings, and other vital infrastructure. Knowing that their work is fundamental to shaping the built environment can be deeply fulfilling for operators.

Pursuing a career as an earthmoving equipment operator can be an enticing choice for individuals seeking hands-on work, job stability, competitive wages, and the chance to make a meaningful impact in construction and development projects.

Chapter Two

Skid Steer Operations

A skid loader, also known as a skid-steer loader or skidsteer, is a compact, engine-powered machine featuring a rigid frame and lift arms designed to accommodate various labour-saving tools or attachments. Numerous manufacturers produce their own versions of this equipment, including Kubota, Bobcat, Terex, Case, Caterpillar, Gehl Company, Hyundai, JCB, JLG, John Deere, Komatsu, LiuGong, New Holland, Volvo, Wacker Neuson, among others.

Skid-steer loaders are versatile machines used across a wide range of industries and applications due to their compact size, manoeuvrability, and ability to accommodate various attachments. Some common uses of skid-steer loaders include:

1. Construction: Skid-steer loaders are extensively used in construction sites for tasks such as digging, grading, trenching, and material handling. They can manoeuvre easily in tight spaces, making them ideal for tasks in confined areas.

2. Landscaping: Landscapers utilize skid-steer loaders for tasks such as grading, leveling, excavation, and moving materials like soil, mulch, and gravel. They are also used for tasks like tree

removal, stump grinding, and brush clearing.

3. Agriculture: Farmers and ranchers use skid-steer loaders for various agricultural tasks, including feeding livestock, cleaning barns, moving hay bales, and maintaining fences. They are also used for tasks like planting, tilling, and harvesting in smaller-scale operations.

4. Snow Removal: Skid-steer loaders equipped with snowblower or snow plow attachments are commonly used for snow removal in parking lots, driveways, sidewalks, and other areas where larger vehicles may not be suitable.

5. Demolition: Skid-steer loaders are used in demolition projects for tasks such as breaking down structures, removing debris, and clearing sites. Their compact size allows them to work efficiently in confined spaces and navigate around obstacles.

6. Utility Work: Skid-steer loaders are used by utility companies for tasks such as digging trenches for laying pipes and cables, repairing utility lines, and general maintenance of infrastructure.

7. Forestry: In forestry operations, skid-steer loaders are used for tasks such as clearing brush, removing tree stumps, and transporting logs. They are often equipped with forestry-specific attachments for these tasks.

8. Waste Management: Skid-steer loaders are used in waste management facilities for tasks such as loading and unloading dumpsters, sorting recyclables, and managing landfill operations.

9. General Maintenance: Skid-steer loaders are valuable for general maintenance tasks in various settings, including parks, golf courses, campuses, and industrial facilities. They can be used for

tasks such as cleaning, landscaping, and light construction work.

Overall, skid-steer loaders offer versatility and efficiency, making them valuable assets in a wide range of industries and applications.

Skid-steer loaders typically feature four-wheel configurations, with wheels mechanically locked in synchronization on each side. The left-side drive wheels can operate independently from the right-side drive wheels, with no separate steering mechanism. Instead, the machine turns by varying the speed of the wheel pairs, causing the vehicle to skid or drag its fixed-orientation wheels across the ground. The robust frame and durable wheel bearings prevent damage from the torsional forces generated by this skidding motion. Steering is achieved by generating differential velocity at opposing sides of the vehicle.

Figure 9: Mustang 2054 skid-steer loader. Orderinchaos, CC BY-SA 4.0, via Wikimedia Commons.

Similar to tracked vehicles, skid steers can cause significant friction on soft or fragile surfaces, potentially damaging them. However, this can be mitigated by using specialized wheels like the Mecanum wheel, which reduces ground friction. Skid-steer loaders excel in manoeuvrability, capable of executing zero-radius turns, making them valuable for compact and agile loading tasks. Some skid-steer loaders can be fitted with tracks instead of wheels, known as multi-terrain loaders.

In contrast to a traditional front loader, the lift arms of these machines run parallel to the operator, with the pivot points positioned behind the driver's shoulders. Due to the operator's close proximity to moving parts, early skid loaders posed safety concerns compared to conventional front loaders, especially during operator ingress and egress. However, modern skid loaders are equipped with fully enclosed cabs and additional safety features to safeguard the operator. Similar to conventional front loaders, they can move materials between locations, transport materials in their buckets, and load materials onto trucks or trailers.

Figure 10: Components of a Skid Steer. Back image - Bobcat S650 skid steer loader, Bob Adams from George, South Africa, CC BY-SA 2.0, via Wikimedia Commons.

A skid steer loader serves as a versatile machine utilized for excavating, gathering, lifting, and relocating various materials, notably dirt and sand. Additionally, it performs tasks such as grading, jackhammering cement, and loading trucks. Popular activities involving skid steers encompass site cleanup, material spreading, road sweeping, backfilling, loading and removing materials, turf preparation, and slab preparation, among others.

Predominantly employed for excavation purposes, the skid steer boasts versatility, agility, and lightness, with an array of attachments available for diverse applications. It is commonly found in construction sites, where its adaptable arms accommodate various landscaping functions.

In Australia, these machines are often referred to as "bobcats," though in countries like America, this term specifically refers to a prominent skid steer brand that gained popularity in the 1970s, remaining one of the largest skid steer brands globally.

Another variant, multi-terrain loaders, comes into play when ground conditions necessitate enhanced traction, such as in snow, mud, sand, or bush. Skid steers feature steering locked on both sides, allowing independent operation of the right and left wheels or tracks. This configuration enables the skid steer to achieve exceptional manoeuvrability and execute sharp turns, known colloquially as "turning on a dime."

Typically, the loader arms operate via hydraulics, enabling the bucket or other attachments to lift either vertically or radially. Radial movement allows the bucket to arc away from the skid steer until reaching heights as high as the cab before retracting inward.

When considering skid steer hire options, choices typically include two-track skid steer hire or four-wheel skid steer hire. In terms of operation, the wheels can be independently operated on either side of the machine, with the front and back axles synchronized. As the wheels maintain a fixed straight alignment and lack the ability to turn, the skid steer operator must increase the speed of the wheels on one side to induce dragging or skidding across the surface. This action prompts the machine to rotate in the opposite direction, hence the name "skid steer."

Skid steer hire is exceedingly popular across construction, landscaping, and mining industries due to its versatile nature. Whether opting for a two-track or four-wheel skid steer hire, understanding the variety of attachment options available is crucial for optimizing project outcomes. Among the most common attachments when hiring a skid steer is a bucket, though a wide range of alternatives exists to facilitate various tasks. These may include stump grinder hire, tree spade hire, wood chipper hire, trench-digging hire, pallet fork hire, bale spear hire, ripper hire, tiller hire, trencher hire, wheel saw hire, pavement miller hire, and cement mixer hire, among others.

Ultimately, skid steer hire offers a multitude of benefits across diverse applications, enabling the completion of tasks that singular plant hire options may not accomplish. Prior to hiring a machine, understanding the potential advantages for budget and project timelines is crucial. Whether undertaking landscaping, excavation, construction, or snow-clearing tasks, skid steer hire presents an efficient and reliable solution, provided the machine is well-maintained, properly serviced, and operated by licensed professionals.

Figure 11: Tracked skid steer. Wikideas1, CC0, via Wikimedia Commons.

There are different types of skid steers, each designed with specific features to suit various applications. These include:

1. Wheeled Skid Steers:

- Wheeled skid steers are equipped with rubber tyres, making them suitable for use on solid surfaces like pavement, concrete, and hard-packed soil.

- They offer excellent manoeuvrability and speed, making them ideal for tasks that require frequent relocation or travel over short distances.

- Wheeled skid steers are commonly used in construction, landscaping, agriculture, and material handling operations.

2. Tracked Skid Steers:

- Tracked skid steers, also known as compact track loaders (CTLs), feature tracks instead of wheels, providing better traction and flotation, especially on soft or uneven terrain.

- These machines are well-suited for operations in muddy, sandy, or rough terrain where wheeled skid steers may struggle.

- Tracked skid steers exert lower ground pressure, reducing soil compaction and minimizing damage to delicate surfaces.

- They are commonly used in forestry, landscaping, agriculture, and construction applications where terrain conditions are challenging.

3. Mini Skid Steers:

- Mini skid steers are compact versions of standard skid steers, designed for applications that require manoeuvrability in confined spaces or where access is limited.

- These machines are smaller in size and lighter in weight compared to conventional skid steers, making them suitable for use in residential areas, urban environments, and indoor spaces.

- Mini skid steers are often used by landscapers, utility contractors, and homeowners for tasks such as digging trenches, moving materials, and performing light construction work.

4. Stand-On Skid Steers:

- Stand-on skid steers are designed for operators to stand on a platform rather than sit in a traditional cab.

- These compact machines offer a smaller footprint and increased visibility, allowing operators to manoeuvre easily in tight spaces and navigate obstacles more effectively.

- Stand-on skid steers are commonly used in landscaping, grounds maintenance, and construction applications where manoeuvrability and efficiency are essential.

Each type of skid steer has its advantages and is suited to different applications based on factors such as terrain, space constraints, and specific job requirements. Choosing the right type of skid steer ensures optimal performance and productivity in various working conditions.

Figure 12: Mini/Stand-on skid steer. Ditch Witch SK 1050, Daderot, CC0, via Wikimedia Commons.

Machine Characteristics

The ratio between tread width and wheelbase is crucial for the efficient operation of a skid steer. If the tyres are positioned too far apart, the skid steer will expend excessive power during turns, leading to faster tyre wear. Typically, the recommended tread width to wheelbase ratio is 1.3 to 1 (Goulet & Anderson, 2007).

Tread width refers to the distance measured from the centre of the left tyre to the centre of the right tyre. Wheel base is measured from the centre of the front tyre to the centre of the rear tyre, see .

Figure 13: Tread width and Wheel base. Back image - Bobcat S570 Skid-Steer Loader, Steven Pavlov, CC BY-SA 4.0, via Wikimedia Commons.

As per the guidelines set by the Society of Automotive Engineers (SAE), the rated operating capacity is determined to be half of the tipping load. This rating indicates the maximum weight the machine can safely carry during typical operational circumstances. For instance, if the tipping load is 1996 kg (4400 lb), then the rated operating capacity would be 998 kg (2200 lb), as per the SAE standards (Goulet & Anderson, 2007).

Operators must ensure not to surpass the rated operating capacity, as doing so can compromise the stability and manoeuvrability of the skid steer, potentially resulting in damage to the equipment. Overloading the bucket or using a heavy attachment in a raised position can cause the skid steer to tip forward. In such instances, failure to utilize the seat restraint may lead to the operator being ejected from the protective cab. This can result in the skid steer running over the operator or causing the operator to be crushed by the bucket or load.

The weight distribution of a skid steer is intentionally unequal between the front and rear wheels, typically set at a ratio of 70% to 30%. This configuration enhances the skid steer's manoeuvrability, particularly when turning. If the weight distribution were to be evenly split between the front and rear wheels, at 50% each, the skid steer would require more engine power and would experience diminished turning capabilities. When the bucket is empty, approximately 70% of the weight rests on the rear wheels, with the remaining 30% on the front wheels (Goulet & Anderson, 2007). Conversely, when the bucket is full, the weight distribution shifts, with around 70% of the weight now borne by the front wheels and 30% by the rear wheels. Refer to Figure 14

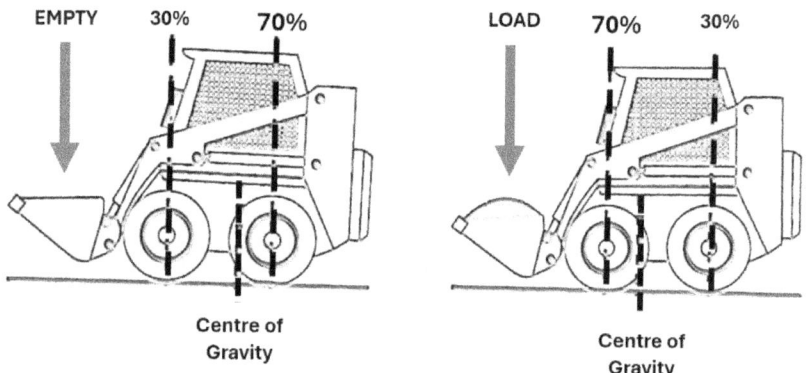

Figure 14: Weight on front and rear wheels loaded and empty.

As an example, A skid steer with a total weight of 2806kg (6185lb) and a rated operating capacity of 794kg (1750lb) will have a weight distribution as shown in Figure 15.

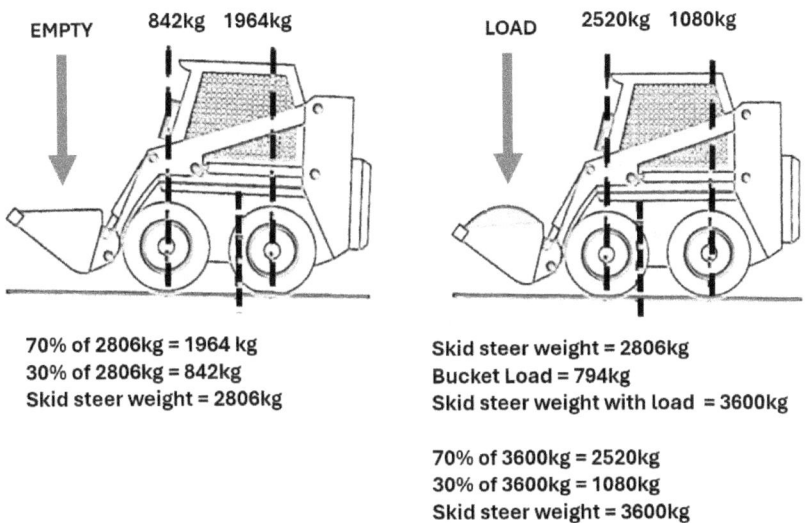

Figure 15: Weight distribution calculations.

The tyres bearing 70% of the weight are the ones upon which the machine pivots during operation. Understanding this dynamic is crucial, especially in tight or crowded spaces. When combined with an understanding of the centre of gravity, this knowledge empowers operators to work safely and efficiently.

The centre of gravity (COG) in a skid steer refers to the point where the majority of its weight is concentrated. It's a crucial concept to understand because it affects the stability and balance of the machine during operation.

In a skid steer, the centre of gravity typically lies somewhere within the chassis, often closer to the rear due to the heavy engine and transmission components. However, the exact location can vary depending on factors such as the weight distribution of attachments, load in the bucket, and the position of the operator.

The centre of gravity represents the equilibrium point of a skid steer, where all forces acting on the machine are evenly balanced, see Figure 16. This point shifts continuously during operation, particularly in response to changes in the weight distribution at the front of the skid steer.

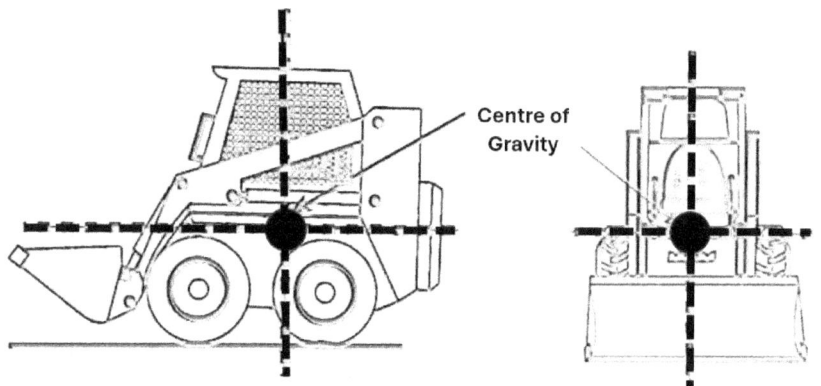

Figure 16: Skid steer centre of gravity.

When the skid steer is stationary on level ground, the centre of gravity is usually positioned low and centred between the four wheels. This configuration maximizes stability, making it less likely for the machine to tip over.

During operation, movements such as turning, lifting, or carrying loads can shift the centre of gravity. For example, when turning sharply or lifting a heavy load high off the ground, the centre of gravity moves towards the outside of the turn or the lifted load, respectively. These shifts can affect the stability of the skid steer and increase the risk of tipping over, especially if the centre of gravity moves beyond the machine's stability limits.

When you load the bucket, the centre of gravity shifts forward. Additionally, the centre of gravity adjusts vertically depending on the height and weight of the bucket. As you lift the bucket, the centre of gravity ascends, and the act of lifting transfers weight to the front wheels. Consequently, the centre of gravity rises with the elevation of the load, with heavier loads resulting in a higher centre of gravity. See Figure 17.

EARTHMOVING EQUIPMENT OPERATIONS

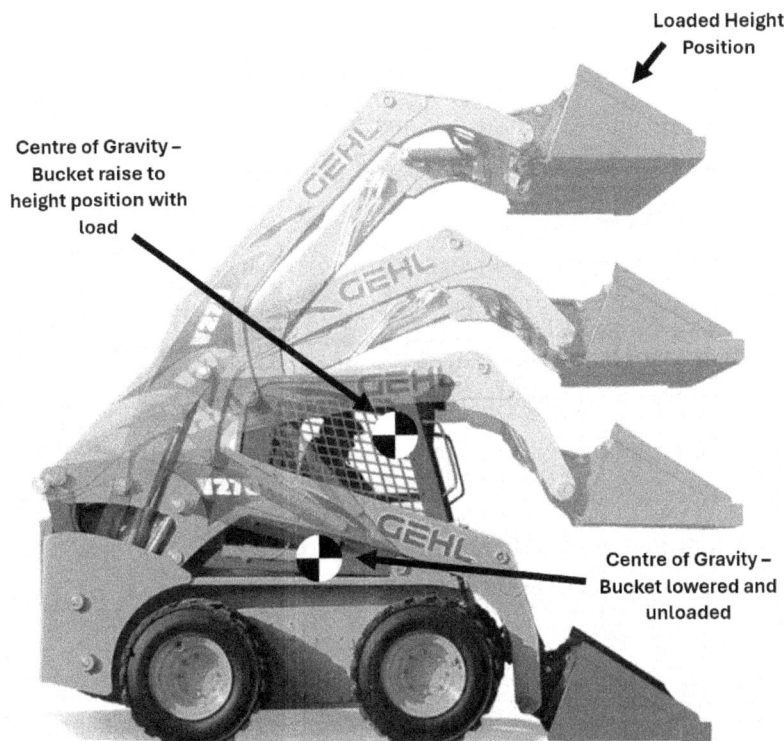

Figure 17: Shift in centre of gravity with load and lift height. Nack image - Zralok1, CC BY-SA 3.0, via Wikimedia Commons.

Operators must be aware of the skid steer's centre of gravity and understand how their actions impact its stability. Proper training and adherence to safe operating practices, such as avoiding sudden movements and operating within the machine's capacity limits, are essential for maintaining stability and preventing accidents. Additionally, manufacturers often provide guidelines and recommendations for safe operation based on the skid steer's centre of gravity and stability characteristics.

Various attachments are available for skid steers, including buckets, backhoes, augers, chippers, trenchers, and pallet forks. The weight of each attachment affects the center of gravity differently.

For instance, pallet forks, being elongated, cause the centre of gravity to shift forward when loaded to the normal rated operating capacity. To maintain stability, the rated operating capacity must be decreased to ensure that the centre of gravity remains behind the front wheels. If the centre of gravity shifts too far forward, the machine becomes unstable and risks tipping over.

Additional counterweights can be installed at the rear of the loader to prevent tipping. This may increase stress on the arms. Avoid driving with a high load. Keep the load as low as possible.

Before using a new attachment, carefully review the operator's manual. It outlines potential hazards associated with the attachment and provides instructions for safe operation. Ensure that attachments are securely mounted and fastened. A sudden release of an attachment can result in a dropped load, potentially destabilizing the loader and causing injury to bystanders.

Preparing and Planning for Operations

Planning and preparing for skid steer operations involves several key steps to ensure efficiency, safety, and successful completion of tasks. Here's a comprehensive guide on how to plan and prepare for skid steer operations:

1. Understand the Task Requirements: Begin by thoroughly understanding the requirements of the task or project that the skid steer will be used for. Consider factors such as the type of materials to be moved, the terrain of the work area, and any specific challenges or constraints.

2. Select the Right Skid Steer: Choose the appropriate skid steer for the task based on factors such as the size of the machine, its lifting capacity, and the type of attachments needed. Ensure

EARTHMOVING EQUIPMENT OPERATIONS

that the selected skid steer is well-suited to handle the demands of the job effectively.

3. Check Regulations and Requirements: Familiarize yourself with all relevant regulations, standards, and safety requirements governing skid steer operations in your jurisdiction. Ensure compliance with these regulations to maintain a safe and legal work environment.

4. Conduct a Site Assessment: Perform a thorough assessment of the work site to identify any potential hazards, obstacles, or risks that may impact skid steer operations. Take necessary measures to mitigate these risks and ensure a safe working environment.

5. Inspect the Skid Steer: Before beginning operations, conduct a comprehensive prestart inspection of the skid steer to ensure that it is in good working condition. Check all mechanical, hydraulic, and electrical components, as well as safety features, for any signs of damage or malfunction.

6. Prepare Attachments: If the skid steer will be used with attachments, ensure that the appropriate attachments are selected and properly installed. Inspect the attachments for any defects or damage that could affect their performance during operation.

7. Establish Communication Channels: Establish clear communication channels with other personnel involved in the task, such as ground workers, supervisors, and equipment operators. Ensure that everyone understands their roles and responsibilities and can communicate effectively during operations.

8. Develop a Work Plan: Develop a detailed work plan outlining the sequence of tasks, operational procedures, and safety measures to be followed during skid steer operations. Consider

factors such as work schedules, equipment utilization, and contingency plans for unforeseen circumstances.

9. Provide Training and Instruction: Ensure that all operators and personnel involved in skid steer operations receive adequate training and instruction on safe operating practices, equipment usage, and emergency procedures. Address any gaps in knowledge or skills through additional training as needed.

10. Prepare for Emergencies: Develop a comprehensive emergency response plan that outlines procedures for responding to accidents, injuries, equipment malfunctions, and other emergencies. Ensure that all personnel are familiar with the plan and know how to implement it effectively.

Understanding and being aware of the contract's requirements is paramount. The contract specification outlines the responsibilities for different aspects of the sealing process and the desired end result. However, it is often up to the constructor to assess whether the proposed seal meets the specified performance criteria. Thus, it's crucial that the individual responsible for sealing comprehends both the 'defects liability' and 'performance' requirements stipulated in the contract.

Prior to planning, safety and environmental considerations concerning the site must be evaluated. This includes addressing issues such as traffic safety, fire hazards, noise impacts, and potential pollution of stormwater and air. Adequate measures should be put in place to mitigate risks, including providing firefighting equipment, spillage kits, and first aid facilities.

Upon completing the induction program, familiarizing oneself with the safety features of the immediate work area is essential. This includes identifying the location of fire extinguishers, emergency stops, first aid stations, and emergency evacuation procedures. Although the induction program provides general safety training, workplace orientation specific to the immediate work area ensures readiness to respond to emergencies effectively.

Effective planning is crucial for the successful execution of tasks. Depending on the scale of the operation, daily work requirements may be communicated through verbal briefings or written instructions from supervisors. It is imperative that these instructions are received and clearly understood. If there is uncertainty regarding the task requirements, seeking clarification from the supervisor is recommended. Additionally, conducting a site visit before commencing work allows for a thorough inspection of the job and ensures proper preparation of equipment.

Planning plays a vital role in managing projects, ensuring they are completed on time, within budget, and according to the required standards. It establishes a sequence of activities, clarifies roles and responsibilities, and provides direction for action. Effective planning reduces uncertainty, eliminates duplication of effort, and allows for better control over costs. Organizing work efficiently ensures tasks are carried out in a logical sequence, optimizing resources and minimizing waste.

Planning and organization are essential for achieving project objectives and ensuring a safe and productive work environment. Adhering to established procedures and safety protocols enhances efficiency and minimizes risks, ultimately contributing to the successful completion of projects.

Planning serves as a fundamental framework for guiding actions towards a specific goal, providing clarity and direction for supervisors, managers, and employees alike. It entails organizing and sequencing activities necessary to achieve objectives, ensuring everyone understands what needs to be done, who is responsible, where, when, why, and how it should be done. By anticipating change and preparing for it, planning helps reduce uncertainty, prevent duplication of efforts and expenses, and lays the groundwork for effective monitoring and evaluation of performance and achievements.

Moreover, planning enables better control over costs by ensuring proper allocation of resources and materials, facilitating smoother operations, and preventing last-minute shortages. Failure to plan adequately can lead to increased difficulty in performing tasks, unexpected challenges, and missed opportunities. Those who plan effectively can proactively address challenges and seize opportunities, while those who do not may face setbacks and obstacles.

In the construction industry, planning and organizational skills are especially crucial for efficiently managing workloads and projects. Whether as an employee, contractor, or project manager, effective planning involves considering various factors such as sequencing of trades, management of delays and disruptions, and cost management. These skills are essential for accurate estimates, prioritizing projects, adapting to unforeseen circumstances, and ensuring increased productivity and profitability.

For supervisors and employers, successful project planning and organization result in numerous benefits, including increased efficiency, reduced waste, improved communication among workers, enhanced safety, and better hazard identification. Following a well-organized work program not only maximizes the utilization of resources but also fosters a sense of pride and satisfaction among employees, leading to higher morale and overall success.

Even for seemingly simple tasks, planning is essential for ensuring efficiency and effectiveness. Whether washing a car or managing an entire department, having clear objectives and well-defined plans increases the likelihood of success. While plans may sometimes fail due to unforeseen circumstances, maintaining flexibility and monitoring progress allows for timely adjustments and ensures progress towards desired objectives.

In summary, planning is a straightforward yet essential process that involves determining tasks, anticipating challenges, and considering various approaches to achieving goals. By adhering to a structured planning process and fostering clear communication, individuals and organizations can enhance productivity, mitigate risks, and achieve desired outcomes.

When instructions are not clearly explained, it's easy for things to go awry. In addition to understanding precisely what tasks you're expected to perform, it's important to grasp how your role fits into the broader picture and why certain tasks are necessary. Fair allocation of work is also crucial for maintaining morale; feeling overburdened compared to your colleagues or constantly assigned less desirable tasks can be disheartening.

Communication is key:

- If you encounter any uncertainties regarding work instructions, don't hesitate to discuss them with your supervisor.

- When instructions are unclear or you require clarification on specific issues, seek assistance from someone who can provide clarity.

- When you're the one delivering instructions, ensure that your message is conveyed clearly and comprehensibly.

Work instructions can be conveyed through various channels, including:

- Written documentation: Official documents such as reports, memos, manuals, and service standards.

- Verbal instructions: Directives communicated orally by supervisors or managers.

- Team meetings: Gatherings where work teams receive instructions, report progress, and discuss upcoming tasks.

- Plans/specifications: Detailed drawings and documents outlining job requirements, including construction, mechanical, and electrical aspects, as well as material lists and written instructions.

Key Components of Work Instructions:
Effective work instructions should include:

- The job's purpose.

- Sequence of tasks.

- Hazard assessment.

- Emergency procedures.

- Personal protective equipment (PPE) requirements.

- Timeframes.

- Priorities.

Comprehensive instructions provide valuable insights into safety measures, efficiency, and planning. If you find yourself unsure about any aspect of the instructions, don't hesitate to seek clarification from your supervisor to prevent potential errors.

Planning involves assessing tasks, allocating time, determining equipment and materials needed, and outlining work methods and risk analyses. It's essential to ensure that the company possesses the necessary expertise to carry out the work effectively.

Considerations for Work Environment:

- Equipment and materials utilized should be appropriate for the project's scale.

- Adherence to waste management plans to avoid fines from local authorities or environmental agencies.

- Consideration of weather conditions and noise restrictions imposed by regulations or local councils.

- Dust suppression methods and good housekeeping practices to maintain a clean and safe work environment.

Good Housekeeping Practices:
- Stacking materials neatly.
- Proper waste disposal.
- Separating waste products.
- Preventing contamination.
- Ensuring cleanliness of facilities.
- Regular maintenance of work areas.

General safety guidelines for operating a Skid Steer Loader:

1. Only authorized personnel, or those under the instruction of authorized personnel, should operate the Skid Steer Loader.

2. Utilize the provided steps and handrails and maintain three-point contact when getting on and off the machine; avoid jumping off.

3. Keep steps, rails, and walkways clear of grease and debris to prevent slips and falls.

4. Wear the seatbelt at all times and consider using hearing protection while operating or being around the machine.

5. Ensure windows and mirrors are clean; sound the horn five seconds before starting or moving the truck to alert nearby

personnel.

6. Before leaving the operator's seat or allowing anyone to board the machine, apply the park brake.

7. Familiarize yourself with the location, function, and use of all instruments, controls, indicator lights, and safety devices in the cab.

8. Read and understand all safety, warning signs, and labels; report any damaged or missing safety signs to your supervisor or trainer.

9. Follow all Company Regulations and Site Procedures to ensure a safe work environment.

10. Refrain from smoking around flammable liquids and checkpoints.

11. Be vigilant for any broken or frayed wiring or hoses; report them immediately to prevent accidents.

12. Watch out for damaged or missing shields and guards covering electrical components and sharp, hot, or moving parts; report any issues promptly.

13. Avoid handling or smoking around batteries.

14. Minimize skin contact with oils or fuels; if contact occurs, wash off immediately. Be cautious around oil and fuel lines operating under pressure and heat.

15. Be aware of the potential for falling rocks from the trays of loaded Skid Steer Loaders and other working equipment at any time.

Inspections:
1. Perform a full pre-start and operational check before starting the Skid Steer Loader.

2. Note that oil and coolant can become hot during operation; check the coolant level during prestart when the machine is cool to prevent scalding.

Safe Operation:
1. Prior to starting any work with the skid steer, consider:

   - Awareness of surrounding machinery, light vehicles, and personnel.

   - Using correct two-way radio protocol when manoeuvring around other machines.

   - Inspecting and reporting potential hazards in the work area.

   - Maintaining full operational control of the Skid Steer Loader at all times.

   - Adhering to Skid Steer Loader speed limits and driving cautiously based on road conditions.

   - Preventing tyre damage and following approved shutdown and park-up procedures.

   - Using Personal Protective Equipment (PPE) as instructed.

Figure 18: Assess the work environment prior to commencing operations. ŠJů, Wikimedia Commons, CC BY 4.0, via Wikimedia Commons.

Compliance Documentation:

1. Compliance documents outline information, processes, and procedures that must be followed and serve as a guide for workplace tasks.

2. These documents may include legislative, organizational, and site requirements, manufacturer's guidelines, operational manuals, Australian standards, and OHS requirements, among others.

Interpreting Requirements:

1. Understand the terminology used to rank compliance levels, such as "should," "consider," and "must."

2. Apply the relevant requirements based on the specific work location and situation.

EARTHMOVING EQUIPMENT OPERATIONS

Applying Requirements and Procedures:

1. Familiarize yourself with applicable compliance documents and procedures and apply them from planning through completion of work.

2. Seek assistance if you encounter difficulties in understanding or applying the requirements.

Obtaining and Applying Work Instructions:

1. Obtain work instructions from plans, drawings, specifications, project documents, or supervisors.

2. Confirm understanding by asking questions and repeating back your understanding of the instructions.

3. Identify hazards in the work area and formulate safe work procedures accordingly.

Be Alert To:

1. Ground conditions, power lines, trees, manholes, trenches, service lines, people working overhead, wind direction, and bridges.

2. Always ensure relevant permits are obtained before starting any excavation work.

If in Doubt, Ask.

Operator vigilance is crucial, with attention directed towards:

- Assessing ground and road conditions.

- Identifying the presence of power lines.

- Being mindful of trees and other obstacles.

- Noting the locations of manholes and open excavations.

- Recognizing the existence of service lines.

- Being aware of window locations and blind spots.

- Monitoring wind direction and weather conditions.

- Considering the time of day and lighting conditions.

- Being cognizant of bridge load capacities and width restrictions.

During machine operation, operators should always be on the lookout for:

- Communication networks.

- Presence of barricades and signage.

- Control personnel and pedestrians.

- Traffic lights and other signals.

Regarding power lines:

- Maintain a minimum clearance from high voltage power lines.

- For low voltage power lines, maintain the same clearance unless specifically trained in electrical assets.

- Clearance requirements may vary if power lines are insulated to local authority standards.

- Ensure the presence of spotters, permits, and Safe Work Method Statements (SWMS) as required for site-specific operations.

- In the event of contact with power lines, it is safest to remain inside the Skid Steer loader until power is turned off and the area is deemed safe.

- If help does not arrive and evacuation becomes necessary, jump clear of the equipment, avoiding contact with the ground and loader simultaneously to prevent electric shock.

For identifying potential underground hazards:
- Utilize cable locators and review maps and plans.

- Seek guidance from supervisors and contact relevant supply authorities for further information.

Working in Low Light or at Night Time: Working during low light conditions or at night exposes workers to various risks, including the potential for being struck by moving vehicles and the increased likelihood of slipping, tripping, and falling.

Examples of Controls: To mitigate these hazards, measures such as ensuring at least two workers are present at all times, providing additional lighting, and outfitting workers with fluorescent or retroreflective clothing like vests and gaiters can be implemented.

Sun and Heat: Prolonged exposure to the sun poses risks such as skin cancer, skin disorders, eye injuries, heat stress, and heat-related illnesses. Each workplace should conduct its own assessment of sun exposure risks and implement measures to control workers' exposure to sunlight.

Examples of Controls: Controlling sun exposure can involve using personal protection like sunscreen and sunglasses, scheduling outdoor tasks during cooler parts of the day, and providing ample shaded areas and hydration.

Fatigue: Fatigue, caused by prolonged periods of physical or mental exertion without sufficient rest, can impair a person's ability to function normally, leading to decreased performance and an increased risk of incidents and injuries.

Examples of Controls: Controlling fatigue risks may include limiting night shift workers' responsibilities to core duties, scheduling low-risk work during periods of high fatigue, and providing adequate supervision and emergency response plans.

Slips, Trips, and Falls: Factors such as contaminants, floor surfaces, obstacles, and footwear contribute to the risk of slips, trips, and falls in the workplace.

Examples of Controls: Measures to control these risks include removing hazards at the design stage, implementing good housekeeping practices, and ensuring adequate lighting for tasks.

Noise: Excessive noise levels can cause hearing damage, and controlling noise exposure involves identifying sources of excessive noise, reducing noise at the source, and providing hearing protection for workers.

Examples of Controls: Controlling noise may involve redesigning machinery, scheduling noisy work for times when fewer people are present, and providing hearing protection devices.

Recycled Water: Water from non-potable sources, including recycled water, may contain biological hazards, and workplaces must take measures to prevent harm from exposure to such water.

Inclement Weather: Wet weather conditions can create hazards such as slippery surfaces and electrical hazards, requiring workplaces to implement safe systems of work to mitigate these risks.

Hazardous Manual Tasks: Manual tasks involving lifting, carrying, and moving objects can lead to musculoskeletal disorders, and controlling these risks involves modifying tasks and obtaining assistance when necessary.

There are several methods for creating a work plan to ensure adherence to site procedures and safe work practices. An informal risk assessment is one such method, simplifying the identification of hazards and implementing control measures. This process may involve basic tools like pocket notebooks and a set of procedures.

One common risk assessment process in mining and construction industries is SLAM, which stands for STOP, LOOK, ASSESS, and MANAGE. It's a straightforward and effective system used globally, offering documented evidence of identified health and safety risks.

STOP

The job plan starts with a risk assessment, asking critical questions to identify potential hazards and determine the safest and most productive way to complete tasks. Considerations include the environment, required skills, necessary equipment, and relevant procedures.

LOOK

After stopping, employees must assess the workplace for potential hazards, including ergonomic and health risks that could lead to accidents and injuries.

ASSESS

Next, employees evaluate the identified hazards based on their consequences and likelihood of occurrence, using a risk matrix to determine the level of risk associated with each task.

MANAGE

Finally, employees implement controls to minimize risks to As Low As Reasonably Possible (ALARP) levels. This involves reducing energy, isolating hazards, enhancing knowledge and skills, planning tasks, and using effective tools and processes.

Daily SLAM

Workers should conduct this assessment daily or before starting new tasks. Monitoring processes for quality and environmental factors should also be considered, with attention to existing systems, monitoring frequency, and feedback management.

SAM

Preventing accidents and illnesses is preferable to reacting after incidents occur. Simple approaches like SLAM or SAM (Spot the Hazard,

Assess the Risk, Make the Changes) provide effective frameworks for managing hazards and risks in the workplace.

Spot the Hazard (S)

Identify workplace hazards, including environmental, chemical, biological, ergonomic, and electrical risks.

Assess the Risk (A)

Evaluate the seriousness of identified hazards and report risks to management or OHS representatives for appropriate action.

Make the Changes (M)

Implement measures to control risks, such as removing hazards, improving work routines, or providing training to minimize risks.

When planning any project, it's crucial to assess its environmental impact and take steps to mitigate any adverse effects. In many countries, there exist laws, regulations, policies, and guidelines aimed at safeguarding the environment. Within the general construction industry, key environmental concerns include stormwater pollution, litter, dust, and sediment runoff. Construction activities must be conducted in a manner that prevents pollution from entering water bodies.

Stormwater runoff can transport pollutants to water bodies and coastal areas, while sediment runoff can suffocate aquatic life and lead to the silting up of water systems. Additionally, litter can contaminate stormwater.

Implementing effective litter and waste management practices, along with erosion, sediment, and dust control measures, offers numerous benefits. These include cost savings on cleanup efforts, reduced hazards from mud and dust, improved working conditions during wet weather, enhanced occupational health and safety, better drainage, minimized stockpile losses, fewer public complaints, and a positive community image.

Dust control is not only an environmental concern but also a matter of occupational health and safety (OHS). Construction activities inherently produce dust, posing risks to workers, especially from materials like cement or gypsum-based products.

Various controls can mitigate dust hazards, including the use of water sprays and mists, wet methods for concrete cutting, prompt debris cleanup, wearing approved masks in high inhalation risk areas, and employing industrial vacuum cleaners.

Effective site drainage practices can significantly reduce the environmental impact of stormwater runoff. Measures such as diverting upslope water, discharging stormwater onto stable areas, and avoiding discharge towards site entrances/exits are essential.

Recycling materials whenever possible is vital for sustainable construction practices. Materials like steel, aluminium, timber, concrete, bricks, plastics, glass, and carpet can all be recycled, reducing the demand for new resources and minimizing landfill waste.

To further minimize environmental impact, steps should be taken to reduce building material usage. This includes strategies like consuming fewer materials, reusing existing ones, recycling resources, utilizing renewable materials, and opting for products with high recycled content.

Proper management of sand and soil stockpiles is crucial to prevent environmental degradation. Controls such as designating delivery areas, avoiding storage on footpaths or road reserves, locating stockpiles behind sediment controls, and maintaining a safe distance from hazard areas should be implemented.

Sediment fencing plays a vital role in controlling sediment runoff. These fences help prevent sediment from leaving the site and should be placed along contours, regularly inspected and repaired, and properly installed to ensure effectiveness.

A variety of attachments equips a single machine to tackle various landscaping and construction tasks with ease. Farmers often utilize skid steer loaders across their properties for diverse purposes, benefiting from their adaptability and functionality.

Primarily designed for digging, skid steer loaders boast lightweight construction and exceptional manoeuvrability. Beyond digging, these versatile machines can perform a multitude of functions including lifting, grading, debris removal, demolition, clearing, and leveling. They excel in various tasks such as acting as an all-terrain forklift, executing bulk earthmoving, and facilitating automated soil distribution with precision. Additionally, they prove efficient in road profiling, concrete work, and hard surface tasks, including concrete sawing.

Skid steer loaders come in two configurations: four-wheeled or equipped with two tracks. Wheeled skid steer loaders utilize a chain case drive system, while tracked variants employ hydrostatic drives. Although skid steer loaders are generally standardized, they are available in various sizes, categorized as small frame, medium frame, and large frame, each differing in weight and power capacity.

The extensive array of attachments for skid steer loaders enhances their versatility and utility across different applications. Some available attachments include augers for efficient hole drilling, rock breakers for robust concrete and rock breaking, and grapple buckets for moving large objects. Additionally, there are rock buckets for effective stone and rock removal, forks for material handling, and slashers for vegetation clearing. Tillers prepare soil for planting, while trenchers create trenches of various sizes. Rakes gather debris, and brooms power sweep areas, while spreaders and smudge bars are suitable for soil leveling and spreading.

Figure 19: Skid steer with fork attachments lifting a pallet. The Official CTBTO Photostream, CC BY 2.0, via Wikimedia Commons.

Choosing the appropriate attachment is crucial to optimizing productivity and efficiency for each task. Choosing the right equipment, whether a skid steer loader or an excavator, is crucial for ensuring efficiency and effectiveness in construction tasks, often considered among the most challenging and labour-intensive endeavours. Unsure about which machinery suits your upcoming project—skid steer loader, excavator, or a combination? The decision hinges on factors such as application, job site conditions, spatial limitations, urgency, and utilization potential.

Skid steer loaders, renowned for their compactness and versatility, excel in digging, pushing, and moving dirt, making them indispensable in various applications like backhoeing, pavement milling, tilling, cement mixing, site cleaning, rubbish removal, and wood chipping. Unlike excavators, skid steer loaders feature a fixed carriage, enhancing their adaptability.

Selecting the appropriate skid steer loader involves considering several factors. First, assess the size of the machine, ensuring it matches your project's requirements and the site's surface capacity. Small frame skid steers are ideal for demolition work and manoeuvring in narrow spaces, while medium to large frames handle heavier tasks efficiently. Additionally, factor in the job surface—whether flat or uneven terrain—and choose between wheeled or tracked skid steers accordingly.

Controls play a pivotal role, with traditional pedal and lever controls being common in conventional skid steers, while modern variants feature joystick controls for smoother operation. The diverse range of attachments available for skid steer loaders further enhances their utility, but compatibility with specific machines must be ensured. Attachments such as buckets, ground engaging tools, fork attachments, concrete mixers, vegetation control tools, grapples, and brooms offer versatility in handling various tasks.

To maximize efficiency and versatility, opt for a skid steer loader capable of accommodating a wide range of attachments compatible with your project needs. Assessing the machine's attachment compatibility ensures optimal performance and versatility, making it a worthwhile rental investment for your construction endeavours.

Before operating any machinery, it's imperative to acquaint oneself with all safety and isolation protocols.

Fire Fighting Procedures: Machines engaged in heavy-duty operations, running continuously, often operate at elevated temperatures. While machine fires are rare, they can lead to complete destruction if not swiftly controlled.

Understanding the fire tetrahedron, which comprises fuel, heat, an oxidizing agent, and a chemical chain reaction, is crucial. Any alteration to these factors can prevent, suppress, or manage a fire.

The principle of fire extinguishing revolves around removing one side of the fire triangle, thereby hindering ignition. Operators, often positioned several meters above the ground, should avoid immediately abandoning the machine during a fire incident and instead follow specific steps to minimize harm:

- Completely shut down the machine to prevent the engine fan from exacerbating the fire.

- If equipped with a two-way radio system, use emergency radio procedures to signal for assistance.

- Activate the fire suppression system within the cab or utilize a handheld extinguisher if safe to do so.

- Ensure a clear path for retreat and move away from the machine if the fire persists after extinguishing attempts.

Fire Suppression Systems: Machines equipped with fire suppression systems require specific protocols during fire incidents:

- If flames are visible, immediately pull over, stop the engine, and activate the fire suppression system. Await further assistance with a handheld extinguisher.

- If smoke is detected, halt operation, investigate the cause, and activate the fire suppression system if necessary. Report any incidents to the supervisor promptly.

Incident Management: All incidents must be reported, investigated, and managed following the organization's WHS Incident Reporting, Investigation, and Escalation Procedure.

Emergency Response and Preparedness: For construction or roadside sites, competent individuals should develop and implement emergency response procedures and plans. These plans should be tested, and workers educated on their content and responsibilities. Fixed worksites must adhere to specific emergency evacuation plans and guidelines outlined in site-specific manuals and WHS standards.

The prestart check for a skid steer involves a systematic inspection of various components to ensure that the machine is in safe working condition before operation. Here's a detailed explanation of each step typically involved in a prestart check for a skid steer:

1. Exterior Inspection: Begin by visually inspecting the exterior of the skid steer. Look for any signs of damage, such as dents, scratches, or leaks. Check the tyres or tracks for wear and tear, ensuring they are properly inflated and free from any visible defects.

2. Fluid Levels: Check the fluid levels, including engine oil, hydraulic fluid, coolant, and fuel. Ensure that each fluid is at the appropriate level according to the manufacturer's specifications. If any fluid levels are low, top them up as needed.

3. Belts and Hoses: Inspect the belts and hoses for any signs of wear, cracks, or leaks. Make sure they are securely fastened and free from any damage that could lead to malfunction during operation.

4. Controls and Instruments: Test all the controls and instruments to ensure they are functioning properly. This includes the steering, pedals, joysticks, gauges, lights, horn, and any other control mechanisms. Ensure that they respond correctly and smoothly to inputs.

5. Safety Features: Check all safety features, such as seat belts, rollover protection system (ROPS), and falling object protection system (FOPS), if equipped. Ensure that they are in good condition and functioning as intended to protect the operator during operation.

6. Attachments: If the skid steer is equipped with attachments,

inspect them for proper installation and condition. Ensure that they are securely mounted and free from any defects that could affect their performance.

7. Brakes and Steering: Test the brakes and steering to ensure they are responsive and effective. Check for any unusual noises or resistance that could indicate a problem with these systems.

8. Fluid Leaks: Look for any signs of fluid leaks around the skid steer, including oil, hydraulic fluid, coolant, or fuel. Address any leaks immediately to prevent potential hazards or damage to the machine.

9. Structural Integrity: Finally, inspect the overall structural integrity of the skid steer, including the frame, chassis, and body. Look for any signs of damage, corrosion, or fatigue that could compromise the safety or performance of the machine.

By conducting a thorough prestart check according to these steps, operators can ensure that the skid steer is in safe and optimal working condition before beginning any tasks or operations. This helps prevent accidents, malfunctions, and downtime while maximizing productivity and efficiency on the job site.

To start and control the skid steer, firstly consult the owner's manual for essential instructions. Typically, it contains safety guidelines for operators and operational procedures for the skid steer. Additionally, it holds the code necessary to unlock the vehicle, a prerequisite for operation.

Ensure proper seating. Situate yourself comfortably in the skid steer and grasp the safety bar, pulling it down over yourself. Note that the safety bar is designed to rest in the downward position without locking, resembling a seatbelt.

Before operating the skid steer, conduct a thorough visual inspection of your surroundings, checking the front, rear, and sides for any obstacles or hazards.

Start the skid steer by turning the key to the right. Once the code panel illuminates, enter the correct code provided in the manual. Then, turn the key fully to start the skid loader. Ensure the idle speed is not set too high before initiating. In steps starting a Skid Steer involves:

1. Grip the exterior handles firmly with both hands, ensuring three points of contact as you ascend the steps.

2. Enter the cab, turning around as you step inside.

3. Take a seat and adjust the seating and other features to your preference for comfort.

4. Secure your seat belt; note that certain models require the seat belt to be fastened before starting.

5. Reach overhead and lower the roll cage using both hands; newer models mandate securing the roll cage before starting.

6. Turn the ignition key a quarter turn and await the audible signal.

7. Release the parking brake by pressing the overhead button.

8. Turn the ignition key fully to start the engine.

9. Override the safety mechanism by pressing the green "ready" button, which unlocks the gears.

10. Push the arm controls forward to initiate motion and set the skid steer in motion.

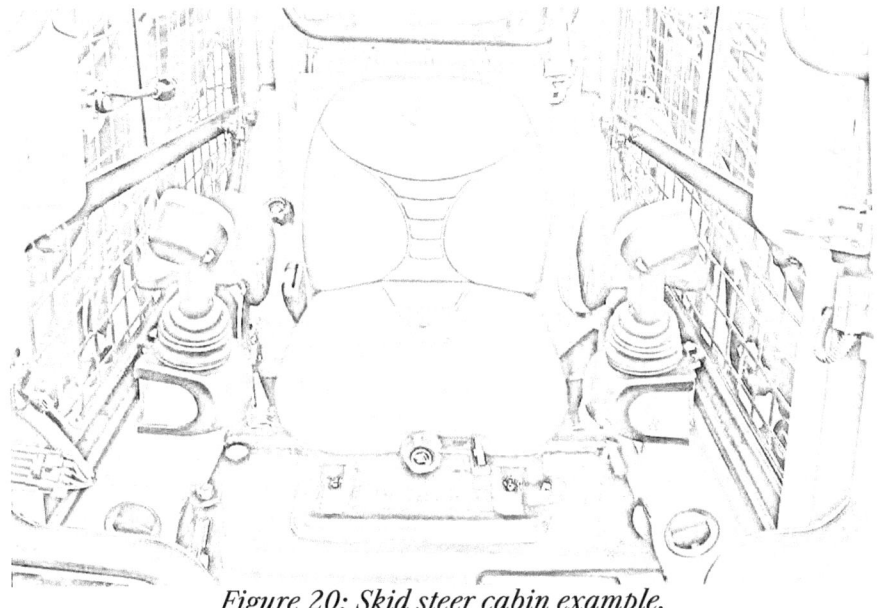

Figure 20: Skid steer cabin example.

Familiarize yourself with the joysticks, which enable control of the skid loader. There are two joystick patterns: ISO and H patterns. In the ISO pattern, the left joystick manages vehicle movement, while the right joystick controls the arms and attachments, see Figure 21 and Figure 22. Conversely, the H pattern combines joystick movements for seasoned operators.

Utilize the skid steer for the intended task, ensuring the appropriate attachment is mounted on the control arms, such as forks for lifting pallets or a bucket for moving materials.

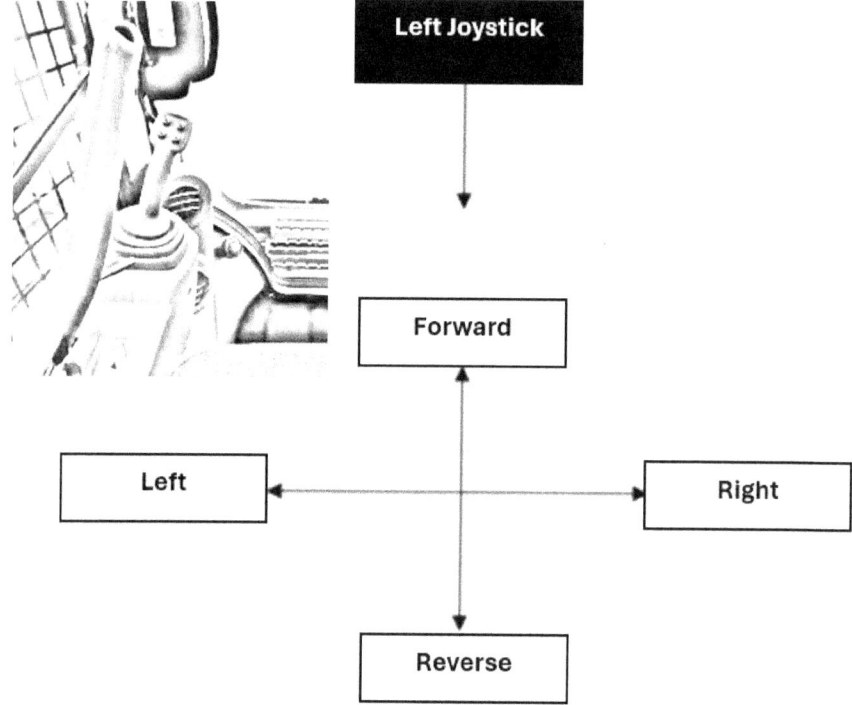

Figure 21: ISO pattern - Left joystick control.

Adjust the idle speed, either through a foot pedal or a lever typically located on the right-hand side of the skid steer. Set the RPM to the highest setting for maximum power.

Raise the bucket or forks at least 12" (30cm) off the ground to prevent them from hitting the ground when the skid steer is in motion. In the ISO pattern, pull the right joystick back in a southwest direction to lift the control arms and tilt the attachment upward.

Navigate the skid steer by pushing the left joystick in the desired direction. Pushing forward moves straight ahead, while pushing left or right turns the skid steer accordingly. To reverse, pull the left joystick backward, either straight back for a straight reverse or diagonally for turning.

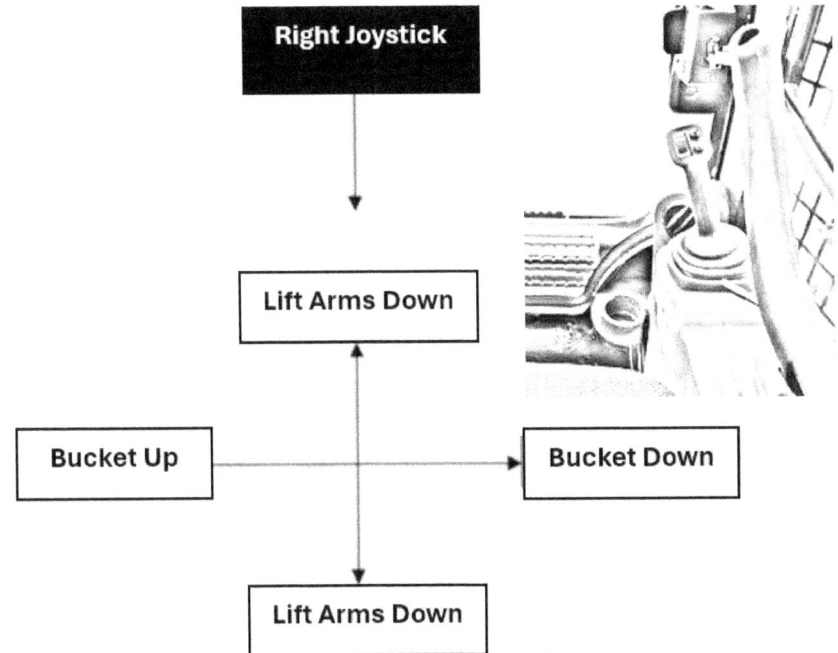

Figure 22: ISO pattern - Right joystick control.

Operating a Skid Steer

In contrast to standard automobiles, skid steer loaders typically utilize separate right and left arm controls, often referred to as joysticks, to manage steering and acceleration (Lane, 2022).

Each side's arm controls dictate the speed and direction of the respective wheels or tracks:

- To turn or move left: push the left arm control forward.

- To turn or move right: push the right arm control forward.

- To move straight forward: push both arm controls forward.

- To move in reverse: pull both arms back toward you.

Some skid steers employ a single arm control to execute all steering manoeuvres. For single arm controls, the joystick's movement determines the direction:

- To turn or move left: push the arm control forward and to the left.

- To turn or move right: push the arm control forward and to the right.

- To move straight forward: push the arm control forward.

- To move in reverse: pull the arm control back toward you.

Basic features and gauges every skid steer should possess include:

- Temperature Gauge: Indicates engine heat levels.

- Fuel Gauge: Displays remaining fuel.

- Hour Gauge: Records machine usage hours.

- Auxiliary Pressure Release: Used to release hydraulic pressure in attachments with hydraulic hoses.

- Variable Flow: Adjusts hydraulic pressure flow for varying attachment needs.

- High Flow: Provides additional hydraulic power for specific attachments.

- Max Flow: Activates maximum hydraulic power for heavy-duty attachments.

- Bob-Tach: Facilitates attachment addition or release via overhead button controls.

Certain attachments may operate effectively across multiple flow settings. It's advisable to consult the manufacturer's manual to determine the ideal gallons per minute (GPM) requirements for optimal attachment performance.

When operating a Skid Steer During Lifting and Dumping:

Utilizing Foot Pedals Each foot pedal manages a specific function of your attachments through foot movement. The left foot pedal governs the boom, while the right foot pedal controls the bucket.

Left (Boom) Pedal

- To lower the boom: gently push your left forefoot (toe) forward on the pedal.

- To raise the boom: gently push your left heel back on the pedal.

Right (Bucket) Pedal

- To dump the bucket: gently push your right forefoot (toe) forward on the pedal.

- To curl the bucket for digging: gently push your right heel back on the pedal.

Boom & Bucket Controls for Single Arm Control Skid Steers

When operating a skid steer equipped with single arm control for steering, the unused arm control is utilized for operating the bucket and the boom.

- To dig with/curl the bucket: move the arm control to the left.

- To dump the bucket: move the arm control to the right.

- To lower the boom: pull the arm control back.

- To raise the boom: push the arm control forward.

Skid Steer Loaders come equipped with up to seven different safety mechanisms to safeguard the operator. These include:

1. Seat Belt

2. Safety Guards and Covers

3. Warning Devices

4. Supplementary Steering and Emergency Brakes

5. Warning Labels

These devices serve as controls to prevent harm to both the operator and others, emphasizing the importance of vigilant inspection and maintenance by a competent operator.

Typically, Skid Steer Loaders are equipped with seat belts to prevent the operator from falling off the seat in the event of a tip-over. Some seat belts feature an electrical connection that prohibits machine operation unless the seat belt is fastened.

It is imperative to remember that seat belts must be worn at all times. The highest chance of survival in an accident is ensured by being inside the cab with a securely fastened seat belt.

Before starting the machine, operators must thoroughly inspect the seat belt for any defects, including frayed webbing, damaged buckles, proper anti-creep slide operation, and secure belt mounting hardware. If any defects are identified, the machine should not be operated until the necessary replacements are made.

Additionally, seat belts must be worn by all personnel traveling in company vehicles and mobile equipment, with passengers seated in approved seating and their seat belts fastened before movement. Failure to wear seat belts may lead to legal consequences and loss of entitlement to workers' compensation.

Operator protection bars, including roll-over protection (ROPS) and falling objects protective structures (FOPS), are specifically designed to provide crush protection to the operator in the event of a tip-over or rollover by allowing controlled bending of the structural members.

It is crucial to note that the design of the cab must not be altered in any way, as doing so could render the protection system inoperative during a rollover and potentially void the manufacturer's warranty.

Keep in mind the importance of weight distribution and centre of gravity as you manoeuvre the machine, especially in tight or confined spaces. Ensure that the hydraulic operation is smooth and fluid, without any abrupt movements or loud impacts when the arms or bucket reach their limits. Aim for a consistent and smooth speed when operating the hydraulic lift arms and bucket.

Maintain movement in all tyres, with the inside tyres rotating slowly to minimize power consumption and ground disturbance. Avoid letting the inside tyre stop turning, particularly on harder surfaces where maintaining traction is crucial for control.

Leverage the machine's power effectively and avoid oversteering, especially when navigating corners. Maintain control of the machine at all times and release the steering levers if the machine starts to feel uncontrollable, as your actions may contribute to the problem.

Ensure stability and visibility by keeping the centre of gravity as low as possible, particularly when traveling or turning. Keep the bucket positioned low to the ground to maintain stability. Remember to position the heavy end uphill when traversing slopes, with the rear heavier when unloaded and the front heavier when loaded.

Avoid side-hilling the skid steer and instead drive up and down slopes slowly and cautiously. Prohibit riders from being on the machine, whether in the bucket or on the operator's lap. Refrain from using the skid steer as a makeshift man lift or personnel carrier, as hydraulic failure may occur.

Never start the engine or operate the controls from outside the cab, as the loader or lift arm attachments could move unexpectedly, posing a crushing hazard. Always check for obstacles and coworkers before backing up, and use the armrests to maintain control on rough terrain.

When encountering ditches or obstacles, approach them at an angle to maximize tyre contact with the ground and ensure stability. By adhering to these guidelines, you can enhance safety and efficiency when operating the skid steer.

Any of the following can cause a loss of stability during operations:

1. Quick acceleration

2. Sudden braking

3. Traveling with the load too high

4. Dumping load too quickly

5. Dropping lift arms too quickly

6. Uneven terrain

7. Drains

8. Inclines

9. Turning on inclines

10. Turning too quickly

11. Uneven load

12. Obstructions

13. Trenches

14. Horse-play

15. Low tyre pressure

16. Overloading the bucket

Maintaining stability in skid steer loaders is crucial for the safety of the operator, bystanders, the load, and the work environment. To ensure stability:

1. Maintain recommended tyre pressure.

2. Avoid overloading the machine with excessively large loads, especially wet material which can be heavier.

3. Ensure the load is evenly distributed in the bucket.

4. Adjust operations according to ground and weather conditions.

5. Travel at appropriate speeds based on ground and weather conditions.

6. Reduce speed on rough surfaces and use the machine to clear hazards where possible.

7. Avoid driving sideways on slopes.

8. Keep the work area clean and free from obstacles.

9. Maintain a smooth operational flow.

10. Stay vigilant of obstacles and peripheral equipment.

11. Exercise caution when driving into water; verify the depth beforehand.

12. Plan tasks thoroughly.

13. Keep hands clear of obstructions on the loader.

As a loader operator, familiarity with basic calculations for area and volume is essential. Area is determined by multiplying length by width, while volume is calculated by multiplying area (length x width) by depth.

Before lifting any load, it's crucial to calculate its weight accurately. This can be achieved by:

- Checking weight markings on the load.

- Reviewing delivery dockets or information documents.

- Referring to weighbridge documents if available.

- Calculating the weight of the material if necessary.

When uncertain about the weight, seek guidance from a supervisor or colleague, or opt for smaller loads within the loader's safe load limits.

To estimate the amount of material within safe load limits, refer to the operator's manual or data plates for bucket capacity. Alternatively, use the following formula as a rough guide:

Length x Height x Width ÷ 2

During loading, ensure all four wheels remain on the ground while loading. Adjust the bucket angle based on the material type, increasing it for hard compact materials. Excessive angle may cause bucket chatter, while insufficient angle may result in bouncing and gliding over the material.

EARTHMOVING EQUIPMENT OPERATIONS

Figure 23: Correct bucket angle is important during loading. SFC ORBE, USA, Public domain, via Wikimedia Commons.

Maximize throttle and drive into the stack, adjusting speed by squeezing levers and maintaining consistent pressure. Maintain forward thrust while rolling the bucket to prevent improper filling or engine overload.

The skid steer is not intended for dozing, Focus on gentle and consistent pushing into the pile while crowning and lifting the bucket to ensure complete filling.

While rolling the bucket with forward thrust, elevate the arms, considering that some materials may not necessitate this operation.

Before reversing or changing direction, always check over your shoulder.

Transporting the Load: Keep the load as low as possible with the bucket fully rolled back, adjusting height considering terrain and positioning the truck or loader to minimize movement. Consider wind conditions, ground surface, material weight, and centre of gravity to maintain loader stability.

Figure 24: Transporting load as low as possible. Aktron, CC BY 3.0, via Wikimedia Commons.

Shifting the Load: Before lifting and shifting the load, ensure attachments are correctly secured, and slings, if used, are positioned for balance. Communicate intentions clearly, monitor for any shifting or hazards, use a tag line to steady the load, and deposit it safely before removing attachments or slings.

Dumping: Raise arms when approaching the truck/hopper, keeping the top of the bucket level, and dump the load slowly.

Figure 25: Dump load slowly. ŠJů (cs:ŠJů), CC BY-SA 3.0, via Wikimedia Commons.

Visibility is often limited on heavy equipment due to the elevated position of the operator. It is the operator's responsibility to maintain clear windows, lights, and reflectors on any vehicle to ensure maximum visibility at all times. Before moving forward or reversing, the operator must ensure the area is clear of obstructions and consider using horn signals as necessary. Operators should also be mindful of their field of vision and blind spots, as well as the blind spots of other equipment, to make necessary adjustments. Parking directly behind other mobile equipment should be avoided, and operators should ensure they are visible or use radio contact before proceeding.

Effective policies and procedures should be established for managing site safety. These should be part of an overarching management system that effectively identifies and controls risks associated with the work being done. A comprehensive safety system should include processes for identifying individuals with occupational health and safety responsibilities, managing the health and safety of contractors and subcontractors, establishing consultation procedures for health and safety matters, identifying hazards and controlling risks, locating underground services, developing site safety rules, monitoring site activities and enforcing safety rules, establishing site amenities, implementing ongoing maintenance, providing site-specific induction for workers and others, ensuring only trained and competent workers are allowed to work onsite, ensuring all plant and equipment is safe and without risks to health before use, identifying requirements for a mobile plant compound and vehicle parking, developing traffic management plans, identifying and controlling risks to the public, and developing emergency response plans for foreseeable emergency situations.

Each employer on-site must effectively manage the safety of their workers, mobile plant, and equipment. Processes and procedures should be in place to ensure the development of safe work method statements for high-risk construction work, the development of safe work procedures for other tasks with risks to workers or the public, competent workers or direct supervision of workers, emergency response plans for foreseeable emergency situations, including procedures to manage risks associated with a person becoming engulfed by soil or other material, and monitoring the health and conditions of workers. If powered plant is used, it must be mechanically sound, safe for use, and have the required safety documentation.

Hazards on-site may include moving materials and equipment, rough ground, falls, close proximity of mobile plant and other vehicles, excessive noise or dust, utility services, contaminated soil, and weather conditions and UV radiation. Employers should strive to eliminate risks to health and safety so far as reasonably practicable, such as by de-energizing power lines if necessary. If risks cannot be eliminated, they must be reduced through measures like implementing mandated controls specified by law, substituting new activities or equipment, isolating persons from hazards, using engineering controls, or employing a combination of these methods. Any remaining risks should be controlled through administration controls such as specific safety training and PPE like hearing protection and high visibility clothing.

Skid Steer Attachments

Skid steers are versatile machines capable of performing various tasks. Typically equipped with a scoop bucket for moving soil, gravel, feed, and similar materials, skid steers can easily switch between different attachments to adapt to different tasks.

One of the key advantages of skid steer loaders or multi-terrain loaders is the wide range of work tools available. Caterpillar Work Tools, for example, are specifically designed to interface with the machine's universal quick coupler system, allowing for fast and secure attachment changes without the operator leaving the cab. Some of the work tools offered include dirt buckets, utility buckets, pallet forks, utility grapple buckets, landscape rakes, and more.

Figure 26: Sample attachment - Forks. Wikideas1, CC0, via Wikimedia Commons.

Removing an attachment involves finding a flat surface, ensuring no distractions, locating the release button or lock pins, and reversing the device until the mounting plate releases. Adding an attachment with a quick attach system involves aligning the mounting plate, sliding it into the saddle of the new attachment, locking the arms into place, and pressing the engagement button. Manual systems require securing the new attachment with lock pins and ensuring proper alignment without resistance.

Figure 27: Sample attachment - Auger.

Skid steer attachments come in various types, including buckets, backhoes, brooms, rakes, trenchers, brushcutters, tillers, augers, hammers, mulchers, and forks. Each attachment serves specific purposes, such as excavation, landscaping, demolition, drilling, and material handling.

Skid steer attachments are considered universal due to their interchangeability among different models and brands. This universality is facilitated by the "quick attach" system, a standard attachment mechanism used worldwide in skid steer loaders.

Figure 28: CASE SR210 skid steer loader with grapple attachment. Case Construction Equipment, CC BY-SA 4.0, via Wikimedia Commons.

The Bob-Tach system is a quick attachment mounting system used in skid steer loaders and compact track loaders manufactured by Bobcat Company. It allows operators to rapidly change buckets and attachments without leaving the cab, enhancing efficiency and versatility on the job site.

The Bob-Tach system typically consists of two levers located on the loader arms that control the locking mechanism of the attachment. By pulling these levers, the locking mechanism is disengaged, allowing the operator to remove or install attachments quickly and easily. This system is designed to be user-friendly and ensures a secure connection between the attachment and the loader arms, minimizing the risk of accidents or detachment during operation.

Overall, the Bob-Tach system simplifies the process of switching between various work tools, such as buckets, pallet forks, augers, and more, making the skid steer loader or compact track loader more adaptable to different tasks and applications on the work site.

Where a loader is equipped with the Bob-Tach system, designed for rapid changing of buckets and attachments:

1. Pull the Bob-Tach levers upwards completely.

2. Tilt the Bob-Tach forward and drive the loader forward until the top edge of the Bob-Tach is fully under the flange of the bucket. Avoid hitting the Bob-Tach levers on the bucket.

3. Tilt the Bob-Tach backward until the bucket is off the ground, and then stop the engine.

Warning: To prevent injury or death, turn off the machine before leaving the operator's seat. Before exiting:

- Lower the lift arms to place the attachment flat on the ground.

- Stop the engine.

- Engage the parking brake.

- Raise the seat bar and adjust the pedals until both lock securely.

To lock the Bob-Tach wedges, push down on the levers as demonstrated. Always refer to your owner's manual for attaching different auxiliary attachments to your machine to avoid injury or death.

Note: Always consult the operator's manual or contact the dealer when operating or fitting new attachments.

Boom mounted attachments can be swiftly changed. The system comprises:

A. Pivoting mounting plate affixed to the boom lift arms.

B. Latch handles to secure the attachment to the pivoting mounting plate.

C. Attachment saddle (part of the attachment).

To mount an attachment, ensure the latching handles are fully in the "up" position to retract the lock pins. Align the skid steer mounting plate with the attachment's saddle by adjusting the skid steer while raising or lowering the top of the mounting plate under the attachment saddle hydraulically. Raise the mounting plate using foot or hand lever controls until the attachment's back surface rests against the mounting plate. Lower the attachment with the bucket rolled forward (ensuring it does not touch the ground). Once in position, turn off the engine, set the parking brake, and exit the skid steer. Firmly push down the locking levers to engage the lock pins into the retaining tabs.

Note: Some skid steers may feature a push-button attachment locking system that electrically activates hydraulic pins from the operator's seat.

To remove the attachment, reverse the installation process. When the attachment is free, lower the boom slightly and slowly back away from the attachment, ensuring it is stable.

Warning: Do not attempt to lock the manual lock pins from inside the operator's cab. Keep all body parts inside the cab.

Removing a Hydraulic Powered Attachment: Disconnecting a hydraulically powered attachment involves not only the mechanical connection but also the hydraulic hoses.

Follow these steps to disconnect the hydraulic hoses:

- Ensure the attachment is in a stable position.

  - Lower the lift boom arms and move the hydraulic control levers back and forth to release the static pressure.

EARTHMOVING EQUIPMENT OPERATIONS

- Push back on the lock ring.

- Remove the hydraulic hoses from the couplings and replace the dust caps on each connector.

- Hang the hoses on the equipment, keeping them off the ground to prevent damage to the machine or injury to yourself.

Warning: Remember to remove the hydraulic lines before pulling away.

The skid steer operates as a hydraulic machine driven by an engine. Upon starting the engine, every action - whether it's ground movement, steering, lift arm control, bucket positioning, or attachment operation - involves hydraulic mechanisms.

Hydraulic Power: The term "hydraulic" pertains to fluids under pressure. While any liquid can be pressurized, not all liquids are suitable for hydraulic work. For instance, a garden hose left in the sun demonstrates pressurized water, but water cannot function effectively as a hydraulic fluid due to its tendency to vaporize at high temperatures. Oil is the typical hydraulic fluid used in farm equipment, as it can effectively flow through systems with minimal openings and withstand high pressure.

Precautions When Using Hydraulics: To operate hydraulic systems safely and efficiently, it's crucial to consider the following points:

- Cleanliness of the hydraulic oil

- Generation of heat during operation

- Risks associated with oil leaks under pressure

Ensure a clear understanding of each point, and if necessary, seek guidance from a supervisor or hydraulic technician.

Clean Oil Requirements: Hydraulic pumps and control valves operate with tiny clearances and close tolerances. Contaminants like grit and dirt can cause wear and damage to these components. Therefore, clean hydraulic oil must be used, and care should be taken to maintain cleanliness around fill areas and connections.

Hydraulic connector covers should always be in place to prevent dust, dirt, grease, and moisture from entering the system, thereby ensuring longer system durability.

Heat Generation Hazards: As hydraulic fluid moves through the system, it encounters resistance from loads, leading to increased pressure and heat buildup. Under heavy load conditions, hoses and connections can become hot. Before touching any connections, it's essential to sense for heat by placing the back of your hand nearby.

If connections are hot, allow the hydraulic system to cool down before making any adjustments.

High-Pressure Oil Leaks: Pressure within hydraulic systems can exceed 2000 psi, posing a risk of leaks from hoses and connections. These leaks may not always be visible and can result in serious injury if oil is injected under the skin. Never check for leaks with your hand, and seek immediate medical attention if oil injection occurs.

Connecting Hydraulic Hoses to Couplers Hydraulic couplers facilitate quick and straightforward connections. Follow these steps:

1. Clean the couplers to remove dirt and grit.

2. Remove the dust covers from the couplers.

3. Push the couplers together until the lock ring snaps the two parts securely. Some systems may feature older-style lock levers or manual pull lock rings.

If connection proves difficult, try the following:

a. Release any static pressure by moving the hydraulic control levers back and forth.

b. Check for any obstructions blocking movement of the locking ring on the female coupler.

In some cases, hoses leading to hydraulic cylinders may be reversed, resulting in unexpected actions from control valves/levers. To correct this, switch the hoses to the opposite female coupler.

Disconnecting Hydraulic Hoses To disconnect hydraulic hoses:

- Relieve static pressure by moving the control lever.

- Push back on the lock ring.

- Remove the hydraulic hose.

- Replace dust caps on each connector.

- Hang the hoses on the implement and keep them off the ground.

Generally, the skid steer is not considered suitable for lifting tasks akin to cranes. As a result, the use of chains, wires, or slings is typically associated with backhoes, excavators, and cranes. However, in the absence of these machines, specific guidelines must be followed when using lifting equipment:

- Never attempt to lift while the equipment hangs over the cutting edge.

- Avoid using the clam of a 4-in-1 bucket to hold a chain sling or rope.

- Ensure that the weight lifted does not exceed the Safe Working Load (SWL) specified in the owner's manual of both the machine and the chain/rope/sling.

- Only attach lifting equipment using a D-shackle attached to an engineer-approved lifting lug welded to the bucket.

- Avoid using drag chains.

- Use only tagged lifting equipment and hooks to attach the load.

- Refer to the manual handling unit for further guidance.

The first step is to determine the SWL of the machine with forks attached, as outlined in the owner's manual and the forks owner manual. This information should be familiar to operators and may also be displayed on the machine for easy reference.

A bobcat, particularly with attachments like the 4-in-1 bucket and engineer-approved forks, can effectively function as a forklift. Forks are typically rated around 1600kg, well within the machine's lifting capability. However, operators must carefully consider the load to prevent tipping over.

There are various methods to estimate the weight of loads, including using delivery dockets, product weight knowledge, manufacturer inquiries, or visual cues such as stamped weights on products. If weights are not readily available, it's essential to err on the side of caution and estimate conservatively.

When lifting loads, operators should ensure the load is low to the ground, within the SWL of the machine, on stable ground, and evenly distributed across lifting arms. Communication between the operator and other workers involved in the operation is crucial for safety. Simple hand and body signals should be established and understood by all involved before commencing the operation.

In cases where communication breaks down, operators should promptly power down the machine, turn it off, and remove hearing protection to address any issues. Effective communication and adherence to safety protocols are paramount in skid steer operations to prevent accidents and ensure the safety of all personnel involved.

Concluding Skid Steer Operations

Before shutting down the skid steer, it's important to follow the proper procedures outlined in the owner's manual. As a general approach, firstly, ensure that the vehicle is parked on a level surface to prevent any unexpected movement. Then, gradually decrease the engine speed and allow it to settle down to a stable state. Lower the lift arms and place any attachments flat on the ground to ensure stability during shutdown.

Next, it's crucial to allow the engine to cool down sufficiently. Shutting down a hot engine prematurely can lead to the thin oil film coating the engine parts burning off, resulting in potential metal-on-metal contact upon restarting. This cooling period is particularly important if the machine is equipped with a turbocharger, as allowing the engine to cool for three to five minutes allows the turbo to equalize its temperature.

After ensuring the engine has cooled adequately, place the controls in the neutral position and engage the parking brake to secure the vehicle. Turn off all lights and accessories to conserve battery power. Then, proceed to shut off the motor completely.

To relieve any hydraulic pressure within the system, it's advisable to cycle the controls before finally removing the ignition key to complete the shutdown process. Following these steps ensures a safe and proper shutdown of the skid steer loader.

When exiting the skid steer, it's important to follow a systematic procedure to ensure safety. Begin by unbuckling the safety belt to free yourself from the seat restraint. Next, raise the seat bar to allow for easier exit from the cab.

Finally, exit the cab using a three-point exit technique. This involves using both hands and one foot or both feet and one hand to maintain three points of contact with the machine as you exit. By following this procedure, you can minimize the risk of slips, trips, or falls when exiting the skid steer.

Maintenance is crucial to ensure the efficient operation of your skid steer loader. Regular maintenance tasks, similar to those required for maintaining a car, can be performed by the machine operator after each shift or approximately every 10 hours of operation. These tasks include cleaning and lubricating the bucket and loader, refuelling, checking and topping up all fluids, inspecting air filters, examining the battery, ensuring a clean work cabin, cleaning windows, reporting any faults to supervisors, completing log book entries, and checking tyre pressures. When inflating tyres, caution must be exercised to avoid hazards associated with split rim wheels.

Scheduled maintenance tasks are essential to maintain the safety and effectiveness of the loader. These tasks can be performed at the end of a job, on a regular basis (e.g., weekly or monthly), or during breaks in work activities. Scheduled maintenance typically involves cleaning, authorized servicing, replacing serviceable parts such as filters and fluids, draining fuel and air tanks, and monitoring and recording any issues.

When undertaking repairs on the skid steer loader, it's crucial to follow certain precautions. Operators must be qualified and authorized, adhere to supplier guidelines, check hour meters and service stickers, and ensure attachments are properly maintained and serviced. Tampering with machinery should be avoided, as most organizations have designated maintenance personnel responsible for such tasks.

The hydraulic system of skid steer loaders is powered by an internal combustion engine, which operates a hydraulic pump. Monitoring hydraulic fluid levels, checking for oil leaks, and exercising caution when working with raised hydraulics are essential for safe operation.

Diesel engines require proper warm-up before starting, and precautions must be taken to prevent issues such as carbon monoxide exposure in enclosed spaces and address oil system problems promptly. Batteries contain sulphuric acid and can explode if mishandled, so care must be taken when changing or disconnecting them.

When refuelling, the engine should be turned off, and spillages should be promptly addressed according to site procedures. When replacing defective parts or equipment, the loader must be securely parked, appropriate replacements and tools must be used, and qualified assistance should be sought if unsure.

Regular inspection of the engine, hydraulic system, and control system is necessary to identify potential issues such as engine starting problems, hydraulic fluid level discrepancies, and control system malfunctions. Addressing these issues promptly ensures optimal performance and safety of the skid steer loader.

While most large machinery is typically transported by a specialized float company, the size of a skid steer often allows for self-transportation. Successful transport includes:

1. Ensure engineer-approved ramps with a Safe Working Load (SWL) larger than the skid steer are used.

2. Have locking bolts for securing ramps into the tipper body.

3. Always reverse up into tippers or floats to prevent the machine from rolling back.

4. Note that ramps into a tipper may be steeper and longer, and planning may be necessary to accommodate all attachments.

5. Ensure the machine does not extend outside of the floating vehicle.

6. Use tie-down chains in flat-sided trucks.

Upon Arrival at a New Site:
- Thoroughly fill in the pre-start checklist sheet, including noting engine hours before moving off.

- Ensure all fire suppression equipment is in place, charged, and serviceable.

- Do not remove radiator or oil tank caps when hot, as contents may be under pressure. (Note: Caps will not be hot if the pre-start occurs at the start of the day as intended.)

- Avoid accumulations of paper, rags, debris, etc., around the radiator, exhaust, engine, ladder, or cab.

- Report all defects and new damage immediately. Ensure all fluid levels (engine oils, hydraulic oils, coolant, and diesel) are topped up. (Note: Hydraulic fluid level will be visible at the bottom of the sight glass at pre-start and rise into the centre of the target during operation as hydraulic oil expands.)

- Do not open the hydraulic oil reservoir cap to check the level, as hydraulic systems are sensitive to contamination. Maximum operating performance is achieved with clean hydraulic fluid.

- Refrain from operating an unsafe or damaged machine.

- Check the general functioning of the machine, including the operation of flashing lights and reverse beepers.

Chapter Three

Loader Operations

A front end loader, also known as a front loader, bucket loader, or simply loader, is a type of heavy equipment commonly used in construction, agriculture, and landscaping. It is characterized by a large, wide bucket at the front of the vehicle that is used for scooping, lifting, and moving materials such as soil, gravel, sand, and debris.

Front end loaders are typically equipped with hydraulic systems that enable the operator to control the lifting, tilting, and dumping of the bucket. They are often mounted on either wheels or tracks for mobility and stability. Front end loaders are versatile machines and can be fitted with various attachments such as forks, grapples, and snow plows to perform a wide range of tasks.

Figure 29: A loader at the Sunrise Dam Gold Mine. Calistemon, CC BY-SA 3.0, via Wikimedia Commons.

These loaders are commonly seen on construction sites for moving earth and debris, in agricultural settings for handling crops and feed, and in landscaping projects for transporting materials and shaping terrain. They are valued for their efficiency, power, and versatility in handling different types of materials and tasks.

The front end loader plays a pivotal role in daily operations at construction sites. These versatile wheel loaders are adept at transferring materials from stockpiles to trucks and transporting them around job sites. They come in various sizes of buckets, with larger models commonly used in mining contexts. Additionally, small and mid-sized wheel loaders often feature attachment couplers, enabling them to utilize a range of work tools like forks, brooms, and lifting jibs.

In quarrying and mining operations, the front end loader serves multiple functions, including digging, leveling, pushing, loading and carrying materials, handling loads akin to a crane, and serving as a tool carrier. It also contributes to tasks such as preparing and leveling stock storage pads, leveling and rehabilitating areas, towing loads and other equipment similar to a tractor, and general cleanup of quarry floor work areas.

The operator of the front end loader holds a crucial responsibility in ensuring the smooth movement of haul trucks and minimizing idle time by systematically managing truck turnarounds. Keeping loading sites free of loose material is essential for reducing tyre damage, wear, and mechanical maintenance on vehicles, thereby enhancing efficiency and cutting costs. Additionally, operators may be tasked with preparing material storage pads and performing general cleanup duties.

Operating a front end loader demands a high level of hand-eye coordination to achieve a level surface. For the purpose of this resource, certain definitions apply: an attachment refers to a bucket or other implement designed for attachment to the FEL (front end loader), while a competent person for any task is defined as an individual with the requisite knowledge, skills, and experience to carry out that task effectively. The FEL itself is a unit comprising lifting arms and fastening devices, intended for mounting on the front of an agricultural tractor and equipped for fitting of a bucket or other attachment. The rated capacity denotes the maximum lift capacity in kilograms at maximum height for the FEL and standard bucket, determined in accordance with ASAE S301. Rollback refers to the loss of control of the load, resulting in the load falling rearwards onto the tractor and/or operator. ROL (rated operating load) signifies the maximum load in kilograms that can be lifted to full height without exceeding the tractor specifications while maintaining stability, determined for a specific tractor, FEL, and attachment combination.

A front end loader, typically consists of several key components that work together to perform various tasks in construction, mining, agriculture, and other industries. These components include:

1. Chassis: The chassis is the base frame of the front end loader, providing structural support and housing for all other components. It is usually mounted on a set of wheels or tracks for mobility.

2. Engine: The engine powers the front end loader and drives the hydraulic system. It provides the necessary energy to move the machine and operate its attachments.

3. Hydraulic System: The hydraulic system is a crucial part of the front end loader, responsible for powering its movements and attachments. It includes hydraulic pumps, cylinders, valves, hoses, and reservoirs. The hydraulic system allows for lifting, lowering, tilting, and other movements of the loader arms and bucket.

4. Loader Arms: Also known as lift arms or booms, the loader arms are connected to the chassis and extend forward to support the bucket or other attachments. They can be raised, lowered, and tilted to manipulate the load.

5. Bucket: The bucket is the primary attachment used for scooping, lifting, and transporting materials. It is mounted at the front of the loader arms and comes in various sizes and configurations depending on the intended application.

6. Attachment Coupler: Many front end loaders are equipped with an attachment coupler, which allows for quick and easy swapping of attachments such as forks, brooms, grapples, and more. The coupler securely locks the attachment in place and ensures

compatibility with the loader arms.

7. Operator Cab: The operator cab is where the operator controls the front end loader and performs various tasks. It typically features a seat, controls for operating the machine and attachments, instrumentation, and safety features such as rollover protection structures (ROPS) and falling object protection structures (FOPS).

8. Counterweight: To maintain stability and balance while lifting heavy loads, front end loaders often include counterweights mounted at the rear of the machine. These counterweights help prevent tipping and ensure safe operation.

These components work together seamlessly to enable the front end loader to perform a wide range of tasks efficiently and effectively, making it a versatile and indispensable machine in many industries.

Figure 30: Wheeled front end loader components. Back image - Grendelkhan, CC BY-SA 4.0, via Wikimedia Commons.

Figure 31: Tracked front end loader components. Back image - U.S. Navy photo by Photographer's Mate 3rd Class John P. Curtis, Public domain, via Wikimedia Commons.

Wheeled loaders and tracked loaders (see Figure 32 and Figure 33) are both types of front end loaders used for material handling, excavation, and other tasks in various industries. While they share similarities in functionality, they differ in their design, performance, and suitability for different applications.

Figure 32: Caterpillar track loader. Kevin M Haddocks, U.S. Navy, Public domain, via Wikimedia Commons.

Here are some key differences between wheeled loaders and tracked loaders:

1. Mobility:

- Wheeled Loaders: Wheeled loaders are equipped with rubber tyres, allowing them to move quickly and efficiently on smooth surfaces such as roads, pavement, and compacted soil. They offer excellent manoeuvrability and are well-suited for applications where frequent travel over longer distances is required.

- Tracked Loaders: Tracked loaders feature tracks instead of tyres, providing superior traction and flotation on soft, uneven, or rough terrain such as mud, gravel, and loose soil. They are more stable and capable of navigating steep slopes, muddy conditions, and rough terrain, making them ideal for off-road applications and challenging working environments.

2. Ground Pressure:

- Wheeled Loaders: Wheeled loaders exert higher ground pressure due to the concentrated weight of the machine being distributed over a smaller contact area of the tyres. As a result, they may cause more soil compaction and surface damage, making them less suitable for soft or sensitive ground conditions.

- Tracked Loaders: Tracked loaders exert lower ground pressure thanks to the larger contact area of the tracks, which distributes the machine's weight more evenly. This reduces soil compaction and minimizes damage to sensitive terrain, making tracked loaders preferable for working in environmentally sensitive areas or soft ground conditions.

3. Stability:

- Wheeled Loaders: Wheeled loaders typically have a higher centre of gravity compared to tracked loaders, which can affect their stability, especially when lifting heavy loads or operating on uneven terrain. However, they offer greater agility and manoeuvrability, making them suitable for applications where tight turning radiuses are required.

- Tracked Loaders: Tracked loaders have a lower centre of gravity and wider track footprint, providing greater stability and traction, particularly on slopes and uneven surfaces. This makes them well-suited for tasks that require lifting and carrying heavy loads in challenging terrain conditions.

4. Maintenance:

- Wheeled Loaders: Wheeled loaders generally require less

maintenance compared to tracked loaders, as they have fewer moving parts and components associated with the track system. Maintenance tasks such as tyre replacement, alignment, and balancing are simpler and more cost-effective.

- Tracked Loaders: Tracked loaders have more complex track systems that require regular inspection, adjustment, and maintenance to ensure proper tension, alignment, and lubrication. Track replacement and undercarriage maintenance can be more time-consuming and expensive compared to wheeled loaders.

Overall, the choice between wheeled loaders and tracked loaders depends on factors such as the specific application, terrain conditions, mobility requirements, and operational preferences. Wheeled loaders are preferred for applications that prioritize speed, manoeuvrability, and versatility on smooth surfaces, while tracked loaders excel in providing traction, stability, and flotation in challenging off-road environments.

EARTHMOVING EQUIPMENT OPERATIONS

Figure 33: Liebherr 631 tracked loader. btr, CC BY-SA 2.5, via Wikimedia Commons.

Wheeled front end loaders, also known as wheel loaders, come in various types, each designed for specific applications and industries. Some of the common types of front end loaders include:

1. Compact Wheel Loaders: These are smaller-sized wheel loaders designed for manoeuvrability in tight spaces and light-duty applications. They are often used in landscaping, construction, and agriculture for tasks such as loading materials into trucks, moving pallets, and clearing debris.

2. Small Wheel Loaders: Small wheel loaders are slightly larger than compact wheel loaders and offer increased lift capacity and bucket size. They are versatile machines suitable for a wide range of applications, including material handling, landscaping, snow removal, and light construction.

3. Medium Wheel Loaders: Medium wheel loaders are larger and more powerful than compact and small wheel loaders, making them suitable for heavier-duty tasks in construction, mining, quarrying, and industrial applications. They have higher lift capacities and larger buckets, allowing them to handle larger volumes of material more efficiently.

4. Large Wheel Loaders: Large wheel loaders are the most powerful and robust type of front end loaders, designed for heavy-duty applications in mining, quarrying, bulk material handling, and large-scale construction projects. They have the highest lift capacities, largest buckets, and are capable of handling the toughest materials and operating conditions.

5. High-lift Wheel Loaders: High-lift wheel loaders are specialized machines equipped with extended lift arms that provide increased lift height and reach. They are commonly used in applications where materials need to be loaded or stacked at greater heights, such as warehouses, ports, and industrial facilities.

6. Integrated Tool Carriers: Integrated tool carriers are front end loaders equipped with a quick coupler system that allows for easy attachment changes. They are commonly used in construction, agriculture, and material handling operations, where multiple attachments such as buckets, forks, grapples, and brooms are required for different tasks.

7. Articulated Wheel Loaders: Articulated wheel loaders feature a hinged joint between the front and rear chassis sections, allowing for greater manoeuvrability and flexibility on uneven terrain. They are commonly used in construction, agriculture, and landscaping for tasks such as loading, grading, and material handling.

Each type of front end loader offers unique features and capabilities to meet the specific needs of different industries and applications, providing versatility, efficiency, and productivity on job sites.

Sample Front Loaders:

Caterpillar 924K, 930K, 938K Wheel Loaders: Caterpillar has enhanced the design of its compact wheel loaders—the 924K, 930K, and 938K—with various new features. These include software improvements enabling the hydrostatic-drive system to operate more similarly to a mechanical-drive machine. Additionally, the left control pedal (decelerator and brake) has been redesigned for enhanced precision, and implement-response levels can now be adjusted through the in-cab secondary display. Other upgrades include thread-to-connect couplers in the auxiliary hydraulic system for easier operation and modified loader linkage to improve forward visibility.

Figure 34: Caterpillar 924K. E911a, CC BY-SA 4.0, via Wikimedia Commons.

Atlas Copco LHD Scooptram: Atlas Copco offers its load/haul/dump (LHD) Scooptram models—ST7, ST1030, and ST14—with an optional side-dump bucket, enhancing versatility and productivity. This addition speeds up the loading cycle, as the loader only needs to position itself parallel to the truck for dumping. Equipped with the side-dump bucket, these LHD models are suitable for various applications, including civil engineering projects, rail- and road-tunnel construction, and mine development.

Kubota R30 Series Wheel Loader: The R30 series of wheel loaders, including models R530 and R630, marks Kubota's entry into the 60-to-80-horsepower range. The R630 boasts a horsepower of 64.4 and a bucket breakout force of 10,415 pounds, while the R530 offers 51 horsepower and 7,761 pounds of bucket force. Both models feature improved visibility and offer hydrostatic transmissions, with the R630 additionally offering an electronic transmission with four modes.

Caterpillar 903C Wheel Loader: The Cat 903C compact wheel loader is equipped with Z-bar loader linkage, hydrostatic drive, maintenance-free propeller shafts, and oscillating axles with planetary reduction. The cab features dual entry doors, tilting steering column, low-effort hydraulic controls, and optional HVAC system. Optional external counterweights and multiple tyre choices allow customization for various applications.

Takeuchi TW65, TW80 Wheel Loaders: The new Series 2 compact wheel loaders TW65 and TW80 meet Tier 4-Final emissions standards with a 73-horsepower Deutz diesel engine. They feature increased performance, improved serviceability, and an enhanced operator's environment. The loaders offer increased attachment compatibility, pilot-operated joystick controls, and a two-speed hydrostatic drive system for precise attachment control.

Volvo L150H, L180H, L220 H Wheel Loaders: The H Series wheel loaders from Volvo, including models L150H, L180H, and L220H, feature Tier 4-Final D13J diesels matched with Volvo powertrain and hydraulics systems. They offer increased fuel efficiency, automatic power shift, and rear axle cradles with maintenance-free components. The cabs can be tilted for easy access, and the loaders are equipped with advanced controls for improved productivity.

Figure 35: Volvo L150H loader. Neuwieser from Germany, CC BY-SA 2.0, via Wikimedia Commons.

Case 21F, 121F, 221F, 321F Tier 4-Final Wheel Loaders The F Series compact wheel loaders from Case are completely redesigned, featuring shorter wheelbases, reduced cab heights, increased breakout force, and enhanced attachment compatibility. They offer improved performance, increased serviceability, and enhanced cab comfort.

Hyundai HL730-9A Wheel Loader: The HL730-9A wheel loader from Hyundai features a 128-horsepower Cummins engine meeting Tier 4-Interim standards. It offers improved transmission control, increased fuel efficiency, and enhanced operator comfort. The loader is equipped with advanced technology for remote management and service access.

Kawasaki 70Z7 Wheel Loader: The Kawasaki 70Z7 wheel loader is a powerful machine with a 173-horsepower Cummins engine meeting Tier 4-Interim standards. It features advanced IntelliTech functions for automated operations and offers high productivity and reliability for various applications.

Front end loader controls (see Figure 36 for an example) typically consist of various levers, pedals, and switches that enable the operator to manoeuvre the loader effectively and perform different tasks. Here's an explanation of common front end loader controls:

1. Steering Wheel: The steering wheel allows the operator to control the direction of the front end loader. Turning the steering wheel left or right directs the wheels accordingly, enabling the loader to move in the desired direction.

2. Acceleration Pedal: Also known as the throttle pedal, this pedal controls the speed of the front end loader. Pressing the pedal increases the engine's RPM (revolutions per minute), allowing the loader to move forward or backward at different speeds.

3. Brake Pedal: The brake pedal is used to slow down or stop the front end loader. Pressing the pedal applies the brakes, reducing the loader's speed or bringing it to a complete stop when necessary.

4. Loader Control Levers: These levers are typically used to operate the loader's hydraulic system, controlling the movement of the loader arms, bucket, and any attached implements. The position of these levers determines the direction and speed of the loader's movements, such as lifting, lowering, tilting, and dumping.

5. Loader Arm Controls: Separate controls may be provided to operate the loader arms independently. These controls allow the operator to extend or retract the loader arms and adjust their height as needed for loading and dumping materials.

6. Bucket Control Levers: Similar to the loader control levers, these levers control the movement of the bucket or other attachments. They allow the operator to open, close, tilt, and rotate the bucket for efficient material handling.

7. Auxiliary Control Switches: In loaders equipped with auxiliary hydraulic systems, auxiliary control switches are provided to activate additional hydraulic functions, such as operating attachments like forks, brooms, or hydraulic grapples.

8. Instrument Panel: The instrument panel typically displays important information such as engine RPM, fuel level, temperature, hydraulic pressure, and warning lights for various systems. It allows the operator to monitor the loader's performance and identify any issues that may arise during operation.

These controls may vary slightly depending on the specific model and manufacturer of the front end loader, but they generally serve similar functions to ensure safe and efficient operation of the equipment.

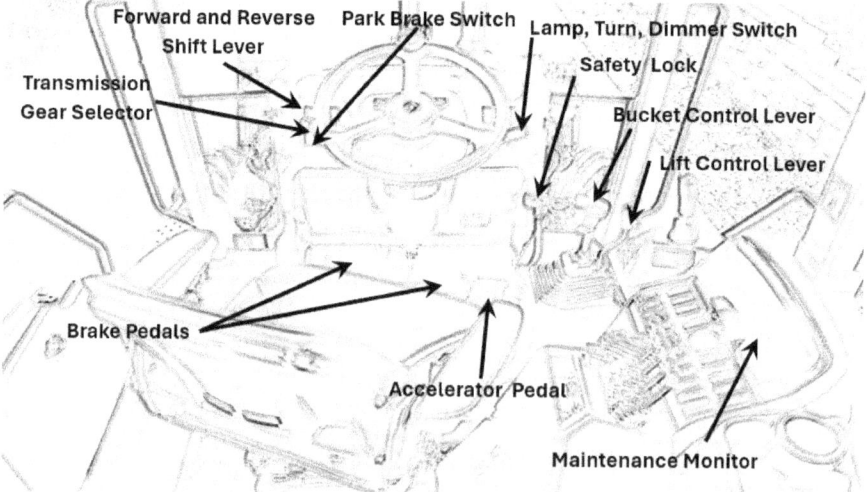

Figure 36: Example of typical controls for a front end loader.

EARTHMOVING EQUIPMENT OPERATIONS

The bucket operation controls encompass two primary functions: lifting and tilting. For lifting, operators can elevate the bucket, maintain its position, lower it, or engage a floating mode. When tilting the bucket, operators can tilt it back, crowd it, or incline it forward, with options to hold the position or initiate tipping or discharge. Additionally, foot controls play a crucial role in manoeuvring the front end loader. The right pedal acts as the service brake, facilitating regular braking actions during movement. Conversely, the left pedal is responsible for activating the brake and disengaging the transmission, enabling engine acceleration to enhance hydraulic speed.

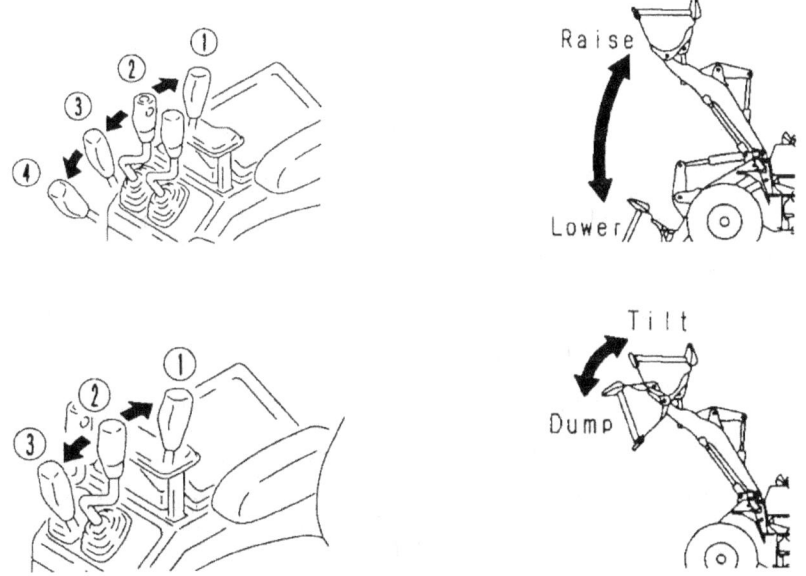

Figure 37: Bucket controls.

Planning and Preparing for Loader Operations

Upon completion of the induction program and readiness to commence work at the actual workplace, it is advisable to request your supervisor for a briefing on the local safety protocols within the immediate work area. This briefing should cover essential safety features including the location and types of fire extinguishers and hoses, emergency stop mechanisms for electrical equipment and fuel supply, emergency tag policy, evacuation procedures, special signage, first aid stations, quarry traffic regulations, emergency phone and communication systems, protocols for handling chemical or oil spills, designated vehicle parking areas, and rules and safety procedures for two-way radios. While the induction program provides a general overview, this workplace orientation is tailored to the specific hazards and safety measures of your immediate work environment, ensuring preparedness to respond safely to emergency situations.

Depending on the scale of operations, daily work instructions may be communicated through verbal briefings or written directives from your supervisor. It is crucial to receive and comprehend these instructions clearly. If uncertain about any task requirements, seek clarification from your supervisor. Additionally, conducting a site visit to inspect the job before preparing the loader for work may be necessary. Inspecting the material to be handled is an integral part of planning operations, considering factors such as whether the material will be moved solely with the loader, loaded onto a haul truck, stockpiled, or excavated directly from the face or a stockpile. Implementation of safe operating procedures specific to the site should be part of the planning process, taking into account considerations like site speed limits, working around overhead power cables, underground utilities, conveyors, other machinery, blasting operations, and site traffic regulations involving loaded vehicles and water trucks.

Safe Operation requires adherence to all safety rules, precautions, and instructions when operating or performing maintenance on the machine. Ensuring safety, both for oneself and others, relies on the careful operation and judgment of the front end loader. A well-trained and vigilant operator significantly mitigates the risk of accidents. Therefore, it is imperative to follow all safety protocols and abstain from operating the machine when feeling unwell, under the influence of medication inducing drowsiness, or after consuming alcohol.

A wheel loader is designed to handle, load, and transport loose material when equipped with the appropriate attachment, such as a bucket, grapple, or lift forks. It is not intended for crushing, ripping apart, or compacting loaded material. It is imperative to ensure that the operator is adequately trained and certified to operate the equipment for the specific material handling application. Only designated and authorized personnel should operate the wheel loader.

The wheel loader operator must possess mental and physical fitness, along with good vision, spatial perception, adequate hearing, and quick reaction time. Adherence to guidelines for the proper use of the wheel loader is essential to prevent hazards, as outlined in the manufacturer's instruction and safety manual. The operator should be thoroughly familiar with the layout and operation of all wheel loader controls, monitors, and indicators, as well as understand its lifting capabilities and limitations.

Before starting up the wheel loader, the operator must meticulously plan the machine's operating procedure based on the existing working conditions and environment. Awareness of the location of all underground and above-ground utilities at the job site is crucial. Both the operator and maintenance personnel should identify a clear and safe approach to the machine.

A daily walk-around inspection of the wheel loader and the job site surroundings is mandatory. This includes checking for secured pin and bolt connections, wear and tear items, hydraulic and fuel leaks, and any structural damage. Attention should also be given to maintenance deficiencies, such as loose wheel lug nuts, incorrect tyre inflation, tyre damage, and issues with clutch or brake functionality, as well as frayed or damaged fuel or hydraulic lines.

Operating a defective or damaged machine is strictly prohibited. When accessing the machine, utilize a three-point stance on ladders, steps, and provided handholds, avoiding the use of the steering wheel or joystick as a handhold. Familiarize yourself with the emergency exit on the machine and perform a thorough inspection and check prior to every shift change, as outlined in the manufacturer's instruction manual.

Ensure that all maintenance tasks have been completed and documented, and that all doors are unlocked but closed and secured to prevent inadvertent movement. Additionally, ensure that all windows and mirrors are unobstructed and clean, with mirrors properly positioned for optimal operator visibility to the rear of the machine. Before operating the wheel loader, take a seat and fasten the seat belt, adjusting the seat and armrests to the most comfortable operating position, and confirm that the area of operation is clear of personnel and obstructions.

Workplace Safety Guidelines:

- When collaborating with another operator or a person managing work site traffic, ensure that all personnel understand the designated hand signals.

- Strictly adhere to all safety rules and regulations applicable to the work site.

- Verify that all guards and covers are correctly positioned, and have them promptly repaired if found damaged.

Caution: Operating under compromised conditions can impair judgment and increase the risk of accidents. Always utilize safety features such as safety lock levers and seat belts correctly. Never remove safety features, and always maintain them in optimal condition to prevent serious injury or fatality due to improper usage.

Avoid wearing loose clothing, jewellery, or long hair that could become entangled in controls or moving parts, posing a significant risk of injury or death. Additionally, refrain from wearing oily clothes as they are flammable. Always wear appropriate personal protective equipment, including a hard hat, safety glasses, safety shoes, mask, or gloves when operating or maintaining the machine. Note that in dusty or hazardous environments, a mask or other breathing protection may be necessary.

Before utilizing the Front End Loader (FEL) and its attachments, conduct a thorough inspection, ensuring all safety features are operational. If any safety feature is found to be malfunctioning, refrain from using the FEL and its attachments until the issue is resolved. Operate the FEL and its attachments in accordance with the manufacturer's instructions.

Prior to commencing operations, consider several factors, including overhead power lines, underground services, terrain, proximity of personnel, load specifications, Roll Over Limit (ROL), travel speed, and counterweights. Familiarize yourself with the specific regulatory jurisdiction's approach distances for work near overhead power lines.

During transportation, ensure that the load is positioned at the lowest feasible level and maintain a safe speed not exceeding 10 km/h, considering the terrain for stability. When operating on slopes, be aware that a tractor's stability and the FEL's ability to prevent roll back are compromised.

Always wear safety goggles, hard hats, and heavy gloves when handling metal chips or minute materials, especially during tasks involving hammers or compressed air cleaning of the air cleaner element. Ensure that no one is near the machine and verify the proper functioning of all protective equipment before usage.

Caution: Always engage the safety lock (if equipped) before leaving the operator's seat. When vacating the seat, securely position the safety lock lever to the LOCK position and the parking brake switch to the ON position to prevent unexpected movement and potential injuries or damage.

Avoid jumping on or off the machine and never attempt to embark or disembark from a moving machine, as these actions can lead to unforeseen injuries. When boarding or alighting, maintain three-point contact with handrails and steps and refrain from holding any control levers.

Before entering or exiting the machine, inspect handrails and steps for any oil, grease, or mud, and promptly clean them to prevent slipping hazards. Additionally, repair any damages and tighten loose bolts to ensure structural integrity.

Precautions for Roll Over Protection System:

- Never operate the machine with the Roll Over Protection System (ROPS) removed, as it is designed to safeguard the operator in the event of a rollover. The ROPS must meet all regulations and standards, and any damage should be reported to the supervisor or equipment distributor for repair. Fasten the seat belt while operating the machine, as the ROPS can only provide adequate protection when coupled with the seat belt.

Ensure proper precautions are taken when handling attachments and accumulators, strictly adhering to manufacturer's instructions and safety protocols to mitigate risks and ensure safe operation of the machine.

Rollback incidents, where the load moves backward onto the operator, pose a significant risk during material handling operations. Hence, it is imperative for all Front End Loaders (FELs) to incorporate a rollback prevention system.

Designers must ensure the elimination of rollback when the tractor, FEL, and attachment combination are used as intended on a level surface. They should also provide guidance on controlling rollback on sloped ground, including specifying load limitations for manufacturer-approved attachments.

In cases where the FEL and its attachments come from different designers, the assembler must ensure compatibility and the elimination of rollback risks. Self-leveling systems should be designed to prevent override and rollback creation.

The angle of the earthmoving bucket attachment relative to the ground increases significantly as the FEL is raised, potentially causing the load to rollback onto the tractor or operator.

With a self-leveling anti-rollback device incorporated into the FEL and its attachments, the angle remains constant, effectively eliminating the risk of rollback when operated correctly.

Similarly, the angle of the pallet fork attachment relative to the ground increases as the FEL is raised, leading to potential rollback onto the tractor or operator.

By integrating a self-leveling anti-rollback device into the FEL and its attachments, the angle remains constant, ensuring that the risk of rollback is eliminated when operated correctly.

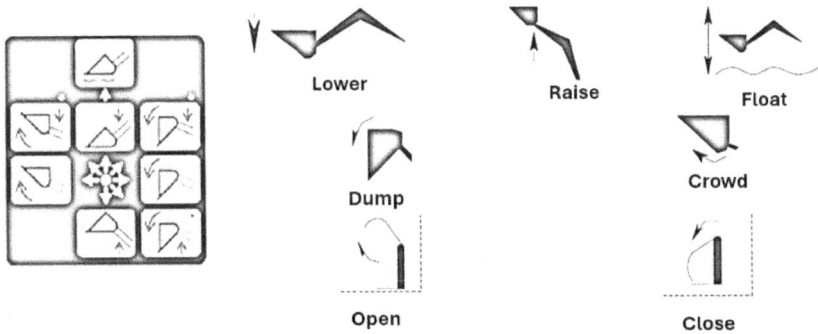

Figure 38: Typical operating control identification.

Shear hazards arising between the moving arm and the stationary structure of the tractor must be identified and, where feasible, eliminated. In cases where a hazard cannot be removed entirely, the manufacturer's instructions must include information and guidelines identifying potential hazards and recommending appropriate controls.

The Front End Loader (FEL) should be designed for easy removal to ensure unobstructed access for tractor maintenance and inspection. When disconnected from the tractor, it should remain stable.

In situations where disconnecting the FEL is impractical, such as during field service, a safe working system must prevent accidental lowering of raised lift arms in the event of hydraulic pressure loss in the FEL. A mechanical or hydraulic safety device must be integrated into the design. If a mechanical safety device is utilized, it should be easily accessible on either the FEL or the tractor.

A hydraulic safety device, if provided, must guarantee that the raised arm cannot lower due to single or multiple hydraulic leaks or failures in the system, such as hose failure, ram seal damage, or valve leakage.

The FEL and its attachments should prominently display pictorial and/or written signs warning against significant safety risks. These signs may include messages such as "Do not exceed ROL," "Crush zone," or "Use of mechanical devices during maintenance." All symbols should conform to locality standards signs for the occupational environment, with all text in English and measurements in metric units.

Furthermore, the FEL must clearly exhibit pictorial and written signs cautioning against serious safety risks. Additionally, FEL attachments may require similar signage warning against their specific safety hazards.

ROPS must adhere to locality standards, both in manufacturing and maintenance. A plate or decal confirming compliance should be affixed to the ROPS frame or inside the tractor cabin.

It's worth noting that while a falling object protective structure (FOPS) is typically not necessary for agricultural tractors, consideration should be given to the potential introduction of falling risks associated with the FEL and its attachments' activities, potentially necessitating the installation of a FOPS.

FEL attachments are specifically designed for particular applications and should only be used for their intended purposes. For instance, lifting large round hay bales using a bucket may not be safe.

The inclusion of an FEL raises the tractor's centre of gravity, resulting in a less stable combination compared to the tractor alone. Additionally, having a raised load in the attachment further increases the centre of gravity.

The centre of gravity (CG) is a crucial concept in understanding the stability and balance of a front-end loader (FEL) during its operation. It represents the point where the entire weight of the loader and any attached load can be considered to act upon. In an FEL, the centre of gravity typically lies within the structure of the loader itself when it is not carrying any load.

However, as the loader lifts or carries a load, the distribution of weight changes, causing the centre of gravity to shift accordingly. This shift in the centre of gravity is influenced by factors such as the weight of the load, its position relative to the FEL, and the height to which it is lifted.

When a load is added to the FEL, the centre of gravity moves towards the load, causing the front of the loader to become heavier. As a result, the stability of the FEL is affected, with a higher risk of tipping forward. Similarly, lifting a load to greater heights raises the centre of gravity, increasing the risk of the FEL overturning backwards.

Understanding how the centre of gravity shifts during operation is essential for operators to maintain stability and prevent accidents. Proper load positioning, adherence to weight limits, and cautious manoeuvring can help mitigate the risks associated with changes in the centre of gravity of a front-end loader. This is demonstrated in Figure 39.

Within Figure 39, the marked point "X" represents the typical centre of gravity when operating a front-end loader. Upon adding a large bale, the centre of gravity shifts to point "Y." Lifting a large round bale further relocates the centre of gravity to point "Z." Elevating the load exacerbates the shift in the centre of gravity, heightening the risk of overturning. Additionally, point "O" denotes the centre of gravity for the round bale itself.

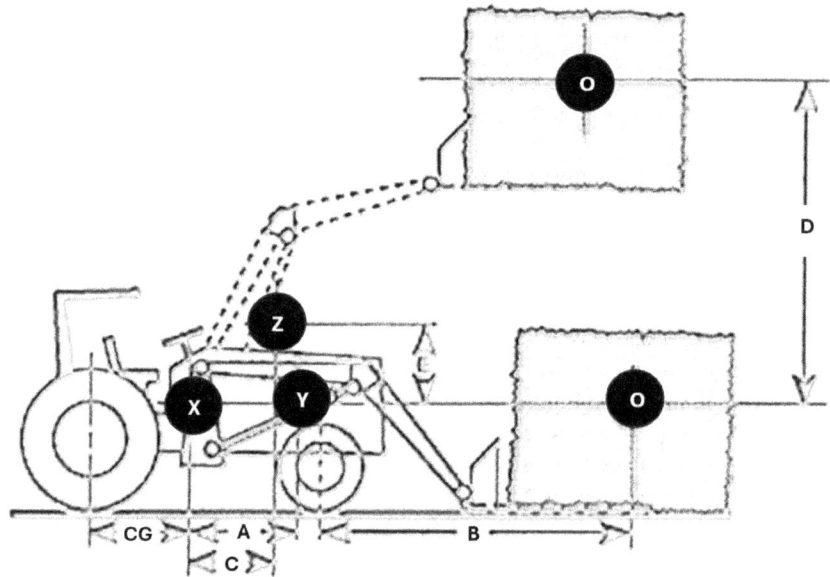

Figure 39: Front end loader centre of gravity.

Performing a pre-start check on a front end loader is essential to ensure that the machine is in proper working condition and safe to operate. This includes:

1. **Exterior Inspection:**

    - Walk around the front end loader and visually inspect the exterior for any signs of damage, leaks, or loose components.

    - Check the tyres or tracks for proper inflation, damage, and signs of wear.

    - Inspect the lights, signals, and reflective markings to ensure they are functioning correctly.

2. **Fluid Levels:**

- Check the engine oil, hydraulic fluid, coolant, and fuel levels using the respective dipsticks or sight gauges. Top up fluids as needed.

3. **Hydraulic System:**

    - Look for any visible leaks in the hydraulic hoses, fittings, and cylinders.

    - Check the hydraulic controls for smooth operation and responsiveness.

    - Ensure that the hydraulic reservoir is adequately filled and that the fluid is clean.

4. **Engine Compartment:**

    - Open the engine compartment and inspect the engine for any signs of leaks, damage, or loose components.

    - Check the air filter and clean or replace it if necessary.

    - Inspect the battery terminals for corrosion and ensure they are securely connected.

5. **Safety Features:**

    - Test the seatbelt to ensure it is functioning correctly and securely fastens.

    - Check the rollover protective structure (ROPS) and ensure it is in good condition.

    - Verify that the fire extinguisher is present, fully charged, and within the expiration date.

6. **Attachments and Controls:**

- Inspect any attachments (e.g., bucket, forks) for damage or wear.
- Test the controls for proper operation, including the lift arm, bucket tilt, steering, and brakes.
- Ensure that all control levers, pedals, and switches are functioning correctly and are not sticking.

7. **Cab Interior:**

- Enter the operator's cab and check the condition of the seat, pedals, and steering wheel.
- Test the visibility by cleaning the windows and mirrors.
- Verify that all gauges, indicators, and warning lights are operational.

8. **Documentation:**

- Ensure that the operator's manual, maintenance records, and any required permits or certifications are present and up to date.
- Check for any safety bulletins or recalls issued by the manufacturer.

9. **Final Checks:**

- Start the engine and listen for any unusual noises or vibrations.
- Test the brakes, accelerator, and transmission by engaging and disengaging them.
- Perform a brief test drive to ensure that the front end loader

operates smoothly and responds correctly to controls.

10. **Shutdown Procedure:**

- Once the pre-start check is complete, shut down the engine and secure the front end loader according to manufacturer guidelines.

- Report any issues or abnormalities discovered during the pre-start check to the appropriate personnel for further inspection or maintenance.

By following these steps, operators can ensure that the front end loader is in optimal condition for safe and efficient operation. Regular pre-start checks are crucial for identifying potential issues early and preventing accidents or breakdowns.

The inspection of the work area involves various methods of devising a work plan to ensure compliance with site procedures and safe work outcomes. An informal risk assessment is one such method, serving as a simplified approach to identifying hazards associated with specific tasks and implementing control measures. This process may entail using basic tools like a pocket notebook to record hazards and a set of procedures.

In industries such as mining and construction, a commonly employed risk assessment process is the SLAM method, which stands for STOP, LOOK, ASSESS, and MANAGE. This systematic approach is widely adopted for its simplicity and effectiveness in managing risks within work sites. It begins with the STOP phase, where a risk assessment is initiated by asking crucial questions about potential hazards and necessary precautions.

Subsequently, in the LOOK phase, employees examine the work environment for specific hazards arising from human interaction, machinery, and surrounding conditions. This includes identifying ergonomic and health hazards that could lead to accidents or injuries.

During the ASSESS phase, risks are evaluated and categorized based on their consequences and likelihood of occurrence. Employees rate the identified hazards and assess the level of risk they pose when performing tasks.

Finally, in the MANAGE phase, all identified risks are mitigated to As Low As Reasonably Possible (ALARP) through the implementation of appropriate controls. These controls aim to reduce the energy or likelihood of hazards, employing strategies such as isolation, guarding, training, and effective work planning.

Workers are encouraged to conduct daily SLAM assessments or similar evaluations when starting new tasks to ensure ongoing safety. Additionally, in the SAM approach—Spot the Hazard, Assess the Risk, Make the Changes—employees are reminded of their responsibility to prevent accidents by proactively identifying hazards, assessing risks, and implementing necessary changes to control them.

Rated Capacity

Determining the rated capacity of a front end loader involves several factors and calculations. Here's a step-by-step explanation:

1. Consult the Manufacturer's Specifications: The manufacturer of the front end loader provides detailed specifications including the rated capacity. These specifications are typically available in the loader's manual or technical documentation.

2. Understand the Rated Capacity: The rated capacity refers to the maximum weight that the loader is designed to lift safely under ideal conditions. It's crucial to understand the conditions under which the rated capacity is valid, including factors like load position, lift height, and stability.

3. Identify Load Position: The rated capacity can vary based on the position of the load relative to the loader. For example, the rated capacity may differ if the load is positioned at ground level versus being lifted to a certain height.

4. Consider Lift Height: The rated capacity may change depending on the lift height. Generally, loaders have a lower rated capacity as the lift height increases due to stability concerns.

5. Evaluate Load Distribution: Load distribution plays a significant role in determining the rated capacity. Unevenly distributed loads or loads with a high centre of gravity may reduce the loader's stability and rated capacity.

6. Account for Operating Conditions: Operating conditions such as terrain, slope, and environmental factors can affect the loader's performance and rated capacity. Ensure that the rated capacity is appropriate for the specific operating conditions.

7. Perform Calculations: Once you have all the relevant information and specifications, you can calculate the rated capacity based on the manufacturer's guidelines. This typically involves applying formulas or using load charts provided by the manufacturer.

8. Verify Safety Factors: Manufacturers often include safety factors in the rated capacity to account for uncertainties and ensure safe operation. It's essential to adhere to these safety factors and never exceed the rated capacity to prevent accidents or equipment damage.

9. Training and Certification: Operators should receive proper training and certification to understand how to operate the loader safely and within its rated capacity limits. This training

includes learning about load limits, stability, and safe operating practices.

The rated capacity may also be shown by the manufacturer in a chart. An example is shown as Figure 40

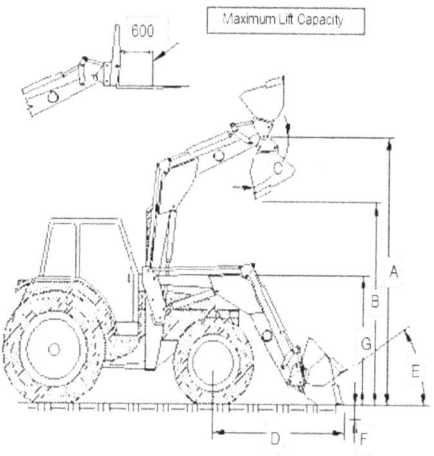

Loader Model	A Max Lift Height	B Clearance when dumped	C Max dump angle (Deg)	D Reach at ground	E Crowd back	F Digging depth	G Overall height	H Heaped Capacity	I Max lift capacity (kg)
60	3260	2400	80	1900	30	240	1565	0.51	1050
80	3490	2540	80	2000	28	240	1660	0.51	1350
120	3825	2855	80	2100	28	240	1760	0.73	1550
140	4050	3080	80	2150	28	240	1870	0.73	1550
160	4050	3080	80	2150	28	240	1870	0.73	2000
180	4310	3310	80	2405	40	280	1900	0.88	3150

Figure 40: Example rated capacity chart for a front end loader.

Load charts, also referred to as rated capacity charts, provide information about the maximum load that a crane or other equipment can safely lift. It is crucial for the operator to have access to the load chart to ensure that the equipment is not overloaded.

In some cases, certain types of powered mobile equipment, such as cranes, may have multiple load charts for different boom and counterweight configurations. These load charts can be intricate and include various conditions that must be followed to ensure safe lifting operations.

The load chart for the mobile equipment should specify the capacity for each lift point location and corresponding configuration. Key information that should be included in the load chart comprises the manufacturer's details, plant model, and manufacturing date, along with lifting point locations and their rated capacities. Additionally, it should indicate boom configurations, maximum lifting loads for each point and configuration, stabilizer requirements, side slope allowances, and deductions for attachments like buckets or quick-hitch devices.

Regarding lifting points, loads should only be suspended from designated lift points or quick-hitch attachments if provided, unless another designated lifting point has been specifically engineered and installed. These lifting points and attachments are typically supplied by the equipment manufacturer or designed by an engineer. They often consist of welded assemblies that attach to the end of the dipper arm when the bucket is not in use.

The design of lifting points should ensure that accidental unhooking of the load is prevented, and that slings cannot become detached. They should also be structured to keep slings clear of the boom or attachments. Hooks should not be used on dipper arms or other attachments of earthmoving equipment, as they may unhook as the arm rotates, even if equipped with a latch.

Moreover, lifting points should not be attached to quick-hitch buckets or buckets in general, as this can lead to unintended loading of pins and linkages, potential overloading of the equipment, sling damage, and bucket damage during excavation activities.

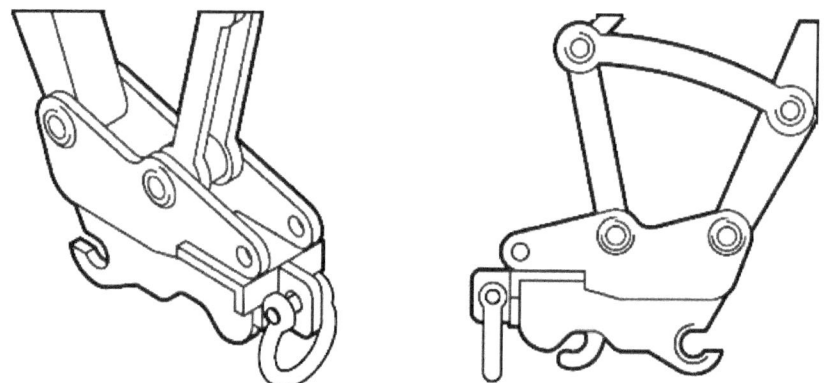

Figure 41: Closed eye lifting points on an excavator.

Quick-hitches are attachments installed on excavator or backhoe arms to facilitate the swift mounting and dismounting of various attachments, necessitating suitable risk management measures.

Burst protection is a crucial safety feature that should be installed on earthmoving equipment utilized as a crane, particularly when the rated capacity exceeds 1 tonne. Guidance on the installation of burst protection should be sought from the original equipment manufacturer. In cases where the rated capacity of the equipment is 1 tonne or more and burst protection is not present, the equipment should not be employed for lifting loads in proximity to workers.

Burst protection is specifically designed to be fitted on critical hydraulic cylinders to prevent potential collapse of the boom or dipper arm. Several conditions must be considered when assessing the need for burst protection:

- Information regarding the installation of burst protection devices should be obtained from the equipment manufacturer.

- The maximum rated capacity of the equipment should comply with the manufacturer's specifications, including both single and variable rated capacities.

- For equipment with variable lifting capacities, the lifting capacity at the minimum radius should be used to determine the necessity of burst protection.

- The equipment must fully adhere to the design requirements applicable to mobile cranes.

- It is imperative that operators are unable to deactivate burst protection devices for enhanced safety measures.

Unlike cranes, earthmoving equipment (EME) such as excavators, front-end loaders, and backhoes are not primarily designed for lifting loads. While manufacturers may configure EME to perform lifting tasks as a secondary function, operators must ensure, to the extent reasonably practicable, that any equipment used for lifting or transporting a freely suspended load is specifically designed for that purpose. EME should only be utilized for lifting where the use of a crane is not feasible and where non-precision lifting suffices.

EME is unsuitable for precision lifting tasks such as structural steel erection or precast concrete panel placement, situations requiring multiple pieces of equipment for a lift, or when stabilizers are necessary for stability, unless the EME is equipped with stabilizers and they are deployed.

Before employing EME for lifting tasks (as a secondary function), several risk control measures should be considered:

- Ensuring the rated capacity, stability, and suitability of the equipment are established.

- Displaying working load limits on the equipment with an appropriate load chart.

- Verifying that the design and location of lifting points comply with the manufacturer's specifications.

- Traveling with the lifting arm fully retracted when transporting loads.

- Using stabilizers to achieve plant stability.

- Prohibiting any person from being under a suspended load.

- Ensuring operators are competent to perform the task.

- Verifying that trip-type catch buckets are securely bolted or positively engaged.

- Developing and implementing safe systems of work.

Loads should only be suspended from the manufacturer's designated lifting point on the boom or quickhitch, ensuring that the lifting point forms a closed eye and is designed to prevent unintended unhooking or detachment of slings. Quickhitches may only be used to support attachments specifically designed for the equipment and must be operated by competent personnel.

Safe systems of work, including the development of Safe Work Method Statements for high-risk construction work, should be established, considering factors such as equipment selection, inspection, maintenance of lifting gear, establishment of exclusion zones, and proper handling of transported loads.

Records should be maintained for all servicing, maintenance, repairs, and equipment malfunctions.

Operating a Loader

Driving a front-end loader requires careful attention to safety procedures and operating principles. Here's a step-by-step guide on how to drive a front-end loader:

EARTHMOVING EQUIPMENT OPERATIONS

1. Pre-Start Check:

   - Before operating the front-end loader, conduct a pre-start check to ensure that all components are in working order. This includes checking fluid levels, inspecting tyres or tracks for damage, and ensuring that all safety features are functional.

2. Start the Engine:

   - Once the pre-start check is complete, start the engine according to the manufacturer's instructions. Allow the engine to warm up before engaging any controls.

3. Seat Adjustment:

   - Adjust the seat and mirrors to ensure proper visibility and comfort during operation.

4. Engage the Parking Brake:

   - Before moving the loader, engage the parking brake to prevent unintentional movement.

5. Select the Transmission:

   - Depending on the model of the front-end loader, select the appropriate transmission mode (forward, neutral, reverse).

6. Operate the Joystick Controls:

   - Familiarize yourself with the joystick controls for raising, lowering, tilting, and dumping the loader bucket. Practice using the controls to manipulate the bucket smoothly and accurately.

7. Drive Forward:

    ◦ To move the front-end loader forward, release the parking brake, shift into the forward gear, and gently press the accelerator pedal. Use the steering wheel to manoeuvre the loader in the desired direction.

8. Drive in Reverse:

    ◦ When driving in reverse, ensure that the area behind the loader is clear of obstacles. Shift into reverse gear, use the mirrors to guide you, and proceed slowly while maintaining awareness of your surroundings.

9. Operating the Bucket:

    ◦ Use the joystick controls to raise, lower, tilt, and dump the loader bucket as needed for loading and unloading materials. Practice operating the bucket to achieve precise control over its movements.

10. Observe Safety Precautions:

    ◦ Always wear a seatbelt while operating the front-end loader.

    ◦ Maintain a safe distance from obstacles, pedestrians, and other vehicles.

    ◦ Avoid sharp turns or sudden manoeuvres that could cause the loader to tip over.

    ◦ Be mindful of overhead obstructions, such as power lines or tree branches.

    ◦ Use caution when operating on slopes or uneven terrain, adjusting your speed and approach as necessary.

- Follow all safety guidelines outlined in the operator's manual and receive proper training before operating the front-end loader.

11. Shut Down:

- Once you have completed your work, return the loader to a safe location, engage the parking brake, and shut down the engine according to the manufacturer's instructions.

Before starting the machine, conduct a visual check around the vehicle to ensure there are no individuals or obstacles in the vicinity. Refrain from starting the engine if a warning sign is displayed on the operating lever. Ensure proper seating position before initiating the engine start. Only authorized personnel, such as the driver, should enter the driving cab or any other area of the vehicle. Verify the functionality of the reverse running buzzer, if installed, before operating the vehicle.

Starting and Operating Procedures for the Wheel Loader:

- Operate the wheel loader solely outdoors or in well-ventilated indoor spaces.

- Maintain clear communication with colleagues and ensure good visibility at all times.

- Alert nearby personnel of machine activation by either sounding the horn twice or activating the beacon light/flasher, if available.

- Provide a signal-person in confined areas with limited visibility, ensuring they remain at a safe distance from the wheel loader.

- Test and confirm radio contact with the operator, if applicable.

- Keep the cab, control levers, and pedals clean, avoiding placing any objects on the control panel.

- Refrain from storing tools, equipment, or flammable liquids in the cab.

- Start the engine following the manufacturer's specifications and monitor the control panel for any abnormalities.

- Activate the servo circuit control before engaging any hydraulic functions.

- Test all wheel loader functions, including steering, brakes, lights, and signals.

- Increase engine speed and allow system components to warm up to operating temperatures.

- Exercise caution during operation, maintaining sufficient clearance from power lines and obstacles.

- Familiarize yourself with the load's weight, dimensions, and centre of gravity.

- Operate within the machine's capabilities and use slow, progressive joystick movements under load conditions.

- Reduce travel speed, particularly in poor visibility or challenging terrain.

- Allow ample time and space for stopping, avoiding abrupt brake applications with a load.

- Adhere to transportation rules and regulations when operating on public roads, considering road conditions, clearances, and load limitations.

- Lower attachments and loads as close to the ground as possible during machine travel.

- Never leave the machine unattended while the engine is running or in motion.

- Prohibit anyone from approaching or being near the machine during operation.

- In case of contact with a high-voltage power line, remain in the cab, warn others, and move the machine away if possible.

- Exit the cab only after the power line is switched off or the machine is at a safe distance.

- Minimize shock loads and machine shaking by reducing travel speed and avoiding road irregularities.

Ventilation in Enclosed Areas:
- Open doors and windows to ensure adequate ventilation when starting the engine or handling fuel, oil, or paint in enclosed or poorly ventilated areas.

- Use fans if additional ventilation is required.

Maintenance and Safety Precautions for Fuels, Oils, and Engine:
- Wear personal protective equipment when handling fuel and oil.

- Wait for engine oil and hydraulic oil to cool down before performing maintenance operations.

- Relieve pressure before removing oil caps to prevent hot oil from spurting out.

- Exercise caution when checking coolant and oil temperatures to avoid burns.

Prevention of Crushing or Cutting Incidents:
- Avoid placing any body part between moving parts or equip-

ment components.

- Keep hands and feet away from moving parts such as engine fans, belts, and hinge points.

Precautions When Working with Raised Equipment:
- Always support raised attachments during servicing or repairs and never walk under them unless properly supported.
- Use stands or supports when the front end loader is raised on a jack.

Articulation Lock:
- Utilize the articulation lock when accessing the chassis area between the wheels, ensuring the engine is shut down during installation or removal.

Operating in Reverse: When operating the machine in reverse, adhere to the following guidelines: Alert individuals in the vicinity by sounding the horn. Ensure there are no individuals present around or behind the machine. Assign a designated individual to oversee safety procedures, particularly when the vehicle is in reverse mode. Assign a designated individual to manage traffic flow in hazardous areas or where visibility is limited. Prohibit individuals from approaching the path of the vehicle while in operation. These protocols should be followed even if the vehicle is equipped with a reverse running buzzer and rearview mirror.

Safety Checks: Before starting the machine, verify that the safety lever is in the neutral position.

Operating Precautions: Maintain a scraper bowl clearance of 40 to 50 cm when driving on level terrain. Exercise caution and reduce speed when traversing uneven terrain, maintaining stable steering and avoiding sudden turns. In the event of engine failure while in motion, refrain from using the steering wheel, immediately apply the brakes, and bring the vehicle to a stop.

Operating on Slopes: Driving on steep slopes, embankments, or hillsides may lead to overturning or slipping. When driving on slopes, embankments, or hillsides, maintain a scraper bowl clearance of 20 to 30 cm (8 to 12 inches). In emergencies, swiftly lower the scraper bowl to the ground to aid in stopping and prevent overturning. Avoid making turns or traversing slopes; these manoeuvres should be performed on level ground. Refrain from driving across grassy areas, areas covered in fallen leaves, or wet steel plates to prevent slipping. When driving near the edge of a slope, maintain a very low speed. When descending slopes, maintain a reduced speed and utilize the engine as a brake. In the event of engine failure on a slope, immediately engage the brakes, lower the scraper bowl, and bring the vehicle to a stop.

Operating on Soft Ground: Avoid working in close proximity to cliffs, steep or deep ditches, as collapse may lead to vehicle overturning and potential injuries or fatalities. Note that soil stability in these areas may decrease following adverse weather conditions. Exercise caution when working near loose or soft soil, as machine weight and vibration may cause collapses. Install a roll-over protection structure (ROPS) when operating in hazardous areas or where the risk of falling debris is present. Utilize both ROPS and safety belts when working in areas prone to falling debris and potential vehicle overturning.

Certain machines feature a dump linkage configuration wherein a bucket that rests flat on the ground automatically tilts when lifted a few feet above ground level. Should the operator wish to prevent this automatic tilt-back, they can utilize the dump control to counteract it. Automatic kickouts are also incorporated to halt the hoist at either maximum height or another preselected height, as well as to return the bucket to its digging angle after dumping. These mechanisms enable operators to manage the machine's functions with both hands on the tractor controls while manoeuvring.

Loading the Bucket

The following outlines safe and effective practices for a range of typical work performed with a front end loader (Symons, 1985).

To load the bucket effectively:

1. Position the speed range control lever in the first (1) gear position and the directional control lever in the forward (F) position.

2. Set the transmission range lever to the low position.

3. Lower the bucket using the lift arm control lever and adjust the bucket's cutting edge and bottom to be parallel to the ground using the bucket control lever (ensuring alignment with bucket indicator pointers).

4. Slowly drive the machine forward to push the cutting edge into the pile until the bucket is nearly full.

5. Alternately pull back the lift arm control lever and the bucket control lever incrementally to raise the lift arm and tip the bucket back, continuing until the bucket is fully loaded.

6. Place the lift arm control lever in the HOLD position.

7. Shift the direction control lever to the reverse (R) position and reverse out of the pile, keeping the load low and the bucket slightly tipped back.

8. Transport the load to the dumping area, maintaining a low load position and a slightly tipped-back bucket. Generally, loaders

perform digging tasks with the bucket either flat or tilted slightly downward, allowing for maximum penetration into banks and high spots while facilitating smooth movement of the machine.

For buckets that do not roll back but remain flat when the dump rams are fully retracted, this position is optimal for both digging and raising and carrying a load.

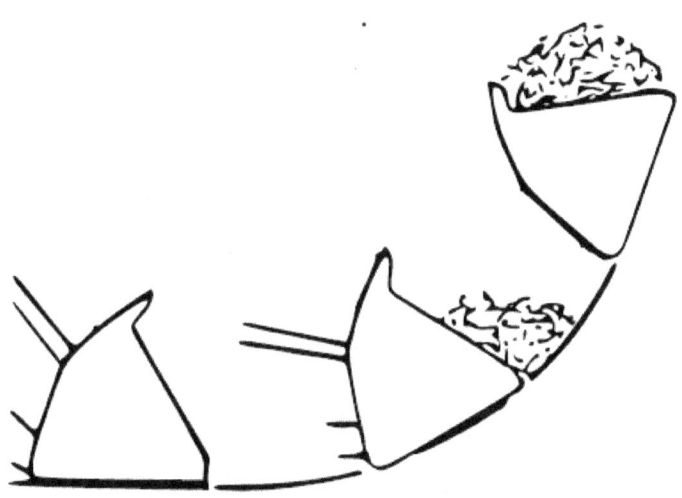

Figure 42: Loading the bucket.

For digging into hard dirt, the bucket should be tipped downward at an angle of ten to thirty degrees. Once it has penetrated to a depth of two to six inches, flatten it entirely while continuing the forward motion of the tractor until the bucket is filled. This approach combines effective initial penetration, a sturdy bucket position for most of the pass, and a potent prying effect during the angle change. In some soil conditions, making continual minor adjustments to the angle while digging can enhance penetration.

Figure 43: Digging with the front end loader.

Ramping Down: When excavating downward, such as when cutting an excavation or a ramp, hard material may necessitate tilting the bucket bottom at an angle of ten to thirty degrees relative to the line of the wheels and cutting in thin slices. It's important for the downward pitch of the ramp to be gradual, as the machine becomes front-heavy with a loaded bucket and may tip forward when reversing out of the hole.

Grading and Excavation: During grading or excavation tasks, adjust the bucket so that the bucket position indicator indicates a level position (with pointers aligned). Tip the bucket slightly forward toward the dump position to facilitate penetration. Once the cutting edge has penetrated, use the bucket control lever to adjust the bucket to the desired depth and to prevent excessive digging. Gradually move the bucket control lever forward and backward to achieve a smooth, even grade. To maintain a proper grade, depress the foot throttle to half throttle in first (1) or second (2) gear, low range. When the bucket is full or the desired depth has been reached, pull back on the bucket control lever until it is in the "TILT-BACK" position and the bucket rests against the stops. Then, raise the push arms slightly off the ground to carry the load.

Transporting the Load: When transporting the load, adjust the machine's travel speed based on the distance of the haul and the condition of the surface. Slow down on rough terrain and when making sharp turns. Maintain the loaded bucket approximately 14 inches above the ground. Avoid transporting a load with the bucket raised more than halfway. Keep the bucket as close to the ground as possible to enhance visibility and machine stability, particularly on slopes or during turns.

Dumping the Bucket: Raise the bucket using the lift control lever until it clears the top edge of the truck side or dumping bin. Ensure the machine is perpendicular to the truck side or bin for even dumping within the designated area. Once the bucket is at the appropriate height, place the lift arm control lever in the "HOLD" position and gradually push the bucket control lever to the "DUMP" position. Avoid abruptly pushing the bucket control lever forward to prevent rapid dumping that could damage the truck body or hydraulic cylinders. After emptying the bucket, return the bucket control lever to the TIP BACK position, check behind the loader, sound the horn, and reverse the machine away from the truck or bin. Lower the bucket by adjusting the lift control lever and return to the pile for another load.

Handling Large Heavy Material: Special care should be taken when loading large heavy materials like riprap or boulders to protect the truck being loaded. Start by loading smaller materials to cushion the box against the impact of larger items. Dump these materials from the lowest possible height and at a slow pace to prevent damage to the bottom or sides of the box.

Traveling without a Load in the Bucket: When relocating the machine to another job site without a load in the bucket, position the empty bucket approximately 14 inches above the ground in the rolled-back position. Adjust the travel speed of the loader according to the surface conditions. Avoid driving the machine in reverse to achieve higher speeds or better steering control. Continuous reverse travel may result in poor visibility over the rear hood and could cause the engine to overheat due to disrupted airflow through the radiator.

Stockpiling Material: Elevate the bucket filled with material to a height where you can see underneath it while seated in the operator's seat on the loader. Avoid raising the bucket too high to prevent material from falling back onto the windshield or operator when driving up onto the pile.

Exercise caution when ascending the pile to dump the loaded bucket, ensuring that the loader's wheels ascend evenly onto the pile. If one wheel climbs onto the pile while the other veers to the side, there is a risk of the loader tipping over. While a ramp may assist, take care to avoid rollovers.

The distance travelled up the pile depends on how high you intend to stack the material. Ascend the pile by the same distance for each bucket load to minimize gaps where water can accumulate and damage the material. Maintain the pile's top as level as possible. Upon reaching the desired height on the pile, dump the bucket and apply the brake simultaneously to stabilize the loader on the pile. After the material has been discharged, shift the direction selector lever into reverse and slowly descend from the pile. Avoid coasting downhill in neutral to prevent rapid descent, which could lead to accidents or loader damage.

Safe stockpiling operations involve adhering to the above guidelines and maintaining vigilance for potential hazards.

For pushing a quantity of loose dirt, the flat bucket position is ideal. However, when spreading and grading dirt, tilt the bucket downward steeply to facilitate free flow off the bottom into holes and prevent adherence by sticky soil. Exercise caution to avoid hooking into solid obstructions at a steep angle, as this places the bucket in its weakest position and maximizes leverage against the dump mechanism.

The depth of cut can be regulated either by the hoist or the dump rams. The edge will be highest when flat and two or more feet lower when fully dumped, depending on the position of the push arms.

Digging Banks: In relation to the machine's power and weight, the bucket demonstrates limited penetration. The hoist operates at a significantly slower pace compared to the loader's speed, causing the bucket to often become buried under more soil than it can effectively dislodge and lift. When dealing with hard material banks, it's advantageous to maintain a sloped orientation to aid in breaking out loads. This can be achieved by excavating in layers from the bank's top and then slicing upward from the bottom, ensuring each cut is parallel to the slope. While this method may lengthen each digging cycle slightly due to the increased distance travelled, it can be gentler on the machine compared to excavating in large chunks.

To dig into the bank, the loader bucket is initially pushed in a flat position until the loader begins to slow down, then alternately hoisted and rolled back. Forward motion should be controlled to keep the bucket within the bank, allowing its tilting action to facilitate excavation. Additional forward force on a rolled-back bucket may risk damage and offer no improvement in excavation efficiency. A smooth combination of crowd, curl, and lift motions is essential for optimal results.

For banks of modest height, around two or three feet, digging can be accomplished by maintaining the bucket at the final grade level and running alongside the bank. The bucket cuts into the bank without excessive shoving, utilizing its side and bottom to perform the excavation. Soil accumulates in the bucket, albeit with more weight on the bank side.

Driving the machine directly into the bank may result in the bucket becoming stuck, causing the back tyres to lift off the ground. In such cases, shifting the loader into reverse and backing out is recommended. As the bucket is pulled back slightly within the bank, it typically dislodges and rises with the load intact.

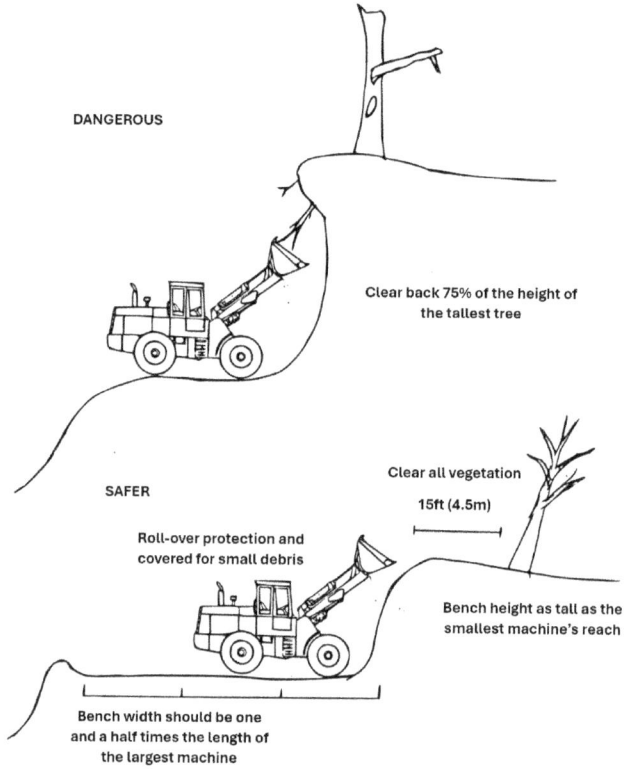

Figure 44: Benching and working face (based on Symons (1985)).

Working beneath high banks and on benches necessitates additional safety precautions to mitigate risks of cave-ins and rollovers.

Payload: The quantity of material collected in the bucket varies depending on factors such as the material's properties, the slope of the bank, the terrain to be traversed, and the operator's proficiency. Typically, a standard one-yard bucket load can range from half a yard to one and a half yards, averaging around seven-eighths to one yard during medium digging. Roll-back buckets generally accommodate larger loads compared to flat ones.

When dumping near the excavation point, speed in completing each cycle is usually prioritized over maximizing loads with each pass, especially when side casting or loading a truck properly positioned. However, as the distance to the dumping point increases, the importance of capacity loads grows.

If the load needs to be transported over rough terrain or uphill, it should be limited to a weight that the machine can handle without tipping over. In case the bucket does not fill adequately, the loader should be reversed, the bucket lowered to ground level, and another pass made. When the load is unevenly distributed, the second cut should be angled to ensure the empty side penetrates first.

It can be challenging for the operator to accurately gauge the amount in the bucket unless the digging conditions allow soil to reach the top of the back of the bucket.

Gouging: In dense soils, a common issue is the bucket's exceptional penetration, which may cause it to be pulled down by the slice it has dug, lifting the back of the loader. This issue can be addressed by keeping the bucket as flat as possible or by positioning the bucket bottom nearly vertically, though this may strain the bucket.

In heavy soils, it may be advantageous for cycle time to allow the bucket to gouge and then make an additional pass to grade the area as necessary.

Transporting Material: If the ground between digging and dumping is hard and smooth, operations such as backing up, turning, and dumping can be performed safely and swiftly with the loaded bucket kept below eye level. However, on rough terrain, the loader must move slowly to avoid tipping forward or causing the bucket to strike the ground over bumps or ridges. Lowering the bucket completely helps shift its weight off the loader, aiding in regaining balance if an upset occurs.

Abruptly dropping a loaded bucket and stopping it in mid-air may damage a hoist ram hose or cause the loader to tip forward again. Keeping the bucket as close to the ground as possible reduces the severity of overbalancing consequences.

The bucket should not be lifted high if there are rocks or protrusions over the back, as they may fall and cause injury or damage, especially when the operator's station is at the front of the loader.

Truck Loading: The following centres around the commonly used small loaders equipped with buckets approximately 2 yards (1.83 metres) in size. All operations are detailed in terms of manual control. While some larger machines in this category and beyond may incorporate automatic kickout devices, these devices simplify operations without altering their underlying principles. Apart from operating the loader, the loader operator bears additional responsibilities. It's their duty to ensure no truck is overloaded, as spillage over the truck's sides not only wastes material but also poses a traffic hazard. Moreover, they must prevent contamination of the stockpile. For instance, spinning tyres carelessly or rutting the work area floor could contaminate a stockpile of graded aggregate. Attempts to rectify this may inadvertently introduce unclean or larger materials into the pile, potentially causing damage to machinery or surfaces where the material is applied.

Manoeuvring the Loader: The typical steps involved in loading a truck are as follows: The loader is directed toward the pile or bank, shifted into low range, the throttle is engaged, and the bucket is lowered until it nearly touches the ground. As the bucket enters the bank, the hoist lever is activated in the UP position to facilitate rising as it penetrates. Upon filling, the direction selector is switched to reverse, and the machine is backed out. The hoist lever may be set to HOLD when the bucket is a few feet above the ground.

During the backing process, the loader should be turned to face the side of the truck to be loaded. It is then shifted into forward gear, the hoist lever is moved upward, and the machine is driven forward. The bucket should be lifted high enough to prevent the bucket lip from striking the truck during dumping, and it's advisable to keep it high enough to clear the truck's side to avoid accidents while backing.

Typically, hoisting is completed before reaching the truck. The control is then set to HOLD, and the loader is positioned so that the bucket is directly above the truck body.

A recommended practice is to time the lift so that the bucket safely clears the truck as it is moved over it, and the control can remain in the UP position during dumping. When the dump valve is opened, it interrupts the hoist valve so that lifting stops, resuming immediately when the dump valve is closed. This "live" bucket is easier to control over the truck body than when the hoist is on HOLD.

In either scenario, the loader is driven forward until the bucket is positioned as desired over the body of the truck. Care should be taken not to impact the truck's side, tyres, or gas tank. The dump lever is then moved forward to unload the load. It's advisable to dump the first bucket or two slowly to minimize shock to the truck. If the soil is sticky, the bucket can be shaken gently by moving the dump valve lever back and forth against the dump stops, but this should be done cautiously to avoid bursting a hose. After ensuring clearance, the machine is shifted into reverse, backed away, and the bucket lip is raised if necessary to clear the body. Once clear of the truck, the machine is stopped, shifted into forward gear, directed toward the bank, and the bucket is lowered into the digging position during the return trip. Favourable conditions such as easy digging, proper truck spotting, and a smooth stockpile area contribute to a faster cycle. Most machines are capable of completing cycles within 15 to 30 seconds.

In scenarios where wheeled loaders encounter challenges like mud, snow, ice, or uneven surfaces causing traction loss and wheel spinning, it's essential to address this issue promptly to avoid premature tyre wear. One solution involves employing a mechanism that synchronizes the rotation of all wheels on an axle, ensuring they move at the same speed. This mechanism effectively "locks" the wheels together, redirecting power to the wheel with the most traction when slippage occurs.

Moreover, using tyres with inappropriate tread for specific surfaces can also contribute to wheel spinning. For instance, concrete surfaces demand tyres with a different tread pattern compared to those required for dirt surfaces. Matching the tyre tread to the surface type enhances traction and minimizes the risk of wheel spin.

Figure 45: Correct typres should be used for the operating surface. JoachimKohler-HB, CC BY-SA 4.0, via Wikimedia Commons.

In the event of an emergency, having established protocols is crucial for minimizing harm. Procedures to follow in case of a tip-over include:

1. Brace – Maintain a firm grip on the wheel and press feet firmly against the floor.

2. Lean – Lean away from the direction of impact as the loader begins to fall.

3. Exit – Exit through a window or door once the loader has come to a stop, avoiding jumping.

In the event of a collision, it is important to securely park and shut down the loader before exiting to assess for any injuries or damage. It is essential to always be aware of the location of fire extinguishers and first aid kits. Implementing proactive accident prevention measures such as designating travel paths, installing barriers, and ensuring clear communication can effectively reduce risks on job sites.

Attachments

General-purpose buckets are versatile enough to handle most loader tasks. However, for specialized jobs, alternative buckets are available to optimize the machine's performance. Lighter material buckets are suitable for lighter loads, supporting a larger volume of substance at the same weight as a general bucket. Rock or sieve buckets feature slim grate designs, allowing loaders to remove rocks while letting soil sift through. For those with multifunctional needs, there are multi-purpose buckets equipped with blades, buckets, and grabs, enabling the loader to manage multiple tasks seamlessly (Cumming, 2017).

Buckets are typically constructed from high-tensile steel to ensure strength and reliability while remaining lightweight. They are engineered to resist roll-back and ensure operator safety without compromising the machine's structural integrity.

Front-end loader bucket teeth: Also known as bull blades, bucket teeth add functionality beyond aesthetics to a loader. Like a Zen gardener tending to a pebble garden, bull blades can transform a hefty loader into a delicate rake. Bucket teeth are invaluable for sites with dense root systems, capable of penetrating challenging surfaces. Grated gap-teeth-style stick rake attachments are available for tasks requiring the removal of shrubs or rocks without disturbing the soil level.

Figure 46: A Caterpillar 930G fitted with a loader rake. Joseph Madden at en.wikipedia, CC BY 3.0, via Wikimedia Commons.

Front-end loader forks: Fork attachments enhance the loader's ability to handle items with finesse. Forks come in various designs for specific or general use. Generic forks mimic forklifts, providing stability when lifting heavy pallets, while specialized forks, like bale forks, feature spikes for handling hay bales efficiently, particularly useful in the agriculture industry.

Front-end loader grapple: Grapple attachments give loaders a voracious appetite for handling diverse items of varying sizes and shapes. For instance, tree grab attachments excel in forestry applications, gripping logs or wooden poles with hydraulic arms for swift handling. Power grab attachments are ideal for silage pits, efficiently transferring large volumes of silage without spillage, with multiple variations available to suit agricultural needs.

Figure 47: Front end loader using a grapple attachment. Robert Kaufmann, Public domain, via Wikimedia Commons.

Front-end loader sweepers and brooms: Sweeping may not be an obvious task for front-end loaders, but attachments like mud scrapers and brooms offer invaluable utility in agriculture and construction. These attachments, such as the Agriclean and Bucketbroom models, can efficiently clear dust and debris from wide areas, akin to street sweepers.

Onboard accessories: Technological advancements have led to the development of intricate tools and devices that enhance loader performance. Onboard scales provide precise weight measurements, improving safety and productivity. Additionally, automatic lubrication systems streamline maintenance, freeing up time for site work rather than manual greasing.

Concluding Loader Operations

Always ensure the wheel loader is parked on stable and level ground. Lower the attachment fully to the ground according to the manufacturer's instructions and deactivate the servo control hydraulics to prevent unintended hydraulic function activation. To depressurize the hydraulic circuits, lower the attachment completely, deactivate the servo system, and move the joystick lever(s) in a circular motion several times before placing them in the neutral position.

If parking the wheel loader on an incline, engage the parking brake, position the bucket into the dump position, lower it entirely to the ground, and use supplied wheel chocks or other blocking devices to prevent downhill movement. Deactivate the wheel loader's servo system, engage the parking brake, gradually reduce the engine speed, and allow it to idle for a few minutes before shutting off. Ensure windows and covers are securely closed and locked. Descend from the machine facing it using a three-point stance, never jump off.

If the machine will be parked for an extended period, remove the battery disconnect switch. Securely lock the machine to prevent unauthorized use or vandalism. Steam-clean the wheel loader before inspections, maintenance, or repairs, avoiding direct spraying on electrical components and connectors, and refrain from using aggressive chemical solvents, except for brakes.

Do not open a hydraulic circuit without depressurizing it completely. Avoid using hands or fingers to align bolts or pins during servicing. Utilize appropriate lifting devices, slings, or chains for heavy parts and components. Always use the correct tools and wear personal protective equipment (PPE) as required by workplace safety regulations. Do not position yourself or others beneath the machine or elevated attachments unless securely blocked, considering potential load shifts.

Use a man lift or platform and wear a full-body harness when working at heights exceeding 2 meters. When transporting the wheel loader, use a trailer with adequate load capacity and comply with transportation weight and height restrictions set by the Department of Transportation. When towing an inoperative wheel loader, use towing equipment designed for the required load capacity, follow the machine's manual, avoid sudden movements, and ensure no one is near the towing equipment or machines.

Never modify the wheel loader's configuration without written approval from the manufacturer. Regularly inspect hydraulic lines and hose assemblies as per the machine's manual and replace defective parts promptly. Do not attempt to repair a damaged accumulator; replace it entirely if defective and only charge accumulators with nitrogen up to the specified pressure limit. Weld load-bearing structures only by experienced and AWS-certified welders.

Display safety signs informing visitors, vendors, and suppliers of hazards and safe distances. Train employees on warning signals and audible alarms and identify areas prone to flying debris. Ensure safety signs are visible and complete, instruct employees to follow their instructions fully, mark off prohibited areas during wheel loader operation, and keep walkways clear of trip hazards. Adhere to good housekeeping practices at all times.

Shutdown and Parking Procedures:

- Always park the wheel loader on stable and even ground.

- Lower the attachment fully to the ground following the manufacturer's instructions and deactivate the servo control hydraulics to prevent unintended hydraulic functions.

- To release hydraulic pressure, lower the attachment completely, deactivate the servo system, and move the joystick lever(s) in a circular motion several times before returning them to the neutral position.

- If parking temporarily on an incline, engage the parking brake, position the bucket for dumping, and lower it entirely to the ground. Use wheel chocks or other means to prevent the machine from rolling downhill.

- Deactivate the wheel loader's servo system and engage the parking brake. Gradually reduce engine speed and allow it to idle for a few minutes before shutting it off.

- Secure and lock windows and covers, and ensure all doors and covers are properly locked.

- Descend from the machine facing it, maintaining a three-point stance. Avoid jumping off the machine at all costs.

- If the machine will be parked for an extended period, remove the battery disconnect switch.

- Secure and lock the machine to prevent unauthorized access or vandalism.

When not in use, store the FEL and its attachments in accordance with the manufacturer's guidelines. For the safest storage, FELs connected to tractors are best placed on the ground. If separated from the tractor, ensure stability to prevent any risk of falling.

Figure 48: Front end loader on a float ready for transport. Bob Adams from George, South Africa, CC BY-SA 2.0, via Wikimedia Commons.

Maintaining loaders consistently is crucial for ensuring optimal functionality and preventing mechanical issues that could compromise safety. Operators should adhere closely to the manufacturer's maintenance instructions provided in the equipment's manual. Regular maintenance tasks include:

- Fluid changes – Regularly changing engine oil, coolant, transmission fluid, and filters based on hours of operation.

- Lubrication – Applying grease to bearings and joints to prevent seizing and potential failures.

- Filter replacement – Replacing clogged air and fuel filters to maintain proper engine function.

- Pressure washing – Cleaning the underside and chassis to remove any mud or debris buildup.

Keeping the loader's manual with the machine ensures operators have easy access to maintenance procedures. Additionally, maintaining a maintenance log provides documentation of proper care.

Chapter Four
Backhoe/Loader Operations

A backhoe is a versatile piece of heavy equipment commonly used in construction, landscaping, and excavation projects. It consists of a tractor-like unit with an articulated arm and a digging bucket or scoop mounted on the back of the machine. The backhoe's design allows it to perform various tasks, including digging trenches, excavating earth, loading trucks, lifting materials, and demolishing structures.

EARTHMOVING EQUIPMENT OPERATIONS

Figure 49: A JCB 3CX backhoe loader. HumongoNationphotogallery, CC BY-SA 2.0, via Wikimedia Commons.

The backhoe's arm has three main components: the boom, the dipper or stick, and the bucket. The boom is the large, vertical arm that supports the other components and provides vertical movement. The dipper or stick is connected to the boom and can extend and retract horizontally. At the end of the dipper is the bucket, which can scoop, lift, and dump materials.

Backhoes are equipped with wheels or tracks for mobility and stability, allowing them to navigate various terrains. They are operated by skilled operators who use hydraulic controls to manoeuvre the arm and bucket with precision.

Overall, backhoes are valued for their versatility, efficiency, and ability to perform a wide range of tasks on construction sites and other work environments.

Backhoe operators are responsible for operating backhoes and their attachments to carry out various tasks such as excavation, breaking, drilling, leveling, and compacting earth, rock, and other materials.

On a day-to-day basis, their duties include preparing and positioning the plant for operation, selecting, fitting, and removing attachments, operating controls, monitoring the operation of the plant, adjusting controls to regulate pressure, speed, and flow of operation while ensuring the safety of other workers, manipulating attachments using manual and hydraulic controls, and performing routine maintenance tasks such as servicing, lubricating, cleaning, refueling, and making minor adjustments and repairs.

Considerations for backhoe operators include the need for driving skills and the requirement to work outdoors.

A backhoe is a type of excavation machine equipped with a digging bucket attached to a two-part articulated arm. Backhoe loaders typically feature a loader-style bucket on the front and a backhoe add-on attached to the rear.

Backhoes are renowned for their stability while moving heavy loads due to the use of hydraulic outriggers, stabilizers, and legs for additional stability. They are commonly employed in various tasks such as laying telephone cables or pipes within mining or civil earthworks projects. Additionally, they are versatile enough to be driven directly to job sites, eliminating the need for transporting the machine using long-bed trucks.

Backhoes find applications in a wide range of projects, including excavation, landscaping, asphalt breaking, construction, demolition, snow clearing, cable lifting, material transport, road paving, ditch digging, trenching, and foundation work.

Backhoe loaders are valued for their ability to combine the functionalities of excavators, wheel loaders, and other construction equipment into one machine, reducing the need for multiple machines on a job site. They can also perform tasks like tree planting and small-scale drilling with the appropriate attachments.

Originally based on tractors, backhoes were invented by tractor and agricultural companies in the 1950s to streamline construction processes and reduce costs associated with hiring multiple machines. Backhoes consist of three main sections: the loader section, the backhoe section, and the tractor section.

The loader section functions similarly to a front loader or skid steer loader, with digging and lifting capabilities. It can be equipped with various attachments such as augers, rippers, hydraulic breakers, compaction wheels, grapples, and fork tynes.

The backhoe section, located at the rear of the machine, acts as an excavator's boom and is capable of excavating a range of materials. It features a narrower bucket than a standard excavator bucket but can be equipped with different bucket attachments for wider digging capabilities.

The tractor section serves as the backbone of the backhoe, housing electronics, a powerful diesel engine, rugged tyres, and operating controls. It is based on a standard tractor body known for its reliability and continuous work capabilities.

A backhoe typically consists of several major components, see Figure 50, each playing a crucial role in its operation and functionality. These components include:

1. Loader Section:

    - The loader section is positioned at the front of the backhoe and resembles a front-end loader or skid steer loader.

    - It features a loader bucket that can be raised, lowered, and tilted using hydraulic controls.

    - The loader bucket is used for lifting, transporting, and loading materials such as dirt, gravel, and debris.

    - Various attachments can be fitted to the loader section,

including augers, rippers, hydraulic breakers, compaction wheels, grapples, and fork tynes, to enhance its versatility for different tasks.

2. Backhoe Section:

- The backhoe section is located at the rear of the backhoe and comprises a two-part articulated arm with a digging bucket attached to the end.
- It functions similarly to an excavator's boom and is used for digging, trenching, and excavation tasks.
- The backhoe arm consists of two main components: the boom and the dipper stick.
- The digging bucket attached to the end of the dipper stick can be raised, lowered, and curled using hydraulic controls to excavate materials.

3. Tractor Section:

- The tractor section serves as the main body of the backhoe and houses essential components such as the engine, transmission, hydraulic system, and operator's cab.
- It is typically based on a standard tractor chassis and provides the power and mobility required for operating the backhoe.
- The tractor section features a powerful, turbocharged diesel engine that generates the necessary horsepower to drive the backhoe and operate its hydraulic systems.
- The operator's cab is located within the tractor section and provides a comfortable and ergonomic workspace for the operator. It is equipped with controls, instrumentation, and

seating for the operator to control the backhoe safely and efficiently.

- The hydraulic system, consisting of hydraulic pumps, cylinders, valves, and hoses, powers the various hydraulic functions of the backhoe, including the movement of the loader and backhoe sections.

4. Stabilizers and Outriggers:

- Stabilizers or outriggers are deployed from the backhoe to provide additional stability and support when operating the loader or backhoe sections.

- These components consist of extendable legs or arms that can be lowered to the ground to stabilize the backhoe and prevent tipping or rocking during heavy lifting or digging operations.

- Stabilizers and outriggers are especially important for maintaining stability on uneven terrain or when lifting heavy loads with the backhoe or loader sections.

These major components work together to enable the backhoe to perform a wide range of tasks efficiently and effectively, making it a versatile and valuable piece of construction equipment.

Figure 50: Backhoe major components. Back image - hodihu, CC BY 2.0 , via Wikimedia Commons.

Choosing between a backhoe and an excavator involves several considerations, as these machines differ in size, rotation, versatility, and suitability for various environments.

Size: The primary distinction between an excavator and a backhoe lies in their size. Excavators are larger and heavier, typically weighing around 15 tonnes, while backhoes usually weigh up to 7.5 tonnes. The size and weight difference can significantly influence machine selection based on the project's environment and requirements.

Environment: Excavators, being heavier, are well-suited for demolition projects, mining, and large-scale industrial endeavours. In contrast, backhoes, being smaller and more adaptable, are preferable for farming, snow removal, and medium-scale construction and excavation projects.

Rotation: Excavators and backhoes have different rotation capabilities, affecting their operational versatility. Excavators can rotate a full 360 degrees, while backhoes have a limited rotation of 200 degrees. Project requirements and the need for rotational flexibility should inform the choice between these machines.

Versatility: Both excavators and backhoes feature a boom, stick, and bucket, enabling them to perform similar tasks. However, backhoes generally offer a wider range of attachments, enhancing their versatility compared to excavators. Additionally, backhoes and mini excavators can be driven on roads, making them suitable for urban projects with spread-out worksites.

Selecting the Right Backhoe: Factors to consider when choosing a backhoe loader include its size, driving capacity (4x4, 2x4, or tracked), and intended workload. Backhoe loaders are versatile machines suitable for various tasks such as small demolition, road paving, pipe laying, and transporting heavy items. They excel in scenarios where multiple machines are required, but hiring individual machines is not cost-effective.

Benefits of Using a Backhoe: Hiring a backhoe offers several advantages over an excavator, including better manoeuvrability on rough terrain and cost efficiency due to its dual functionality as a wheel loader and excavator. Backhoes are ideal for light to medium workloads, smaller construction projects, and industrial sites where space or budget constraints limit the use of multiple machines.

Choosing the Right Size and Drive: Backhoes come in various sizes, categorized based on their operating weight. Larger backhoes (over 10 tonnes) are suitable for construction sites and large agricultural operations, while smaller ones (under 10 tonnes) are ideal for industrial depots and smaller agricultural tasks. Additionally, the type of drive (2x4, 4x4, or tracked) should match the terrain requirements, with tracked backhoes being suitable for challenging ground conditions.

Backhoes come in various types, each designed to suit specific applications and terrains. The main types of backhoes include:

1. Standard Backhoe Loader:

- Standard backhoe loaders are the most common type and are widely used in construction, agriculture, landscaping, and utility work.
- They typically feature a front loader bucket and a rear-mounted digging arm with a backhoe bucket.
- Standard backhoe loaders are versatile machines capable of performing a wide range of tasks, including digging, loading, lifting, and trenching.

2. Mini Backhoe Loader:

- Mini backhoe loaders are smaller and more compact versions of standard backhoes, making them ideal for working in tight spaces and urban environments.
- They offer similar functionality to standard backhoes but with reduced digging depth, reach, and lifting capacity.
- Mini backhoe loaders are commonly used for small excavation projects, landscaping, and light construction work.

3. Extendable Dipper Arm Backhoe:

- Extendable dipper arm backhoes feature a telescoping dipper arm that can extend and retract to increase reach and digging depth.
- These backhoes are particularly useful for tasks that require digging at greater depths or reaching over obstacles.

- Extendable dipper arm backhoes are commonly used in utility work, sewer and water line installation, and deep trenching applications.

4. Side-Shift Backhoe:

   - Side-shift backhoes are equipped with a hydraulic side-shift mechanism that allows the operator to shift the entire backhoe assembly to the side.

   - This feature enables more precise positioning of the digging arm and bucket, making it easier to work in confined spaces and alongside obstacles.

   - Side-shift backhoes are commonly used in landscaping, road maintenance, and urban construction projects where precise excavation is required.

5. Compact Tractor Backhoe Attachment:

   - Compact tractor backhoe attachments are designed to be mounted onto compact tractors, turning them into versatile excavation machines.

   - These attachments typically feature a smaller digging arm and bucket compared to standard backhoes, but they offer similar functionality.

   - Compact tractor backhoe attachments are popular among landscapers, homeowners, and small-scale contractors for digging trenches, planting holes, and light excavation work on residential properties and small job sites.

Regular inspections and preventive maintenance are crucial for ensuring the safe and efficient operation of powered mobile plants. A comprehensive maintenance and inspection program should consider the plant's working environment and usage. It should either adhere to the manufacturer's recommendations or be devised by a qualified individual to achieve similar safety outcomes or compliance with the relevant Australian Standard. When plant is mounted on a carrier vehicle, such as a tipper on a truck, the maintenance program should encompass both the vehicle and plant manufacturers' requirements.

The maintenance program should encompass:

- Daily pre-start checks and tests

- Regular evaluations of plant risk controls

- Routine inspection, servicing, and maintenance at designated intervals

- Major inspections at specified intervals

All inspections, maintenance activities, defects found, repairs undertaken, and structural alterations should be diligently recorded in the plant's service book and maintenance records. These records should be retained for the duration of the plant's lifespan and provided to the purchaser upon its sale.

Warning devices play a critical role in vehicle and mobile equipment operations. While major servicing requirements are typically handled by workshop personnel, drivers/operators are responsible for certain aspects of servicing, such as ensuring fluid levels are correct. It's imperative to maintain the correct type and level of fluid in the appropriate compartments to avoid issues like sludging, corrosion, and reduced lubrication effectiveness caused by incorrect levels or the addition of improper fluids.

Supplementary steering and emergency brake systems provide an additional layer of safety for machines, especially those steered by a differential steer mechanism. These systems utilize a second source of pressurized fluid and an independently controlled brake actuator mechanism to control steering in the event of a primary fluid failure. By interconnecting fluid ports and selectively directing pressurized fluid, these systems enable continued steering even in emergency situations.

Warning labels are essential safety features on machines, indicating specific hazards and precautions. Operators should familiarize themselves with these signs during the pre-start inspection to ensure safe operation.

The centre of gravity (COG) is a crucial concept in understanding the stability and balance of a backhoe, or any other type of heavy equipment. In simple terms, the centre of gravity is the point at which the entire weight of the backhoe is considered to act. It's the theoretical point where the entire mass of the backhoe is concentrated.

In a backhoe, the centre of gravity typically lies somewhere within the machine's frame, usually closer to the heavier components like the engine, transmission, and hydraulic system. However, the exact location of the centre of gravity can shift depending on various factors, including the position of the equipment's components, the load being lifted by the backhoe, and the terrain on which it's operating.

Understanding the centre of gravity is crucial because it directly affects the stability of the backhoe. When the centre of gravity is within the machine's base, it remains stable. However, if the centre of gravity shifts outside the base, such as when lifting a heavy load or operating on uneven terrain, the backhoe becomes unstable, increasing the risk of tipping over.

Operators need to be aware of the backhoe's centre of gravity and how it can change during operation. They must consider factors such as the weight and distribution of the load being lifted, the angle of the backhoe's boom and bucket, and the condition of the terrain. By understanding the centre of gravity and taking appropriate precautions, operators can minimize the risk of accidents and ensure safe operation of the backhoe.

During backhoe operations, the centre of gravity (COG) of the machine can shift due to several factors. Understanding how these factors affect the COG is crucial for maintaining stability and preventing tipping or accidents. Here's how the centre of gravity changes during backhoe operations:

1. Position of the Boom and Bucket: When the backhoe's boom and bucket are extended, the COG shifts towards the extended end. This is because the weight of the load or material being lifted by the bucket adds to the overall weight at that end of the machine. As a result, the COG moves away from the centre of the machine towards the extended end.

2. Load Distribution: The weight and distribution of the load being lifted by the backhoe also affect the COG. If the load is heavy or unevenly distributed, it can cause the COG to shift towards the side or end where the load is situated. This can make the machine more prone to tipping over in that direction.

3. Terrain: Operating on uneven or sloped terrain can significantly impact the COG. When the backhoe is positioned on a slope or an uneven surface, the COG can shift towards the downhill side. This is because gravity acts more strongly on the side of the machine that is lower, causing the COG to move in that direction.

4. Movement and Rotation: As the backhoe moves or rotates, the COG can shift accordingly. Turning sharply or quickly can cause the COG to shift towards the direction of the turn. Similarly, when the backhoe moves forward or backward, the COG can move slightly in the direction of movement.

5. Attachments and Accessories: The addition of attachments or accessories, such as a loader bucket or backhoe attachment, can alter the distribution of weight on the machine. Depending on the weight and position of these attachments, they can affect the COG and make the machine less stable.

Ensuring optimal stability while operating the Backhoe requires the operator to adjust stabilizers individually to maintain steady positioning. The ability to manage stability and control the centre of gravity distinguishes a skilled operator.

When a loader/backhoe is situated on level ground with the backhoe directly aligned behind it, the centre of gravity of the machine is evenly distributed between the wheels, as depicted in the left diagram. However, as the slope incline increases, the machine's stability diminishes due to a reduction in the horizontal distance between the centre of gravity and the wheels on the downhill side. If the slope steepens to the extent that the centre of gravity extends beyond the wheels, the machine risks tipping over.

Traversing rapidly across uneven sloping terrain can result in the machine bouncing and swaying from side to side, consequently elevating the likelihood of a rollover incident.

Rated Capacity

Once you ascertain the weight of the load, it's crucial to ensure that the backhoe/loader you're utilizing has the capability to lift it safely. You can verify the machine's capacity in the operator's manual or manufacturer's specifications.

If you're employing an attachment to lift the load, you must verify that it is also rated to lift the load safely. Keep in mind that using an attachment may potentially diminish the overall capacity of the backhoe/loader.

Always refer to the backhoe/loader load chart to confirm that any load being lifted falls within the machine's capacity. Transmit any pertinent information regarding machine and equipment capacity to the individual responsible for slinging the load.

Attachments

Understanding the diverse array of attachment options for your backhoe is paramount to the success of your project. Identifying the ideal attachment for your specific job requirements is essential to maintain project efficiency while managing costs effectively.

The initial step in choosing the appropriate backhoe attachment is to assess your project's scope and identify the desired functionality for both the backhoe and its attachment. With a multitude of attachments available, selecting the right one is critical to optimizing project efficiency and minimizing costs. Common backhoe attachments include buckets, auger drives, and demolition attachments, among others.

The loader/backhoe comprises the tractor as its fundamental component, designed to accommodate both loader and backhoe attachments. The loader, affixed to the front of the tractor, operates via hydraulic cylinders to raise and lower its arms, supporting a bucket equipped with a hydraulic cylinder for tilting. On the other hand, the backhoe, mounted at the rear of the tractor, utilizes a hinge arrangement enabling the boom and bucket assembly to swing. Hydraulic cylinders facilitate various functions of the backhoe, while stabilizers provide stability during operations.

Several attachments are compatible with the backhoe, each serving distinct purposes:

- Backhoe Bucket: The standard configuration with teeth facing the cab.

- Shovel: Features teeth facing away from the cab, suitable for handling large volumes of material.

- Clamshell Bucket: Opens and closes from the centre, used with the stick perpendicular to the ground.

- Rock Breaker: Functions as a jackhammer for breaking rock and hard ground.

Additional attachments include compactor drums, wheels, rippers, rock grabs, hydraulic grapples, and various bucket types.

Backhoe bucket attachments are designed to enhance digging processes, boasting robust construction for durability under demanding conditions. With variations such as general purpose, mud, tilt, and skeleton buckets, these attachments facilitate efficient digging, filling, and breakout force for different applications.

Auger attachments employ heavy-duty hydraulics to drill into various soil conditions with ease and efficiency. Available in machine-mounted and planetary types, augers offer high torque levels, enabling them to operate effectively in hard or rocky soil conditions.

Rippers are ideal for breaking up hard materials, while hydraulic breakers convert recoil energy to deliver enhanced power for demolition, construction, and excavation tasks. Compaction wheel attachments facilitate soil compaction during trench backfilling, ensuring a smooth finish.

Grapple attachments offer versatility in lifting and shifting tasks, with variations such as multi-tine, demolition, wood, and shell grapples. Thumb attachments, resembling human thumbs, enable secure gripping and rotation of materials, enhancing manoeuvrability and control.

Operator Controls

Prior to commencing operation of a backhoe loader, it is imperative to acquaint oneself with the controls and ensure a comprehensive understanding of their functions.

- Left-arm Controls: Responsible for managing the boom, the left-hand lever facilitates vertical movement. Drawing the lever towards oneself elevates the boom, while pushing it away lowers it. Horizontal movement of the boom is achieved by shifting the lever from left to right.

- Right-arm Controls: Governing the stick, the right-hand lever controls the rear arm, which connects to the bucket. Pulling the lever towards the operator brings the bucket and stick closer to the cab, whereas pushing it away moves them in the opposite direction. To curl the bucket towards oneself, the lever is moved to the left, while moving it to the right extends the bucket away from the operator.

- Stabilizing Controls: Positioned between the right and left arm controls, these regulate the backhoe's stabilizers. Each lever corresponds to a respective stabilizer – the left lever controls the left stabilizer, and the right lever manages the right stabilizer. This enables independent adjustment, particularly useful in challenging terrain.

- Boom Unlock: A mechanism to secure the boom arm in position, typically activated by a pedal on the floor. Unlocking the boom allows for excavation activities to commence after positioning.

- Throttle Control: Governs the engine throttle's revolutions per minute, enabling adjustment as per operational requirements.

Driving a backhoe is akin to operating an automobile, featuring familiar components such as a front-facing steering wheel, gear shift or speed settings, turn indicators, floor throttle pedal positioned to the right, and brakes located to the left.

To adjust the driving speed of a backhoe, look for an adjustable speed control lever typically situated to the left of the steering wheel. This lever, resembling a turn indicator, functions similar to a gear shifter, allowing for the manipulation of speed settings. Newer models offer the convenience of flipping through speed settings while driving, while older backhoes may necessitate engaging a clutch mechanism to shift gears.

Many backhoe models incorporate two brake pedals, one for the right and left sides, which can be utilized together or independently. This dual brake system is often employed to facilitate steering in challenging terrain, with the option to synchronize the pedals for simultaneous braking or disconnect them for individual operation.

Operating the front-end bucket loader on a backhoe follows a straightforward process akin to other front-end loaders. Positioned adjacent to the operator's right knee when seated, the right-hand lever controls the lifting and tilting functions of the boom and bucket. Pulling back on the lever raises the boom and bucket, while pushing it forward lowers them. Tilting the bucket forward or backward is achieved by pushing the lever to the right or left, respectively.

For utilizing a backhoe's digging controls, rotating the operator's seat is often necessary. This process involves several steps, including setting the loading bucket low for stability, engaging the parking brake, and flipping the steering wheel upward. To rotate the seat, a lever located between the operator's legs unlatches it from a forward-facing position, allowing it to pivot for access to rear-facing digging controls.

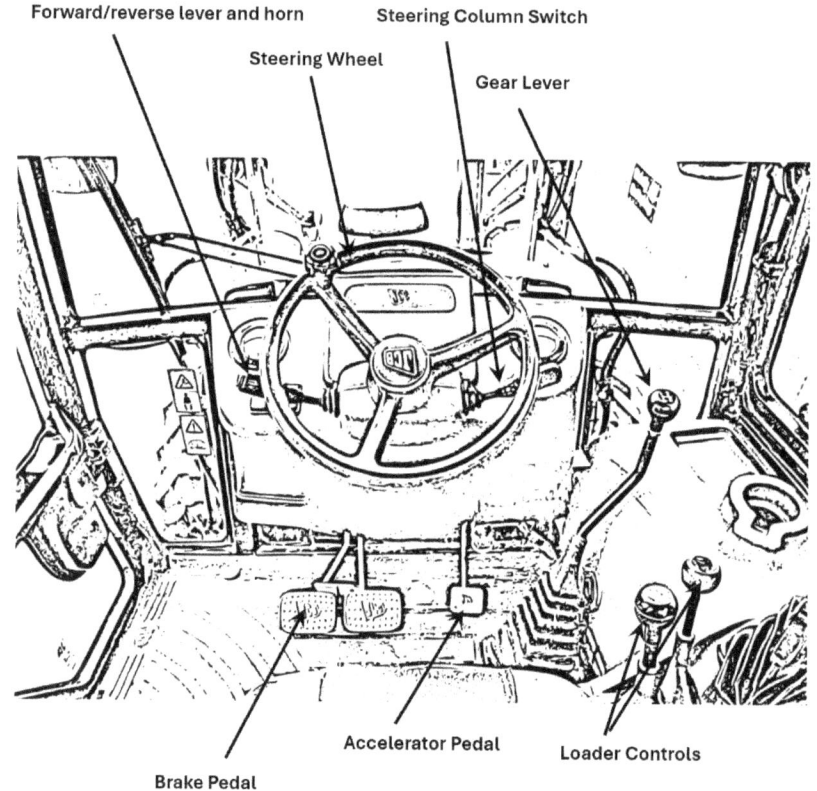

Figure 51: Sample engine and drive controls.

Sample control operations based on the example console/plant shown in Figure 51 follow.

When operating the machine, utilize only the accelerator pedal to regulate the engine speed. Avoid using the hand throttle lever to set the engine speed while in motion.

1. Gear Lever: To select a gear, adjust the lever according to the provided shift pattern. Before choosing a gear while the machine is stationary, ensure the forward/reverse lever is in neutral (N) position and the engine is idling. The machine can initiate movement in any gear based on ground conditions. To change gears while moving: a. Press the transmission dump switch on

the gear lever. b. Choose the desired gear. c. Release the transmission dump switch.

2. Accelerator Pedal: Press down on this pedal to increase the engine speed. Release the pedal to decrease the engine speed. When the foot is off the pedal, the engine will idle at 700-750 revolutions per minute (rev/min).

3. Hand Throttle Lever: Adjust the lever towards the side window to raise the engine speed. Move the lever fully towards the seat for idling speed.

4. Parking Brake Lever: Engage this lever to activate the parking brake before exiting the machine. Note that the transmission drive disengages automatically when the parking brake is engaged. Avoid using the parking brake to decelerate the machine from traveling speed, except in emergencies, to maintain brake efficiency. After using the parking brake in an emergency, always replace the brake pads. To engage the parking brake, pull the lever up (vertical) and ensure the indicator light illuminates. To release the parking brake, squeeze the release lever and lower it fully. Verify that the indicator light goes off.

5. Brake Pedal: Apply pressure on the brake pedal to slow down or halt the machine. Utilize the brakes to prevent over speeding downhill. The stop lights should activate when the brakes are engaged. Do not operate the machine unless both stop lights are functioning correctly. Two brake pedals are present. The left rear brake is controlled by the left pedal, while the right rear brake is controlled by the right pedal. The pedals can be locked together using a steel locking bar. Failure to engage the brake pedal locking bar as recommended can result in fatal or injurious accidents. If only one brake is used for rapid deceleration, the

machine may veer out of control. Separate the pedals only when driving in first gear (1) off-road. Lock the pedals together for driving in any other off-road gear or on-road in any gear.

6. Forward/Reverse Lever and Horn: Caution: Operating the forward/reverse lever while in motion can result in serious injury or fatality, as the machine will abruptly change direction without warning. Adhere to the recommended procedure for safe operation of this selector. Stop the machine before adjusting this lever. To engage forward, reverse, or neutral, 'lift' and shift the lever to the designated position. All four gears are accessible in both forward and reverse. The engine will start only when the lever is set to neutral (N). The lever features 'detent' positions for forward, reverse, or neutral. To transition the lever from the detent position, pull it towards you. For reversing direction:

- Halt the machine and maintain pressure on the foot brakes.
- Allow the engine speed to decrease to idle.
- Choose the new direction.
- Release the foot brake and accelerate away. If the parking brake is activated when the forward/reverse lever is shifted away from neutral (N), an audible warning will sound, and the Parking Brake Engaged Indicator will illuminate.
- Press button located at the end of the lever to activate the horn. This function operates only when the starter switch is set to IGN.

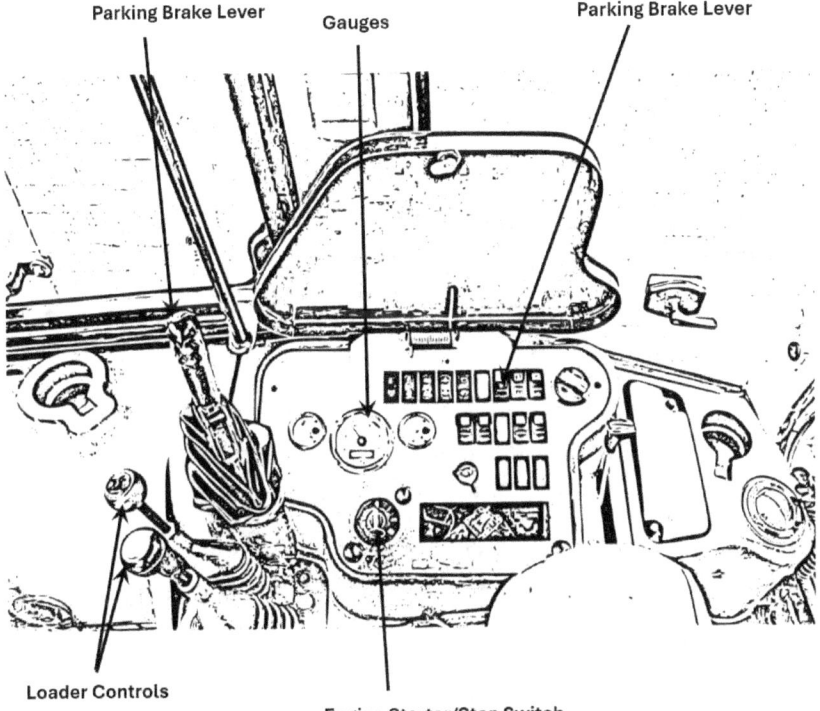

Figure 52: Sample Console.

Console switches include, for example:
- Heater fan
- Side/lights/Headlights
- Hazard Warning Lights
- Rear Window Wash/Wipe
- Rear Work Lights
- Rear Horn
- Rear Fog Light
- Beacon Switch

- Hydraulic Tool Circuit Switch

- Trailer Hitch

As an example of backhoe controls and operation, on machines equipped with JCB X Pattern control feature two backhoe control levers. Lever A, situated on the left-hand side, manages the boom and slew, while lever B on the right-hand side controls the dipper and bucket. The operation of stabilizers follows the instructions outlined in Stabilizer Controls.

Each lever follows an 'X' pattern for executing individual backhoe actions. By manoeuvring the levers between the four primary directions, combined actions can be selected. Simultaneous operation of both levers is possible, enhancing operational efficiency. The speed of backhoe actions is determined by the extent to which the levers are moved; greater movement results in faster action.

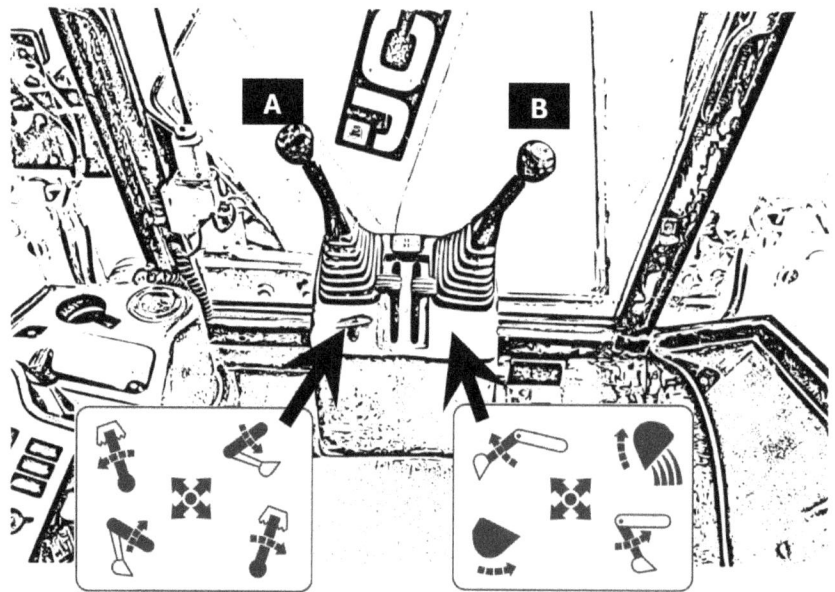

Figure 53: Backhoe operation levers.

Both levers are spring-loaded to return to their central (hold) positions. The backhoe remains in any given position until adjustments are made using the levers. A plastic decal near the controls provides visual guidance, depicting through symbols the corresponding backhoe actions triggered by specific lever movements.

Referring to Figure 53:

- Lift Boom: To elevate the boom (A), pull the lever diagonally left and towards yourself. Prior to raising the boom, ensure there are no obstructions overhead.

- Lower Boom: To lower the boom (B), push the lever diagonally right and away from yourself.

- Slew Left: To pivot the boom to your left (C), push the lever diagonally left and away from yourself. Note: Certain backhoe buckets and attachments may come into contact with the stabilizer legs if pivoted too extensively. Verify this before utilizing different attachments.

- Slew Right: To pivot the boom to your right (D), pull the lever diagonally right and towards yourself.

- Extend Dipper In: To retract the dipper (E), pull the lever diagonally right and towards yourself. Note: Certain backhoe attachments may intersect with the boom if retracted excessively. Verify this before using different attachments.

- Extend Dipper Out: To extend the dipper (F), push the lever diagonally left and away from yourself. If the boom is already elevated, ensure there are no overhead obstructions before extending the dipper.

- Close Bucket: To close the bucket (G), pull the lever diagonally left and towards yourself.

- Open Bucket: To open the bucket (H), push the lever diagonally right and away from yourself.

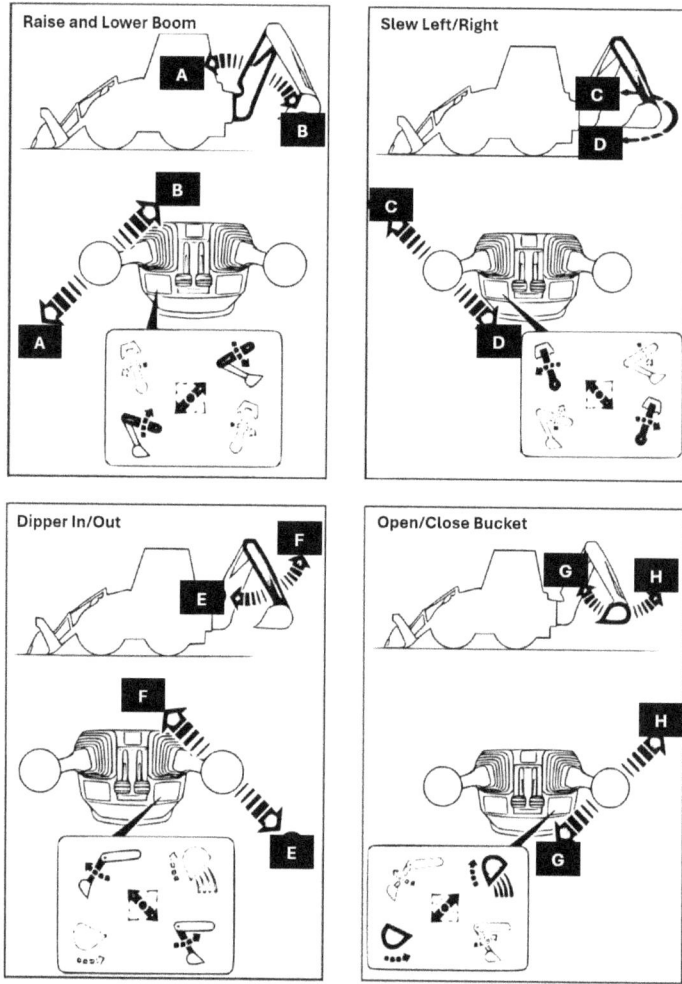

Figure 54: Backhoe control operation.

Planning and Preparing for Backhoe Operations

Understanding the task stipulations outlined in the contract is paramount. The contract specifications delineate the responsibilities for various aspects of the sealing process and delineate the desired outcome. However, it often falls upon the constructor to ascertain whether the proposed seal meets the specified performance criteria. Thus, it is imperative for the individual tasked with sealing duties on the day to have a clear comprehension of the 'defects liability' and 'performance' requirements specified within the contract.

In the planning phase, safety and environmental concerns pertaining to the site demand attention. These may encompass traffic safety, including factors like narrow shoulders or limited passing areas, fire hazards such as flammable vegetation along berms, noise impacts due to proximity to residential areas, and potential pollution risks to stormwater and air quality. Mitigating strategies should ensure the presence of firefighting equipment, strategically positioned fire extinguishers, comprehensive first aid kits, bitumen burns cards, spillage kits furnished with sand for containment, portable textile dams for drain obstruction, an appropriately enclosed catch tank for residue containment, and a designated solids waste receptacle.

Upon completion of the induction program and commencement of work at the designated workplace, familiarity with the local safety protocols in the immediate work vicinity is essential. This includes awareness of the location and types of fire extinguishers and hoses, emergency stop mechanisms for electrical equipment and fuel supplies, emergency tag procedures, evacuation protocols, specialized signage, first aid facilities, traffic regulations specific to the site, emergency communication systems, protocols for chemical or oil spills, designated parking areas, and guidelines for the use of two-way radios. While the induction program provides foundational knowledge, workplace orientation customizes safety protocols to the immediate work area, ensuring adept response in emergency scenarios.

The scale of daily operational requirements dictates the mode of communication, which may range from verbal briefings to written instructions from supervisory personnel. Ensuring receipt and comprehension of work instructions is imperative. In cases of ambiguity, seeking clarification from the supervisor is advisable. Site visits may also be necessary to inspect job sites before preparing equipment for operational tasks.

Efficient management of a company, project, or personal endeavours hinges on meticulous planning and organization. This entails a comprehensive assessment of project parameters to ascertain the optimal approach for timely, budget-conscious, and quality-compliant execution. The absence of structured planning leads to inefficiencies and resource wastage. Consequently, the ability to forecast and adapt to changes, streamline operations, monitor progress, and assess outcomes becomes indispensable.

Failure to plan entails risks ranging from operational inefficiencies to compromised safety and financial ramifications. Effective planning, therefore, serves as a cornerstone for success, offering direction, minimizing uncertainties, and fostering accountability and productivity. Through diligent planning and organizational efforts, individuals and entities in the construction industry can optimize resource utilization, mitigate risks, and achieve desired outcomes efficiently.

Backhoes are equipped with multiple safety mechanisms to ensure operator protection:

1. Seat Belt:

    - A seat belt is a mandatory feature in backhoes. It prevents the operator from being ejected in case of pitching or tipping.

    - Some seat belts have an electrical connection that disables machine operation unless the seat belt is fastened.

Seat belts must be worn at all times. Before starting, inspect the seat belt for any defects such as frayed webbing, damaged buckle, or malfunctioning anti-creep slide operation. If defects are detected, refrain from operating the machine until they are rectified.

1. Operator Protection Bars (ROPS – FOPS):

   - Roll Over Protection Structures (ROPS) and Falling Object Protection Structures (FOPS) are designed to safeguard the operator in the event of a rollover or falling objects by absorbing impact forces.

   - It's imperative not to modify the cab design, as alterations may compromise the effectiveness of these structures and void the manufacturer's warranty.

2. Safety Guards and Covers:

   - These components are installed to shield operators from moving parts and potential hazards, enhancing overall safety during operation.

3. Warning Devices:

   - Backhoes are equipped with warning systems to alert operators of potential dangers or malfunctions, ensuring prompt action can be taken to mitigate risks.

4. Warning Labels:

   - Clearly marked warning labels provide essential safety information and instructions to operators, promoting safe operation practices.

Effective planning is indispensable for providing direction and purpose to actions. It establishes a roadmap for tasks, delineating responsibilities, timelines, and objectives to ensure clarity and alignment among supervisors, managers, and employees. Planning mitigates uncertainty, minimizes duplication of effort, and facilitates performance tracking and assessment. By meticulously planning and adhering to the plan, better cost control, resource utilization, and operational efficiency can be achieved. Failure to plan results in increased difficulty, unforeseen challenges, and diminished prospects for success, potentially leading to job insecurity or demotion. Planning encompasses a systematic approach to task sequencing, resource allocation, and risk management, fostering a conducive environment for achieving desired outcomes efficiently.

Clear communication of work instructions is essential for task execution. Instructions may be relayed verbally by supervisors, outgoing shift counterparts, or documented in written formats such as instruction books, log sheets, or planning schedules. Verbal instructions should be comprehensively understood, and any uncertainties clarified before commencing work. Written instructions should provide clarity on tasks, safety requirements, and necessary equipment, ensuring adherence to safe work practices.

Successful job planning is fundamental for competitive pricing and efficient resource management. It involves meticulous consideration of time, materials, overheads, and expected profit margins to formulate a compelling tender. Clear and comprehensive instructions are imperative for task execution, minimizing the risk of errors or misunderstandings. Effective communication between supervisors and workers fosters a conducive work environment, promoting clarity, efficiency, and accountability.

All work must be meticulously planned in accordance with the site development and operational plan, site work procedures, and legislative requirements. Legal obligations encompass various Acts and regulations governing health and safety.

It is imperative to ensure compliance with the relevant legislation applicable to your site. The procedure for preparing a new excavation area should include:

- Receiving instructions from the shift supervisor regarding the excavation location and equipment requirements.

- Conducting comprehensive checks, including pre-start, pre-engine starting, backhoe controls, engine starting, after-starting, and operation of the backhoe.

- Verifying work area access and ensuring the ground is safe for work.

- Checking for misfires and managing them according to the misfire procedure if found.

All personnel must participate in a start-of-shift meeting to receive and discuss current information, such as (as relevant to the work site):

- Blasting times
- Ground conditions
- Work areas
- Job allocations
- Road conditions

In mining operations, before entering the mine face area, awareness of current conditions is essential. Site rules typically include a shift changeover procedure to update personnel on operational status. A job hazard analysis (JHA) should be conducted before commencing any job without an existing procedure or routine basis. Any identified hazards and risks must be reported using the Company Risk Assessment Process.

Inspection of the work area is crucial to identify hazards and formulate safe work procedures. Potential risks during backhoe operations may include:

- Hazardous materials
- Uneven or unstable ground
- Wet conditions
- Slip, trip, and fall hazards
- Sharp edges
- Access restrictions
- Equipment-related hazards
- Environmental factors such as windrows, buildings, etc.

Operators must remain vigilant regarding:
- Ground and road conditions
- Proximity to power lines, trees, manholes, etc.
- Open excavations and trenches
- Service lines
- Blind spots
- Weather conditions
- Time of day and lighting
- Bridge load capacities and width

Operators should also check for:
- Communication networks
- Barricades
- Signs

- Personnel and pedestrians

- Traffic lights

Operators must also maintain a minimum clearance from power lines as per site-specific regulations. In the event of contact with power lines, follow emergency procedures, remain in the cab, and notify supervisors using the emergency radio procedure. Evacuate the cab only if there is an imminent danger of electrical fire and follow site evacuation procedures.

After identifying hazards, implement control measures such as:
- Barricading the area

- Using traffic control measures

- Posting signs and notices

- Using lights and lighting towers for night work

- Obtaining authorization permits

- Ensuring proper personal protective equipment (PPE)

- Following site procedures and maintaining minimum clearances from services.

In the initial stages of any project, it is essential to assess the environmental impact and take proactive measures to mitigate it. Australia has a comprehensive framework of laws, regulations, policies, and guidelines aimed at safeguarding the environment. Key concerns in the construction industry revolve around stormwater pollution, litter, dust, and sediment runoff, necessitating construction activities to be conducted in a manner that prevents pollution from entering waterways.

Stormwater runoff transports pollutants to water bodies and coastal areas, while sediment runoff can suffocate aquatic flora and fauna, leading to siltation of creeks, rivers, reservoirs, and dams. Litter often ends up in stormwater, exacerbating pollution issues.

Effective management of litter, waste, erosion, sediment, and dust yields several benefits, including decreased cleanup expenses, mitigation of mud/dust-related hazards, enhanced wet weather working conditions, improved occupational health and safety standards, enhanced drainage systems, minimized stockpile losses, reduction in public grievances, and augmented community reputation.

Apart from environmental concerns, dust poses occupational health and safety risks inherent to construction sites. Dust generation is inherent in construction activities, especially with materials like cement or gypsum-based substances. Potential controls include utilization of water sprays and mists, adoption of wet methods for concrete cutting or friction saws, prompt cleanup of debris, use of approved masks in areas with inhalation risks, and deployment of industrial vacuum cleaners.

Site Drainage: Effective site drainage measures can significantly reduce the environmental impact of stormwater. Controls may include diverting uphill water away from the site using turf or geotextile-lined catch drains or diversion banks, directing diverted stormwater to stable areas, avoiding discharge of water towards site entrances/exits, and connecting temporary or permanent downpipes to the stormwater system during roof installation.

Maximizing material recycling contributes to environmental sustainability. Materials such as steel, aluminium, gypsum plasterboard, timber, concrete, bricks, tiles, plastics, glass, and carpet can be recycled. Strategies for reducing building materials include consumption reduction, existing material reuse, resource recycling, utilization of renewable resources, and preference for materials with high recycled content.

Efficient management of sand and soil stockpiles involves implementing controls such as designating specific areas for material delivery on-site, prohibiting stockpile storage on footpaths or within road reserves, locating stockpiles behind sediment controls and protecting them from runoff, ensuring a safe distance from hazard areas, and limiting stockpile height.

Sediment fencing is vital for containing sediment runoff. Key aspects of sediment fencing include preventing sediment discharge from the site, installing fences along contours, conducting weekly inspections for up to six months, ensuring fences remain vertical and securely embedded in the soil, promptly repairing any damages, trenching the fence at least 150mm deep and burying it to allow water flow while preventing seepage, and compacting soil on both sides to prevent seepage.

Boarding and Dismounting Machinery: When boarding or dismounting a machine, it's crucial never to become complacent, as many injuries have occurred due to incorrect boarding or dismounting practices. Here are essential guidelines to follow:

1. Cleanliness: Before climbing, ensure to clean your shoes and wipe your hands.

2. Use Handrails: Utilize handrails, grab-irons, ladders, or steps when mounting the machine.

3. Avoid Controls as Grab-Irons: Never use machine controls as grab-irons.

4. Avoid Boarding Moving Machines: Never attempt to board a machine while it's in motion.

5. Three Points of Contact: Always maintain three points of contact while climbing or descending.

6. Climb Sensibly: Ascend or descend the ladder safely and sensibly.

7. Know Horn Signals: Understand and adhere to the horn signals specific to your site.

Pre-Start Checks: Before conducting walk-around and pre-start inspections, it's essential to fit a tag to the main switch of the machine. Here are the key points regarding pre-start checks:

1. Conduct Full Inspection: Perform a thorough pre-start inspection, including checking the fire system, at each shift change or after any repair or service work.

2. Follow Manufacturer's Instructions: Start the machine according to the manufacturer's instructions.

3. Identify Faults: Conduct pre-start inspections to identify any faults and ensure the machine is ready for operation.

4. Responsibility: Operators are responsible for checking machine repair status before operation.

5. Upper-Level Checks: Perform cab checks and brake tests before moving off.

Walk Around Inspection: A walk-around inspection must be completed before entering and operating equipment. Key points about walk-around inspections include:

1. Timing: Conduct inspections after any absence from the cab, refuelling, repairs, maintenance, or inspections.

2. Safety: Ensure nobody is near the machine before boarding, check for damage to equipment, and verify terrain safety.

Ground Level and Platform Checks: Visually inspect the machine for various aspects, including attachments, superstructure, fluid levels, and cabin conditions, ensuring safety before boarding.

Fluid Checks: Check engine oil, fuel, brake fluid, hydraulic oil, or battery levels without using a naked flame, and use a torch instead.

Cabin Checks: Inspect the cabin for cleanliness, seat belt condition, mirror adjustments, start the engine using appropriate horn signals, and test various controls.

Remember to report any damage or defects to your supervisor and record them on your pre-start checklist to ensure safety and operational readiness.

Before starting the machine, ensure you are wearing appropriate personal protective equipment (PPE). It's advisable to conduct a walk-around inspection of the backhoe after completing the pre-start to check for obstructions. Accidents have occurred due to operators unknowingly reversing into vehicles or individuals.

The start-up procedure is outlined as follows:

1. Check for Maintenance Tags: Ensure there are no maintenance tags on the machine.

2. Climbing into the Cab: Use the ladder and handrails to climb into the cab, maintaining three points of contact.

3. Adjustments: Adjust the seat and fasten the seat belt as necessary.

4. Hydraulic Control Lock: Ensure that the hydraulic control lock/servo switch is applied.

5. Control Checks: Confirm that all controls are in neutral and securely locked.

6. Engine Adjustment: Adjust the engine to start at a low idle.

7. Key Position: Turn the key to the ON position.

8. System Test: Utilize the test functions on the monitoring system.

9. Horn Signal: Sound the horn once to alert others of engine start-up, wait 5 seconds, then start the engine.

After starting the engine, follow these steps:

1. Engine Warm-up: Allow the engine to warm up for 5 minutes from a cold start, following the manufacturer's specifications.

2. Gauge Checks: Verify that all gauges are functioning correctly within 10 seconds of start-up. Ensure dash lights are operational if working at night.

3. Indicator and Light Testing: Test the indicators and lights for proper functionality.

4. Control Function Test: Operate all control levers in all directions to warm up the hydraulic system.

5. Hydraulic Lock Release: Release the hydraulic lockout.

6. Movement Test: Move forward, reverse, and check the reverse beeper.

Before moving the machine, adhere to the following:

1. Clear Surroundings: Ensure the area around the machine is clear of personnel and equipment.

2. Hydraulic Function Test: Perform a hydraulic function test before moving into your work area.

3. Horn Signal: Sound the horn twice for forward or three times for reverse, depending on the direction of movement, and wait five (5) seconds.

4. Machine Movement: To move forward, push the pedals forward with the drive sprockets at the rear.

5. Proceed to Work Area: Proceed to your designated work area and prepare to commence loading.

6. Travel Caution: On rough ground, slow down to avoid damage and aim to travel over smooth areas whenever possible.

All checks should be conducted according to the manufacturer's recommendations, as outlined in the operating manual. Additionally, ensure the engine oil pressure light on the EMS goes off within 10 seconds after starting the engine. If not, shut down the machine and keep engine speed low until the oil pressure indicator is resolved.

Operating a Backhoe

Effective policies and procedures should be established for overseeing site safety, which can be integrated into an overarching management system that adequately manages and mitigates the risks associated with the work being conducted.

A comprehensive safety system should encompass processes for:

- Identifying individuals with Occupational Health and Safety (OHS) responsibilities.

- Managing the health and safety of contractors and subcontractors.

- Developing and managing consultation procedures for health and safety matters.

- Identifying hazards and controlling risks.

- Establishing the location of underground services.

- Developing site safety rules.

- Monitoring site activities and enforcing safety rules.

- Establishing site amenities and implementing ongoing maintenance.

- Developing site-specific induction for workers and others (e.g., delivery drivers and visitors).

- Ensuring only trained and competent workers are permitted to work on-site.

- Ensuring all plant (machinery and equipment) is safe and without risks to health before use.

- Identifying requirements for a mobile plant compound and vehicle parking.

- Developing traffic management plans.

- Identifying and controlling risks to the public. • Developing emergency response plans for reasonably foreseeable emergency situations.

Ensure that powered plant is mechanically sound, safe for use, and accompanied by the required safety documentation.

Hazards may include:

- Moving materials and equipment or manual tasks.

- Rough ground.

- Falls (including climbing in and out of mobile plant and excavations).

- Close proximity of mobile plant and other vehicles (including on-site and road).

- Excessive noise or dust.

- Utility services (e.g., power lines and gas pipes).

- Contaminated soil.

- Weather conditions and UV radiation.

Employers should eliminate risks to health and safety where possible (e.g., de-energizing power lines). If elimination is not feasible, employers must reduce risks as far as reasonably practicable by implementing appropriate controls specified by law, substituting activities or equipment, isolating hazards, using engineering controls, or a combination of these measures.

Prevent common injuries by managing the causes, such as manual handling of materials, slips, trips, and falls. Factors increasing the risk of injury should be addressed through proper planning, storage, access, layout, and use of appropriate force or posture.

Develop a SWMS when working near road traffic and instruct workers accordingly. Implement measures such as wearing high-visibility clothing, using warning devices, deploying traffic controllers, and providing clear emergency procedures and escape routes.

Operators must safeguard pedestrians, cyclists, and others from risks associated with work near public roads. Implement appropriate controls, pedestrian paths, barriers, hoardings, and traffic management measures.

Workers should refrain from using personal electronic devices when working near mobile plant, traffic, or transit routes to avoid distractions and increase awareness of their surroundings.

Effective communication among supervisors, traffic controllers, plant operators, and workers is essential and may include verbal and non-verbal methods.

Identify underground services before mechanical excavating or ground penetration work.

Earthmoving equipment utilized for lifting loads should be equipped with hose burst protection valves on critical hydraulic cylinders, especially if the equipment has a rated capacity exceeding one tonne.

Unless there is a designated lifting point installed elsewhere, loads should only be suspended from the manufacturer's designated lift points on the boom or the quickhitch. The rated capacity must be prominently displayed near the lifting point. Additionally, ensure that the machine's load chart is visibly mounted inside the cabin.

It is essential to inspect lifting gear prior to use and to maintain it regularly.

A sample start-up procedure for a backhoe follows:

1. Ensure Seat Belt and Seat Adjustment: Check that your seat belt (if fitted) is securely fastened and adjust the seat position accordingly.

2. Engage Gear: Select an appropriate gear based on the current conditions and the task at hand. Note that once a gear is engaged, the road wheels will be linked to the engine upon movement of the forward/reverse lever from neutral (N). Be cautious as the machine may attempt to move before you are prepared.

3. Verify Attachment Positions: Confirm that all attachments are in their travel positions.

4. Apply Brake: Press the brake pedal firmly down.

5. Select Drive Direction: Choose either forward (F) or reverse (R). Note that an audible alarm will sound and a warning light will illuminate if the parking brake is still engaged when drive is selected.

6. Release Parking Brake: Release the parking brake by squeezing the release lever and lowering it completely.

7. Ensure Safety and Move Off: Ensure it is safe to proceed, then release the brake pedal and gently press the accelerator pedal to initiate smooth movement. If the engine or steering fails, halt the machine immediately and address the issue before continuing operation.

8. Verify Steering and Brakes: While the machine is in motion, assess the functionality of the steering and brakes. Do not continue driving if these systems are not functioning correctly.

Avoid side hill travel whenever possible, as it significantly increases the risk of tipping the machine over. If you find yourself driving the backhoe/loader on a sloping surface, it's crucial to proceed directly down the slope rather than traversing it horizontally or diagonally. This ensures maximum stability of the machine. When approaching downhill or uphill travel, reduce speed and select an appropriate gear suited to the gradient. Opting for a low gear during downhill travel aids in controlling the descent, often mirroring the gear used for ascending the hill. When crossing a ditch, decrease speed and approach the obstacle at an angle. It's imperative not to coast downhill by putting the backhoe/loader into neutral gear and allowing it to roll freely.

When operating a backhoe/loader, it's essential to feel confident in the machine and understand its capabilities. This is best achieved by thoroughly reading the operator's manual and familiarizing oneself with engine performance, optimal speeds for various tasks, bucket height preferences, and other pertinent factors. This knowledge enables safe operation across diverse terrains and effective adjustment of operating techniques. These techniques encompass general driving, reversing, manoeuvring, braking, attachment operation, bucket loading, and load carrying.

General driving techniques involve maintaining vigilance towards hazards at all times, avoiding trench areas and unprotected edges, and watching out for terrain hazards such as tree stumps. Reversing safely requires ensuring clear visibility behind, continuous monitoring of surroundings, and possibly adjusting the seat orientation for improved visibility and safety. Manoeuvring effectively in confined spaces entails being aware of other equipment, structures, and roadways, understanding machine limitations, and seeking tips from experienced operators.

When it comes to braking, it's essential to exercise caution, avoiding sudden braking unless absolutely necessary and allowing sufficient stopping distance, particularly when carrying a loaded bucket. Braking should not compromise machine balance or stability, especially during turns, and it's crucial to familiarize oneself with the machine's capabilities as outlined in the operator's manual.

Attachment operation involves adhering to design limits and operational recommendations for both the attachment and the backhoe/loader as a whole vehicle. Staying within these specifications, recommendations, and design limits is crucial to prevent damage to either the backhoe/loader or the attachments. The operator's manual provides detailed instructions on how to use each attachment, which will also be demonstrated during equipment induction and familiarization. It's imperative to heed the usage recommendations and design limits outlined for attachments to ensure safe and efficient operation for achieving desired results. If uncertain about how to fit, use, or remove an attachment, referring to the operator's manual or consulting with an authorized mechanic, fitter, or other team members is advisable.

Removing a Bucket:

1. Position the Backhoe: Align the backhoe directly behind the machine. Ensure the bucket rests on level ground with its flat surface facing downwards. Secure the bucket in place to prevent any unintended movement. Maintain a safe distance to one side of the bucket while removing the pivot pins to avoid potential accidents.

2. Remove the Pivot Pins: Be cautious of metal splinters that may cause injury during the removal of metal pins. Utilize a soft-faced hammer or drift for the task, ensuring the use of safety glasses for protection. Unclip and extract the lynch pins, then proceed to remove the pivot pins.

3. Withdraw the Dipper: Using the operational controls, lift the dipper carefully to disengage it from the bucket.

Fitting a Bucket:
Note: This task is preferably performed by two individuals—one to manipulate the controls and the other to align the pivots.

1. Position the Bucket: Place the bucket flat on level ground using an appropriate lifting mechanism. If two people are involved, ensure the control operator is competent. Any abrupt or incorrect movements of the controls could pose serious risks to the other person's safety.

2. Reverse the Machine while Aligning the Dipper End with the Bucket Hinge Area: Manoeuvre the machine in reverse while aligning the dipper end with the bucket hinge area.

3. Engage the Dipper: Exercise caution regarding metal splinters during pin manipulation, using suitable tools and protective gear. Skilfully adjust the controls to align the holes in the dipper and tipping link with those in the bucket. Secure the pivot pins and lynch pins in place.

Bucket Loading Techniques for loading the bucket include:
- Applying the appropriate technique for the specific type of bucket being used.

- Seeking guidance from more experienced operators and requesting mentoring if assistance is needed.

- Avoiding overloading the bucket.

- Improving loading efficiency and effectiveness through regular practice.

Load Carrying Techniques for carrying loads include:
- Keeping the load close to the ground whenever feasible.

- Maintaining a safe traveling speed.

- Ensuring the machine remains balanced while carrying the load.

- Minimizing spillages whenever possible.

Load Discharge Techniques for discharging loads include:
- Discharging the load on level ground to prevent rollovers.

- Exercising care and consideration for the machine's capabilities.

- Adjusting the bucket to the appropriate height for discharge before initiating the movement.

- Rolling the bucket to ensure a clean discharge of materials.

- Applying correct braking or using the hand/load brake to stop movement as necessary.

Mixing Materials Backhoe/loaders are suitable for mixing materials due to their large bucket capacity and ability to move significant amounts of materials efficiently.

A tiller attachment is beneficial for breaking up the ground and mixing topsoil or clay with other materials to prepare the ground for future tasks. Rippers and scarifiers can also be employed to break up the ground before mixing materials.

Loading Techniques: Loading techniques depend on various factors such as material type, excavation method, floor conditions, and wind direction. When loading, consider the following techniques:

- Smoothly swing the load as the bucket is loaded and lifted.

- Tail load trucks whenever feasible to minimize lift height.

- Start dumping the load when the bucket's centre is swinging over the side or end of the truck body.

- Commence the return swing before the bucket is empty.

- Lower the bucket to the next dig area once the teeth clear the truck body.

- Position the stick and bucket before landing.

- If the bucket stalls in the wrong position, slightly lift the boom or extend the stick.

Top Loading: Top loading is applicable for tasks such as finishing a bench, picking up batter trims, starting a drop cut, or digging a sump.

Loading on a Level Surface: Operating the Backhoe on a level surface while loading maximizes productivity, reduces operator fatigue, minimizes machine wear, assists in maintaining levels, and reduces machine instability.

Lifting with a Backhoe: When lifting a load with a backhoe, refer to the operator's manual for specific load ratings at different radii and boom positions. Determine where to attach the lifting sling(s) to the bucket according to the manual's instructions. For buckets without designated lifting attachment points, a chain can be attached, ensuring it is positioned correctly to prevent damage.

Stripping and Spreading Materials Backhoe/loaders are useful for stripping the top layer of earth to excavate or level an area. This is accomplished by using the blade of the bucket to cut and lift a small amount of topsoil.

The excavated topsoil can be transported to another area and spread out. Spreading topsoil can be achieved in various ways, such as discharging the soil bit by bit while moving along or scraping a small pile of topsoil over an area using the bucket blade or a 4-in-1 bucket.

Figure 55: Caterpillar 420E IT backhoe loader stripping topsoil. Shaun Greiner from Creve Coeur, United States of America, CC BY-SA 2.0, via Wikimedia Commons.

Cutting and Boxing Cutting involves removing material above a specified level, such as cutting down to create a floor or design level.

Boxing entails removing material below a level and may include trenching or removing sections of pavement in a "box" shape to the desired level.

Excavating Material: Before excavating material, certain precautions must be taken:

- Conduct a thorough assessment of the work area.

- Ensure all personnel are clear of the work area.

- Determine the location of buried cables, water, and gas lines.

- Identify the location of overhead power lines.

It is crucial to cease machine operation if someone enters the work area and is considered too close until the area is clear.

Ensure smooth operation of the Backhoe attachment at a comfortable engine speed for the task. To enhance efficiency, multiple controls should be utilized simultaneously if necessary.

The machine can be moved forward or backward at any point during the operating cycle to maintain effective digging. If the digging position becomes inefficient, the backhoe must be repositioned.

Digging / Trenching Technique: When conducting digging operations:

- Maintain the machine level.

- Keep travel motors to the rear to safeguard them.

- Use controls to facilitate smooth movement of the attachment.

- Employ the correct bucket digging angle.

- Avoid using the ditch wall to halt the attachment swing, as it can damage the hydraulics.

- Do not overload the bucket.

Workers should refrain from being in a trench being excavated.

When engaging in excavation work, it is essential to keep in mind several key points:

- Before commencing excavation, conduct checks for underground services such as power, telephone, gas, water, sewer, drainage, and fibre optic cable lines. Consult the site supervisor, who will coordinate with supply authorities to obtain council maps of the site.

- When cutting a trench, adhere to the required specifications and deposit full buckets of material away from the trench.

- If cutting a trench across a footpath, obtain necessary information and permits from relevant authorities responsible for services under the footpath. Excavate cautiously towards any underground services and provide appropriate barricades and signs.

- Remove large rocks from trenches as needed.

- For trench excavations deeper than 1.5 meters or where material is prone to collapse, the backhoe/loader operator must bench and batter the sides and lower trench shields before entering the excavation.

- Avoid undercutting a trench, bank, or stockpile, as this could lead to collapse and potentially cause the backhoe/loader to overturn, trapping the operator underneath.

- When operating on soft or uneven ground, the safe load-carrying capacity will be reduced.

- Maintain a safe distance between loads and the trench—material should be placed no closer than 1 meter, with the material coming to rest at least 0.5 meters from the excavation.

- Employ barricades, guardrails, fencing, and warning signs to prevent workers from falling into the trench or vehicles/machines from approaching too closely. Ensure that nobody stands within the operating radius of the backhoe/loader.

- Keep an eye out for signs indicating proximity to previous excavations or underground services. If any of the following signs are observed during excavation, cease operations immediately and conduct hand digging to investigate: crushed blue metal or plastic tape, clean sand or sandbags, broken tiles, moisture, or any other unusual material.

Figure 56: Backhoe digging a trench. Defense Visual Information Distribution Service, Public domain, via picryl.

Backfilling with the backhoe/loader involves filling trenches or small excavations once the work is finished. It's crucial to ensure that the correct materials are deposited into the excavation and that the proper level of compaction is attained.

Loose materials within a trench or excavation may settle over time, causing the ground to sink. Therefore, it's important to ensure that enough material is packed into the trench to maintain an even surface after the work is completed.

When backfilling trenches, remember to:

- Maintain a 90-degree angle unless site plans specify otherwise.

- Steer clear of edges and drop-offs.

- Avoid soft edges and deep holes.

- Trenches exceeding 1.5 meters in depth must be shored up to prevent collapse, especially if personnel will be working within the trench area or alongside it.

As you engage in work and transport materials, the environment around you will undergo changes.

Adjusting to Light Variations: During twilight hours, fatigue may affect your vision, making it challenging to discern terrain features and judge distances accurately. Installing temporary lighting where feasible and proceeding cautiously becomes imperative in such situations.

Consideration of Weather Conditions: Rain, sleet, snow, wind, and humidity can all impact both your loader and the materials being handled. Increased moisture content from any source alters material composition, potentially rendering them heavier and more slippery. Consequently, your ability to lift or transport loads may be compromised, necessitating adjustments in load quantities.

Adapting to Shifting Work Environments: As materials are relocated or cleared from a site, the work environment undergoes changes. Material composition may vary throughout the project's duration. As excavation deepens or transitions occur to other stages such as landscaping or road base preparation, you'll encounter different materials, attachments, and workforce configurations. Adjusting techniques accordingly becomes essential to ensure efficiency and safety.

Finishing Backhoe Operations

When preparing to park the backhoe, follow these steps:

- Positioning: Park the machine away from the working face and avoid parking on a slope.

- Attachment Safety: Ground the attachment and engage the hydraulic lock lever.

- Engine Adjustment: Turn the engine throttle switch towards the turtle character to reduce engine speed.

- Idle Time: Allow the machine to idle for a minimum of five minutes before shutting it down.

- Shutdown: Once the machine has idled for the required time, turn the key start switch to the OFF position.

- Walk-Around Inspection: At the end of a shift, conduct a brief walk-around inspection.

- Pedal Position: Ensure that the travel pedals are in the neutral position when parking.

It's important to note that supervisory permission is necessary to park on a slope, except in cases of emergency.

When parking the vehicle, strive to do so on level ground whenever feasible. However, if parking on a slope is necessary, utilize wooden pads to block the wheels and prevent unintended movement.

As a sample Parking Procedure:

1. Bring the Machine to a Stop: Gradually ease off the accelerator pedal and apply the brake pedal to smoothly halt the machine.

2. Engage Parking Brake: Pull the brake lever upward fully to engage the parking brake. Confirm that the parking brake indicator illuminates and release the foot brake.

3. Disengage Drive: Set the forward/reverse lever to neutral.

4. Lower Stabilisers: Lower the stabiliser legs until they lightly touch the ground.

5. Lower Attachments to Ground: Before lowering attachments, ensure the machine surroundings are clear of individuals. Use the control levers to lower the attachments to the ground, allowing them to bear the machine's weight slightly.

6. Stop the Engine: Turn the starter key to the '0' position. If leaving the machine unattended, remove the starter key.

7. Switch Off Unnecessary Controls: Turn off all unnecessary switches. If required, leave hazard warning lights or side lights activated.

8. Exit and Secure Machine: Before exiting, ensure the parking brake is engaged and prevents unintended movement. Use handholds and steps for safe descent. If leaving the machine unattended, close and secure all windows, lock the door, and consider locking the filler cap.

When the backhoe and its attachments are not in use, adhere to the manufacturer's storage instructions. Backhoes attached to tractors are safest when resting on the ground. If detached, ensure stability and mitigate the risk of falling.

Facilities and sheds should be situated on level, sturdy ground, free of obstructions, allowing workers to access them safely, without slip, trip, or fall hazards, and away from site traffic. Considerations for location selection include proximity to neighbouring residences, access to utilities, restrictions near overhead power lines, and proximity to water drainage systems. Once established, maintain facilities by ensuring regular cleaning, waste removal, and storing materials and equipment away from access areas.

Employers must mitigate risks to the public by implementing appropriate site security measures. Factors influencing the level of security required include site location, nearby pedestrian routes, type of work, mobile plant usage, and materials stored on-site. Adjust site security measures as necessary to contain hazards within smaller areas and utilize temporary perimeter fencing for most situations. Ensure security measures are firmly fixed, regularly inspected, and maintained to prevent collapse.

Establish safe work practices for servicing and cleaning plant equipment based on manufacturer's procedures and factors such as the type of work, chemicals used, and prevention of manual handling injuries, slips, trips, and falls. Develop Safe Work Method Statements (SWMS) for tasks involving significant risks, such as working at heights or adjacent to public roads or railways. Regularly inspect and maintain powered plant equipment according to specified intervals, ensuring necessary repairs are carried out promptly.

Conduct an annual major inspection of powered mobile plant equipment to verify sound mechanical condition, adherence to maintenance programs, adequacy of risk controls, and functionality of safety devices and operator controls. The inspection report should include details of the competent person overseeing the inspection, plant identification, confirmation of safety for continued use, and the date for the next major inspection.

Chapter Five

Excavator Operations

An excavator is a heavy construction machine primarily used for digging and moving large quantities of earth, debris, or other materials. It consists of a rotating cab mounted on tracks or wheels, with a hydraulic arm and bucket attachment. Excavators are versatile and widely used in various construction, demolition, mining, and landscaping applications. They can perform tasks such as digging trenches, foundations, and holes, as well as loading and unloading materials, lifting heavy objects, and demolishing structures. Excavators come in different sizes and configurations to suit different job requirements, ranging from small compact excavators for tight spaces to large crawler excavators for heavy-duty operations.

Excavation work typically involves the removal of soil or rock from a site to create an open face, hole, or cavity, utilizing tools, machinery, or explosives.

An excavator is a self-propelled vehicle, available in crawler or wheeled configurations, featuring an upper structure capable of rotating a full 360 degrees.

EARTHMOVING EQUIPMENT OPERATIONS

This equipment is designed to excavate, swing, and discharge materials. These actions are achieved through the movement of the boom, independent of the chassis or undercarriage of the machine.

Resembling a person's upper arm, forearm, and hand, the excavator boom comprises three segments. The machine digs into the ground below ground level using the bucket to extract materials. As the bucket lifts or swings, it transports the materials towards the machine before depositing them into the discharge area.

Excavators play a crucial role in open-cut mining operations, serving as versatile tools for various tasks such as excavating overburden, extracting coal, clearing batters or rills, digging ramps, and preparing dig faces for shovels. In the accompanying images, excavators are often depicted loading trucks from an elevated position on a bench, providing a strategic height advantage. While excavators may not match the digging capacity of shovels, their superior manoeuvrability and transportability make them indispensable assets in mining operations.

Figure 57: A Hitachi excavator loads a CAT 789C haul truck with overburden at an opencut coal mine. Peabody Energy, Inc., CC BY-SA 4.0, via Wikimedia Commons.

In mining, excavators are used for:

1. Overburden Removal: Excavators are used to remove overburden, which refers to the layers of soil, rock, and other materials covering the mineral deposit. By excavating and removing the overlying material, excavators expose the mineral deposit for extraction.

2. Coal Extraction: In coal mining, excavators are employed to extract coal seams from the earth. Excavators dig into the coal seam, loosen the material, and load it onto trucks or conveyors for transportation to processing facilities.

3. Batt Clean-up: Excavators are used to clean up batters, which are inclined slopes or walls created during mining operations. They remove loose material, debris, and other obstructions from batters to maintain stability and safety.

4. Ramps Construction: Excavators are utilized to construct ramps or access roads within the mine site. These ramps provide access to different mining areas and facilitate the movement of equipment, vehicles, and personnel throughout the site.

5. Dig Face Preparation: Excavators prepare the dig face, which is the exposed surface of the mineral deposit where excavation or mining activities take place. They create a suitable working surface by leveling, shaping, or excavating the area as needed.

6. Truck Loading: Excavators are responsible for loading trucks with excavated material, whether it be overburden, coal, or other minerals. They use their bucket attachment to scoop up material from the dig face and deposit it into trucks for transport to processing or disposal sites.

7. Mobility and Versatility: Excavators offer high mobility and versatility in mining operations. Their ability to rotate 360 degrees

and maneuver in tight spaces makes them well-suited for various tasks across the mine site.

Excavators are indispensable equipment in mining operations due to their efficiency, versatility, and capability to perform a wide range of tasks involved in excavation, material handling, and site preparation.

Excavators are extensively utilized in civil construction, including road construction, due to their versatility and efficiency. Here are several ways in which excavators are commonly used in civil construction projects:

1. Excavation: Excavators are primarily employed for digging and excavating earth, soil, rock, and other materials to prepare the construction site. They can create trenches, foundations, drainage systems, and utility trenches required for various infrastructure projects, including roads.

2. Trenching: Excavators are used to dig trenches for laying underground utilities such as water pipes, sewer lines, electrical conduits, and telecommunications cables. They can efficiently excavate narrow trenches with precise depth and width specifications required for utility installations.

3. Road Construction: Excavators play a crucial role in road construction projects by performing various tasks, including:

a. Clearing and Grubbing: Excavators are used to clear vegetation, trees, debris, and obstacles from the construction site before road construction begins. They help prepare the site by removing vegetation and creating a clear path for road alignment.

b. Earthwork and Grading: Excavators are utilized to cut and fill earthwork to achieve the desired road profile, grade, and slope. They excavate soil from high areas (cuts) and deposit it in lower areas (fills) to create a level roadbed. Excavators equipped with grading attachments can precisely shape and grade the road surface to meet design specifications.

c. Culvert and Drainage Installation: Excavators are involved in installing culverts, stormwater drainage systems, and other drainage structures necessary for road construction. They excavate trenches for installing culverts, pipes, and drainage channels to manage surface water runoff and prevent erosion.

d. Embankment Construction: Excavators are used to construct embankments and road shoulders by compacting fill material and shaping the terrain to support the road infrastructure. They distribute and compact soil, gravel, or aggregates to build stable embankments alongside roads.

e. Utility Installation: Excavators assist in installing underground utilities such as drainage pipes, culverts, manholes, and utility conduits alongside roads. They excavate trenches for laying utility lines and backfill the trenches once installation is complete.

1. Demolition: Excavators equipped with hydraulic breakers or demolition attachments are utilized for demolishing existing structures, pavements, and obstacles obstructing road construction. They can efficiently break concrete, asphalt, and other materials, allowing for the removal and disposal of debris.

EARTHMOVING EQUIPMENT OPERATIONS

Figure 58: Excavator engaged in road construction. PT Kiw, CC BY-SA 3.0, via Wikimedia Commons.

An excavator is a complex piece of heavy machinery designed for digging, earthmoving, and construction tasks. Its components work together to perform various functions efficiently. Here are the main components of an excavator:

1. Upper Structure: The upper structure of an excavator houses the operator's cab, engine, hydraulic system, and the slew mechanism. It is mounted on the undercarriage and can rotate 360 degrees.

2. Operator's Cab: The cab is where the operator controls the excavator's functions. It typically contains a seat, controls for operating the machine, instrumentation, and safety features such as seat belts and rollover protection.

3. Engine: The engine provides power to the excavator's hydraulic system and other components. It is usually located within the upper structure and can be powered by diesel fuel or other

sources.

4. Hydraulic System: The hydraulic system of an excavator is responsible for powering the various hydraulic cylinders and actuators that control the movement of the boom, arm, bucket, and other attachments. It consists of hydraulic pumps, valves, hoses, and cylinders.

5. Boom: The boom is the large, telescoping arm that extends from the front of the excavator's upper structure. It provides reach and elevation for the attachment mounted at its end.

6. Arm (or Dipper): The arm, also known as the dipper or stick, is attached to the end of the boom and provides additional reach and flexibility for digging and reaching objects. It can be extended or retracted using hydraulic cylinders.

7. Bucket: The bucket is the attachment mounted at the end of the arm and is used for digging, loading, and lifting materials. Buckets come in various sizes and configurations, including digging buckets, ditching buckets, and specialized attachments for specific tasks.

8. Undercarriage: The undercarriage is the base of the excavator and includes the tracks (in a crawler excavator) or wheels (in a wheeled excavator), track or wheel frames, drive motors, and rollers. It provides stability, traction, and mobility for the excavator.

9. Counterweight: The counterweight is located at the rear of the excavator's upper structure and provides stability and balance by offsetting the weight of the front-mounted components, such as the boom and arm.

10. Attachments: Excavators can be equipped with a variety of attachments besides the standard digging bucket. These may include hydraulic breakers, grapples, augers, compactors, thumbs, and shears, which enhance the excavator's versatility for different applications.

These components work together seamlessly to perform a wide range of excavation and construction tasks efficiently and safely.

Figure 59: Excavator components. Back Image - Kahvilokki, CC BY-SA 4.0, via Wikimedia Commons.

Excavator components encompass various sizable elements. Among these are the boom, bucket, and tracks. Additionally, numerous engine and hydraulic system components contribute to the excavator's assembly. Given the demanding tasks undertaken by an excavator, its parts tend to be substantial and weighty. Constructed from heavy gauge steel, these parts often necessitate the use of a small tractor for movement within the workshop.

Although certain track components of an excavator may resemble those found on a bulldozer, excavator parts and tracks serve distinct functions. Unlike bulldozer tracks designed for forward traction, excavator tracks are intended primarily for positioning the excavator at the work site. They are not engineered to propel the excavator through challenging terrains like mud or snow but rather to distribute the machine's weight over a larger area than tyres would allow.

The bucket, or scoop, affixed to an excavator is crafted from exceptionally robust steel, enabling it to break through sizable rocks and hard soil. In some cases, excavators are employed to fracture large areas of concrete or paved roadways. As the operator manoeuvres the bucket through tough materials, its sturdy teeth, welded onto the bucket, effectively chew into the material, facilitating its fragmentation.

Despite the bucket's formidable strength, an excavator's ability to fracture hard materials is largely attributed to its potent hydraulic system. A robust engine powers a hydraulic pump, endowing excavator parts with considerable strength. Hydraulic cylinders on the boom function akin to human arm muscles; when contracted, they manipulate the bucket and boom, much like muscles manipulate an arm and hand. Operators regulate these movements by manipulating levers within the cab.

Hydraulics also power the tracks and undercarriage of the excavator. The same engine driving the hydraulic pumps for the boom and bucket also powers a separate hydraulic pump controlling the track drive system. Pedals situated in the cab propel the machine forward and backward, while turning involves braking one track while powering the other, causing the excavator to pivot around the track with applied brakes.

The upper section of the excavator, known as the house, can pivot a full 360 degrees, facilitated by its attachment to the undercarriage via a central pin. This pivotal movement enables the excavator to access a wide workspace without relocating.

Modern hydraulic excavators are available in various sizes, ranging from compact mini excavators to colossal models. Mini excavators, for instance, are smaller and more manoeuvrable, making them suitable for confined spaces and lighter-duty tasks, whereas larger excavators excel at heavy-duty operations. Engines in hydraulic excavators primarily drive hydraulic pumps, providing high-pressure oil for various functions, including arm movement, swing motor operation, and accessory control.

Figure 60: Dragline Liebherr HS 835 excavator. François GOGLINS, CC BY-SA 4.0, via Wikimedia Commons.

Excavators come in various types, each designed for specific applications and environments. Here are the different types of excavators commonly used in construction and earthmoving projects:

1. Crawler Excavator:

- Also known as track excavators, crawler excavators are equipped with tracks instead of wheels, providing excellent stability and traction on rough terrain and soft ground.

- They are ideal for heavy-duty digging and earthmoving tasks, such as excavation, trenching, demolition, and mining.
- Crawler excavators are known for their robustness, durability, and ability to operate in challenging conditions.

2. Wheeled Excavator:

- Wheeled excavators feature wheels instead of tracks, offering greater mobility and speed on paved surfaces and urban environments.
- They are commonly used in road construction, utility work, urban development, and landscaping projects where frequent movement between job sites is required.
- Wheeled excavators are more manoeuvrable than crawler excavators and can travel at higher speeds on roads.

3. Mini Excavator:

- Mini excavators, also known as compact excavators or mini diggers, are small-sized excavators designed for compact spaces and light-duty tasks.
- They are highly versatile and can be used for tasks such as digging trenches, landscaping, demolition in confined areas, and utility work.
- Mini excavators are typically equipped with tracks for stability and can be easily transported on trailers.

4. Long Reach Excavator:

- Long reach excavators feature an extended boom and arm configuration, allowing them to reach greater depths and heights compared to standard excavators.

- They are used for tasks requiring extended reach, such as dredging, deep excavation, slope stabilization, and material handling in water bodies.

- Long reach excavators are commonly used in marine construction, bridge construction, and environmental remediation projects.

5. Dragline Excavator:

- Dragline excavators are large, specialized excavators used primarily in mining, quarrying, and civil engineering projects.

- They feature a long boom and bucket suspended from a cable system, allowing them to excavate materials from deep pits and quarries.

- Dragline excavators are highly efficient for bulk excavation, overburden removal, and material handling over long distances.

6. Backhoe Loader:

- Backhoe loaders combine the capabilities of a loader and an excavator in a single machine, featuring a loader bucket at the front and a backhoe attachment at the rear.

- They are versatile machines used for digging, loading, backfilling, trenching, and material handling in various construction, landscaping, and utility applications.

- Backhoe loaders are commonly used in road construction, utility work, excavation, and landscaping projects due to their compact size and versatility.

Each type of excavator has its advantages and is chosen based on the specific requirements of the project, including site conditions, accessibility, and the type of tasks to be performed.

Figure 61: Doosan DX160W wheeled excavator. Kahvilokki, CC0, via Wikimedia Commons.

Excavator Size: If your excavator lacks sufficient size, power, or lifting and digging capacity, it won't meet your needs. However, there are other crucial factors to consider beyond size and capacity, including:

- The specific type of work required

- Necessary attachments

- Manoeuvrability and site access

- Reach of the boom arm

- Maintenance demands

While this list isn't exhaustive, it highlights the range of considerations when selecting the appropriate excavator for your task. If you're uncertain about your requirements, consult the professionals at Solution Plant Hire. We offer excavators for every application, and our experts are always available to assist you in finding the perfect match.

Skid Steer Excavators: Skid steer excavators, though not the largest, are commonly seen on construction sites across Australia. They are smaller than standard excavators and feature a boom arm and bucket positioned away from the operator. Operating on wheels instead of tracks, they boast excellent manoeuvrability in confined spaces but are less suitable for muddy, sandy, or uneven terrain. Typically used for site clearing, debris removal, and residential landscaping.

Mini Excavators: Larger than skid steers but smaller than standard excavators, mini excavators are prevalent on Australian construction sites. Operating on tracks, they offer versatility on various terrains that skid steers cannot handle. While their track system reduces manoeuvrability somewhat, their reduced tail swing makes them suitable for smaller sites with limited access. Despite having less capacity, their lightweight design makes them fuel-efficient and easy to transport over long distances.

Standard Excavators: Excavators weighing above 5.5 tonnes are classified as standard, ranging from 8 to 30 tonnes. Within this category, various types such as knuckle boom and long-reach excavators are available. Standard excavators offer increased versatility, allowing for the use of multiple attachments like augers, post drivers, buckets, and rock breakers. With various sizes to choose from, they provide the perfect combination of precision and power for handling diverse tasks.

Large Excavators: Large excavators, reaching up to 80 tonnes, are employed for heavy-duty tasks, albeit with reduced precision and manoeuvrability due to their size and power. Typically used in mining or projects requiring substantial material movement, they necessitate special trailers for transport, resulting in higher operating costs compared to smaller excavators.

Specialist Excavators: Specialist excavators serve specific purposes and include:

- Long-reach excavators: Featuring an extended arm and boom for projects with challenging access.

- Hydraulic shovels: Powerful but lacking precision, suitable for lifting extremely heavy materials.

- Spider excavators: Operating on legs for terrain where traditional options are impractical.

- Knuckle boom excavators: Equipped with an additional arm joint for reaching difficult areas.

Figure 62: Longreach excavator - Caterpillar 330C L crawler excavator with a long arm. m.prinke, CC BY-SA 2.0, via Wikimedia Commons.

Excavator attachments are utilized to enhance work performance and efficiency, tailored to the specific task at hand.

Bucket: The bucket is the most common attachment for excavators. Various bucket types serve different purposes: a narrow bucket is typically employed for digging, while wider or smoother ones are better suited for scooping or transporting materials.

Thumb: This attachment increases the bucket's capacity and improves grip when handling larger objects, enhancing excavating capabilities.

Augers: Primarily used in landscaping and construction, augers feature hydraulic spiral blades to swiftly and conveniently dig holes.

Hydraulic breaker: Also known as hammers, hydraulic breaker attachments are utilized to demolish structures, pavements, or other solid surfaces, expediting the demolition process.

Figure 63: Hitachi eco excavator with hydraulic breaker attachment. Daderot, CC0, via Wikimedia Commons.

Shears: Ideal for demolishing buildings, steel structures, and scrap/recycling applications, shears excel at cutting through metal beams, sheets, and wires.

Hydraulic quick coupler: Enhancing efficiency, hydraulic quick couplers facilitate swift attachment changes without requiring manual assistance, increasing operational versatility.

Ripper: Similar to hydraulic breakers, rippers expedite structure demolition by tearing through robust materials, even in challenging conditions or frozen surfaces.

Tilt-rotator: Initially popular in Nordic countries, tilt-rotators are gaining global traction. Acting as a connection between the arm and attachment, they enable 360-degree rotation and ±45-degree tilt, along with a grapple function, allowing excavators to perform a wide array of tasks in diverse conditions.

Excavator operations present various hazards that can pose risks to both operators and other workers on the site. Some of the key hazards associated with excavator operations include:

1. Collapse and Overturning: Excavators can overturn due to uneven terrain, unstable ground conditions, or improper operation. Overturning can result in serious injuries or fatalities to the operator and nearby workers.

2. Struck-By Accidents: Workers can be struck by moving parts of the excavator, such as the bucket or boom, leading to injuries or fatalities. Additionally, objects or debris ejected from the bucket can strike workers nearby.

3. Caught-In or Between: Workers can become caught between the excavator and other objects, such as walls, trenches, or other equipment, leading to crush injuries or fatalities.

4. Falls from Height: Working at heights on the excavator, such as climbing onto the machine or accessing the cab, can lead to falls resulting in injuries.

5. Electrical Hazards: Excavators may come into contact with

overhead power lines, posing electrocution hazards to operators and nearby workers.

6. Pinch Points and Crushing Hazards: Moving parts of the excavator, such as hydraulic cylinders and tracks, can create pinch points where workers' limbs or body parts can become trapped, leading to crushing injuries.

7. Visibility Issues: Limited visibility from the operator's seat can result in blind spots, increasing the risk of striking nearby workers, objects, or structures.

8. Hazardous Materials: Excavating in areas with buried pipelines, utilities, or hazardous materials can pose risks of striking or rupturing these lines, leading to gas leaks, chemical spills, or other hazardous incidents.

9. Noise and Vibration: Prolonged exposure to noise and vibration from the excavator can lead to hearing loss, musculoskeletal disorders, and other health problems for operators and nearby workers.

10. Inadequate Training and Supervision: Operators who are not properly trained or supervised may lack the skills and knowledge to operate the excavator safely, increasing the likelihood of accidents and injuries.

It's essential for employers to identify and assess these hazards, implement appropriate control measures, provide adequate training to operators and workers, and ensure compliance with safety regulations and standards to mitigate the risks associated with excavator operations. Regular inspections, maintenance, and risk assessments are also critical to maintaining a safe work environment during excavator operations.

Planning for Excavation Work

Before commencing excavation work, thorough planning is essential to ensure safety. This entails identifying hazards, assessing risks, and devising suitable control measures in collaboration with all pertinent stakeholders, including the principal contractor, excavation contractor, designers, and mobile plant operators. Structural or geotechnical engineers may also need to be involved in this planning phase.

Consultation should encompass discussions on various aspects, including:

- The nature and condition of the ground and working environment
- Weather conditions
- The scope of work and potential impacts on health and safety
- Static and dynamic loads near the excavation site
- Coordination with other trades
- Site accessibility
- Site-specific Work Method Statements (SWMS)
- Management of vehicular traffic and ground vibration in the vicinity
- Selection of excavation equipment
- Public safety considerations
- Identification and location of existing services
- Duration of excavation operations

- Provision of adequate facilities

- Emergency response procedures.

Understanding the sequence of work activities is crucial in civil construction. For instance, in earthworks, the process typically involves marking out the work area, followed by vegetation removal (clearing and grubbing), topsoil removal, and creating contours, drains, or proceeding to the next step in the construction process. Roadwork construction builds upon these steps by forming drain lines or contours, executing cut and fill operations to achieve the required level, carrying out compaction activities, and applying pavement layers. Similarly, drainage projects encompass the steps of earthworks but additionally involve forming drain lines, building the frame to hold the drain system, laying pipes, box drains, or culverts, backfilling, and landscaping appropriately.

It's important to note that all civil construction tasks must meet project quality requirements, outlining specific expectations and standards. Compliance with these requirements relies on following project quality plans and specifications precisely. Any difficulties encountered in meeting these requirements should be promptly communicated to your supervisor or site quality officer for resolution.

Land survey data provides specific site information crucial for construction tasks. Survey marks define work areas or indicate exclusion zones. Survey data includes cut and fill levels, layer thicknesses, and finished levels, including cross-falls for water drainage. Various surveying controls for excavators, such as dig crest pegs, dig toe pegs, RL pegs, coal edge pegs, drop-in pegs, and clear line pegs, aid in accurate excavation.

Soil technology data pertains to material characteristics and their conditions on the site, such as clay, topsoil, gravels, etc., including their wetness, dryness, or stickiness. This data assists in determining the best approach to handle materials for optimal outcomes.

Lastly, safety is paramount in excavation work due to inherent risks. It's essential to be aware of safety protocols to prevent injuries and fatalities. Each year, people working in excavations face risks, emphasizing the need for thorough knowledge and adherence to safety measures to ensure personal safety and well-being.

Notwithstanding appearances, it's important to recognize that soils vary significantly, a fact you may already be aware of. Soils consist of a blend of clay, sand, and rock, with different combinations yielding soils with distinct characteristics. Here's a basic guide to help identify the type of soil you may encounter:

Clay:

- Very Soft Clay: Easily penetrated 40mm with fist
- Soft Clay: Easily penetrated 40mm with thumb
- Firm Clay: Moderate effort needed to penetrate 30mm with thumb
- Stiff Clay: Readily indented with thumb but penetrated only with great effort
- Very Stiff Clay: Readily indented by thumbnail
- Hard Clay: Indented with difficulty by thumbnail

Sand:

- Loose Clean Sand: Takes footprint more than 10mm deep
- Medium-Dense Clean Sand: Takes footprint 3mm to 10mm deep
- Dense Clean Sand or Gravel: Takes footprint less than 3mm deep

Rock:

- Broken or Decomposed: Diggable. Hammer blow "thuds". The joints (breaks in the rock) are spaced less than 300mm apart
- Sound Rock: Not diggable with pick. Hammer blow "rings". The joints (breaks in the rock) are spaced more than 300mm apart

A mound of excavated soil, also known as spoil, naturally assumes a particular slope depending on the soil type, referred to as the "angle of repose." The approximate angles for various soil types are as follows:

- Granular soils: crushed rock, gravel, non-angular, poorly graded sand, loamy sand
  - Slope Ratio (Width to Height): 1.5:1
  - Slope Angle: 34 degrees
- Weak cohesive soils: angular well-graded sand, silt, silty loam, sandy loam
  - Slope Ratio (Width to Height): 1:1
  - Slope Angle: 45 degrees
- Cohesive soils: clay, silty clay, sandy clay
  - Slope Ratio (Width to Height): 0.75:1
  - Slope Angle: 53 degrees

The angle of repose serves as a useful indicator for estimating the angle of shear planes within the soil profile. Shear planes represent potential lines of breakage through which the unexcavated soil forming the excavation walls may collapse. It is crucial to minimize pressure on this vulnerable area, and the angle of repose aids in estimating the distance that equipment and materials should be from the edge of the excavation to mitigate the risk of wall collapse.

The angle of repose, also referred to as the critical angle of repose, denotes the steepest angle at which a granular material can be stacked on a horizontal plane without collapsing. At this specific angle, the material on the slope's face is poised to slide. The angle of repose spans from 0° to 90° and is influenced by the morphology of the material; smoother, rounded sand grains permit a shallower stacking compared to rough, interlocking sands. Moreover, the addition of solvents can alter the angle of repose. When poured onto a flat surface, bulk granular materials form a conical pile, with the internal angle between the pile's surface and the horizontal surface representing the angle of repose. This angle is contingent upon factors such as particle density, surface area, shape, and the material's coefficient of friction. Materials with a lower angle of repose yield flatter piles in contrast to those with a higher angle of repose.

For instance, in sandy loam soil with an angle of repose of 1:1, equipment and materials should be positioned at a distance equal to the depth of the excavation away from the edge. In a 2-meter-deep excavation in sandy loam soil, equipment and materials should be kept at least 2 meters away from the excavation edge. For rocky soils, with a ratio of 1.5:1, the safe distance is 3 meters, while for clay soils, it is 1.5 meters.

It's important to note that this angle may decrease if the soil becomes wet, particularly if it becomes saturated. Therefore, it is advisable to err on the side of caution and maintain safe distances, especially in adverse weather conditions.

Ground support systems refer to safety measures implemented to mitigate the risk of ground collapse in excavation sites. Typically applied in excavations deeper than 1.5 meters (5 feet) and in shallower depths where soil conditions are unstable, such as loose or wet soil, or in areas with a history of previous excavations, these systems aim to ensure the stability of excavation walls. There are three commonly accepted methods for preventing excavation collapse:

1. Battering: This technique involves sloping the sides of the excavation to the angle of repose, thereby reducing the likelihood of soil collapse into the excavation.

2. Benching: Involves cutting the side walls of the excavation into steps with no vertical face exceeding one meter (3 feet) in height, matching the angle of repose.

3. Shoring: This method entails the insertion of mechanical devices into the excavation to reinforce the side walls and prevent collapse. Different types of shoring are available depending on the specific circumstances, and seeking expert advice is crucial to ensure the correct type is selected and installed properly.

Regular inspections of excavation sites are essential to monitor changing soil conditions and assess their impact on wall stability. Some warning signs indicating potential collapse include tension cracks, sliding of soil into the excavation, toppling of soil blocks, subsidence, bulging of side walls, heaving or squeezing of the excavation floor, and the presence of water pooling in the excavation. If any of these signs are observed, work should cease immediately, and expert advice sought to determine the appropriate corrective measures.

It's important to recognize that soil conditions may vary within an area and can change over time, emphasizing the need for ongoing vigilance and precautionary measures. Additionally, not all buried services may be accurately marked, necessitating thorough checks before excavation begins. By remaining vigilant and taking necessary precautions, workers can ensure their safety and prevent potential accidents or incidents in excavation sites.

Upon completion of your induction program and before commencing work at your designated workplace, it's essential to request your supervisor to provide a detailed orientation of the immediate work area, emphasizing local safety protocols. Key aspects to cover during this orientation include:

- Identification and location of fire extinguishers and hoses.

- Emergency stop mechanisms for electrical equipment, including buttons and lanyards, as well as those for fuel supply, such as gas and liquids.

- Familiarization with the emergency tag policy.

- Procedures for emergency evacuation.

- Recognition of special signage indicating safety hazards or protocols.

- Location of the first aid station.

- Understanding of quarry traffic regulations.

- Awareness of emergency phone and communication systems.

- Protocols for handling chemical or oil spills.

- Designated parking areas for vehicles.

- Guidelines for utilizing two-way radios and adherence to safety procedures.

While you have already undergone the induction program, this workplace-specific orientation is crucial for your immediate work area, ensuring you can respond effectively and safely in emergency situations.

Depending on the scale of operations, daily work tasks may be communicated through verbal briefings or written instructions from your supervisor. It's imperative to receive and comprehend these instructions clearly. If any aspect is unclear, do not hesitate to seek clarification from your supervisor. Additionally, a preliminary visit to the work site may be necessary to inspect the job before preparing the loader for operation.

When preparing the loader for work, it's essential to consider the nature of the work and the material to be handled. Part of the planning process involves implementing any necessary safe operating procedures at the site. Consider the following factors:

- Destination of the material to be moved and whether it will be handled exclusively with the loader.

- Whether the material will be loaded onto a haul truck or stockpiled.

- Whether the material will be excavated directly from the face or from a stockpile.

Safety considerations should encompass:

- Adherence to site speed limits.

- Safe practices around overhead power cables and underground utilities such as power, water, gas, and telephone lines.

- Awareness of overhead conveyors and associated equipment.

- Ensuring safe operations around other machinery and personnel.

- Understanding of blasting operations if applicable.

- Compliance with site traffic regulations, including the movement of loaded vehicles and water trucks.

Below are examples of excavating procedures:

- Prioritize checking for underground services (power, telephone, gas, water, sewer, drainage, and fibre optic cable lines) before commencing excavation. Consult the site supervisor, who will contact the relevant supply authorities for council maps of the site.

- Verify state/territory standards for safe operating distances from power lines.

- Cut trenches to required specifications and deposit full buckets of material away from the trench.

When excavating across a footpath, adhere to the following steps:
- Obtain information and permits from relevant authorities concerning services under the footpath.

- Excavate slowly towards any underground services.

- Provide appropriate barricades and signs.

- Remove any large rocks from the trench when necessary.

- Avoid undercutting banks or stockpiles to prevent collapse and potential hazards.

Exercise caution when boarding or dismounting a machine to prevent injuries. Follow these guidelines:
- Clean shoes and wipe hands before climbing.

- Utilize handrails, grab-irons, ladders, or steps for mounting.

- Never use controls as grab-irons.

- Avoid boarding a moving machine.

- Maintain three points of contact at all times.

- Safely climb or descend the ladder.

- Familiarize yourself with horn signals for the site.

Pre-Start Checks: Before conducting walk-around and pre-start inspections, fit a tag to the machine's main switch. Perform a comprehensive pre-start inspection at each shift change or after repair or service work to check for damage or component wear. Pre-start checks are critical for ensuring the machine is in good repair and ready for operation.

Walk-Around Inspection: A walk-around inspection must be completed before entering and operating equipment:

- After any absence from the cab, refuelling, or completion of repairs or maintenance.

- To ensure nobody is in, under, behind, or around the machine before boarding.

- To check for damage to the equipment's bodywork, lights, indicators, and other components.

- To verify the terrain's suitability for operation.

Ground Level and Platform Checks: The operator must visually inspect the machine for various components before operation. These checks include undercarriage, attachment, and superstructure checks, among others. Ensure no persons are in the cab during these inspections. It's advisable to use the machine or site's pre-start checklist if available.

Fluid Checks: Before operation, inspect engine oil, fuel, brake fluid, hydraulic oil, and battery levels. Never use a naked flame for these checks; instead, use a torch to ensure safety.

Cabin Checks: Prior to operation, conduct a cabin inspection, ensuring cleanliness and functionality of various components such as the operator's seat, seat belt, mirrors, and controls.

It's imperative to report any damage or defects to your supervisor and record them on your pre-start checklist to maintain a safe working environment.

Excavators are equipped with various controls that allow operators to manoeuvre the machine effectively and perform tasks with precision. Here's an explanation of the common controls found in an excavator:

1. Main Control Levers: These levers are typically located in the operator's cab and are used to control the movement of the excavator's boom, stick (also known as the arm), and bucket. By manipulating these levers, the operator can extend, retract, raise, and lower each component to perform digging, lifting, and loading operations.

2. Boom Control Lever: This lever controls the vertical movement of the excavator's boom, which is the large arm that extends from the machine's body. Pulling the lever towards the operator raises the boom, while pushing it away lowers the boom.

3. Stick Control Lever: Similar to the boom control lever, the stick control lever adjusts the angle of the stick (arm) attached to the boom. Moving the lever towards the operator retracts the stick, while pushing it away extends the stick.

4. Bucket Control Lever: This lever controls the opening and closing of the excavator's bucket, which is attached to the end of the stick. Pulling the lever towards the operator closes the bucket, while pushing it away opens the bucket.

5. Swing Control Lever: The swing control lever allows the operator to rotate the upper structure of the excavator, including the boom and cab, in a clockwise or counterclockwise direction. This movement enables the excavator to reach different areas without repositioning the tracks.

6. Travel Control Pedals: Excavators are equipped with pedals that control the machine's movement on tracks. Pressing the left pedal makes the excavator turn left, while pressing the right pedal makes it turn right. Pressing both pedals simultaneously moves the machine forward, and releasing them moves it backward.

7. Throttle Control: The throttle control adjusts the engine speed of the excavator, allowing the operator to increase or decrease the power output as needed for different tasks. Higher engine speeds provide more power for heavy digging, while lower speeds conserve fuel and reduce noise.

8. Auxiliary Hydraulic Controls: Many excavators are equipped with auxiliary hydraulic circuits that allow attachments such as hydraulic breakers, grapples, or thumbs to be operated. These controls typically consist of switches or levers that activate hydraulic functions beyond basic digging and lifting.

9. Monitor and Display Panel: Modern excavators often feature a digital display panel or monitor that provides important information to the operator, such as engine RPM, fuel level, hydraulic pressure, temperature, and diagnostic alerts. The monitor may also include settings for customizing machine performance and preferences.

10. Emergency Stop Button: Located within easy reach of the operator, the emergency stop button instantly halts all machine functions in case of an emergency or safety hazard.

These controls work together to give operators precise command over the excavator's movements and functions, allowing them to perform a wide range of tasks efficiently and safely on construction sites.

Proper training and familiarization with these controls are essential for operators to operate excavators effectively and minimize the risk of accidents.

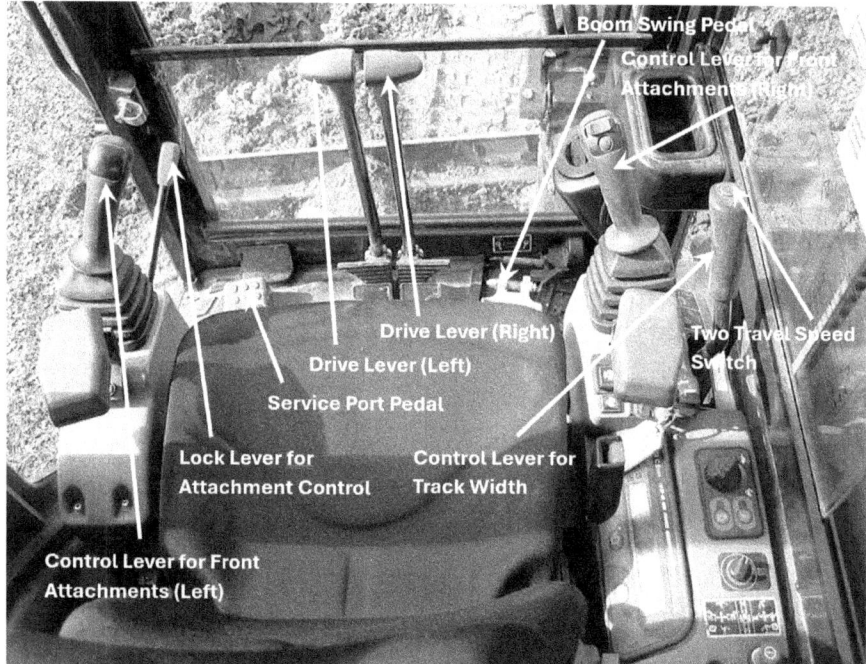

Figure 64: Sample excavator controls. Back image - Hans Haase, CC BY-SA 4.0, via Wikimedia Commons.

To operate the excavator, identify whether the excavator is configured in an ISO or SAE control pattern, which are the two standard configurations for excavator controls. In the ISO pattern, the left hand manages swing and boom movements, while the right hand controls stick and bucket motions.

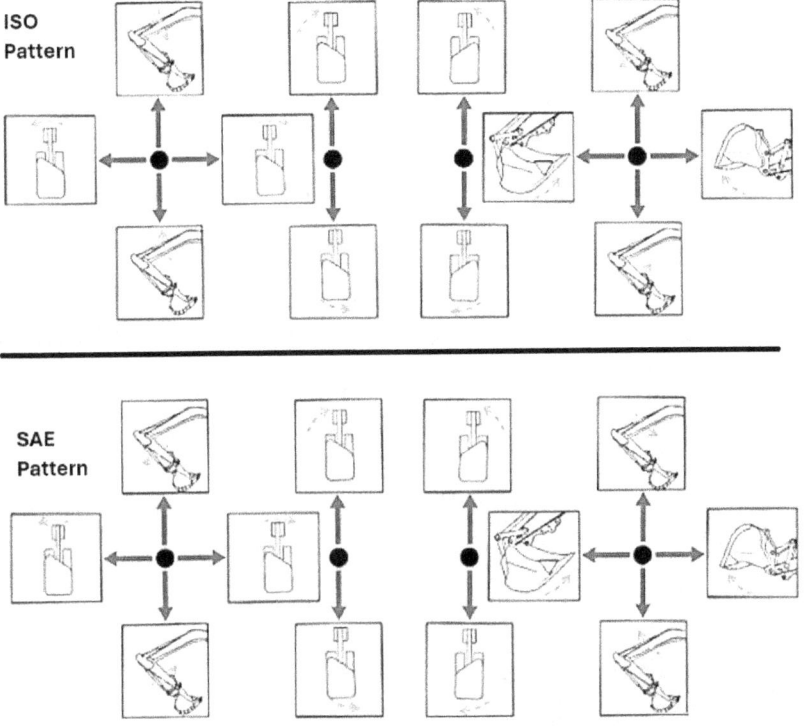

Figure 65: ISO and SAE control configurations.

Conversely, the SAE pattern reverses this setup, making it challenging to switch between patterns if you're accustomed to one. Many modern excavators feature a display in the cab indicating the control pattern. Ensure the pattern matches your preference before operating the machine.

- If necessary, adjust the control pattern setting. Some excavators offer a button or switch within the cab for this purpose. Check the display screen for a control pattern switch button.

- Alternatively, on some excavators, the control pattern lever is located at the rear near the engine. Open the rear section and locate a blue or red lever marked with each pattern setting. Slide the lever to switch between patterns.

- Always refer to the owner's manual before adjusting the control pattern to ensure the correct procedure is followed.

- For beginners, it's advisable to start with the ISO pattern as it's more commonly used in excavators. Enter the cab and adjust the seat position accordingly. Excavator seats are adjustable and can be moved back and forth using a lever located beneath the seat to accommodate operators of different heights. Verify the seat position upon sitting down, ensuring your feet can comfortably reach the pedals and you can access all handles. Adjust the seat using the lever if needed and fasten your seatbelt for safety.

- If you're not operating the excavator with the door open, close it securely. Most excavators have a door handle lock, so ensure it's engaged before starting the machine.

- Many operators prefer to run the machine with the door closed to prevent debris ingress, although some may keep it open for communication with other workers. Start the machine by turning the key and allowing it to idle to warm up. Within the cab, locate the key and a knob with various positions near the right armrest. Ensure the knob is set to "I" for Idle, then turn the key to start the engine.

- Let the machine idle for 5-10 minutes before operating to warm up adequately.

- In cold weather conditions, perform several hydraulic control cycles before engaging in any digging activities.

To move the boom and cab:
- Release the controls by lifting the red lever located on your left side. Every excavator is equipped with a locking lever positioned on the left side of the cab, typically coloured red and attached to

the armrest. When the lever is in the down position, the joystick controls remain locked. Lift the lever upward until it clicks to unlock the controls, allowing movement of the arm and cab. Always ensure the surroundings are clear of people or objects before unlocking the controls. If anyone approaches the cab or if there's a risk of damaging nearby objects, lower the lever until the area is clear again.

- Utilize the right joystick to raise and lower the boom by moving it back and forth. The boom, located nearest to the cab, is controlled by the right joystick in ISO configuration. Locate this joystick in front of the right armrest. Pushing the joystick forward raises the boom, while pulling it backward lowers it. Note that instructions are provided based on ISO configuration, as it's the more commonly used setting. For SAE configuration, simply reverse the controls to the opposite side.

- Control the opening and closing of the bucket by shifting the right joystick right and left. Positioned at the end of the digging arm, the bucket's position is also controlled by the right joystick. Push the joystick to the right to open the bucket and to the left to close it.

- Manoeuvre the stick forward and backward by pressing the left joystick in the corresponding direction. Located in front of the left armrest, the left joystick manages the stick and swing movements for the excavator. The stick, which is the lower part of the arm connected to the boom, resembles a shin attached to a knee. Push the left joystick forward to extend the stick away from the cab, and pull it backward to retract the stick closer to the cab. Ensure smooth motions when operating the stick and boom, as they are hydraulically controlled. Avoid suddenly releasing the joysticks to prevent rapid rocking of the machine.

- Rotate the cab by shifting the left joystick left and right. Lastly, use the left joystick to rotate the cab using the excavator's swing control. Pushing the joystick left or right rotates the cab accordingly. The cab can freely complete a 360-degree turn, and holding the joystick in one direction will continue the rotation.

It's imperative to establish appropriate policies and procedures to ensure site safety management. These should be integrated into an overarching management system that effectively addresses and controls the risks associated with the work being carried out.

A comprehensive safety system should encompass processes for:

- Identifying individuals with occupational health and safety (OHS) responsibilities.

- Managing the health and safety of contractors and subcontractors.

- Developing and managing consultation procedures for health and safety matters.

- Identifying hazards and controlling risks.

- Determining the location of underground services.

- Establishing site safety rules.

- Monitoring site activities and enforcing safety rules.

- Providing and maintaining site amenities.

- Conducting site-specific inductions for workers, delivery drivers, and visitors.

- Allowing only trained and competent workers to work on-site.

- Ensuring all plant (machinery and equipment) is safe and free from health risks before use.

- Determining requirements for a mobile plant compound and vehicle parking.

- Developing traffic management plans.

- Identifying and controlling risks to the public.

- Developing emergency response plans for foreseeable emergency situations.

For each employer on-site, there should be effective safety management systems in place, including processes to ensure:

- Development of safe work method statements (SWMS) for all high-risk construction work.

- Establishment of safe work procedures for tasks posing risks to workers or the public.

- Competent workers or direct supervision of workers.

- Implementation of emergency response plans for foreseeable emergencies.

- Monitoring the health and conditions of workers.

When using powered plant, ensure it is in good mechanical condition, safe for use, and accompanied by the necessary safety documentation.

Controlling Risks from Hazards: Various hazards may arise, including moving materials and equipment, falls, rough ground, noise, and weather conditions. Employers should aim to eliminate these risks as much as possible. If elimination is not feasible, employers should implement controls mandated by law, substitute activities or equipment, isolate persons from hazards, and use engineering controls. Remaining risks should be managed through administrative controls and personal protective equipment (PPE).

Planning for Safety: Preventative measures should be taken to address common injuries such as manual handling, slips, trips, and falls. Factors contributing to these injuries, such as poor planning, inadequate access, and excessive force, should be mitigated through proper planning and layout considerations.

Working Near Road Traffic: When working near road traffic, a SWMS should be developed, and relevant traffic management plans (TMPs) should be referenced to control vehicle-related risks. Workers should be briefed on safety measures outlined in the SWMS and TMP, including the use of high visibility clothing, warning devices, traffic controllers, and emergency procedures.

Protecting the Public: Employers have a responsibility to protect the public from risks associated with work on or near public roads. This involves setting up pedestrian controls or diversions, creating alternative pedestrian paths away from road traffic, providing appropriate barriers, maintaining clear signage, and ensuring suitable controls for disabled individuals.

Personal Electronic Devices: Workers should refrain from using personal electronic devices when working near mobile plant or traffic to avoid distractions and reduce the risk of accidents. Communication between workers should be facilitated through non-verbal (e.g., signage, hand signals) and verbal means, ensuring workers are aware of potential risks when using radios or mobile phones.

Contact with Powerlines: Training should be provided to workers on emergency procedures in the event of accidental contact with overhead powerlines. If contact occurs, the plant should be removed from service until inspected and verified safe for use.

Underground Services: Before mechanical excavation or ground penetration work, underground services should be identified using services such as Dial Before You Dig. Excavation near underground assets should be approached cautiously, with hand digging or non-destructive methods used to confirm asset locations.

Controlling Risks in Excavation: Common hazards associated with excavation work include ground collapse, water inrush, falls, and buried contaminants. Employers should implement control measures such as ground support systems, dewatering systems, access ramps, and training programs to mitigate these risks effectively. Additionally, materials should be stored away from excavations, and proper planning should guide the placement of excavated material to reduce the risk of ground collapse.

Excavator blind spots refer to areas around the excavator where the operator's visibility is limited or obstructed, making it difficult to see people, objects, or vehicles in those areas. These blind spots pose a significant safety risk, as they can lead to accidents, injuries, or property damage if not properly managed.

Blind spots in excavators typically include areas:

1. Behind the Excavator: The rear of the excavator is often a significant blind spot for the operator, especially when the excavator is in motion or rotating. Objects or people directly behind the machine may not be visible to the operator, increasing the risk of collisions or crushing incidents.

2. Along the Sides: The sides of the excavator, particularly towards the rear, can also have blind spots where the operator's view is obstructed. Objects or individuals positioned alongside the excavator may not be visible to the operator, increasing the risk of side collisions or accidents during manoeuvres.

3. Below the Operator's Line of Sight: Certain areas directly below the operator's line of sight, particularly towards the front and sides of the excavator, may also be blind spots. Objects or

individuals in these areas may not be visible to the operator, especially when the excavator's bucket or arm obstructs the view.

4. Overhead: Excavator operators may have limited visibility of objects or structures directly overhead, such as power lines, tree branches, or building eaves. Failure to detect these hazards could result in contact with overhead obstacles, posing a risk of electrocution, entanglement, or structural damage.

To mitigate the risks associated with excavator blind spots, operators and site managers can implement several safety measures:

- Use of Spotters: Employing dedicated spotters or signallers to assist the operator in identifying hazards and guiding manoeuvres, especially when operating in areas with poor visibility.

- Installation of Cameras and Sensors: Equipping excavators with cameras, proximity sensors, or radar systems to provide additional visibility and alert operators to potential hazards in blind spot areas.

- Clear Communication: Establishing clear communication protocols between operators, spotters, and other workers on the site to ensure everyone is aware of potential blind spots and can coordinate movements safely.

- Training and Awareness: Providing comprehensive training to operators on recognizing and managing blind spots, as well as raising awareness among workers about the risks associated with working near excavators.

- Site Planning and Signage: Designing worksites to minimize blind spots where possible, and using appropriate signage and barriers to indicate hazardous areas around excavators.

Essential safe practices during operations include:

Equipment Inspection: Maintaining the excavator in optimal condition is crucial for safe operation. Before commencing any work, contractors should conduct thorough inspections and tests to ensure the excavator's functionality. Any identified issues should be promptly reported for necessary corrective measures.

Use of Protective Gear: Operators should prioritize personal safety by wearing appropriate protective equipment (PPE). This includes high-visibility reflective vests, sturdy work boots, hard hats, and either clear or tinted safety glasses. Gloves and ear protection may also be necessary in certain situations to safeguard hands and ears.

Maintain Situational Awareness: Operators must remain vigilant of their surroundings while operating machinery, particularly in residential areas where various hazards exist, such as overhead power lines, pedestrians, and traffic. Several safety measures can help maintain a secure environment:

- De-energizing electrical lines to prevent accidents near homes or operators.

- Contacting local utility companies before digging to ensure utility shutdowns.

- Clearly marking areas of heavy equipment use to deter unauthorized entry.

- Restricting access of workers and pedestrians from active work areas whenever feasible.

Establish Communication Channels: Effective communication between operators and ground personnel is essential for ensuring safe operations. Spotters equipped with two-way radios can relay crucial information to operators throughout the workday. In the absence of radios, hand signals or signs can be used for communication. Spotters should wear appropriate PPE and redirect pedestrians and traffic to enhance safety.

Select Proper Attachments: Using manufacturer-approved attachments suitable for the task at hand is imperative for safe excavator operation. Heavy-duty buckets are ideal for various soil types and demanding digging tasks. Operators should adhere to load capacity guidelines to prevent overloading, which could lead to tipping hazards.

Seat Belt Usage: Operators must wear seat belts at all times while operating excavators to minimize injury risks in the event of overturns or collisions. Despite the excavator's slower speed compared to cars, seat belts are essential for operator protection and comfort.

Blade Positioning: Proper blade positioning contributes to excavator stability and balance. For larger excavators weighing over 8 tons, keeping the blade in front is recommended. Smaller excavators weighing less than 3 tons should position the blade at the back to prevent cab tipping during digging operations.

Establish Buffer Zones: Construction sites near busy highways or pedestrian-heavy areas require buffer zones to ensure safety. Physical barriers, warning signs, and cautionary measures should be employed to separate heavy equipment from traffic and pedestrians, following location guidelines.

Before moving any material, the excavator must be driven to the designated work area. It is essential to ensure that the route is clear and travel is conducted at a safe speed. Additionally, ensure that any attachments are raised to the appropriate height or stowed securely.

When reversing the excavator, thoroughly check the path behind by looking over both shoulders. Sound the horn twice before reversing unless a reversing/motion alarm is installed. Maintain awareness of the direction of travel throughout the reversing process.

Whenever feasible, avoid traveling on side hills to minimize the risk of tipping the machine over. If driving the excavator on a sloped surface is necessary, descend directly down the slope rather than traversing diagonally for enhanced stability.

Approaching uphill or downhill travel, reduce the speed of the excavator and select an appropriate gear suitable for the grade. When descending, opt for a low gear to effectively control the descent, typically the same gear used for ascending the hill.

When crossing a ditch, slow down and approach the ditch at an angle to ensure safe traversal. Never coast the excavator downhill by shifting into neutral gear and allowing it to roll freely.

The centre of gravity in relation to an excavator is a crucial concept in understanding its stability and safe operation. The centre of gravity refers to the point within the excavator where the entire weight of the machine and its load is considered to act. It is essentially the balance point of the excavator.

In an excavator, the centre of gravity typically lies somewhere within the body of the machine, often towards the lower portion due to the heavy components like the engine, hydraulic systems, and counterweights. When the excavator is stationary and on level ground, the centre of gravity is positioned centrally, contributing to its stability.

However, as the excavator moves, lifts loads, or operates on uneven terrain, the position of the centre of gravity can shift. For example, when the excavator's boom is extended or when it's digging a trench, the centre of gravity moves forward. Similarly, when the bucket is loaded with material, the centre of gravity shifts depending on the weight and position of the load.

It's important for operators to be aware of the location of the centre of gravity at all times because any shift in its position can affect the stability of the excavator. If the centre of gravity moves outside the base of support—defined by the tracks or wheels—there is a risk of the excavator tipping over, especially on uneven or sloped terrain.

Operators must consider the position of the centre of gravity when manoeuvring the excavator, particularly during lifting, digging, or operating on slopes. By understanding and managing the centre of gravity, operators can ensure safe operation and minimize the risk of accidents due to tipping or instability.

When the weight in the bucket becomes the centre of gravity, causing the rear rollers to lift off the track trails, your excavator reaches its tipping point. The tipping load is the specific load that brings the excavator to this tipping point at a defined radius. This radius is measured from the axis of upper structure rotation to the centre of the vertical load line, denoted as the radius from the swing centreline (Figure 66 A). The height is determined by the bucket lift point height (Figure 66 B), which represents the distance from the bucket lift point to the ground.

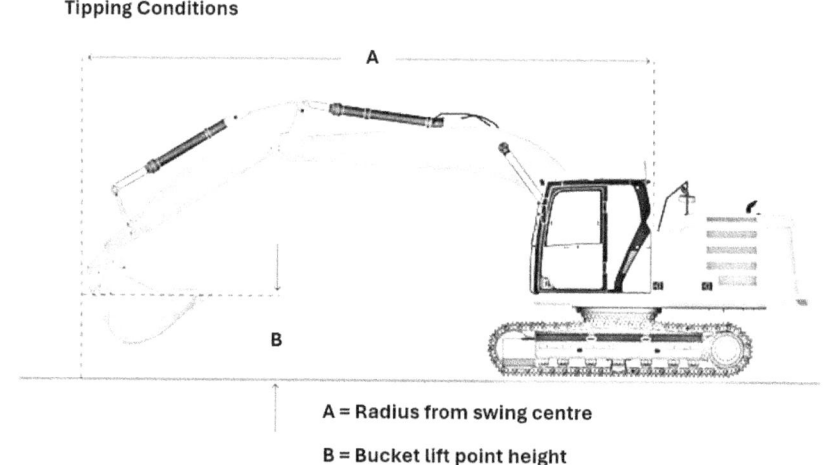

Figure 66: Excavator tipping conditions.

The rated capacity of an excavator refers to the maximum weight or load that the excavator is designed to safely lift or handle under specific conditions. Determining the rated capacity involves considering several factors:

1. Manufacturer's Specifications: The first step in determining the

rated capacity is to refer to the manufacturer's specifications for the particular model of excavator. Manufacturers provide detailed information regarding the maximum lifting capacity for various configurations of the excavator, including boom length, arm length, and bucket size.

2. Load Chart: Excavators typically come with a load chart provided by the manufacturer. This load chart displays the rated capacity of the excavator under different operating conditions, such as boom length, arm length, and angle of operation. Operators should consult the load chart specific to their excavator model to determine the rated capacity for their intended task.

3. Configuration: The rated capacity of an excavator can vary depending on its configuration, including the length of the boom and arm, the type and size of the bucket, and any attachments or accessories used. Operators must ensure that the excavator is configured correctly for the task at hand and that the rated capacity is not exceeded.

4. Operating Conditions: The rated capacity of an excavator is based on certain operating conditions, such as ground stability, slope angle, and environmental factors like wind speed. Operators must assess the operating conditions at the job site and ensure that they comply with the specifications provided by the manufacturer.

5. Safety Factors: It's essential to consider safety factors when determining the rated capacity of an excavator. Manufacturers typically include safety margins in their specifications to account for variations in operating conditions and unexpected loads. Operators should never exceed the rated capacity of the excavator to avoid accidents and equipment damage.

6. Operator Training: Proper operator training is crucial for accurately determining and adhering to the rated capacity of an excavator. Operators should be familiar with the manufacturer's specifications, load chart, and safe operating practices to ensure the safe and efficient use of the excavator.

By considering these factors and following the manufacturer's guidelines, operators can determine the rated capacity of an excavator and safely perform lifting and handling tasks on the job site.

Excavator load charts are graphical representations or tables provided by the manufacturer that detail the safe operating capacities and lifting capabilities of an excavator under various conditions. These load charts are essential for ensuring the safe and efficient use of the excavator on construction sites and other job locations.

Key components of excavator load charts include:

1. Boom Length and Angle: Load charts typically include different boom lengths and angles to provide information on the machine's lifting capacity at various configurations. The boom angle refers to the angle of the boom relative to the horizontal plane.

2. Radius: The load radius, also known as the working radius or reach, represents the horizontal distance from the excavator's rotation centre to the load being lifted. Load charts often provide capacities for different radii to accommodate lifting operations at various distances from the machine.

3. Lift Capacities: Load charts display the maximum allowable lifting capacities for the excavator based on the combination of boom length, angle, and load radius. Capacities are usually presented in terms of weight or load in pounds or kilograms.

4. Operating Conditions: Load charts may include information on

EARTHMOVING EQUIPMENT OPERATIONS

operating conditions that can affect the machine's lifting capacity, such as ground conditions, slope angles, and counterweight configurations. These factors are important considerations for safe operation.

5. Attachment Considerations: Load charts may also account for the use of attachments, such as buckets, grapples, or lifting hooks, and provide adjusted lifting capacities accordingly.

6. Charts and Graphs: Load charts may be presented in graphical or tabular format, making it easy for operators to reference the appropriate capacity for specific operating conditions quickly.

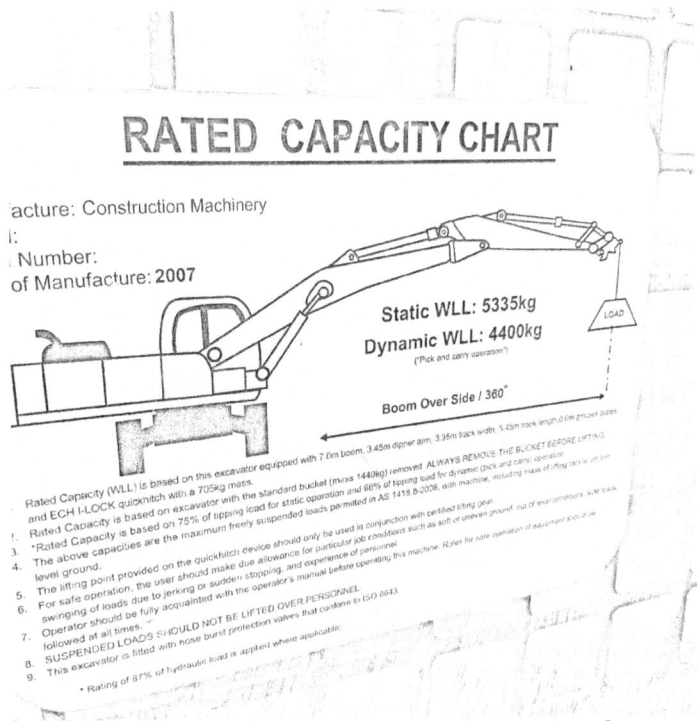

Figure 67: Sample excavator rated capacity chart.

An excavator working range diagram, also known as a working envelope or working radius diagram, is a graphical representation that illustrates the maximum reach and operational capabilities of an excavator. It typically includes various parameters such as the maximum digging depth, maximum reach, and maximum dumping height.

The diagram usually consists of a series of arcs or lines that depict the excavator's reach and movement in different directions, often categorized by the machine's rotation angle. These diagrams are essential for operators to understand the machine's limitations and ensure safe and efficient operation, especially when working in confined spaces or around obstacles. Figure 68 shows an example.

EARTHMOVING EQUIPMENT OPERATIONS

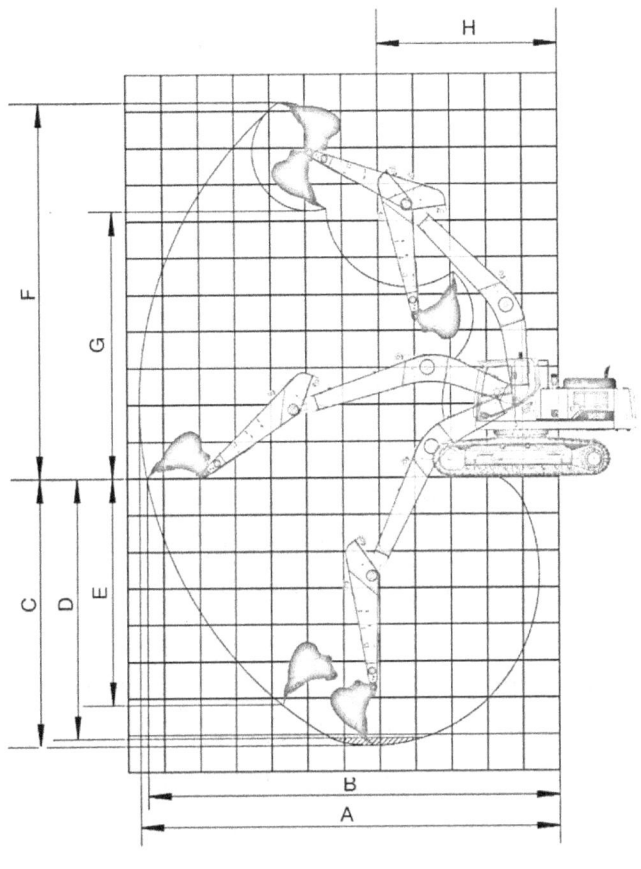

Boom Length	6,500 mm
Arm Length	2,550 mm
A Max. Digging Reach	10,625 mm
B Max. Digging Reach on Ground	10,388 mm
C Max. Digging Depth	6,521 mm
D Max. Digging Depth,	2.44 m (8') level 6,337 mm
E Max. Vertical Wall Digging Depth	5,204 mm
F Max. Cutting Height	9,977 mm
G Max. Dumping Height	7,038 mm
H Min. Front Swing Radius	4,645 mm

Figure 68: Sample excavator working range diagram.

Excavators possess remarkable versatility, largely owing to the extensive range of attachments available for these machines. Those who are familiar with or operate excavators can attest to their capability to address diverse tasks with the appropriate attachment. While certain attachments are more commonly used, there exists a wide array of options to choose from, including attachments from various Original Equipment Manufacturers (OEMs) featuring slight variations in design.

Some prevalent attachments include:
- Buckets
- Screening buckets
- Rock grabs
- Augers
- Rippers

Attachment Installation and Removal Previously, attaching and detaching attachments was a largely manual process involving unattaching, aligning the next attachment, and then reattaching. Clearly, this manual approach was not the most efficient method, and given that time equals money, significant improvements have been made to excavator attachments over time. For instance, many modern excavators now feature a quick hitch, facilitating swift attachment and detachment of attachments. Also referred to as a quick adaptor or quick coupler, a quick hitch can serve as a front attachment or a permanent fixture for your machine. Various types of quick hitches exist, including the half hitch, mechanical hitch, semi-automatic hitch, and automatic hitch. Most of these hitches can be operated from within the cab, ensuring optimized efficiency and enhanced Return on Investment (ROI).

With the plethora of options available, determining which attachments will work with your excavator or which specialized attachment is most suitable for your specific requirements can be challenging. Periodic innovations in excavator attachments, such as screening buckets, further contribute to this complexity. The compatibility of attachments with your machine is influenced by factors such as equipment weight, hitch size, pin size, pin layout, and hydraulic requirements. While there may be some overlap between brands, excavator sizes, and other factors, not all attachments are universally compatible across all excavators. To ascertain whether an attachment will suit your excavator, it is advisable to consult the seller or conduct research on the attachment's dimensions, and inquire about its compatibility with (or without) a quick hitch.

Operating an Excavator

Excavation operations have the potential to compromise the stability or security of any neighbouring buildings or structures. This could result in structural failures or collapse. Therefore, excavation activities should not commence until appropriate measures have been taken to mitigate the risk of collapse or partial collapse of any nearby buildings or structures.

Any excavation below the footing level of a structure, including retaining walls, must undergo assessment by a competent individual. It should be secured with a suitable ground support system, designed by a competent person, to prevent structural instability. Additionally, suitable supports may be necessary to brace the structure, as identified by a competent person.

Special consideration should be given to the impact of excavation activities on nearby buildings, particularly those housing sensitive equipment like hospitals. Measures must be taken to prevent adverse effects from vibration or concussion during excavation work.

Excavation work must be conducted in a manner that does not cause flooding or water infiltration into adjacent buildings.

The principal contractor is responsible for managing risks associated with essential services such as gas, water, electricity, etc. Specific precautions must be taken when operating excavators near overhead electric lines, with consultation and implementation of appropriate control measures.

Information regarding underground essential services should be provided to relevant parties, including workers, contractors, and subcontractors. This information must be readily available for inspection and retained for a specified period.

The excavation area must be secured to prevent unauthorized access, considering potential health and safety risks and the likelihood of unauthorized entry. This is essential to safeguard workers and prevent accidents.

The excavation contractor must develop an emergency plan to address unforeseen incidents such as ground slip, flooding, or gas leaks. This plan should be integrated into the broader construction project emergency plan coordinated by the principal contractor.

To drive the excavator:

Determine whether you prefer to operate the machine using your hands or feet. Excavators feature two pedals equipped with handles positioned in front of the cab, extending upwards for easy access. These pedals can be manipulated either by stepping on them with your feet or grasping the handles with your hands. Both methods function identically, so the choice depends on personal preference.

- Beginners may find driving with their hands easier.

- Experienced operators typically favour using their feet for control.

Engage both pedals upward to initiate forward motion. Operating the driving controls of an excavator is straightforward. To move forward, simultaneously push both pedals forward. This action can be executed with either your hands or feet. The pressure applied determines the speed at which the excavator moves.

- If using your feet, position them atop the pedals and push downward.

- Always ensure the surrounding area is clear before manoeuvring the excavator in any direction.

- Excavators typically have a maximum speed of around 8 mph (13 km/h), so even with maximum pressure, movement remains relatively slow.

Pull both pedals back to execute reverse movement. Conversely, to move backward, simply perform the reverse action. Pull back on both handles simultaneously to initiate reverse motion.

- When using your feet, press down on the bottom portion of the foot pedals to move in reverse. Position your feet downward with your heels resting on the cab floor, then press down with your toes against the pedal bottoms.

- Prior to reversing, always check the area behind the excavator. Some modern excavators are equipped with rear cameras to aid in reversing manoeuvres.

Utilize one pedal at a time to execute turns with the excavator. Each pedal governs the movement of one of the excavator's tracks. When turning, depress the pedal on the opposite side of the desired direction. Depressing the left pedal causes the excavator to turn right, while pressing the right pedal prompts a left turn.

- If already in motion, gradually release pressure from one pedal rather than releasing both and pressing one again, resulting in smoother turns.

- The same principles apply whether turning in reverse or forward motion. Depress the left pedal to turn right while moving backward, and press the same pedal forward to turn right while moving forward.

Digging with the excavator involves:

Position the cab directly over the tracks to ensure stability. Utilize the left joystick to align the cab with the tracks, aiming for a square orientation.

- Although excavators may remain stable even when not perfectly centred, it's advisable for beginners to maintain a square cab position until more experience is gained.

- Once positioned, refrain from operating the foot pedals to prevent accidental movement during digging.

- Avoid attempting to drive and dig simultaneously until proficient in operating the excavator.

Fully extend the stick forward to its maximum position. Employ the left joystick to push forward until the stick reaches its limit, setting up the initial position for digging.

- Advanced operators may vary the stick position for digging tasks. However, beginners should extend the stick completely before commencing digging activities.

Align the bucket teeth with the stick for optimal digging. Strike a balance between fully opening and closing the bucket when excavating soil. Visualize an imaginary line extending from the end of the stick and adjust the bucket position using the right joystick to align the teeth with this line.

- Avoid digging with the bucket fully extended to prevent potential damage to the machine's joints caused by debris accumulation.

Lower the boom until the bucket penetrates the soil surface. Employ the right joystick to lower the boom by pushing it backward until the toothed portion of the bucket enters the soil, stopping at this point.

- Aim to enter the soil with the bucket approximately halfway up to ensure an effective scoop.

Curl and elevate the bucket to gather the soil. Initiate the curling motion by pushing the right joystick to the left. As the bucket nears closure and the ground forms a mound, cease curling and lift the boom by pushing the right joystick upward to complete the scoop.

Step 6: Rotate the cab and open the bucket to release the soil. After scooping the dirt, manoeuvre the cab using the left joystick to the desired dumping location. Position the bucket over the spot and, using the right joystick, open the bucket to release the dirt.

- Keep the dumped soil nearby in case backfilling is required, and repeat the process as necessary to complete the excavation.

Square the cab with the tracks before shutting down the machine. Upon finishing the task, rotate the cab to align with the tracks, facing forward. Disengage the joystick controls by lowering the control lever, then reduce the throttle to idle using the knob near the right hand. Allow the engine to idle for a minute for cooling before turning off the machine by removing the key.

- Exercise caution when exiting the cab to prevent falls, as construction sites pose inherent risks of injury.

Most excavators are equipped with an electronic monitoring system (EMS), although the specific features may vary between machines. Some excavators include a test function for the EMS, which typically comprises a monitor light, fault/action light, fault alarm, and a monitoring panel with individual indicators for each machine system. It is advisable to test this system as part of the start-up procedure.

Below are some warning lights commonly found on the EMS:

Parking Brake: Indicates the parking brake is engaged and the transmission is in neutral. It should illuminate during start-up and extinguish when the brake is released.

Alternator: Indicates a malfunction with the alternator. If this light comes on, stop the machine and investigate the cause before operating further.

Fuel: Indicates low fuel level (10% of tank capacity). Refuel as soon as possible if this light comes on.

Coolant Temperature: Indicates excessive coolant temperature. Stop the machine and investigate the cause if this light illuminates. Do not continue operating if the fault persists.

Transmission Oil Temperature: Indicates excessive transmission oil temperature. Reduce load on the machine and investigate the cause. Cease operation if the fault persists.

Hydraulic Oil Temperature: Indicates excessive hydraulic oil temperature. Take similar precautions as with transmission oil temperature.

Engine Oil Pressure: Indicates low oil pressure. Stop the machine immediately, investigate the cause, and rectify before further operation.

Transmission Oil Filters: Indicates a clogged oil filter. Stop the machine and investigate the cause before resuming operation.

Coolant Flow: Indicates a failure in the coolant system. Cease operation and rectify the issue before continuing.

Engine Coolant Temperature: Indicates the temperature of the engine coolant. If the needle reaches the red range, cease operation and seek assistance to avoid engine failure.

Warning Categories: The EMS provides three warning categories:

- Level 1: Operator Awareness

- Level 2: Operator Response Required

- Level 3: Immediate Shutdown Required

Key Start Switch: OFF: Turn the key to this position to stop the machine. ON: Turn the key clockwise to activate all cab circuits. START: Crank the engine by turning the key to this position. Release the key once the engine starts. If the engine does not start after 30 seconds, return the switch to OFF for two minutes before attempting to START again.

Ground Level Engine Shutdown Switch: This switch, usually located at ground level, stops the engine when placed in the off position. The engine will not start unless this switch is in the on position.

Emergency Stop Button: Depress this button inside the cab only in emergency situations. Do not use it for routine machine shutdown.

When engaging in digging operations, it's crucial to follow proper technique to ensure safety and efficiency. Here are some guidelines to keep in mind:

- Maintain machine stability by keeping it level during operation.
- Position travel motors to the rear to safeguard them.
- Operate controls smoothly to ensure the attachment moves seamlessly.
- Use the correct bucket digging angle for optimal performance.
- Avoid using the ditch wall to halt the swing of the attachment, as it can cause hydraulic damage.
- Do not overload the bucket.

In case the machine's tracks lift off the ground while digging, gently lower the machine back down to prevent damage. Never allow the machine to drop abruptly to the ground.

Here's a step-by-step process for effective digging:

1. Position the stick at approximately a 70° angle to the ground.

2. Manoeuvre the cutting edge of the bucket to a 120° angle to maximize break force.

3. Move the stick inward, toward the cab, while keeping the bucket parallel to the ground.

4. Gradually raise the boom while simultaneously closing the bucket when the stick stops moving.

5. Continue the pass with the bucket traveling horizontally to scoop the material effectively.

6. Close the bucket and raise the boom once it's full.

Note: To achieve the greatest break force at the cutting edge, decrease downward force as the stick moves toward the cab.

Loading Techniques

There are four main loading techniques used with excavators:

- Straight Loading

- Tail Loading

- Corner Loading

- Top Loading

The choice of technique depends on various factors such as material type, floor conditions, machinery match, wind direction, and lighting plant position. Depending on these factors, operators may choose to load trucks parked along the bench, requiring a longer swing angle of approximately 20° on the arc.

When loading, follow these techniques:

- Smoothly swing the load as the bucket is loaded and lifted.

- Preferably tail load trucks for less lift height.

- Start dumping the load when the bucket's centre is over the side or end of the truck body.

- Begin the return swing before the bucket is empty.

- Lower the bucket to the next dig area when the teeth clear the truck body.

- Position the stick and bucket before landing, and adjust if needed.

Note: Raise the boom when loading trucks to allow them to reverse under the bucket, optimizing loading time and reducing turnaround time.

Excavation Methods

The nature of excavation work dictates the choice of excavation method and a safe work system. Consider health and safety issues carefully, especially for excavations beyond shallow trenching and small material quantities.

For trenching:

- Ensure all trench sides are adequately supported using shoring, benching, or battering methods.

- A combination of support measures may be necessary based on site conditions.

- Consider the risk of engulfment when workers enter trenches, implementing control measures regardless of trench depth.

- Consult a geotechnical engineer for stability assessments and design support systems if needed.

Preparation and excavation:

- Utilize bulldozers, scrapers, and excavators for preparatory work and trenching.

- Manual trimming may be necessary, controlled to mitigate fall and powered mobile plant risks.

Tunnelling: Tunnelling work requires meticulous planning, design, and construction to ensure safety and effectiveness.

- Conduct thorough pre-construction engineering investigations to inform tunnel design.

- Design tunnels considering ground conditions, excavation methods, and support requirements.

- Address potential hazards such as tunnel stability, changing ground conditions, and limited space.

- Implement control measures like ground support systems, fall protection, and ventilation to manage risks effectively.

Shafts: Shafts provide access or ventilation to tunnels and require careful design and construction.

- Consider shaft dimensions, stability, and access control to manage risks.

- Utilize appropriate support systems, fall protection, and ventilation measures.

- Obtain expert advice for shaft design and construction, especially for special features or challenging conditions.

Excavators often work in conjunction with other earthmoving plant. These operations include loading to a haul truck.

EARTHMOVING EQUIPMENT OPERATIONS

Figure 69: Loading a dump truck. Oto Zapletal, CC BY-SA 4.0, via Wikimedia Commons.

Straight Loading: Straight loading occurs when the excavator operates parallel to the working bench. Haul trucks approach the excavator in a clockwise direction, swinging directly out from the excavator and then reversing straight back to align with the excavator cab.

Tail Loading: Tail loading involves the excavator still operating parallel to the working bench. Haul trucks approach the excavator in a clockwise direction, swinging out at a 45° angle, then aligning with the excavator teeth and reversing back.

This loading technique allows the excavator operator to shorten the swing cycle, thus increasing productivity.

Corner Loading: Corner loading occurs when the excavator completes the current cut it is working on. As the excavator reaches the end of the cut, it is necessary to remove the corner dirt on which the machine is situated. At this point, the truck will be positioned in the corner parallel to the face as the excavator works around the corner. Once the corner dirt is removed, the excavator resumes digging parallelly in the opposite direction and continues straight loading.

Top Loading: Top loading is a loading method where the haul truck and the excavator are at the same level. It is used when finishing the remains of a bench, picking up batter trims, starting a drop cut, or digging a sump.

Loading on a Level Surface: Ensuring that the excavator is on a level surface when loading trucks offers several benefits:

- Maximizes productivity

- Reduces operator fatigue

- Minimizes machine wear

- Assists in maintaining levels

- Reduces machine instability.

Note: Operating an excavator on uneven ground can lead to excessive wear and make the machine unstable.

Tramming: Tramming refers to the process of moving the excavator over a distance. Before tramming the excavator, the operator must:

- Ensure that the excavator sprockets are positioned to the rear.

- Disengage the hydraulic safety lock.

- Select full throttle.

- Raise the bucket 500mm off the ground using the boom (or as per manufacturer's specifications).

- Bring the stick towards the excavator.

- Sound the horn twice and wait 5 seconds before tramming.

Tramming should not exceed 20 minutes at a time, after which the excavator should be allowed to cool down. During this cooling down period, carry out the following inspection:

- Allow engine RPM's to run at high idle.
- Position hydraulic implements (bucket) on the ground.
- Place hydraulic safety lock into ON position.
- Inspect excavator for oil, coolant, and diesel leaks.
- Visually inspect rollers and idlers for damaged or missing components and excessive heat.
- Ensure the excavator is functional. If not, inform your supervisor.

Always take extreme care to protect the track adjustments when tramming off a bench.

Note: A water cart may be used to cool tracks while tramming long distances to prevent overheating.

Manoeuvring the Excavator Between the Bench and Pit Floor:

To manoeuvre an excavator from a bench to the pit floor and vice versa, follow these steps:

- Create a ramp approximately 1.5 times the machine length from the bench to the pit floor.
- Ensure that the ramp has a gradient of approximately 45 degrees.
- Ensure the ramp is safe and firm.
- Ensure the tracks have the correct tension, adjusted using a ram.
- Idlers must be to the front of the excavator.

- Allow track motors to support the weight of the excavator.

Tramming Off the Bench:
1. Descend from benches by pushing the edge of the bench over and placing the boom on the floor of the dig.

2. Walk the machine to the edge and start the decline from the bench keeping the tracks 90° to the bench.

3. Keep weight on the boom and stick and decline slowly.

4. Lift the front of the excavator slightly to clear the ground off the front idlers when they reach the bottom of the ramp by bringing the stick forward.

5. Keep walking out, lifting the boom as you go for clearance.

6. Complete the climb off the working bench.

Tramming Onto the Bench:
1. Approach at 90° to the bench and pull the top section down to lessen the angle of the climb.

2. Place the bucket on the top of the bench.

3. By pulling the stick in and tramming at the same time, the machine will climb up the ramp.

4. When near the top of the bench, start raising the boom keeping it close to the ground.

5. Once at the top of the climb, push the bucket out to maintain balance.

6. When tracks are level on top of the bench, the climb is complete.

Note: Some excavators require a ramp created at a grade where they can walk up using their track motor alone.

Before tramming onto a bench, please check manufacturer specifications and site requirements.

Drop Cuts: When initiating a new bench, a ramp is crafted to connect one level to another, known as a drop cut. Typically, a drop cut is formed at the base of the main ramp to the pit, but it can be executed at any point within the pit for operational convenience.

The drop cut should maintain a moderate slope and span approximately 2.5 trucks wide, ensuring ample space for trucks to manoeuvre safely. Position the excavator bucket over the designated area where the truck is to be stationed. The truck operator will then reverse the truck down the drop cut, aligning it squarely with the ramp underneath the bucket.

Cutting Batters: A batter refers to the vertical wall of the pit. When cutting batters, adhere to the following procedure:

- Maintain the bucket square to the face.

- Ensure the bucket aligns with the wall at the specified angle determined by the site.

- Orient the boom toward the batter edge for a swift exit in case of wall collapse.

- Place all trimmings away from the wall to facilitate cleanup by the dozer.

- Utilize an incline meter or spotter if needed to achieve the correct angle.

Excavator operators sometimes cut batters while mining, a process referred to as cutting the batter on the run. To execute this:

- Keep the tracks parallel to the high wall.

- Remove the majority of dirt from the high wall.

- Trim the high wall according to the angle specified by the site.

- Ensure the truck is positioned parallel to the high wall.

Note: Leave sufficient material on the bench to enable safe batter cutting by the excavator.

Maximizing Productivity: Several factors contribute to maximizing productivity, including:

- Optimizing truck cycle times.

- Maintaining clean haul roads and loading areas.

- Achieving efficient digging, with the optimal boom/stick configuration at a 15-degree angle on either side from the right angle.

- Ensuring speedy excavator loading cycle times by utilizing hydraulics to their maximum capacity.

- Loading the bucket to its maximum capacity.

Note: If a trainee truck driver encounters difficulty reversing under the excavator, supervisors should consider allowing them to observe correct procedures from the excavator cab.

Remember:

- Avoid using "impact" force to prevent damage to the bucket and equipment.

- Load only rocks within the excavator and haul truck's capacity.

- Never sweep rocks away with the bucket; gently nudge them aside or use another machine for removal if necessary.

- Avoid excavating over the track motors.

Slew Brake: If the excavator is equipped with a slew brake:
- Avoid excessive use to prevent overheating.
- Engage the slew or park brake when leaving the machine unattended.

To prevent engine or hydraulic overheating when digging in heavy material:
- Reduce material output.
- Pause digging periodically to allow the machine to cool down.

Night Time Operating Rules and Tips:
- Equip excavators with effective headlights when operating in the pit at night.
- Avoid direct glare from oncoming traffic headlights.

Important: Always adjust operations according to prevailing conditions. For instance, in extremely dusty or low-visibility conditions, slow down or halt operations altogether to prevent accidents.

Completing Excavator Operations

Procedure for Parking and Shutting Down the Excavator - When preparing to park the excavator:
- Choose a parking spot away from the work area;
- Avoid parking on an incline;
- Align the excavator body with its tracks;
- Lower the attachment to the ground and engage the hydraulic lock lever;

- Adjust the engine throttle switch to reduce engine speed;

- Allow the machine to idle for at least five minutes before shutting it down;

- Turn the key start switch to the OFF position once the machine has stopped running;

- Perform a brief walk-around inspection at the end of each shift;

- Ensure the travel pedals are in the neutral position before parking. Permission from a supervisor is necessary to park on an incline, except in emergency situations.

Preventing Machine Fires: To prevent machine fires, it is important to:

- Maintain cleanliness by avoiding the accumulation of dust and debris, particularly around the engine and exhaust areas;

- Avoid welding or flame cutting near pipes and hoses containing flammable liquids;

- Know and follow proper extinguisher handling procedures.

To prevent fires related to flammable fluids such as fuel or oil:

- Avoid spillage onto hot surfaces (such as engines and exhausts) during servicing;

- Do not smoke while refuelling;

- Promptly repair any oil and fuel leaks;

- While refuelling, the operator must exit the cab and remain on the ground.

To ensure optimal performance and minimize downtime, proper maintenance of your excavator is essential. Here's a brief guide to maintaining your excavator:

- Regularly check the fluids, including coolant, hydraulic fluid, and engine oil.

- Inspect the dust ejector in the air filters.

- Examine the undercarriage and side compartments for any signs of leaks.

- Check the tracks for missing bolts or bent shoes.

- Ensure the coolers are free of debris.

- Inspect the attachments for any wear and tear or broken teeth. Additionally, keep the undercarriage clean to prevent debris from damaging moving parts. If you operate your excavator in harsh conditions, schedule regular servicing. Please note: These are general maintenance guidelines. Consult your machine's manual for specific instructions. Alternatively, contact your local dealer, service technician, or the manufacturer for tailored advice.

Chapter Six

Dozer Operations

A bulldozer, often simply referred to as a "dozer," is a heavy-duty construction machine primarily used for earthmoving and leveling tasks on construction sites, mines, quarries, and agricultural land. It typically features a large metal blade at the front, known as a dozer blade or a blade, which can be raised, lowered, and tilted to push, lift, and move various materials such as soil, sand, gravel, rocks, and debris.

Bulldozers are equipped with powerful engines and tracks or wheels for mobility and stability, allowing them to operate effectively in rough terrain and adverse conditions. They are commonly used for tasks such as clearing land, grading, excavation, backfilling, road construction, and snow removal.

Bulldozers come in various sizes and configurations, ranging from small utility models suitable for light-duty tasks to large, heavy-duty machines capable of handling massive earthmoving projects. They are essential pieces of equipment in the construction, mining, and agricultural industries, contributing to efficient and productive operations across a wide range of applications.

The term "bulldozer" typically refers to heavy machinery like loaders or excavators, but specifically, it denotes a tractor equipped with a blade. A bulldozer is a tracked vehicle with an integrated metal blade used to move large quantities of soil, sand, debris, etc., typically encountered in construction work. Typically, bulldozers are large and sturdy tracked machines. The tracks provide excellent traction and manoeuvrability on uneven terrain. The wide tracks distribute the weight of the bulldozer over a large area, reducing the pressure exerted and preventing sinking in sandy ground. Bulldozers feature a torque converter that enhances engine power for increased pulling capacity, enabling them to tow heavy loads effortlessly. Due to these capabilities, bulldozers are utilized for clearing debris, obstacles, constructing roads, clearing vegetation, and land preparation tasks. Bulldozers are also employed for digging trenches, agricultural activities, and military operations.

Figure 70: Caterpillar D10N bulldozer. MathKnight, CC BY-SA 3.0, via Wikimedia Commons.

Designed to push or demolish obstacles in their path, these robust vehicles find application in construction, agriculture, and military sectors.

The core of bulldozer functionality lies in its powerful engine and tracks, which enable it to push, pull, and carry heavy loads consistently. The tracks provide excellent traction and weight distribution, preventing the bulldozer from getting stuck or slipping on challenging terrain. This, combined with the significant torque produced by the diesel engine and torque converter, facilitates the manipulation of substantial loads effortlessly. Modern bulldozers are capable of towing tanks weighing over 70 tons.

A bulldozer comprises several components, but the most notable are its blade, tracks, and ripper. Attached to the front of the vehicle via a push frame, the blade is a heavy metal plate used for pushing objects and scooping up large volumes of material like sand and earth. Blades typically come in three designs: an S blade, which is short and lacks lateral curvature and side wings; a U blade, which is tall with pronounced side wings for gathering more material; or an S-U blade, combining features of the other two types.

Figure 71: A Zettelmeyer ZD 3001 wheeled-bulldozer in the brown coal open pit mine Vereinigtes Schleenhain. High Contrast, CC BY 3.0 DE, via Wikimedia Commons.

Bulldozer tracks also come in various configurations, with oval and triangular arrays being common. A popular track system is Caterpillar's triangular high-drive system, designed to elevate the cab position for better visibility during operation and enhance balance and traction across all tasks. For instance, high-drive bulldozers offer consistent stability and grip whether pushing, pulling, or carrying heavy loads.

The ripper is another essential component attached to the rear of the bulldozer and powered by a hydraulic cylinder. Typically resembling a toothed blade or series of blades, the ripper breaks up hard ground for scooping or pushing by the blade. Equipped with replaceable tungsten steel alloy tips, rippers remain sharp, and variants like stump-buster rippers are tailored for specific tasks like splitting and shredding tree stumps.

Figure 72: Wheeled dozer.

Bulldozers come in various types, each tailored for specific applications and terrain conditions. Here are some common types of bulldozers:

1. Standard Bulldozers: Standard bulldozers are versatile machines used for a wide range of earthmoving tasks. They typically feature a large, straight blade mounted on the front for pushing soil, debris, or other materials. Standard bulldozers are suitable for general construction, grading, and leveling projects.

2. Crawler Bulldozers: Crawler bulldozers, also known as track-type bulldozers, are equipped with tracks instead of wheels. These tracks provide excellent traction and stability, making crawler bulldozers well-suited for rough or uneven terrain. They are commonly used in heavy construction, mining, and forestry applications.

3. Wheel Bulldozers: Unlike crawler bulldozers, wheel bulldozers are equipped with wheels instead of tracks. They are more manoeuvrable and faster than crawler bulldozers, making them suitable for tasks that require frequent movement over shorter distances. Wheel bulldozers are commonly used in road construction, land clearing, and landscaping projects.

4. Mini Bulldozers: Mini bulldozers, also known as compact or mini-dozers, are smaller and lighter than standard bulldozers. They are ideal for tasks in confined spaces or areas with limited access. Mini bulldozers are commonly used in landscaping, residential construction, and utility work.

5. Hydrostatic Bulldozers: Hydrostatic bulldozers utilize a hydrostatic transmission system instead of a traditional mechanical transmission. This system provides smoother operation and precise control of speed and direction, making hydrostatic bull-

dozers suitable for fine grading and delicate earthmoving tasks.

6. Swamp Bulldozers: Swamp bulldozers, also known as marsh or wetland bulldozers, are specially designed for working in soft, muddy, or swampy terrain. They typically feature wide tracks or specialized track designs that distribute the machine's weight over a larger area, reducing the risk of getting stuck in wet or unstable ground.

7. Waste Handling Bulldozers: Waste handling bulldozers are equipped with features specifically designed for working in landfill or waste management applications. They may include protective guarding, specialized tyres or tracks, and enhanced cooling systems to withstand harsh operating conditions and protect against debris damage.

8. Specialized Bulldozers: Specialized bulldozers are customized or modified for specific applications or industries. These may include forestry bulldozers equipped with protective cages and specialized attachments for clearing trees, or military bulldozers designed for combat engineering tasks such as building fortifications or clearing obstacles.

Overall, the choice of bulldozer type depends on factors such as the nature of the terrain, the specific tasks at hand, and the desired level of performance and efficiency.

The primary components of a bulldozer consist of the blade and the ripper. Positioned at the rear of the bulldozer, the ripper is an extended device that can either have a single shank or be grouped into multiple shank rippers. Typically, single shank rippers are preferred for deep ripping, which involves breaking up hard earth for agricultural purposes. Heavy bulldozers can even crush lava to facilitate agriculture or rip other hard soils to enable the planting of orchards in otherwise inhospitable land. Meanwhile, the blade, located at the front, is a robust metal plate used for pushing objects, soil, sand, and debris.

Various components are necessary to assemble a complete bulldozer. Engine parts, chassis, and hydraulic components form some of the more intricate elements of the bulldozer. Unique to this type of earth-moving equipment are components such as the blade, tracks, and control levers. Other parts, such as the seat, muffler, and hydraulic cylinders, may bear similarities to those used in other heavy equipment.

Comprising many solid steel components, bulldozers are typically among the heaviest pieces of earth-moving machinery on job sites. The weight of a bulldozer is significantly contributed by its large diesel engine, housed in a heavy cast-iron engine block. This engine block contains water passages for coolant circulation, providing cooling for various moving parts such as the rotating crankshaft, pistons, and connecting rods.

The radiator on a bulldozer plays a crucial role in cooling not only the engine but also the hydraulic fluid, engine oil, and transmission fluid, making it an essential part of the machine's cooling system. Notable components of a bulldozer include the tracks and the large front blade. The tracks, constructed by linking heavy steel sections with solid steel pins, enable the bulldozer to operate on soft ground while providing traction. The large blade, mounted on heavy arms, allows the machine to push substantial amounts of earth, rock, and debris.

Controlled by large hydraulic cylinders, the movement of the blade—up, down, and sometimes tilting fore and aft—is facilitated. The operator manipulates these movements using control levers mounted in the operator's compartment, with newer bulldozer designs incorporating blade controls, transmission, and steering controls into a single joystick. Optional computer-assisted features interact with various components of the bulldozer, enabling precise level finish work.

EARTHMOVING EQUIPMENT OPERATIONS

The distinguishing features of a crawler dozer include a cab, a set of caterpillar tracks, a blade positioned at the front, and occasionally, a ripper at the rear.

Figure 73: Main bulldozer components. Back image - Shaun Greiner, CC BY-SA 2.0 , via Wikimedia Commons.

The operator's cabin in a crawler dozer typically integrates joystick controls for optimal manoeuvrability, along with a variety of other controls and gauges to ensure the operator remains informed about the machine's status at all times. The cabin must provide a reasonably comfortable and spacious environment for the operator, who may spend several hours at a stretch inside it. It should also be equipped with air conditioning and soundproofing to mitigate the noise generated by the machine and the work site, which can strain the operator's ears.

The tracks of a crawler dozer serve as substitutes for tyres or wheels, boasting heavy-duty material and a ridged design that enables the machine to traverse the work site regardless of rugged terrain or obstacles. Crawler dozers come with small, medium, or large tracks, depending on the nature of the work they are intended for.

Small track dozers are typically swifter and more agile in navigating through work sites due to their narrower tracks. They find application in tasks that involve confined spaces and require precise operations, such as road construction, landscaping projects, and the erection of residential structures, driveways, small-scale buildings, and parking lots.

Medium track dozers offer versatility and can be deployed in both residential and larger-scale construction projects. They serve as a suitable choice for companies operating across diverse work sites and conditions. Their medium-sized tracks facilitate significant manoeuvrability while delivering the requisite power for handling heavy loads.

Featuring the widest tracks among all dozer types, large track dozers offer enhanced stability and shock absorption for tackling the most challenging and rugged tasks. These substantial machines boast a higher blade capacity and can manage considerably heavier loads compared to their smaller counterparts. Larger dozers often come equipped with a ripper at the rear, capable of crushing rocks and other hard objects encountered in rough terrain. Moreover, the most powerful dozers with high horsepower ratings are frequently employed in mining operations.

Different bulldozers are equipped with various types of blades, each suited to specific construction tasks. Depending on the blade type employed, bulldozers find application across different construction sites. For surface grading and soil leveling tasks, straight blade bulldozers prove most effective. Conversely, bulldozers outfitted with U blades, also known as universal blades, excel in tasks requiring pushing, hauling, and scooping capabilities. However, for heavier tasks beyond the capacity of straight or U blade bulldozers, a combination blade is necessary. Combination blade bulldozers are versatile, capable of handling tasks ranging from pushing and debris clearance to managing heavy loads simultaneously.

The prominent metal structure at the front of a bulldozer, known as the blade, serves to gather and relocate various materials such as dirt, rocks, rubble, and sand within construction sites or work areas. While some crawler dozers feature fixed blades, others incorporate blades with adjustable angles to facilitate precise grading on sloped terrain.

Bulldozer blades are available in different configurations, including universal, straight, and combination blades.

Universal Blade Characterized by its curved design and side panels or wings, forming a scooped shovel shape. These panels retain materials within the dozer blade during machine operation.

Straight Blade Considerably shorter than a universal blade, lacking its curvature and side panels. Ideal for tasks requiring fine grading precision.

Combination Blade Blending features of both universal and straight blades, primarily used for moving stones, rocks, and similar large debris. Short in length with a slight curve and small side wings.

Various work tools can be installed at the rear of the machine to complement the functionality of the front blade:

- Large steel slabs can be mounted to the rear to increase weight, aiding in heavy dozing applications.

- A drawbar and CCU (Cable Control Unit) are utilized for pulling towed scrapers and trailed implements. In more recent models, hydraulic systems have replaced the CCU for operating scrapers.

- A hydraulic winch can be installed at the rear for towing or pulling purposes, particularly useful in forestry work where a lighter front blade may also be employed for pushing brush and trees.

- A ripper with single or multiple shanks can be attached to the rear to break up hard soil or rock.

- Equipped with a linkage (three-point hitch) for agricultural use with mounted implements like plows.

Typically installed on large-track bulldozers utilized in mining and similarly challenging environments, a ripper is an attachment affixed to the rear of the machine. Rippers are tasked with breaking apart rocks, stones, and densely packed soil, rendering them into smaller pieces that can be easily scooped up, transported in trucks, and relocated. In agricultural settings, farmers sometimes employ rippers to fracture compacted, rocky soil, facilitating the fertilization and planting of crops.

Rippers come in two main types: single-shank or multi-shank, both featuring durable tips made of tungsten steel alloy that can be replaced when necessary due to wear and tear.

In some cases, bulldozers may be equipped with a stumpbuster instead of a ripper. A stumpbuster is a long spike designed to split tree stumps into more manageable pieces for removal, particularly useful in land clearing operations for construction or farming purposes. Contrary to common belief, rear implements such as rippers may see more use than the dozer blade itself in certain scenarios. Another frequently employed rear implement is the winch, adding versatility to the tractor and influencing the need for counterweights based on the chosen rear attachment.

Cat Medium Track-Type Tractors are engineered to optimize productivity while accommodating rear implements. The selection of rear implements should consider factors such as tractor horsepower, gross weight, and penetration force required for the task at hand.

Common Rear Implements for Cat Medium Track-Type Tractors:

Ripper Configurations: Choosing the appropriate tractor for a ripping job is crucial, considering factors such as flywheel horsepower, gross weight, and available penetration force at the ripper tip. With increasing urbanization and environmental concerns surrounding alternative methods like drilling and blasting, the use of ripping has seen a rise in popularity.

Multi-Shank Fixed Parallelogram Linkage Ripper: These versatile rippers are suitable for various sites and applications without requiring frequent changes. The fixed parallelogram linkage ensures consistent tooth angles at different ripping depths, making them ideal for tasks like pre-ripping for scrapers.

Multi-Shank Ripper with Hydraulically Variable Angle: Offering the flexibility of angle adjustment via hydraulic controls, these rippers enhance productivity by allowing operators to adapt to varying material conditions.

Single-Shank Ripper with Hydraulically Variable Angle: Designed for demanding ripping tasks and deep penetration requirements, these rippers are selected for production ripping applications where the machine spends a significant amount of time working in tough materials.

Reverse Rippers: Commonly used in the petroleum industry, reverse rippers are mounted to the backside of the blade, enabling ripping operations while the tractor reverses in preparation for the next dozing pass.

Other Tractor Attachments include:

- Winches: Winches, whether hydrostatically or mechanically powered, are affixed to the rear of the tractor, providing towing capabilities. They are utilized for vehicle retrieval, logging operations, setting up and dismantling oil fields, as well as various utility towing tasks.

- Specialized Tools: Caterpillar offers a diverse range of tractor tools tailored for specific applications, including:

- Woodchip Blade: This high-capacity blade boosts dozing efficiency when dealing with lightweight woodchips.

- Cable Plow: Mounted to the rear of the tractor, cable plows, available in both static and vibratory models, facilitate high-production below-grade installation of copper and fiber optic cables.

- Log Arch: When connected to a winch, a log arch enables the tractor to tow a bundle of logs off the ground.

- Street Pads: Rubber or polyurethane street pads, either bolted or clamped onto the tracks, enable track-type tractors to traverse paved surfaces with minimal damage.

- Fireline Plow: Towed behind a tractor, fireline plows create firebreaks, eight feet or wider, to aid in wildfire suppression efforts.

- Blade Rake: Also known as "root rakes," these attachments mount to the blade and feature tines that extend below the cutting edge, facilitating the removal of tree roots below the soil surface.

- Sideboom: Suitable for lighter pipe-lifting tasks and smaller pipes, sidebooms allow tractors to handle small pipeline projects efficiently.

- Slopeboard: Mounted to the side of a dozer blade, slopeboards feature hydraulic controls that enhance the efficiency of dozing on sloped surfaces.

- Foldable VPAT Blade: This versatile blade is ideal for situations where transport width is a concern.

- V-Blade (Clearing): Featuring a steeply angled V shape and sharp cutting edges, V-blades are robust attachments designed for clearing medium to larger vegetation.

- Coal Blade: These high-capacity blades are specifically designed to boost dozing productivity in coal and petcoke stockpile applications.

- Drawbar: Attached to the rear of the tractor, a drawbar facilitates towing implements and pulling other machines from stuck or mired positions. It is a requisite attachment if no other rear attachment is specified.

- Front and Rear Striker Bars: Striker bars are essential in waste applications to shield the tractor's fuel tank, fenders, and other sheet metal components from damage. Positioned to deflect hazards away from the tractor, rear striker bars are typically mounted on a rear striker box, which can also serve as storage for shovels, tools, or CO_2 cylinders for a fire-suppression system.

In a bulldozer, the levers and pedals control various functions essential for operating the machine effectively. Here's an overview of what these controls typically do:

1. Blade Control Lever: This lever controls the movement of the blade attached to the front of the bulldozer. It allows the operator to raise, lower, tilt, and angle the blade to perform different tasks such as pushing or spreading material.

2. Throttle Lever or Pedal: The throttle control regulates the engine speed and power output. By adjusting the throttle, the operator can increase or decrease the speed at which the bulldozer moves and the force it exerts.

3. Transmission Lever: The transmission lever or gear shift lever is used to select the appropriate gear for forward or reverse movement. It allows the operator to control the speed and direction of the bulldozer.

4. Steering Clutches and Brake Pedals: Bulldozers typically use

steering clutches and brake pedals to control the steering and braking. By pressing the brake pedal, the operator can stop the bulldozer or slow it down. Steering clutches are engaged or disengaged to control the turning of the bulldozer.

5. Hydraulic Controls: These controls operate various hydraulic systems in the bulldozer, such as those for raising and lowering the ripper, adjusting the blade, or operating any attachments. They usually consist of levers or joysticks that allow precise control over hydraulic functions.

6. Track Control Pedals: In a tracked bulldozer, there are pedals for controlling the tracks. Pressing one pedal causes the bulldozer to turn by slowing down one track while the other continues moving, enabling it to pivot.

7. Attachments Control: If the bulldozer is equipped with additional attachments such as a ripper or winch, there may be separate controls for operating these attachments. These controls allow the operator to engage, disengage, and manipulate the functions of the attachments as needed.

Overall, these levers and pedals provide the operator with the necessary control and manoeuvrability to perform various tasks efficiently and safely with the bulldozer.

Steering is achieved by decelerating or halting one track while the other continues its motion. Direct drive machines utilize a steering clutch and brake on one track to achieve this, effectively disengaging power application. While this method has been prevalent for many years and is effective, it reduces pushing force by half during turns. Operators mitigate this limitation by employing techniques emphasizing straight pushing under load with minimal turning, aligning the machine when empty, and executing turns before fully loading the blade or while reducing the load. Additionally, adjusting ground engagement to favour the required turn direction is another practiced technique. Understanding these principles enhances the efficiency of operating modern hydrostatic drive machines.

Hydrostatic drive systems enable variable speed control for each track without significant power reduction. This permits slowing either track for turning without disrupting power transmission. While this feature substantially enhances turning power under load, operators should recognize that straight pushing optimally utilizes available power. Turns demand traction and draw power from the blade's forward thrust irrespective of the drive system.

A joystick regulates the flow and pressure of oil to each track, offering control through four directions of stick movement, occasionally involving stick rotation for direction control or buttons for incremental speed adjustments. Generally, increased stick movement results in greater oil flow and speed if the load permits. Adjusting speed and power to each track facilitates turns, with counter-rotation of tracks (one forward and the other backward) occasionally employed for spot turns.

Figure 74: Typical dozer cabin layout.

Planning and Preparing for Bulldozer Operations

As a Bulldozer operator, it is essential to prioritize both personal safety and the safety of others in the vicinity, as mandated by legal requirements. Safe operation of a Bulldozer heavily relies on the application of common sense, with operators remaining vigilant of potential hazards that could compromise their well-being, the safety of co-workers, or the integrity of the machine. The operator bears the responsibility for ensuring the safety of the Bulldozer and its load at all times.

Implementing straightforward safety measures in collaboration with the employer and adherence to basic rules can significantly reduce risks. Operators should adhere strictly to instructions provided by site managers and supervisors, as well as abide by the manufacturer's guidelines outlined in the operator manuals specific to the Bulldozer being operated. It is crucial to exercise caution by taking safety measures before, during, and after operating the machine, ensuring it is operated within its designated capabilities.

Operators should refrain from operating any machinery without appropriate training and authorization, and must not disregard potential hazards or engage in the misuse, tampering, or interference with the Bulldozer and its associated safety equipment. Negligence that compromises personal safety or that of others should be avoided at all costs.

Before commencing work, operators must ensure that the Bulldozer is in proper working condition and safe for use by conducting routine daily checks and maintenance procedures. Additionally, they should survey the work areas for hazards and obstacles that could impede the Bulldozer's operation.

In terms of construction safety tips, it is imperative to conduct a comprehensive inspection of ground conditions before commencing work to identify any potential risks. Installing markers to delineate the edge of the road can enhance visibility and awareness, while pushing earth at the correct angle relative to the road shoulder can minimize the risks of collapse and other hazards.

Planning for bulldozer operations involves several key steps to ensure safety, compliance, and efficiency:

1. Access, interpret, and apply dozer operations documentation: Begin by accessing relevant documentation, such as manufacturer's manuals, safety guidelines, and regulatory requirements. Interpret this information to understand proper operating procedures, safety precautions, and legal obligations. Apply these guidelines to ensure that bulldozer operations comply with industry standards and regulations.

2. Obtain, read, interpret, clarify, and confirm work instructions: Obtain clear work instructions from supervisors or project managers regarding the scope of work, objectives, and specific tasks to be performed. Read and interpret these instructions carefully, seeking clarification if needed to ensure understanding. Confirm the details of the work instructions to avoid misunderstandings and errors during bulldozer operations.

3. Identify and address risks, hazards, and environmental issues: Conduct a thorough risk assessment of the worksite to identify potential hazards, risks, and environmental concerns associated with bulldozer operations. Implement appropriate control measures to mitigate these risks, such as barriers, signage, and safety protocols. Address environmental issues by minimizing disturbance to sensitive areas and complying with environmental regulations.

4. Select and wear personal protective equipment (PPE): Identify the appropriate PPE required for bulldozer operations, such as helmets, high-visibility clothing, gloves, and steel-toed boots.

Ensure that all personnel involved in bulldozer operations wear the necessary PPE to protect against injuries and hazards.

5. Identify, obtain, and implement traffic management signage requirements: Assess the need for traffic management signage to control vehicular and pedestrian traffic around the worksite during bulldozer operations. Obtain the required signage and implement it according to regulatory standards to ensure the safety of workers and the public.

6. Select and check for faults, tools, equipment, and/or attachments: Choose the appropriate tools, equipment, and attachments needed for specific bulldozer tasks, such as blades, rippers, or winches. Conduct pre-operation checks to identify any faults or defects in the bulldozer, tools, or equipment. Rectify any issues or defects before commencing operations to prevent accidents or breakdowns.

7. Obtain and interpret emergency procedures: Familiarize yourself with emergency procedures for the worksite, including fire, accident, and medical emergencies. Understand the evacuation routes, assembly points, and communication protocols in case of an emergency. Be prepared to respond effectively to emergencies and provide assistance as needed to ensure the safety of personnel and property.

Accessing, interpreting, and applying dozer operations documentation involves several steps to ensure safe and compliant operations. Firstly, it's essential to access all relevant documentation related to bulldozer operations, which includes manufacturer's manuals, safety guidelines, and regulatory requirements mandated by local authorities or industry standards organizations. Ensuring that all relevant documents are readily available to personnel involved in bulldozer operations sets the foundation for safe practices.

Once the documentation is obtained, the next step is to interpret the information contained within it. This requires a careful reading and review of the documentation to understand the content thoroughly, including operating procedures, safety precautions, and legal obligations. Paying close attention to details such as equipment specifications, maintenance procedures, and safety guidelines is crucial. The information must be interpreted in a manner that is clear and comprehensible to all personnel involved in bulldozer operations to ensure effective implementation.

After interpreting the information, the guidelines outlined in the documentation must be applied to ensure compliance with industry standards and regulations. Proper operating procedures, safety precautions, and maintenance practices should be implemented as prescribed in the documentation. It's essential to ensure that all personnel are trained and equipped to adhere to these guidelines effectively to mitigate risks and hazards.

Regularly reviewing and updating the documentation is necessary to ensure ongoing compliance with changing regulations or industry standards. Conducting periodic audits or inspections helps verify that bulldozer operations align with the guidelines outlined in the documentation. Any non-compliance issues should be addressed promptly, and corrective actions implemented as necessary to maintain safe and compliant operations.

Obtaining, reading, interpreting, clarifying, and confirming work instructions is essential for ensuring that bulldozer operations are carried out efficiently and effectively. Firstly, obtain clear work instructions from supervisors or project managers before commencing any tasks. These instructions should outline the scope of work, objectives, and specific tasks to be performed using the bulldozer. Clear communication between supervisors and operators is crucial to ensure that everyone understands their roles and responsibilities.

Next, carefully read and interpret the provided work instructions. Pay close attention to details such as the location of the work site, the type of terrain, and any specific requirements or constraints. It's essential to fully understand the objectives and expectations outlined in the instructions to perform the tasks accurately.

If there are any uncertainties or ambiguities in the work instructions, seek clarification from supervisors or project managers. Asking questions and seeking clarification demonstrates a proactive approach to understanding the requirements and ensures that potential misunderstandings are addressed before work begins.

Once the work instructions have been understood, confirm the details to avoid misunderstandings or errors during bulldozer operations. This may involve summarizing the instructions verbally or in writing to ensure that both parties are on the same page. Confirming the details helps to establish clear expectations and reduces the likelihood of mistakes or rework.

In summary, obtaining clear work instructions, reading and interpreting them carefully, seeking clarification if needed, and confirming the details are essential steps in preparing for bulldozer operations. Effective communication and understanding between supervisors and operators are key to ensuring that tasks are performed safely, accurately, and in accordance with project requirements.

Identifying and addressing risks, hazards, and environmental issues is necessary for ensuring the safety of bulldozer operations and minimizing adverse impacts on the environment. Firstly, conduct a comprehensive risk assessment of the worksite before initiating bulldozer operations. This involves identifying potential hazards, such as uneven terrain, overhead obstacles, buried utilities, or nearby structures. Ad-

EARTHMOVING EQUIPMENT OPERATIONS

ditionally, assess risks associated with factors like weather conditions, visibility, and the presence of other workers or vehicles in the vicinity.

Hazards associated with bulldozer operation include:

1. Collision: Bulldozers are large and heavy machines that can cause significant damage or injury in the event of a collision with other vehicles, equipment, or personnel on the worksite.

2. Overturning: Bulldozers can tip over if operated on uneven or unstable terrain, leading to serious injury or death for the operator and nearby workers.

3. Entanglement: Moving parts of the bulldozer, such as tracks, blades, and attachments, pose a risk of entanglement, which can result in severe injuries or fatalities.

4. Falling objects: Materials or debris being pushed or lifted by the bulldozer can fall onto workers or bystanders, causing injuries or fatalities.

5. Crush injuries: Workers can be caught between the bulldozer and other objects or crushed by the machine itself, leading to severe injuries or death.

6. Visibility issues: Limited visibility from the operator's cab can make it difficult to see workers, equipment, or obstacles in the bulldozer's path, increasing the risk of accidents.

7. Environmental hazards: Bulldozers may encounter hazardous materials or conditions, such as chemical spills, unstable ground, or steep slopes, which can pose risks to the operator and the environment.

8. Noise and vibration: Prolonged exposure to high levels of noise and vibration from bulldozer operation can cause hearing loss,

musculoskeletal disorders, and other health problems for operators and nearby workers.

9. Fire and explosion: Bulldozers may encounter flammable materials or ignite fires due to friction or overheating, posing a risk of fire or explosion on the worksite.

10. Mechanical failures: Malfunctions or failures of bulldozer components, such as brakes, hydraulics, or steering systems, can lead to accidents or loss of control of the machine, resulting in injuries or fatalities.

Once hazards and risks have been identified, implement appropriate control measures to mitigate them effectively. This may include installing barriers or warning signage to alert personnel of potential dangers, establishing clear communication channels between operators and ground personnel, and implementing safety protocols such as wearing personal protective equipment (PPE) and adhering to designated operating procedures.

Environmental issues should also be taken into consideration during bulldozer operations. Minimize disturbance to sensitive areas, such as wetlands, water bodies, or wildlife habitats, by adhering to designated work zones and avoiding unnecessary disruption to the natural environment. Additionally, ensure compliance with environmental regulations and permits to mitigate potential impacts on air and water quality, soil erosion, and wildlife.

Regular monitoring and review of risk management strategies are essential to ensure ongoing effectiveness and address any emerging hazards or environmental concerns. By proactively identifying and addressing risks, hazards, and environmental issues, bulldozer operators can maintain a safe working environment and minimize their ecological footprint during construction activities.

Selecting and wearing personal protective equipment (PPE) is essential to ensure the safety of personnel engaged in bulldozer operations. To begin with, identify the specific PPE required for bulldozer operations based on the potential hazards and risks present in the worksite. This may include items such as helmets to protect against head injuries from falling objects or overhead hazards, high-visibility clothing to enhance visibility and minimize the risk of collisions with other vehicles or workers, gloves to protect hands from cuts, abrasions, or pinch points, and steel-toed boots to safeguard feet from crushing injuries or punctures.

Once the appropriate PPE has been identified, ensure that all personnel involved in bulldozer operations are equipped with the necessary protective gear. Provide clear instructions and guidelines on the correct use and maintenance of PPE to ensure maximum effectiveness and compliance with safety regulations.

Regularly inspect and replace PPE as needed to ensure that it remains in good condition and provides adequate protection against hazards. Encourage personnel to report any damaged or defective PPE promptly to facilitate timely replacement and prevent potential injuries.

Additionally, emphasize the importance of wearing PPE consistently and correctly throughout bulldozer operations, regardless of the duration or intensity of the task. Properly fitted and maintained PPE can significantly reduce the risk of injuries and ensure the safety and well-being of personnel working in and around bulldozers.

Identifying, obtaining, and implementing traffic management signage requirements is important to ensure the safety of workers and the public during bulldozer operations. Begin by conducting a thorough assessment of the worksite to determine the need for traffic management signage. Consider factors such as the volume of vehicular and pedestrian traffic, the layout of the worksite, and any potential hazards or obstructions that may affect the safe flow of traffic.

Once the signage requirements have been identified, obtain the necessary signage materials and equipment. This may include signs indicating speed limits, pedestrian crossings, lane closures, and other relevant information to guide traffic around the worksite safely.

Ensure that the traffic management signage meets regulatory standards and requirements specified by local authorities or industry guidelines. Select signs that are clearly visible, durable, and weather-resistant to ensure effectiveness in various environmental conditions.

Implement the traffic management signage according to the established plan and regulatory standards. Place signs strategically at key locations around the worksite to provide clear guidance and direction to vehicular and pedestrian traffic. Consider factors such as visibility, placement height, and distance from the worksite to maximize the effectiveness of the signage.

Regularly monitor and maintain the traffic management signage to ensure that it remains in good condition and continues to provide accurate information to road users. Replace or update signage as needed to address changing traffic patterns, worksite conditions, or regulatory requirements.

By identifying, obtaining, and implementing traffic management signage requirements effectively, organizations can enhance safety and minimize the risk of accidents or injuries during bulldozer operations.

Selecting and checking for faults, tools, equipment, and/or attachments for bulldozer operations is essential to ensure smooth and safe task execution. Begin by assessing the specific requirements of the bulldozer tasks to determine the appropriate tools, equipment, and attachments needed. Consider factors such as the type of terrain, the nature of the material being handled, and the desired outcome of the operation. Choose tools and attachments such as blades, rippers, or winches that are suitable for the task at hand.

Once the tools, equipment, and attachments have been selected, conduct thorough pre-operation checks to identify any faults or defects. Inspect the bulldozer, tools, and equipment for signs of wear and tear, damage, or malfunction. Pay close attention to critical components such as hydraulic systems, engine performance, and structural integrity.

During the inspection, check for leaks, loose or damaged components, worn-out parts, or any other issues that may affect the performance or safety of the bulldozer and associated equipment. Use manufacturer's manuals and guidelines to ensure that the inspection is comprehensive and systematic.

Rectify any identified faults or defects promptly before commencing operations. Repair or replace damaged or faulty components, tighten loose fittings, and address any other issues to ensure that the bulldozer and associated equipment are in optimal working condition. Document any maintenance or repairs performed for record-keeping and accountability purposes.

Regularly monitor and maintain the bulldozer, tools, equipment, and attachments to prevent issues from arising during operations. Conduct routine inspections and maintenance procedures as recommended by the manufacturer to prolong the lifespan of the equipment and ensure continued reliability and safety.

By selecting and checking for faults, tools, equipment, and attachments diligently, operators can minimize the risk of accidents, breakdowns, and delays during bulldozer operations, contributing to efficient and effective task execution.

Performing pre-start checks on a bulldozer is necessary to ensure its safe and efficient operation. Some common pre-start checks include:

1. Visual Inspection: Conduct a visual inspection of the bulldozer's exterior and interior components to check for any visible damage, leaks, or loose parts. Look for signs of wear and tear on the tracks, undercarriage, blade, hydraulic hoses, and engine

compartment.

2. Fluid Levels: Check the levels of essential fluids such as engine oil, hydraulic fluid, coolant, and fuel. Ensure that all fluids are at the recommended levels and top up if necessary. Look for any signs of leakage around fluid reservoirs or hoses.

3. Hydraulic Systems: Test the bulldozer's hydraulic systems by operating the controls to raise, lower, and tilt the blade. Listen for any unusual noises or vibrations that may indicate hydraulic issues. Check for leaks in the hydraulic lines and cylinders.

4. Electrical Systems: Test the lights, gauges, and warning indicators to ensure they are functioning properly. Check the battery terminals for corrosion and ensure that all electrical connections are secure.

5. Controls and Instruments: Check the operation of all controls, levers, and switches to ensure they are functioning smoothly. Test the steering, brakes, transmission, and blade controls to verify their responsiveness.

6. Undercarriage and Tracks: Inspect the undercarriage and tracks for signs of damage, excessive wear, or misalignment. Check the track tension and adjust it if necessary to ensure proper tracking and alignment.

7. Safety Equipment: Verify the presence and condition of safety features such as seat belts, rollover protection structures (ROPS), and fire extinguishers. Ensure that all safety equipment is in good working order and readily accessible to the operator.

8. Documentation and Paperwork: Review the bulldozer's maintenance records, service history, and inspection logs to ensure

that it has been properly maintained and serviced. Confirm that all required documentation, including operating manuals and safety guidelines, is present and up to date.

To ensure optimal performance and prevent potential issues, it's crucial to regularly monitor and adjust the track tension on a tracked bulldozer. A loose track can risk slipping off the rollers, while excessive tension may lead to engine strain, power loss, and track damage.

Follow these steps to adjust the tracks on a bulldozer:

1. Bring the bulldozer to a gentle stop without using the brakes.

2. Park the bulldozer and switch off the engine.

3. Clear away any dirt or debris from the track surface.

4. Place a straight edge or string from the grousers on the front idler to the sprocket.

5. Measure the distance from the string to the grouser tip at the lowest point of the sag. If there's a carrier roller between the idler and sprocket, measure both sides and calculate the average.

6. Refer to the operator's manual to determine the recommended sag for your specific bulldozer model, typically ranging from 2 to 3 inches.

7. If adjustment is necessary, locate the hydraulic adjustment valve.

8. To tighten the track, apply grease to the valve and operate the machine back and forth. Re-measure until the desired tension is achieved.

9. To loosen the track, gradually release grease by turning the

valve. Close the valve when the correct track tension is reached.

Note that the specific procedures may vary depending on the make and model of your bulldozer. For precise instructions tailored to your equipment, consult the operator's manual provided by the manufacturer. For example, if you need guidance on adjusting the tracks of a John Deere dozer, refer to the corresponding section in the operator's manual.

Obtaining and interpreting emergency procedures is essential for ensuring the safety of personnel and property on a worksite. Here's how to do it effectively:

1. Access Emergency Procedures: Obtain copies of the emergency procedures specific to your worksite from supervisors, safety officers, or posted signage. These procedures typically include protocols for various emergencies such as fires, accidents, medical incidents, or natural disasters.

2. Review Documentation: Read and review the emergency procedures thoroughly to understand the steps to take in different emergency scenarios. Pay close attention to details such as evacuation routes, assembly points, emergency contact information, and specific actions to be taken in each type of emergency.

3. Seek Clarification: If any aspects of the emergency procedures are unclear or ambiguous, seek clarification from supervisors, safety officers, or colleagues who are familiar with the procedures. It's crucial to have a clear understanding of the protocols to ensure an effective response in case of an emergency.

4. Interpret Procedures: Interpret the emergency procedures in the context of your specific worksite and job responsibilities. Consider how the procedures apply to your role and what ac-

tions you need to take to fulfill your responsibilities during an emergency situation.

5. Be Prepared to Respond: Familiarize yourself with the location of emergency exits, fire extinguishers, first aid kits, and other emergency equipment on the worksite. Be prepared to respond promptly and appropriately in case of an emergency, following the procedures outlined in the documentation.

6. Practice Drills: Participate in emergency preparedness drills or training sessions conducted on the worksite to practice implementing the emergency procedures. Practice drills help reinforce knowledge of the procedures and ensure that personnel are prepared to respond effectively in real emergency situations.

7. Stay Informed: Stay informed about any updates or changes to the emergency procedures and be proactive in keeping your knowledge up to date. Regularly review the procedures and communicate any updates or revisions to colleagues to ensure everyone is informed and prepared.

Inspecting and starting the bulldozer involves several steps to ensure safe and efficient operation:

- Begin by scanning the exterior of the machine for any visible signs of damage, such as cracks in the windows or dents on the body. Check the blade and ripper for cracks and wear, recording your observations on a pre-operation checklist sheet. This step is particularly important if you're renting the bulldozer to protect yourself from liability for pre-existing damages.

- Next, check the bulldozer for any oil or hydraulic fluid leaks. Look for oil leaks on the ground under the engine and inspect the lift cylinders and hydraulic hoses for leaks or cracks. Refer to the user manual for guidance on repairing any identified leaks.

- Ensure that all door and hood latches are securely locked in place to prevent them from opening during operation due to vibration. Close the hood and doors securely, giving them a few tugs to confirm that they're properly latched. If a door opens while operating, park the bulldozer before attempting to close it.

- Maintain proper levels of fuel, oil, engine coolant, transmission oil, and hydraulic fluid. Wipe the oil dipstick clean before checking levels, and ensure that the engine is cooled down before inspecting the coolant. Refer to the owner's manual for specifications on fluid levels and how to check them accurately.

- Use the safety rails and steps to climb into the cab of the bulldozer. Exercise caution while climbing to avoid slipping, especially considering the height of the machine. Be mindful of the large teeth on the tracks to prevent your boots from getting trapped.

- Once seated in the cab, buckle the seatbelt securely around your waist to prevent bouncing around while operating the bulldozer. Replace the seatbelt if it's damaged or faulty.

- Turn the ignition key to the right, ensuring that your foot is on the brake if required by the machine. Listen for the engine to turn over and begin idling, being attentive to any abnormal sounds like clanking or squealing. Keeping your foot on the brake prevents unwanted movement.

- Allow the bulldozer to warm up for a few minutes before operating to ensure optimal performance. This allows the oil to lubricate all parts and the cooling system to reach its operational temperature. Monitor the temperature and fluid gauges to ensure they enter the safe zone while the engine warms up.

Operating a Bulldozer

Moving the bulldozer forward and backward involves a series of steps to ensure smooth and safe operation:

- Begin by adjusting the speed control on the left joystick. The method of adjusting speed control may vary depending on the bulldozer model, such as a button or a small wheel. Gradually decrease the speed to ensure smooth adjustment. Some newer models feature a digital gauge indicating when the speed is set to zero.

- Turn the throttle knob to the run position. Rotate the throttle knob to the right to increase engine power. Some knobs may have symbols like a turtle for idle mode and a rabbit for run mode. Adjusting the throttle while keeping the speed down is crucial for proper engine control.

- Shift the left joystick forward for drive or backward for reverse. Handle the joystick gently to engage the transmission smoothly, ensuring no damage occurs. A subtle click should be felt when the transmission is properly engaged.

- Manoeuvre the left joystick left or right to control the bulldozer's direction. Once in drive or reverse, moving the joystick dictates the machine's movement direction. Exercise caution and remain vigilant of your surroundings to prevent accidents.

- Verify the functionality of the controls by testing each direction individually. Ensure smooth and responsive movement without any sticking or jerking. Familiarize yourself with the machine's response before attempting faster speeds.

- Utilize the foot brake to halt the bulldozer's movement when necessary. Apply pressure with your right foot on the foot brake, akin to braking in a car. Use the foot brake only for immediate stops, and exercise caution due to its sensitive nature.

By following these steps, you can effectively operate the bulldozer forward and backward while maintaining safety and control.

Operating the blade and ripper of the bulldozer requires careful control and coordination:

- Adjust the height of the blade by moving the right joystick forward or backward. Hold the joystick with your right hand and push it forward to lower the blade. Conversely, pull the joystick backward to raise the blade. Ensure smooth movement of the blade without any abrupt jerks. Avoid placing the blade on the ground until you are ready to start pushing dirt.

- Control the tilt of the blade by moving the right joystick horizontally. Shift the joystick to the right to tilt the blade in that direction and to the left to tilt it to the left. This tilting capability allows you to control which side of the blade is closer to the ground. It proves particularly useful when working on uneven terrain to achieve the desired dirt scraping.

- Adjust the angle of the blade using the angle control knob to fan it either to the right or left. Utilize your thumb to manipulate the knob in your preferred direction. Depending on the bulldozer model, this adjustment can be done via a button system or a small dial. Angling the blade determines the direction in which the dirt will flow, either to the right or left side of the bulldozer.

- Activate the ripper by moving the ripper joystick backward. Grip the joystick with your right hand and adjust it up or down as needed. Typically located behind the right joystick closer to the operator, the ripper features forks that penetrate the ground to loosen hard dirt or materials. Note that not all bulldozers are equipped with a ripper attachment, and its activation may not always be necessary for the task at hand.

Operating under diverse conditions presents various challenges that require careful consideration and precautionary measures. When resuming operations after rainfall, it's essential to exercise caution due to the altered conditions. Particularly, when approaching road shoulders or cliffs, which may have become unstable, vigilance is crucial.

Navigating uneven terrain or areas with obstacles necessitates adherence to specific guidelines:

- When traversing uneven ground, maintain a low speed and avoid sudden changes in direction to ensure stability.

- Where feasible, steer clear of large obstacles like rocks or fallen trees. Alternatively, utilize the equipment to remove them or manoeuvre around them.

- In cases where obstacles are unavoidable, shift the gear to low, reduce speed, and cross over them carefully to minimize impact.

Certain situations demand additional attention:

- Before crossing bridges, verify load limits.

- Following earthquakes or blasting activities, confirm ground stability and ensure no unexploded charges remain.

Unexpected increases in speed pose risks:

- When dumping soil over a cliff or passing incline summits, sudden acceleration can occur. To counter this, promptly reduce speed using the decelerator pedal or fuel control lever.

- Avoid mounting obstacles at an angle or disengaging steering clutches when crossing obstacles.

Operating near edges or road shoulders requires heightened vigilance:
- Extreme caution should be exercised when working near the edge of cliffs or road shoulders to avoid accidental falls.
- On river embankments or piled soil areas, be wary of potential sinking due to machine weight or vibration.

Inclines necessitate specific operating techniques:
- Always travel directly up or down inclines to prevent rollovers or sideways slipping.
- When descending, utilize the engine and lower gear as brakes. Avoid coasting with the gear shift lever in neutral.

Operating in water or muddy terrain requires careful assessment:
- Before entering water or muddy areas, assess soil condition and water depth and flow speed to prevent exceeding safe limits.
- In case of mud entrapment, avoid spinning tracks or rocking the machine excessively. Instead, reduce load by raising the blade and exit slowly.

In forested regions, caution is paramount:
- Avoid mounting fallen trees or logs and exercise caution on slippery surfaces like leaf piles.
- Prioritize frequent cleaning of the belly plate and radiator to prevent debris accumulation.

Operating at night introduces additional challenges:
- Ensure adequate lighting for visibility.

- Beware of misjudging distances and heights at night, and exercise caution in foggy or misty conditions.

- Stop work in poor visibility conditions and wait for improved visibility to resume operations.

In snowy conditions:
- Refrain from sudden stops using the steering brake on inclines; lowering equipment is a safer braking method.

- Utilize seat belts during operation, as mandated by ROPS standards, to enhance safety.

Stockpiling with a bulldozer involves several steps to efficiently and safely store materials for later use. Here's a guide on how to stockpile with a bulldozer:

1. Assess the Site: Begin by inspecting the site where the stockpile will be located. Consider factors such as accessibility for removal and future operations, distance from the proposed stockpile to the work area, and whether any clearing is needed before stockpiling.

2. Choose Stockpiling Method: Select the appropriate stockpiling method based on factors like material type and ground/weather conditions. Common methods include windrow method and forming a mound for storage.

3. Prepare the Area: Clear the designated area for the stockpile if necessary, ensuring it is free from obstacles and debris that could interfere with stockpiling operations.

4. Start Stockpiling: Begin by pushing material with the bulldozer to form the initial windrow or mound. Use the bulldozer's blade to control the placement and shape of the stockpile.

5. **Build Height and Length:** Continue pushing material to the top of the stockpile, gradually increasing its height and length. Use successive passes to add more material, ensuring that the stockpile is built up evenly and compactly.

6. **Level and Compact:** Once the desired height and length are achieved, use the bulldozer to level and compact the top of the stockpile. This helps seal the surface and prevent moisture absorption.

7. **Ensure Accessibility:** Ensure that the stockpile is accessible to loading machinery if it needs to be loaded out later. Position the stockpile in a location that allows easy access for loading equipment.

8. **Follow Safety Precautions:** Throughout the stockpiling process, follow all necessary safety precautions, such as maintaining the correct angle of the stockpile, ensuring there is sufficient material under the bulldozer's tracks for stability, and practicing safe reversing manoeuvres.

9. **Minimize Passes:** Aim to minimize the number of passes required to build the stockpile efficiently. Take a methodical approach to the job to reduce unnecessary movements and optimize productivity.

When choosing a stockpiling method with a bulldozer, it's essential to consider various factors such as the type of material being stored and the prevailing ground and weather conditions. Different methods offer distinct advantages and are suitable for specific scenarios. Here's a breakdown of the two common stockpiling methods:

1. **Windrow Method:** The windrow method involves creating long, narrow piles or rows of material. This method is particularly

useful when dealing with materials like soil, gravel, or debris that need to be stored in an organized manner. Windrows are typically formed by pushing the material with the bulldozer into long rows, allowing for easy access and retrieval when needed. It's important to note that drainage should be considered to prevent water buildup, especially if the material is susceptible to erosion or degradation.

2. Mound Formation: Forming a mound involves creating a single, large pile of material. This method is often used for storing bulkier materials such as earth, rocks, or construction debris. Mounds are built by continuously adding layers of material and compacting them using the bulldozer's blade. Mounds are ideal for maximizing storage capacity in areas with limited space, as they can be built upwards rather than spreading out horizontally. Additionally, mounds offer better protection against moisture absorption compared to windrows, as the compacted surface helps seal the pile.

When selecting the appropriate stockpiling method, operators should assess factors such as the volume and type of material to be stored, the available space, drainage conditions, and the need for accessibility. By carefully considering these factors, operators can choose the most suitable method to ensure efficient storage and easy retrieval of materials while minimizing the risk of damage or deterioration.

Changing Environments

After rainfall, it's crucial to be aware that conditions may have changed, requiring caution when resuming operations. Exercise extra care when approaching road shoulders or cliffs, as they may become unstable due to the rain. Additionally, when operating in uneven terrain or areas with obstacles, remember to maintain a slower speed and avoid sudden changes in direction to mitigate risks effectively.

To minimize risks, it's advisable to steer clear of large rocks, fallen trees, tree stumps, and similar obstacles whenever feasible. Either utilize working equipment to clear them or navigate around them. In instances where avoidance isn't possible, switch the gear shift lever to low gear, decrease speed, and approach the obstacle. Prior to the front of the machine tipping down, further reduce speed to mitigate the impact of hitting the ground.

When encountering obstacles that cannot be avoided, it's essential to take certain precautions. Before crossing bridges, ensure to check their load limits for safety. Additionally, following earthquakes, verify that the ground remains stable, and after blasting activities, confirm the absence of any unexploded charges to prevent potential hazards.

When the machine reaches the moment of dumping soil over a cliff or crossing the summit of an incline, there's a sudden surge in speed, which can be hazardous. To mitigate this risk, promptly apply pressure to the decelerator pedal or adjust the fuel control lever to decrease the speed. Additionally, it's crucial to never approach obstacles at an angle while mounting over them, and avoid disengaging one steering clutch for obstacle traversal.

When disposing of soil over a cliff, it's essential to follow a specific method. Initially, refrain from directly dumping the first excavated soil over the cliff edge; instead, utilize subsequent excavated soil to gradually push the earlier piles over. Take care not to inadvertently approach the edge, ensuring a perpendicular approach while leaving a raised lip (bern) to facilitate the process. When working near cliff edges or road shoulders, exercise utmost caution, especially when there's a risk of the machine tipping over the side. Avoid any accidental approaches to the cliff or road shoulder edges to mitigate potential hazards effectively.

When operating in areas constructed with piled soil such as river embankments, there's a risk that the weight or vibrations from the machine could lead to sinking. Hence, exercise extreme caution when working in such locations. When navigating inclines, keep the following considerations in mind:

- Operating On Inclines: When traversing an incline, always ascend or descend directly along its slope. Avoid traversing horizontally or diagonally across the incline to prevent potential rollovers or sideways slipping of the machine.

- Descending An Incline: Utilize the engine as a brake and shift to a lower gear when descending an incline. If additional speed control is necessary, engage the steering brake. Never descend an incline with the gear shift lever in NEUTRAL.

- Avoid Turning On An Incline: Whenever feasible, refrain from making turns while on an incline to prevent potential rollovers or sideways slipping of the machine. When operating in water or muddy areas, it's essential to consider the following points:

When working in water or crossing shallow areas, begin by assessing the condition of the riverbed soil, as well as the depth and flow rate of the water. Proceed cautiously, ensuring not to exceed the allowable depth.

When the machine becomes trapped in mud, attempting to boost engine speed or rocking the machine back and forth won't be effective. Instead, raise the blade to alleviate the load and cautiously drive out at a slow pace. Occasionally, rocking the bulldozer back and forth might aid in breaking the suction grip.

In forested areas, it's important to avoid mounting fallen trees or logs, as well as being cautious when navigating through piles of leaves or branches due to their slippery nature. Regularly clean the belly plate and radiator of any debris to maintain optimal performance. Before ascending or descending inclines, carefully select a suitable travel speed and refrain from changing gears while on the incline to ensure stability. If the engine stalls on an incline, use the brake to halt the machine, engage the park brake, lower any raised equipment, shift the gear lever to NEUTRAL, and restart the engine. When manoeuvring through narrow spaces, exercise caution regarding side and overhead clearances, avoiding contact with obstacles. If needed, have someone outside the machine provide guidance.

When working during nighttime hours, it's important to consider the following factors: ensure the implementation of a sufficient lighting system to maintain visibility. Additionally, bear in mind that it's easier to misjudge distances and heights of objects and terrain in low light conditions, thus exercising extra caution is necessary to prevent errors.

In conditions of poor visibility such as fog, mist, or smoke, it's crucial to exercise heightened caution and assess the safety of operations beforehand. If visibility falls below a safe threshold, it's advisable to halt work and wait for conditions to improve. Additionally, even minor inclines can lead to unexpected side slipping, necessitating careful operation and extreme caution in such areas.

When working in snowy conditions, it's essential to adhere to specific precautions. Avoid using the steering brake to abruptly stop on inclines; instead, employ the more effective method of lowering the working equipment. Additionally, during operation, ensure to utilize the seat belt if the equipment is equipped with one, as it's a mandatory safety measure in ROPS standard equipment.

When leveling onto a fill, it's important to avoid advancing the fill at maximum height, as this can diminish downhill travel and complicate maintaining the desired grade. Instead, gradually taper the fill to zero height while preserving its full width, which ensures consistent downhill travel and facilitates achieving the intended grade line with greater ease. Additionally, this approach aids in compacting the fill effectively to achieve desired stability.

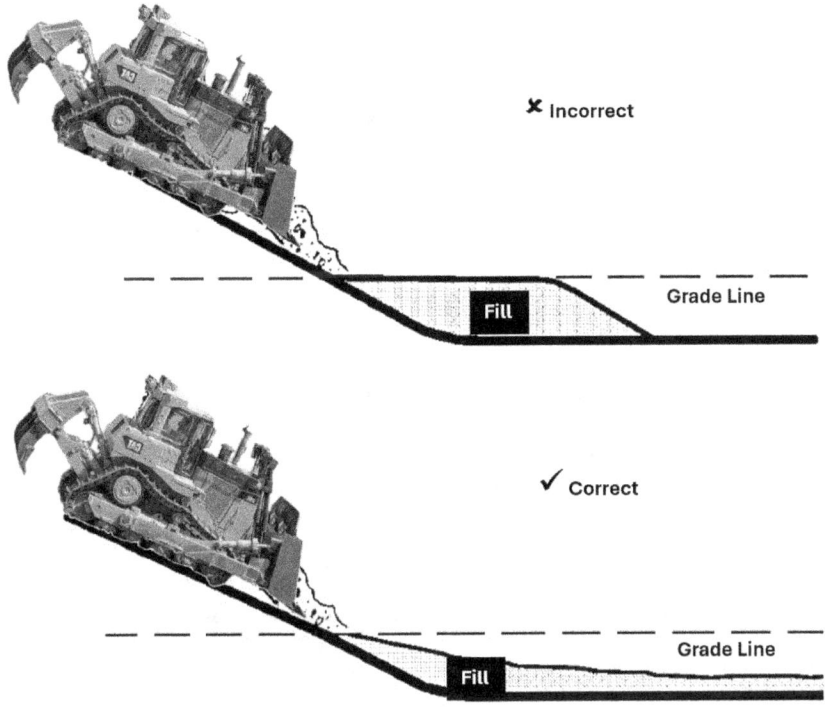

Figure 75: Levelling onto a fill.

When leveling raised areas such as hills or mounds, avoid excavating dirt in horizontal layers. Depending on the incline angle, soil pushed from these areas may be necessary to construct a ramp with a suitable incline, allowing the bulldozer to access the grade line on the downward slope. Remember to begin at the top and load dirt towards the fill while maintaining the downward grade, as this approach saves time, fuel, and engine power.

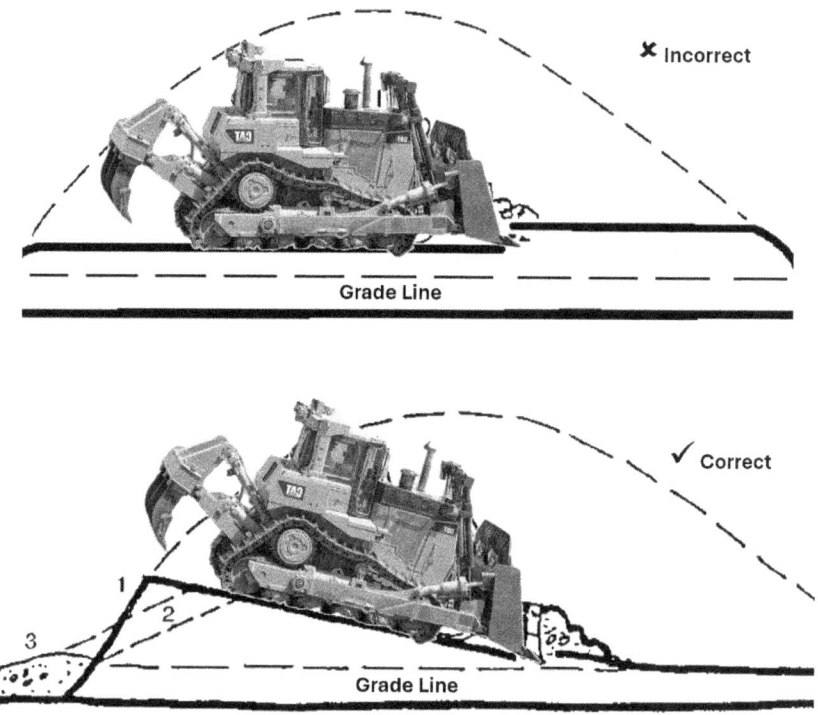

Figure 76: Levelling raised areas.

Building an embankment, such as a levee used for water containment, follows a construction method akin to building a small dam. When employing a bulldozer for levee construction, several steps are essential. First, the site must undergo vegetation clearance, followed by the careful selection of suitable material, typically impermeable clay, for the levee. Utilizing the bulldozer, this selected material is pushed into layers to form the levee wall, as shown in Figure 77.

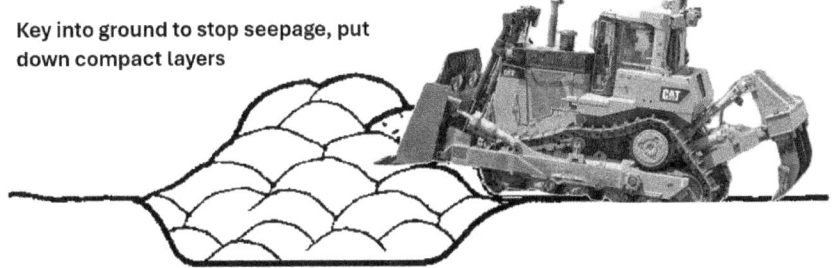

Figure 77: Constructing an embankment.

Pushing material into a levee wall: As the levee wall increases in height, the bulldozer can be employed to compact the material effectively by rolling each layer as it's added.

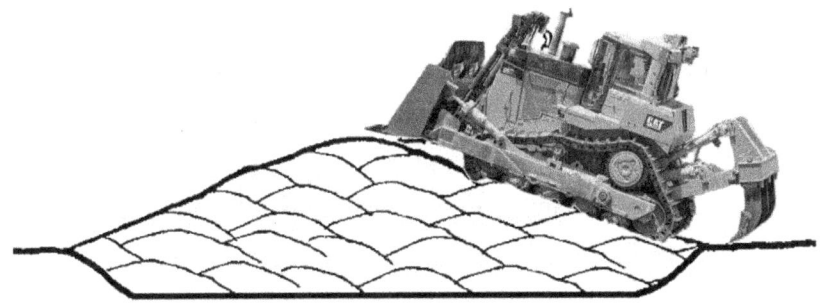

Figure 78: Pushing material into a levee wall.

Creating a stockpile involves accumulating material into a mound for future use. The shape and size of the stockpile are influenced by the type of soil being piled. For instance, sand-dominated materials typically result in long, low piles, while clay-based materials allow for higher stacks. In wet conditions, it's crucial to leave the top of the stockpile undulating to facilitate water collection and absorption into the material, aiding in spreading and compaction later on. Steep sides should be avoided to prevent erosion and material loss. The method of removal dictates the size and slope of the stockpile, with considerations for safety; for instance, using a scraper necessitates keeping the pile long and low to prevent hazards. Material separation according to job specifications is essential to prevent mixing, unless materials are being stockpiled for disposal purposes.

Single layer stockpiles are created by pushing material up to the designated endpoint, continuing this process for a distance of no more than 50 meters. Successive rows of material are then added until the desired volume is achieved. This method involves forming a pile of material during the initial pass, with the machine operating in low gear and the blade fully engaged as it approaches the starting point of the stockpile. The first pass should conclude before reaching the anticipated end of the stockpile to account for potential overflow. Subsequent passes are made in higher gears, with caution exercised while reversing. This process continues until the required volume of material is accumulated. Single layer stockpiles are typically employed in "Borrow Pits" or small quarries for future use or maintenance purposes, with no compaction applied. The peaks of these stockpiles remain intact, allowing rainwater to collect and seep down, keeping the material damp for extended periods, which aids in spreading and compaction upon use.

EARTHMOVING EQUIPMENT OPERATIONS 315

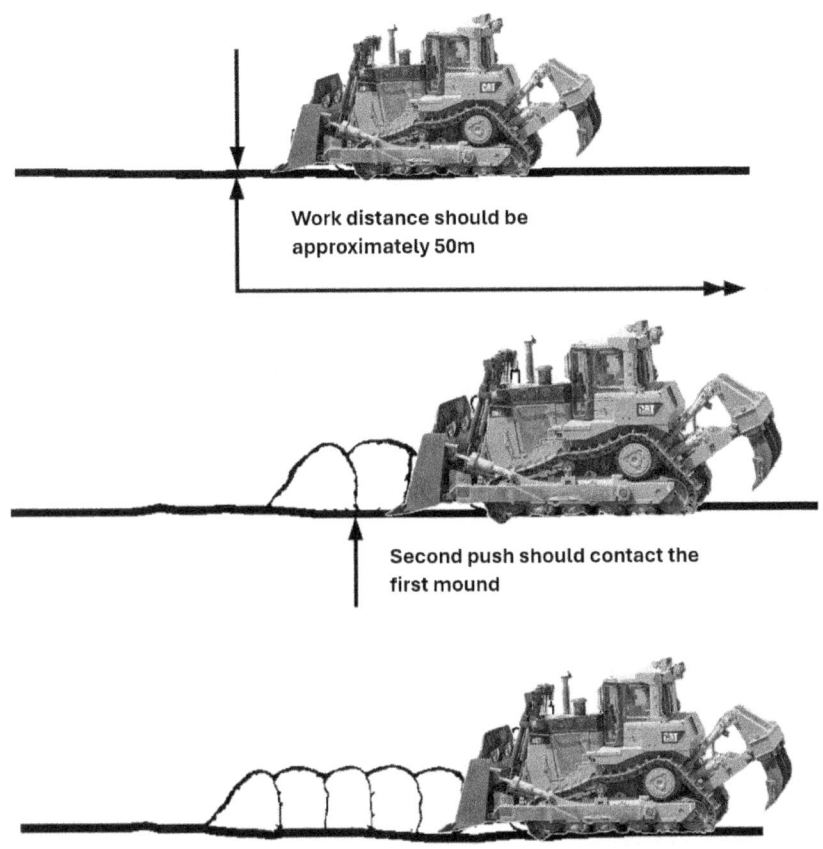

Figure 79: Single layer stockpile procedure.

Multi-layer stockpiles are constructed in stages, beginning with the formation of a single layer stockpile, typically extending to about three-quarters of the material length. The tops of the pile are then pushed over to create a ramp, facilitating the addition of material to the top of the stockpile. As the pile height increases, the ramp must be extended backward towards the completed length of the stockpile until further material cannot be added without extending the pile further. Maintaining a gentle slope on the ramp is essential to optimize production efficiency and prevent excessive compaction of the material, which could hinder removal later on. Another crucial consideration is the separation of material, with larger particles settling at the bottom and smaller particles remaining on top as material is pushed over the end of the pile. Utilizing the multi-layer method minimizes particle separation and is particularly suitable for stockpiling road building materials. When reversing down the stockpile, it's important to maintain power and avoid coasting. As the stockpiling nears completion, the final step involves pushing material up the ramp and leaving it on the ramp path, with subsequent passes incorporating the previous material until the entire ramp is also stockpiled. Finally, leveling and compacting the top of the stockpile is necessary to seal it and prevent moisture absorption.

EARTHMOVING EQUIPMENT OPERATIONS

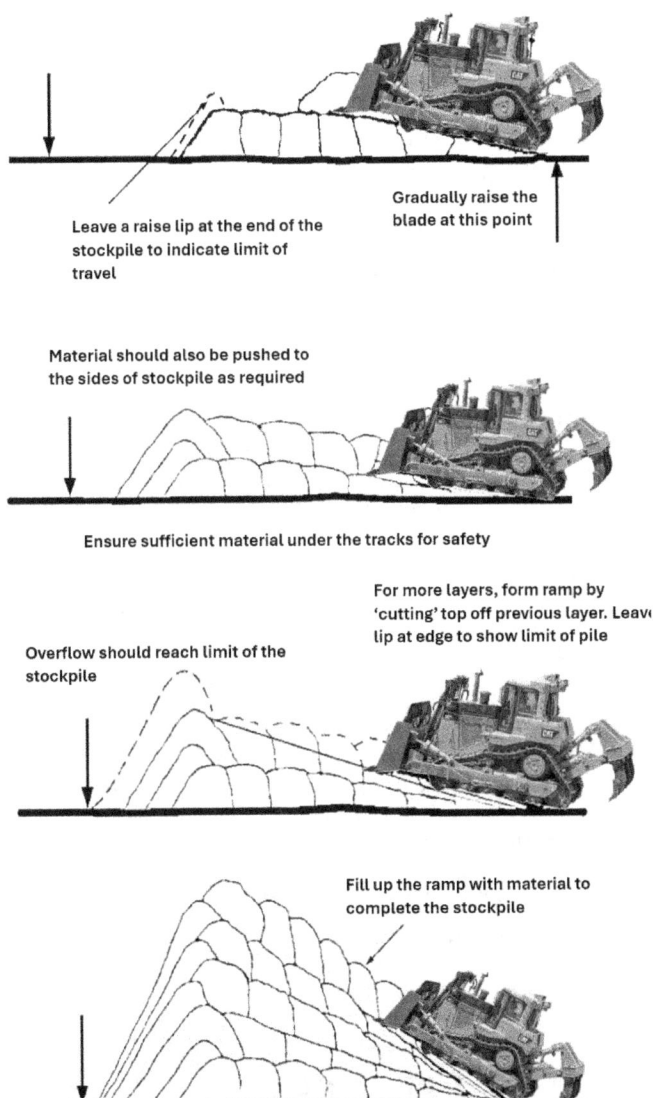

Figure 80: Multilayer stockpiling technique.

To effectively spread a stockpile, maintain the blade slightly above the original surface and drive the machine through the heap, ensuring the blade picks up a full load of material across the job. It's crucial to gradually lose material before reaching the boundaries of the fill area to achieve even distribution. Pushing with only a partial blade full is uneconomical, so if material depletes quickly due to deep fill areas, backing up to gather another full blade load is recommended. Any leftover material from the first pass will be picked up and spread during subsequent passes until all material is evenly distributed. On the final pass, lose all the material across the entire area, leaving it level and contained within the fill boundaries.

When breaking down stockpiles from the side, avoid undercutting material to prevent collapse onto the machine. Constructing a ramp to the pile's summit and pushing downwards is an effective method, requiring attention to maintaining sufficient material under the tracks and avoiding loose edges. Always exercise caution while reversing and remain aware of other machinery and personnel in the area.

For smaller stockpiles, the preferred method is to push down one side first, followed by the other side, leaving the middle portion untouched to ensure an even level surface. It's essential not to cut into the subsoil during spreading to prevent material mixing.

With larger stockpiles, there's a risk of undercutting and collapse when pushing from the sides. In such cases, it's necessary to break down the pile from the top by constructing a ramp for safe access. Once on top of the pile, downhill passes can be made through the layers to the bottom for efficient dismantling.

Completing Bulldozer Operations

Upon completion of use, it is essential to follow proper procedures:
- Park the bulldozer on solid, flat ground, activate the parking brake, and disengage drive and controls.

- Shut down the engine according to the manufacturer's guidelines.

- Remove any debris or material from the track assembly.
- Refill the fuel tank to the appropriate level to ensure readiness for the next operation.

Turning off the bulldozer involves several steps to ensure proper shutdown and safety:

- Lower the blade and ripper gently onto the ground using the designated joysticks for each. This action reduces stress on the machine's components, ensuring longevity.
- Adjust the throttle knob to the lowest position by turning it to the left with your fingers. This step ensures that the next operator will find the machine in the correct starting condition, and it prevents potential engine damage.
- Shift the machine's transmission into neutral by moving the left joystick to the neutral position, located between drive and reverse. Leaving the bulldozer in drive or reverse can hinder proper starting, so shifting gently is essential to avoid damaging the transmission.
- Activate the parking brake by pressing the parking brake button with your hand. Engaging the parking brake is a vital safety measure after using heavy machinery, although its location may vary depending on the bulldozer model.
- Turn the key off by grasping it and turning it to the left or off position. If leaving the job site for the day, remove the key to prevent theft or accidents involving inexperienced operators. Handle the key gently to avoid breakage.
- Exit the machine carefully by unbuckling your seatbelt, gathering your belongings, and using the safety rails and steps to

descend to the ground. Exercise caution as some parts of the machine may be hot, ensuring you place your hands and feet safely. Employ the same safety precautions when exiting as when entering the machine.

Chapter Seven

Water Truck Operations

Water trucks stand apart from conventional trucks due to their specialized tank configurations, custom chassis designs, and mounting equipment. They play a crucial role in mining and construction operations, serving various purposes such as dust control, compaction, and fire prevention.

A water truck driver is tasked with operating a water truck primarily for construction projects, oil rigs, and crews in remote areas, responsible for filling the truck at designated locations and transporting the water to the construction site to hydrate machinery or clear dusty roads. They adhere to company directives for water transportation, often navigating diverse terrain and weather conditions. Additional responsibilities include conducting daily inspections of the water truck, documenting inspection outcomes, ensuring compliance with local and national safety regulations, utilizing machinery for loading and unloading, and navigating remote areas using maps to locate specific destinations.

In terms of functionality, water trucks vary in size and design, with some capable of carrying up to 36,000 litres of water. Certain models are specifically tailored for mining applications, featuring off-road tyres, safety enhancements, and reinforced structures for stability on rough terrain.

The filling and spraying capabilities of water trucks differ depending on their intended use. Typically, filler pipes are positioned on the truck's side or through an opening atop the tank, while spray nozzles can be found at the front, side, or rear, controlled from within the driver's cab. Additional features such as drip bars, hose reels, and water cannons further enhance their versatility.

Water trucks predominantly serve purposes like dust control, road construction, and water delivery for irrigation and potable use. Unlike conventional trucks designed for static loads, water trucks are engineered to transport liquids, necessitating specific designs to safeguard both the vehicle and its tank.

These trucks come in various sizes ranging from 1,000 to 50,000 litres and are equipped with pumps, sprayers, hose reels, fill points, and outlets tailored to their respective applications.

In mining and construction contexts, water trucks are indispensable for dust suppression, crucial in mitigating hazards to workers posed by dry and dusty conditions. They also facilitate compaction by moistening soil, making it easier to compress and achieve a smooth surface, often working in tandem with large roller compactors.

Figure 81: Jabula Transport Bell 35 000 Litre Water Tanker. Bob Adams from Amanzimtoti, South Africa, CC BY-SA 2.0, via Wikimedia Commons.

Given the arid climate of certain work sites, effective dust management is imperative to mitigate environmental hazards and the associated risks to personnel. Unsealed roads necessitate regular spraying to prevent dust accumulation, while water is essential in road construction to aid soil compaction.

Water trucks are deployed in the mining sector primarily for dust suppression and environmental restoration efforts. Typically utilized off-road, these trucks must adhere to rigorous mine specification standards.

Water trucks are frequently utilized for delivering potable water, ensuring it meets safety standards for drinking. This requires tanks approved for food-grade applications.

Water trucks play a crucial role in both proactive and reactive firefighting efforts. Although not designed explicitly for firefighting, they contribute significantly by supplying water to fire trucks at the frontline. In remote inland mining operations, water trucks also help prevent the spread of fires and support firefighting efforts during bushfires.

Additionally, they may be employed to wet areas pre-emptively during severe fire danger conditions.

Utilizing professional water truck services offers numerous advantages for the construction industry, often overlooked initially. Besides facilitating high-pressure water cleaning, water trucks can address and prevent various complex issues. Considerations include:

1. Dust Control: Water trucks effectively minimize the impact of dust by preventing its buildup and clearing airborne particles, thereby safeguarding the health of workers and the environment.

2. Tailored Solutions: Water trucks equipped with heavy water and solutions incorporating liquid polymer surfactants penetrate soil deeply, pre-emptively addressing dust issues and averting interruptions in construction processes.

3. Water Usage Risks: Proper handling of high-pressure hoses and quality water pumps by trained professionals is crucial to avoid unnecessary water damage and wastage. This ensures targeted water delivery to the site with minimal overflow, preventing surrounding areas from being inundated with mud.

4. Workplace Safety: Water truck hire is vital for maintaining emergency protocols, minimizing fire risks, and mitigating potential damages. Adherence to stringent workplace health and safety standards is essential, particularly concerning heavy machinery and road works, to mitigate accidents and ensure a safe working environment.

"Side spray" refers to a feature or functionality commonly found in water trucks or irrigation systems. This feature allows the water to be sprayed horizontally from the side of the truck or equipment.

In practical terms, side spray is beneficial for various applications. For instance, it can be used to water a row of plants growing alongside roads. By spraying water horizontally, the side spray ensures that the plants receive adequate moisture without wastefully spraying water onto the road surface.

Figure 82: Water truck side sprays crawlerway ahead of CT-2 and MLP-2. Cory Huston, Public domain, via Wikimedia Commons.medium confidence

Additionally, side spray is useful for dust suppression purposes. When water trucks are equipped with side spray capabilities, they can effectively dampen dusty areas alongside roads or construction sites. This helps mitigate airborne dust particles, contributing to improved air quality and creating safer working conditions for personnel.

Figure 83: Covil cleaning with side spray. Lanremabaoamne, CC BY-SA 3.0, via Wikimedia Commons.

Side spray functionality offers versatility and efficiency, making it a valuable feature for a range of applications, including watering plants and dust suppression.

"Rear spray" refers to a feature commonly found in water trucks or similar vehicles, where the water spraying mechanism is located at the rear end of the truck.

In practical terms, rear spray functionality serves various purposes. One primary application is dust suppression on dirt roads and construction sites. By positioning the spray nozzles at the rear of the vehicle, the water can be effectively dispersed behind the truck as it moves forward. This helps dampen the road or site surface, reducing the amount of airborne dust particles stirred up by vehicular traffic or construction activities.

Figure 84: Rear spray used for dust suppression. , CC BY-SA 3.0, via Wikimedia Commons.

The rear spray is particularly useful in areas where dust control is essential for environmental reasons or to maintain visibility and safety. By efficiently distributing water across the surface, the rear spray assists in keeping dust levels manageable and minimizes the impact of dust-related hazards on workers, nearby residents, and the surrounding environment.

The rear spray feature enhances the versatility and effectiveness of water trucks, making them valuable assets for tasks such as dust suppression on dirt roads and construction sites.

A "dribble bar" is a specialized attachment or component often found on water trucks or similar vehicles used for road maintenance and construction.

The dribble bar is designed to distribute water evenly and deeply penetrate the ground surface. This makes it particularly effective for tasks such as washing roads and soaking the road base.

Figure 85: Water truck with dribble bar. Hunini, CC BY-SA 3.0, via Wikimedia Commons.

In practical terms, the dribble bar releases water in a controlled manner along its length, allowing the water to seep into the road surface or base material. This helps to thoroughly wet the area, facilitating cleaning of the road surface by removing debris, mud, or other contaminants. Additionally, soaking the road base with water can help improve its stability and compaction, ensuring a solid foundation for the road.

The dribble bar is a valuable tool for road maintenance and construction activities, providing efficient and effective water distribution for tasks such as cleaning roads and preparing the road base.

"Full rear and side spray" refers to a comprehensive water spraying system typically found on water trucks or similar vehicles. This system allows for simultaneous spraying from both the rear and the sides of the vehicle.

In practical terms, full rear and side spray capabilities provide extensive coverage and efficient water distribution, making it suitable for large-scale tasks that require quick completion.

For example, in construction or road maintenance projects where extensive areas need to be watered or dampened for dust suppression, the full rear and side spray system ensures rapid and thorough coverage. The rear spray covers the area behind the vehicle, while the side spray covers the areas alongside the vehicle, effectively minimizing the time and effort required to complete the task.

The full rear and side spray system is ideal for tackling significant projects efficiently, ensuring that ample water is distributed across the work area to meet the requirements of the job at hand.

A "handheld hose spray" refers to a portable water spraying tool that is manually operated and typically connected to a water source, such as a water truck or a stationary water supply.

In practical terms, the handheld hose spray allows for a more targeted approach to water distribution compared to larger, fixed spraying systems. It offers flexibility and precision, making it suitable for tasks that require a focused application of water.

For example, in situations where specific areas need to be watered or dampened with precision, such as watering plants in a garden or providing moisture to localized sections of a construction site, the handheld hose spray provides the ability to direct the water exactly where it is needed.

The handheld hose spray is a versatile tool that offers control and accuracy, making it ideal for jobs that require a more targeted approach to water distribution.

Types and sizes of water tanks include skid tanks and an array of fixed tanks.

Skid Tanks: Skid tanks are mounted onto the tray of a truck using appropriate lifting equipment and securely restrained at both the front and rear. They are either fastened with chains and binders or bolted to the tray using manufactured anchor points. It's crucial to position the tank in the centre of the tray to ensure even weight distribution across the truck.

Each skid tank features a butterfly valve at its outlet, which controls the flow of water. Typically, this valve is operated by threading a strong rope through pulleys, with one end positioned near the operator of the truck. Pulling the rope opens the butterfly valve, releasing water, and upon release, a spring mechanism automatically closes the valve. Care must be taken to ensure that operating the rope does not interfere with driving the vehicle.

The size of a skid tank varies depending on the gross vehicle mass of the truck.

Tandem Water Carts (or Semi-Trailers Tanks): Tandem water carts consist of tanks permanently affixed to the vehicle. The tank size varies depending on the gross vehicle mass. The primary method of releasing water from the tank to the spray bar is through a switch mounted in the cab of the vehicle. Activating this switch triggers an air ram that opens and closes a valve on the tank outlet, allowing water to flow into the spray bar.

Similar to skid tanks, the size of tandem water carts depends on the gross vehicle mass of the truck.

Planning and Preparing for Water Truck Operations

Accessing, interpreting, and applying water vehicle operations documentation: To begin, it is essential to access pertinent manuals, guidelines, and procedures tailored to water truck operations. These resources encompass manufacturer's manuals, workplace policies, and regulatory requirements, offering comprehensive guidance. Next, meticulously read and interpret the documentation to grasp operational procedures, safety protocols, and maintenance requisites linked with water truck operation. Finally, apply the insights gleaned from the documentation by implementing operational techniques, adhering to safety guidelines, and ensuring compliance with relevant regulations and workplace procedures during water truck operation.

Obtaining, interpreting, clarifying, and confirming work instructions and compliance: Start by obtaining clear work instructions from supervisors, managers, or experienced operators concerning specific tasks and responsibilities related to water truck operation. Subsequently, interpret these instructions to comprehend outlined tasks, procedures, and safety measures. If any instructions appear unclear, seek clarification promptly to ensure a precise understanding of the tasks at hand. Additionally, confirm compliance with documentation and workplace procedures by verifying that planned activities align with established protocols and policies before initiating work.

Identifying hazards, assessing risks, and implementing control measures: Identify potential hazards and environmental issues associated with water truck operations, which may include uneven terrain, overhead obstructions, or adverse weather conditions. Conduct a thorough risk assessment by evaluating the likelihood and severity of identified hazards and environmental impacts. Subsequently, implement control measures aligned with workplace policies to mitigate identified risks, such as utilizing safety barriers, signage, or adjusting work methods to minimize environmental impact and ensure worker safety.

Water truck operations entail several hazards that pose risks to both the operator and others in the vicinity. These hazards include:

1. Vehicle Accidents: Water trucks are large vehicles that may be difficult to manoeuvre, especially in confined spaces or on uneven terrain. Accidents such as collisions with other vehicles, objects, or pedestrians can occur, leading to injuries or fatalities.

2. Roll-over Risks: Due to their high centre of gravity, water trucks are prone to tipping over, especially when navigating slopes or making sharp turns. A rollover can result in serious injuries to the operator and bystanders, as well as damage to property.

3. Falling Objects: Water trucks are often used to transport and distribute heavy materials such as soil, gravel, or construction debris. Improper loading or securing of cargo can lead to objects falling off the truck, posing a risk of injury to workers or damage to property below.

4. Slippery Surfaces: During water spraying operations, excess water may accumulate on the ground, creating slippery surfaces. This increases the risk of slips, trips, and falls for both the operator and others working nearby.

5. Chemical Exposure: Water trucks may be used to transport and spray chemicals such as herbicides, pesticides, or fertilizers. Improper handling or accidental spills can result in exposure to harmful chemicals, leading to health hazards for workers and environmental contamination.

6. Electrocution: Water trucks equipped with overhead spraying systems may come into contact with overhead power lines or electrical equipment. This poses a risk of electrocution to the operator and others in the vicinity.

7. Heat-related Illness: Operating a water truck in hot and humid conditions can lead to heat-related illnesses such as heat exhaustion or heat stroke. Prolonged exposure to high temperatures without adequate hydration and rest breaks can be detrimental to the operator's health.

8. Traffic Hazards: Water trucks often operate in areas with moving vehicles and heavy equipment. Failure to follow traffic management procedures or signalling inadequacies can result in accidents or collisions with other vehicles.

9. Equipment Malfunctions: Mechanical failures or malfunctions

in water truck components such as brakes, steering systems, or spraying mechanisms can pose hazards during operation. Regular maintenance and inspections are essential to minimize the risk of equipment failures.

10. Environmental Impact: Improper disposal of wastewater or chemical runoff from water truck operations can lead to environmental contamination, affecting soil, water bodies, and vegetation in the surrounding area.

To mitigate these hazards, it is crucial for water truck operators to undergo thorough training, adhere to safety protocols and procedures, conduct regular equipment inspections, and communicate effectively with coworkers and supervisors. Additionally, proper personal protective equipment should be worn at all times, and emergency response plans should be in place to address unforeseen incidents effectively.

Selecting and wearing personal protective equipment (PPE): Start by identifying the necessary PPE for water truck operations, encompassing high-visibility clothing, safety boots, gloves, and hearing protection. Ensure the appropriate selection and use of PPE by donning the required protective gear before commencing work activities, thereby safeguarding against potential hazards and enhancing personal safety.

Following traffic management signage requirements: Adhere rigorously to established traffic control measures and signage while operating the water truck in public or workplace areas. Comply with speed limits, adhere to designated routes, and obey traffic signals and signs to uphold personal safety and ensure the safety of others in the vicinity.

Obtaining and interpreting emergency procedures: Acquaint yourself with protocols for responding to fire, accidents, or other emergencies encountered while operating the water truck. Familiarize yourself with accessing emergency equipment, executing evacuation procedures if necessary, and identifying whom to contact in case of an emergency, thereby ensuring preparedness for unforeseen circumstances.

Coordinating and communicating planned activities with others: Engage in effective liaison with supervisors, coworkers, and other relevant personnel to coordinate tasks and ensure clear communication before initiating work activities. Facilitate discussions on work plans, resource allocation, and potential safety concerns to promote seamless and efficient operations while prioritizing safety and productivity.

When accessing the water truck tank for loading or unloading, workers often need to climb onto the tank, exposing them to the risk of falling or slipping. These hazards can be mitigated through the use of appropriate safety equipment, such as cages or enclosures, or by utilizing flat top tanks that minimize the risk of falls and slips.

Workers and drivers may also be at risk of tripping and falling over various types of equipment, such as loading hoses. Even a minor trip can result in strains, sprains, back injuries, or fractures. It is therefore essential to adhere to proper safety procedures and exercise caution when working with any specialized vehicle, including the water truck.

Water trucks are commonly used for dust control, but improper usage can lead to the creation of mud and puddles, increasing the risk of slipping. Workers should be knowledgeable about adjusting and using the spray nozzles correctly to minimize slipping hazards and avoid overspraying.

While modern water trucks can hold significant amounts of water, it is crucial to adhere to loading recommendations to prevent accidents. Overloading a water truck can lead to loss of vehicle control, mechanical failures, premature wear and tear, and increased operating expenses due to heightened downtime and maintenance requirements.

Before starting the engine, it is the operator's responsibility to conduct a thorough daily check on the truck. This includes:

- Keeping a log of daily Pre-Start Checklists to ensure all checks are completed.

- Checking the tyre pressures daily, referring to the tyre manufacturer's specifications.

- Verifying fluid levels such as engine oil, transmission oil, and coolant.

- Applying grease to all moving parts daily, including the drive shaft and suspension.

- Checking the water level in the water tank.

- Inspecting for leaks under the truck, including oil, water, and coolant.

- Examining hoses on the water tank for signs of wear or rubbing.

- If the water pump operates hydraulically, checking the hydraulic oil level.

- Ensuring the hydraulic oil cooler fan is operational, listening for its engagement when the PTO is activated. Reporting any malfunctions to maintenance immediately.

- Lubricating the PTO Shaft daily, which connects the PTO to the water pump or hydraulic pump.

- Reporting all faults to the maintenance department before starting work.

Upon starting the truck, it's essential to check the AIR PRESSURE gauges to gauge air pressure. If the pressure is insufficient due to leaks in the air system, allow the truck to idle until full air pressure is reached, as indicated on the gauges.

In automatic trucks, low air pressure may prevent gear selection. Engaging the PTO with low pressure may cause water leaks from the tank sprays, requiring a full air supply to close them properly. Operators must be aware of the truck's height, including any mounted equipment, to prevent damage.

Referencing warning and advisory stickers above the driver's seat contributes to safety. Ensuring the truck has adequate fuel is crucial to prevent engine damage and potential accidents.

After checking and observing the above procedures, operation of the truck or water cart may commence. When selecting gear in automatic transmission trucks, firmly press the brake pedal and select the gear required on the transmission pedestal. For manual transmission trucks, follow standard manual gear selection procedures.

To engage the PTO, ensure the truck speed is very low (no more than 10kph), locate the PTO switch on the dash, and switch it to the ON position. Engaging the PTO requires sufficient water in the tank to prevent water pump failure.

After verifying water levels and engaging the PTO, select the appropriate switch on the control box for the desired operation. Water volume depends on engine RPM, with optimal performance between 1800-2000rpm.

To disengage the PTO, turn off all switches on the control box and, at low truck speed, around 10kph, switch the PTO to the OFF position.

It is crucial to switch off the PTO when not in use, as they are not designed for long-distance travel at high speeds.

TANK FILLING PROCEDURE (Example): There are three methods available for filling the water tank:

OPTION 1: Hydrant Fill The hydrant fill port is situated at the rear of the tank on the passenger side, identifiable by the 3" brass valve. To fill the tank, remove the camlock cap, attach the fill hose to the camlock, and connect the other end to the hydrant. Turn on the hydrant and monitor the tank's water level using the water level indicator.

NOTE: Utilizing hydrants necessitates permits; ensure yours is up-to-date to avoid potential fines.

Figure 86: Water truck filling from hydrant. User:Vmenkov, CC BY-SA 3.0 , via Wikimedia Commons.

OPTION 2: Overhead Fill Primarily used on large construction sites, the overhead fill method requires compliance with site regulations. A large funnel installed atop the water tank facilitates this filling technique.

OPTION 3: Self Fill / Dam Fill The water truck is equipped with this filling option. Please refer to the Self Fill/Dam Fill procedure page located in this folder. It is important to carefully review the instructions provided for this procedure.

Figure 87: Filling an OceanaGold water tanker mining truck working the Macraes mine, Otago, New Zealand. Benchill, CC BY-SA 3.0, via Wikimedia Commons.

As an example of a fill sequence (Custom Truck, 2018), and referring to Figure 88:

1. Start the engine and engage the parking brake while the truck is in park.

2. Attach the fill hose to the creek nipple.

3. Submerge the opposite end of the hose into the water supply.

4. Open valves (A) and (C), keeping valve (B) closed.

5. Open valve (B) to allow the suction hose to fill from the tank.

6. Activate the PTO for mobile operation.

7. Shut valve (C) and let the tank fill up.

EARTHMOVING EQUIPMENT OPERATIONS 339

8. Deactivate the PTO.

9. Close valves (A) and (B), and open valve (C).

10. Disconnect and store the fill hose.

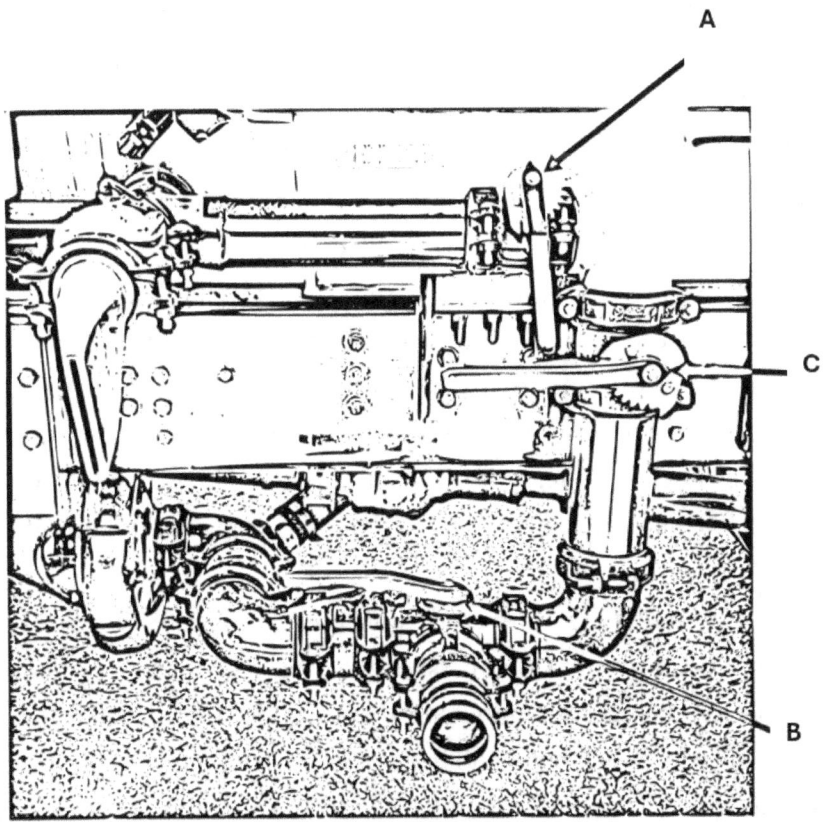

Figure 88: Load King filling valves.

The spray heads installed on the tank feature adjustable collars, enabling users to regulate the water volume output according to their requirements. Initially, the spray heads come with the collar set at its finest adjustment. Users can customize the spray volume by adjusting the collar to suit their needs. If the water volume proves insufficient for the task, simply loosen the single bolt securing the collar and adjust it downwards to increase the spray head's water flow, or remove the collar entirely.

Optimum Moisture Content (OMC): The moisture content at which a specified amount of compaction will produce the maximum dry density. The increase in the dry density of soil resulting from compaction depends primarily on the soil's moisture content and the level of compaction applied. For each type of soil, there exists an Optimum Moisture Content (OMC) at which the maximum dry density is achieved.

The behaviour of soil at different moisture contents can be explained as follows: When the moisture content is too low, the soil is rigid and difficult to compress, resulting in low dry densities and high air contents. As the moisture content increases, water acts as a lubricant, softening the soil and making it more workable, leading to higher dry densities and lower air contents. However, as the air content decreases, the combination of air and water tends to keep the particles apart, preventing significant decreases in air content. Nonetheless, the total voids continue to increase with moisture content, causing the dry density of the soil to decrease.

When operating the water cart, a quick test to identify if the soil is at the Optimum Moisture Content is to take a handful of soil and squeeze it. If the soil maintains its moulded shape, hold it between the thumb and forefinger of each hand and break it in half. If the break is even and the soil doesn't squash or crumble, it indicates that the soil is close to OMC. This method provides a quick and reasonably accurate assessment of soil moisture content, indicating whether additional water is required.

Achieving Maximum Dry Density includes:
- Hydration: This moisture percentage, firmly attached to the soil particle, does not aid compaction as a lubricant. Additional water brings the soil to a point where a slight change in the moisture content begins to produce a large increase in density,

indicating the next phase of compaction.

- Lubricant: Moisture acting as a lubricant enhances densities and cohesiveness, reaching an ideal moisture content for compaction.

- Swelling: Increased moisture creates a film around the soil particles, pushing them apart and decreasing dry density.

- Saturation: Further increases in moisture content replace solids with water, further decreasing dry density.

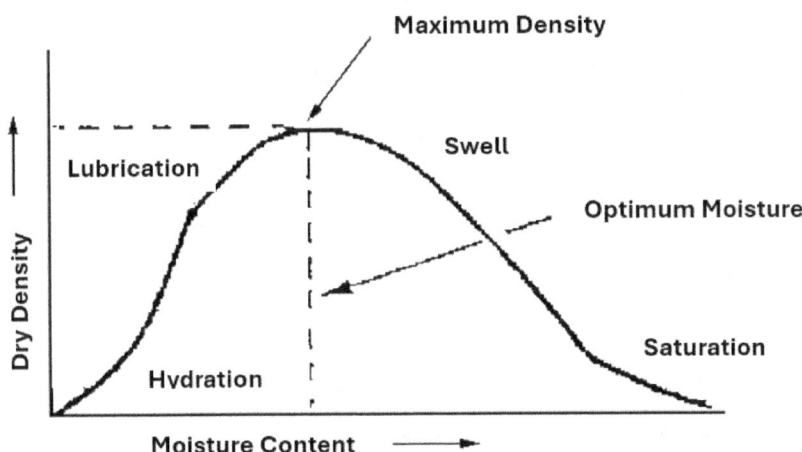

Figure 89: Behaviour of soil at different moisture content.

During summer, haul roads tend to accumulate significant dust, which can be managed by employing the water cart to dampen the road surface. However, caution must be exercised to avoid over-application, as excessive water can lead to slippery and hazardous conditions. It's advisable to only water half of the road at a time, allowing vehicles to maintain traction by driving on a dry surface with either the left or right wheels. Once one side is adequately treated and deemed safe, the other side can be watered accordingly. Additionally, special attention should be given to crossroads and junctions to prevent double-watering, which can create excessively slippery conditions. It's important to note that the primary objective is not to achieve Optimum Moisture Content but rather to suppress dust and ensure the safety of vehicles using the haul road.

Figure 90: Haul road watering. MINING.com, CC BY 2.0, via Wikimedia Commons.

In addition to its primary functions, the water cart is versatile enough to facilitate tree watering. This task can be accomplished by either attaching a hose with a tap to the tank outlet or installing a specialized device on the front of the truck, controllable from within the cab. Once a job is finished and topsoil has been reinstated to promote natural regrowth, the water cart's role includes watering the area. This can be achieved by employing a pump mounted on the tank outlet to distribute water onto the designated area, either through a hose or a spray nozzle.

Operating a Truck Cart

EARTHMOVING EQUIPMENT OPERATIONS

Water truck controls typically consist of various components and systems designed to operate and control the vehicle's functions effectively. Here's an explanation of common water truck controls:

1. Steering Wheel: The steering wheel allows the driver to control the direction of the water truck. It is used to turn the front wheels, enabling the vehicle to manoeuvre left or right.

2. Accelerator Pedal: The accelerator pedal, also known as the gas pedal, is used to increase the engine speed and propel the water truck forward. Pressing the accelerator pedal increases the vehicle's speed, while releasing it slows down the vehicle.

3. Brake Pedal: The brake pedal is used to slow down or stop the water truck. Pressing the brake pedal activates the vehicle's braking system, which reduces speed or brings the truck to a complete stop.

4. Transmission Controls: Water trucks equipped with automatic transmissions typically have gear selection controls, allowing the driver to shift between drive (D), reverse (R), neutral (N), and park (P) modes. Manual transmission trucks have a gear stick for gear selection.

5. Water Pump Controls: Water trucks are equipped with water pump controls to regulate the flow of water from the tank. These controls may include switches or valves to turn the pump on or off, adjust the water flow rate, and control the direction of water discharge.

6. Spray Nozzle Controls: Water trucks used for dust suppression or irrigation purposes often feature spray nozzle controls. These controls allow the driver to adjust the spray pattern, angle, and intensity of the water discharge to suit specific application re-

quirements.

7. Tank Level Gauge: A tank level gauge provides information about the amount of water remaining in the truck's tank. It helps the driver monitor water levels and plan refilling or replenishment as needed.

8. Instrument Panel: The instrument panel displays vital information about the water truck's operation, including engine speed (RPM), vehicle speed, fuel level, engine temperature, and other diagnostic indicators.

9. Lighting Controls: Water trucks are equipped with lighting controls to operate headlights, taillights, turn signals, and other lighting systems. These controls ensure visibility and safety, especially during low-light conditions or when operating on public roads.

10. Horn: The horn is used to alert pedestrians, other vehicles, or workers to the presence of the water truck. It is an essential safety feature for signalling warnings or emergencies.

To operate a water truck safely and efficiently, follow these steps:

1. **Carry out prestart and start-up checks in line with workplace procedures**:

    - Begin by conducting prestart checks as outlined in the workplace procedures and the manufacturer's manual.

    - Check fluid levels, inspect tyres for proper inflation, examine hoses and nozzles for damage, and ensure all safety devices are functional.

    - Start the water truck according to the recommended procedure in the manufacturer's manual and workplace protocols.

2. **Identify faults or defects and rectify or report within the scope of own responsibility and according to workplace procedures:**

    - During prestart checks, carefully inspect the water truck for any faults or defects.

    - If you identify minor issues within your capability, rectify them following workplace procedures.

    - Report any significant faults or defects beyond your scope of responsibility to the appropriate personnel immediately, following workplace reporting procedures.

3. **Operate the water vehicle to original equipment manufacturer requirements, and according to workplace procedures:**

    - Follow the original equipment manufacturer (OEM) requirements and workplace procedures while operating the water truck.

    - Adhere to speed limits, vehicle capacity, and operational guidelines specified by the OEM to ensure safe and efficient operation.

4. **Manage engine power to ensure distribution of water to complete work activity, and in line with workplace procedures:**

    - Adjust engine power based on the water distribution requirements for the specific work activity.

    - Ensure that the water flow rate is sufficient to complete the task effectively while conserving water resources.

- Follow workplace procedures for managing engine power and water distribution to achieve the desired outcomes.

5. **Coordinate engine power with gear selection to ensure smooth transition and operation within the torque range**:

    - Coordinate engine power with gear selection to maintain smooth operation and prevent strain on the engine.

    - Select appropriate gears based on the terrain, load, and operational requirements to optimize fuel efficiency and performance.

    - Operate within the torque range specified by the OEM to prevent engine damage and ensure optimal power output.

6. **Monitor hazards and risks, and ensure safety of self, other personnel, plant, and equipment**:

    - Continuously monitor the work environment for hazards and risks associated with water truck operations.

    - Take proactive measures to mitigate identified hazards and ensure the safety of yourself, coworkers, and equipment.

    - Follow workplace safety procedures, wear appropriate personal protective equipment (PPE), and communicate effectively with others to minimize risks and prevent accidents or injuries.

7. **Position water vehicle at loading and/or distribution points**:

    - Approach the loading or distribution point with caution, considering the terrain and any obstacles.

- Position the water truck in a safe and accessible location that allows for efficient loading or distribution of water.

- Ensure that the truck is parked securely with the brakes engaged and any necessary safety measures in place before proceeding with loading or distribution.

8. **Load water vehicle to within the authorized carrying capacity and to suit the site and task conditions:**

    - Determine the authorized carrying capacity of the water truck based on manufacturer specifications and workplace regulations.

    - Load the water vehicle with the appropriate amount of water to avoid exceeding the authorized carrying capacity while ensuring it is sufficient for the site and task conditions.

    - Monitor the loading process carefully to prevent overloading and maintain stability while on the move.

9. **Operate water vehicle according to site conditions to avoid surge and sway:**

    - Drive the water truck smoothly and steadily, especially when carrying a full load of water, to minimize surge and sway.

    - Maintain a safe speed and avoid sudden acceleration, deceleration, or sharp turns that could cause the water in the tank to slosh and create instability.

    - Be mindful of uneven terrain, slopes, and obstacles that could affect the stability of the water truck and adjust driving techniques accordingly.

10. **Discharge or distribute water efficiently in accordance**

with work requirements and workplace procedures:

- Activate the water discharge system according to the specific work requirements and workplace procedures.

- Adjust the water flow rate and nozzle settings as necessary to achieve the desired coverage and distribution pattern.

- Ensure that water is discharged evenly and efficiently to effectively address the task at hand, such as dust suppression or soil compaction.

11. **Monitor discharge of water throughout the operations:**

- Continuously monitor the discharge of water from the truck to ensure it is functioning properly and meeting the intended objectives.

- Adjust the water flow and distribution as needed based on changing site conditions or task requirements.

- Be attentive to any signs of malfunction or issues with the water discharge system and take prompt action to address them to prevent disruptions to operations.

Adapting driving behaviour according to road conditions is crucial. Assess the on-site and on-road conditions for any potential hazards, particularly avoiding roads with potholes, damage, or deterioration.

It's essential to have the weight of a fully loaded water truck documented for reference purposes. This information enables adjustments to be made, especially when considering weight restrictions on bridges or crossings.

Preferably, plan the route well in advance to ensure safe passage of the truck. Despite the presence of modern alarms and cameras, it's imperative to train spotters to assist when the water truck needs to reverse.

When transporting a fully loaded water truck, the increased weight requires careful handling during acceleration and deceleration. Adjusting the speed appropriately helps prevent excessive surging of water in the tank, which can lead to hazardous road accidents by destabilizing the truck's centre of gravity.

Priming the pump of a water truck or water cart is essential to prevent breakdowns and minimize downtime, especially concerning centrifugal pumps. But why is pump priming necessary? Water truck pumps are designed to pump liquid, not gases or vapours. Therefore, it's crucial to fill the pump with water before operation to safeguard the seals and impeller from damage. Even self-priming pumps require partial filling to operate effectively.

A properly primed pump exhibits a fully water-filled chamber, ensuring efficient operation. Conversely, if air remains trapped within the pump, it impedes performance and poses risks. Thus, it's imperative to expel any air and replace it with water to enable the pump to function optimally.

Priming a self-priming pump involves several steps. If there's still water in the tank, the priming plug atop the pump is removed, and the valve to the tank outlet on the suction system is opened to allow water to flow through. Once the pump is initiated, the impeller mixes the air with the water until the air is expelled, enabling the tank to fill. Alternatively, if the tank is empty, the tank outlet valve is closed, and water is manually introduced into the pump and suction system using a bucket or hose.

For non self-priming pumps, the process differs slightly. If water remains in the tank, a valve on the pressure side of the pump is opened to facilitate water flow. Simultaneously, the hand valve at the tank outlet on the suction system is opened to allow water to flow from the tank. Once the pump is filled with water, the plug is replaced, indicating successful priming. In cases where the tank is dry, water is poured manually into the top of the pump and suction system until both are fully filled. After priming, the plug is replaced, and the pump can be started, initiating the tank-filling process.

Water plays a dual role in soil compaction, acting as both a facilitator and a potential obstacle. When water is applied, the objective is to attain the optimum moisture content, which varies depending on the soil's composition of sand, silt, and clay. To ensure even distribution, water should be sprayed directly onto the surface, allowing it to permeate the material. Alternatively, a more efficient method involves trailing the grader, which distributes material, and spraying water over it on subsequent passes, allowing for better mixing. The process continues until the material reaches a state where it can be moulded in hand without crumbling or becoming excessively muddy, indicating proximity to its Optimum Moisture Content. At this stage, further watering is unnecessary unless the material begins to dry out.

Refurbishing Shoulders: This task necessitates a grader, a multi-wheeled roller, and a water cart. Before commencement, appropriate road site signage, as per Australian Standards, must be installed. The required material can either be picked up or delivered to the site, adhering to specified moisture content. A simple hand test can be conducted on the delivered material: if it crumbles upon opening the hand, it's too dry; if it squashes out through fingers upon closing the hand, it's too wet. Ideally, the material should retain its shape when moulded. The grader prepares the site and instructs the water cart driver on when to apply water. During mixing, the material may dry out, necessitating additional water to maintain an optimal moisture content. The quantity of water applied depends on the ground speed of the truck. Excessive speed can result in insufficient moisture for compaction, while slower speeds can oversaturate the material, rendering it uncompactable. Maintaining a consistent pace is crucial to achieving the right moisture balance throughout the job.

Finishing up Water Truck Operations

To successfully complete water truck operations, follow these steps:

1. **Park up, shut down, secure, and carry out post-operational inspection of equipment**:

   - Safely park the water truck in a designated area, ensuring it is on level ground and away from any hazards.

   - Shut down the engine and any auxiliary systems following manufacturer and workplace procedures.

   - Secure the water truck by engaging the parking brake, turning off the ignition, and locking the cab and any compartments.

   - Conduct a post-operational inspection of the equipment, checking for any signs of damage, leaks, or abnormalities.

   - Report any faults or defects identified during the inspection to the appropriate personnel and document them as per workplace procedures.

2. **Clear work area and dispose of or recycle materials**:

   - Remove any debris, tools, or equipment from the work area and return them to their designated storage locations.

   - Dispose of waste materials in accordance with workplace procedures, ensuring proper recycling or disposal of any recyclable materials.

- Clean up any spills or residues resulting from the water truck operations, taking care to prevent environmental contamination.

3. **Manage and/or report hazards to maintain a safe working environment:**

    - Continuously monitor the work area for any potential hazards or risks, such as slippery surfaces, uneven terrain, or overhead obstructions.

    - Take appropriate measures to mitigate identified hazards, such as erecting warning signs, implementing safety barriers, or removing obstacles.

    - Report any hazards or safety concerns to supervisors or relevant personnel to ensure a safe working environment for yourself and others.

4. **Complete and file or distribute documentation:**

    - Fill out any required documentation related to the water truck operations, including work logs, inspection reports, and incident reports.

    - Ensure that all documentation is completed accurately and legibly, following workplace practices and procedures.

    - File the completed documentation in the designated location or distribute it to the appropriate personnel as per workplace protocols.

Figure 91: FAP 1823 water tank truck parked in safe and designated area. Srđan Popović, CC BY-SA 4.0, via Wikimedia Commons.on automatically generated

When it comes to loading a water cart onto a float, it's imperative to adhere to the manufacturer's guidelines regarding loading and unloading procedures. Several precautions apply universally to all machines in such scenarios. First and foremost, loading and unloading should take place on a level, firm surface. Additionally, the transport vehicle should be securely blocked to prevent any movement during the process. It's essential to verify that the transport vehicle has a sufficient gross combination weight rating to handle the load and is wide enough to accommodate it. Properly constructed loading ramps of adequate size and strength should be used, with the ramp angle kept as low as possible to ensure safe manoeuvring. Furthermore, it's crucial to keep the trailer bed and ramps free from any materials that could cause slipping, such as clay, oil, ice, or snow. While driving the water cart up the ramps, having someone to guide the process can be beneficial. Once loaded, the water cart should be positioned to evenly distribute the weight over the transport vehicle. Using approved chains and load binders, the water cart should then be securely fastened to prevent sliding during transportation. Prior to transport, it's essential to check the overall transport height. When unloading the water cart, the procedure should be reversed to ensure safety.

When floating the water cart, additional safety procedures and regulations must be followed. Firstly, it's crucial to ensure that the safe working load of the float is not exceeded. Checking the condition of the deck and securely tying down the machine with approved chains are essential steps. Warning signs indicating a wide load should be provided, and any protruding parts of the load should be clearly marked with red flags. Depending on the circumstances, providing escorts may be necessary for added safety. Additionally, all brakes and locks on the machine being transported must be applied to prevent any unexpected movement during transit.

Regarding the transport truck itself, several requirements must be met to ensure legal compliance and safe operation on the road. The truck must be registered and adequately insured, meeting all state and territory road traffic regulations. Furthermore, it should be roadworthy and in compliance with all relevant safety standards. The driver operating the truck must possess a current driver's license for the appropriate class of truck, ensuring competency and legal authorization for road travel.

Chapter Eight

Haul Truck Operations

The purpose of a haul truck is to transport large quantities of materials, such as earth, rock, or minerals, from one location to another within a mining, construction, or quarrying site. These trucks are specifically designed for heavy-duty operations and are equipped with a robust chassis, powerful engines, and large-capacity beds or haul bodies to carry significant loads efficiently. Haul trucks play a crucial role in the logistics and material handling processes of various industries, facilitating the movement of extracted or excavated materials to processing areas, stockpiles, or transportation facilities.

Figure 92: Haul truck (Continental Mine, Butte, Montana, USA). James St. John, CC BY 2.0, via Wikimedia Commons.

When it comes to off-road hauling, two primary truck types exist: Rigid and Articulated. Although they share similar technological features, their applications differ significantly. Rigid Haulers are engineered for transporting large, rocky, and abrasive materials over well-maintained roads, while Articulated Haulers excel in adverse conditions and operate on varying grades regardless of weather.

Figure 93: Articulated haul truck. Jon Lavis from Seaford, CC BY 2.0, via Wikimedia Commons.

Choosing the right off-road hauler for your operations involves considering five main factors. Firstly, ground conditions dictate whether a Rigid or Articulated Hauler is more suitable. Articulated Haulers' manoeuvrability in restricted spaces, narrow roads, and slippery terrain makes them ideal for challenging conditions. Conversely, Rigid Haulers are better suited for job sites with large, well-maintained roads, such as rock quarries or surface mines.

Secondly, the size of the jobsite plays a crucial role. Rigid Haulers are preferred for larger sites with extensive, hard-packed roads, whereas Articulated Haulers' versatility suits smaller sites with tighter working conditions.

Thirdly, the type of material and volumes being hauled influence the choice between Rigid and Articulated Haulers. Rigid Haulers handle large rock, ore, or shale efficiently, thanks to their high carrying capacity and faster speeds. On the other hand, Articulated Haulers excel in hauling various materials under different conditions, offering greater flexibility.

Fourthly, considerations about where the material is being dumped come into play. Rigid Haulers are suitable for dumping into high and wide capacity hoppers, while Articulated Haulers are preferred for narrow hoppers.

Lastly, the loading impact is an important factor to consider. Rigid Haulers are resilient and can withstand high-impact loads, making them suitable for loading under large shovels or drag-lines.

It's crucial to weigh all these factors when deciding between a rigid or articulated dump truck. While Rigid Trucks may seem more profitable due to their higher payload and faster cycle times, Articulated Trucks' superior traction and manoeuvrability make them advantageous in challenging terrains and inclines.

Sample Rigid Haulers:

Volvo R45D: Equipped with a Cummins QSK19-C525 engine generating 370 kW of net power at 2,000 RPM and a maximum torque of 2,407 Nm at 1,500 RPM, the Volvo R45D boasts impressive performance specifications. Its transmission features an Allison 5620 ORS system, while it rides on tyres ranging from 21 to 35 inches. The braking system includes front dry disc brakes and rear full enclosed multiple wet disc brakes. With a heaped load capacity of 26 m^3 and a maximum payload of 41,000 kg, the Volvo R45D is a reliable choice for hauling operations.

Caterpillar Haul Trucks: Caterpillar 785: The Caterpillar 785 Haul Truck, also known as an off-road truck, remains a staple in open-cut mining operations worldwide. Often serving as an entry-level truck for new operators, the Caterpillar 785 has established its reliability over the years. Operators typically progress to larger Caterpillar dump trucks as they gain competence, gaining confidence and proficiency in handling larger load capacities across various mine sites. It is essential for operators to become intimately familiar with these trucks to optimize their performance and efficiency.

Figure 94: Caterpillar 785C haul truck. Roy Luck, CC BY 2.0, via Wikimedia Commons.

CAT 789, CAT 793, CAT 797: Among the prominent models in Caterpillar's haul truck lineup are the CAT 789, CAT 793, and CAT 797. The CAT 797, in particular, stands out as one of the largest dump trucks on mine sites, featuring a ladder stairway that leads operators directly into the cockpit, presenting challenges akin to working at heights during pre-start checklists. These machines serve as the backbone of the mining sector, tirelessly hauling loads day in and day out, often operating round the clock in shifts to maximize productivity. With their robust two-axle design and powerful torque engines, these ultra-class mining trucks are well-suited for the diverse range of mine sites.

Figure 95: Caterpillar 789B. TZorn, CC BY-SA 3.0, via Wikimedia Commons.

Given their substantial cost of construction and operation, mining companies prioritize skilled operators who understand the importance of treating these vehicles with utmost care and respect. With a price tag of around 7 million dollars each and tyres costing approximately $45,000 per piece, maintaining these machines is paramount. The CAT 797F, capable of transporting about 400 tons, ranks among the largest haul trucks in the world, boasting a top speed of 67.6 km/h and the power to conquer challenging terrains and driving conditions. In some of the highest mines globally, the CAT 797 has been transported in pieces and assembled on-site to meet operational demands.

EARTHMOVING EQUIPMENT OPERATIONS

Figure 96: Caterpillar 797 haul truck. Lechhabmed, CC BY-SA 4.0, via Wikimedia Commons.

A rigid haul truck typically consists of several major components, each playing a crucial role in its operation and functionality:

1. Chassis: The chassis serves as the foundation of the haul truck, providing structural support and housing various components. It is designed to withstand the immense weight and stress encountered during hauling operations.

2. Cab: The cab is the enclosed compartment where the operator sits and controls the vehicle. It contains essential features such as the steering wheel, pedals, instrument panel, and operator's seat. The cab is equipped with safety features to protect the operator from hazards encountered during operation.

3. Engine: The engine is the power source of the haul truck, responsible for generating the necessary energy to propel the vehicle. It is typically a large, high-powered diesel engine capable of producing significant torque to move heavy loads over rugged terrain.

4. Transmission: The transmission transfers power from the engine to the wheels, allowing the operator to control the speed and direction of the haul truck. It may be manual or automatic, depending on the model and manufacturer.

5. Axles and Wheels: Rigid haul trucks are equipped with multiple axles and wheels to distribute the weight of the vehicle and its payload evenly. These components are designed to withstand heavy loads and provide stability during operation.

6. Bed: The bed, also known as the dump body or tray, is the rear portion of the haul truck where the payload is carried. It is typically made of durable steel and can be raised hydraulically to unload materials at the desired location.

7. Suspension: The suspension system helps absorb shocks and vibrations encountered while driving over rough terrain, providing a smoother ride for the operator and reducing stress on the vehicle's components. It consists of springs, shock absorbers, and other components.

8. Braking System: The braking system allows the operator to slow down or stop the haul truck safely. It typically includes air brakes or hydraulic brakes, along with various control mechanisms such as brake pedals and levers.

9. Hydraulic System: Rigid haul trucks rely on hydraulic systems to power essential functions such as raising and lowering the bed, steering, and operating auxiliary equipment. These systems use hydraulic fluid under pressure to transmit force and control movement.

10. Electrical System: The electrical system provides power to various components of the haul truck, including lights, sensors, and

control panels. It includes a battery, alternator, wiring harnesses, and other electrical devices.

These major components work together seamlessly to ensure the efficient and reliable operation of a rigid haul truck in demanding mining and construction environments.

Figure 97: Major components of an articulated haul truck. Back image - Wusel007, CC BY-SA 3.0, via Wikimedia Commons.

An articulated haul truck consists of several major components, each serving a vital function in its operation:

1. Cab: The cab is where the operator controls the articulated haul truck. It contains the steering wheel, pedals, instrument panel, and operator's seat. The cab is designed for comfort and safety, providing a comfortable environment for the operator during long shifts.

2. Articulated Hitch: The articulated hitch is a pivotal connection

between the front and rear sections of the haul truck, allowing for articulation or bending at the joint. This design enables the truck to navigate rough terrain and tight spaces by providing greater manoeuvrability.

3. Engine: The engine is the power source of the articulated haul truck, generating the necessary energy to propel the vehicle. It is typically a large, high-powered diesel engine capable of producing significant torque to move heavy loads over challenging terrain.

4. Transmission: The transmission transfers power from the engine to the wheels, enabling the operator to control the speed and direction of the haul truck. It may be manual or automatic, depending on the model and manufacturer.

5. Axles and Wheels: Articulated haul trucks are equipped with multiple axles and wheels to distribute the weight of the vehicle and its payload evenly. These components are designed to withstand heavy loads and provide stability during operation.

6. Bed: The bed, also known as the dump body or tray, is where the payload is carried. It is typically made of durable steel and can be raised hydraulically to unload materials at the desired location.

7. Suspension: The suspension system helps absorb shocks and vibrations encountered while driving over rough terrain, providing a smoother ride for the operator and reducing stress on the vehicle's components. It consists of springs, shock absorbers, and other components.

8. Braking System: The braking system allows the operator to slow down or stop the articulated haul truck safely. It typically in-

cludes air brakes or hydraulic brakes, along with various control mechanisms such as brake pedals and levers.

9. Hydraulic System: Articulated haul trucks rely on hydraulic systems to power essential functions such as raising and lowering the bed, steering, and operating auxiliary equipment. These systems use hydraulic fluid under pressure to transmit force and control movement.

10. Electrical System: The electrical system provides power to various components of the haul truck, including lights, sensors, and control panels. It includes a battery, alternator, wiring harnesses, and other electrical devices.

The following provides overview of the typical controls found in a haul truck:

1. Steering Wheel: The steering wheel allows the operator to control the direction of the haul truck. It is used to turn the front wheels, enabling the truck to navigate around obstacles and follow designated paths.

2. Accelerator Pedal: The accelerator pedal, also known as the throttle pedal, is used to increase the speed of the haul truck. Pressing down on the accelerator pedal delivers more fuel to the engine, increasing its RPM and propelling the vehicle forward.

3. Brake Pedal: The brake pedal is used to slow down or stop the haul truck. When pressed, it activates the braking system, which applies friction to the wheels, slowing down the vehicle. The haul truck may be equipped with air brakes or hydraulic brakes, depending on the model.

4. Transmission Controls: The transmission controls allow the operator to select the desired gear ratio for the haul truck. This may

include options such as forward, neutral, and reverse gears, as well as high and low ranges for different driving conditions.

5. Dump Bed Controls: If equipped with a dump bed or tray, the haul truck will have controls to raise and lower the bed hydraulically. These controls typically include levers or buttons located within easy reach of the operator.

6. Lights and Wipers: Controls for lights and windshield wipers are essential for ensuring visibility in various lighting and weather conditions. The operator can turn on headlights, taillights, and auxiliary lights as needed, as well as activate windshield wipers for clearing the windshield of rain, snow, or debris.

7. Horn: The horn is used to alert other vehicles, pedestrians, or workers of the haul truck's presence. It is an important safety feature for signalling warnings or emergencies.

8. Engine Shutdown: A control for shutting down the engine is provided for stopping the haul truck when it's not in use. This control may involve turning a key, pressing a button, or toggling a switch, depending on the specific model.

9. Gauges and Instrument Panel: The haul truck's instrument panel displays vital information such as engine RPM, vehicle speed, fuel level, temperature, and hydraulic pressure. Gauges and indicators provide real-time feedback on the truck's performance and status, allowing the operator to monitor its condition.

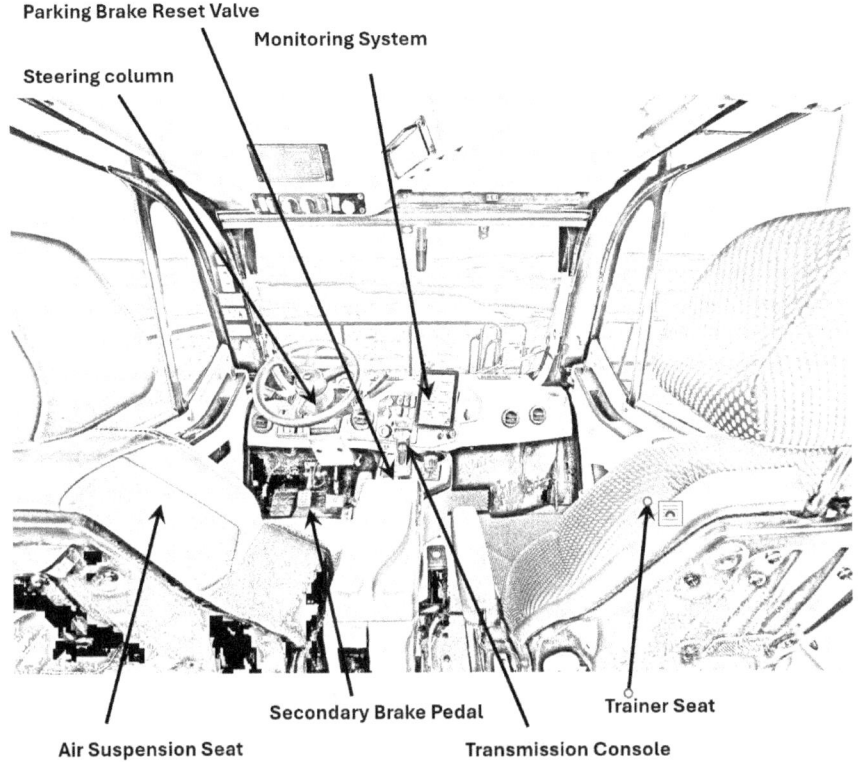
Figure 98: Typical operator cab.

Working with a dump truck, whether on a mine site or a construction site, demands strict adherence to safety protocols to ensure success and mitigate risks. Prioritize safe practices, such as wearing appropriate protective gear and thoroughly familiarizing yourself with the dump truck's manual before operation. Here are some essential tips to ensure safety when working with a dump truck.

Daily Inspections: Regular maintenance of dump trucks is crucial to prevent breakdowns and ensure safe operation. Conduct daily inspections to identify any potential issues or damage before commencing operations. Check tyre pressure, suspension, lift cylinders, and lubricate pins and bushings. Additionally, ensure the windshield is clean to maintain clear visibility of the road ahead.

On-Site Safety Measures: Once daily inspections are complete, ensure compliance with on-site safety regulations. Verify that the operator wears a reflective protective vest, hard hat, and appropriate footwear. Keep safety equipment, such as a first-aid kit and fire extinguisher, easily accessible for emergencies. Utilize alarms, lights, and warning signals when reversing or entering the work site.

Level Ground Offloading: Ensure the dump truck is on a level surface or that the ground beneath it is level before offloading the load. A stable surface prevents the truck from tipping over when raising the bed. Check the ground's stability, particularly for longer beds, and opt for firm soil or gravel for offloading to enhance stability and prevent accidents.

Beware of Electrical Hazards: Exercise caution regarding low-hanging electrical wires or loose wires on the ground. Before lifting the bed, inspect the area for any overhead wires to avoid potential electric shocks. Consider assigning a signaller to work alongside the operator to identify power lines and guide safe manoeuvring. Avoid moving the truck with the bed raised to minimize the risk of contact with electrical wires.

Even Load Distribution: Ensure the load in the dump truck is evenly distributed between the rails of the truck bed to improve balance and stability. Uneven distribution can lead to operational difficulties and pose safety risks, particularly when navigating uneven terrain. Prioritize even loading to maintain truck stability and prevent accidents.

Basic Safety Principles: Adhere to four fundamental safety principles:

1. Safety Consciousness: Prioritize safety, and halt operations if unsure.

2. Common Sense: Exercise competence and caution at all times.

3. Knowledge of Danger Areas: Familiarize yourself with work areas to eliminate surprises and recognize hazards.

4. Recognition of Hazards: Identify potential hazards associated with large machine size, restricted operator vision, difficult working conditions, protruding attachments, and communication difficulties.

Causes of Accidents: Accidents are often attributed to errors in judgment, including carelessness, ignorance, or equipment failure. Prioritize safety through proper training, adherence to safety procedures, regular equipment maintenance, and thorough inspections.

Briefings: As a haul truck operator, possess comprehensive knowledge of the work site, geological features, and operational tasks. Your driving skills will be continuously tested, navigating challenging terrains with varying slopes. Stay vigilant and adaptable to complete assigned tasks safely and efficiently.

Remember to follow instructions provided through various channels, including work instruction sheets, verbal communication, radio, or documentation, to ensure task completion while prioritizing safety at all times.

Planning and Preparing for Haul Truck Operations

Mining trucks present a considerable hazard to workers, as well as other vehicles and equipment, due to their sheer size, weight, power, and the restricted visibility experienced by drivers from the cabin.

Injuries or fatalities can occur due to various circumstances, including:

- Collisions resulting from:
  - Light vehicles or personnel being in blind spots
  - Poor visibility or unexpected obstacles

- Steering or brake failures
- Driving at excessive speeds given the road conditions
- Other vehicles and machinery encroaching into the truck's operational space
- Lack of concentration or driver drowsiness

- Accidental reversing over the edge of a stockpile
- Truck rollovers attributed to excessive speed or adverse road conditions
- Falls by personnel while accessing the cabin and service areas
- Truck fires caused by ruptured oil hoses
- Tyre fires or explosions occurring after contact of the raised tray with overhead power lines
- Tyre explosions due to damage or resulting from a truck fire
- Jolting and jarring stemming from inadequate road maintenance or loading procedures.

When hauling materials, it's essential to consider their various physical attributes, such as maximum lump size, density, grading, and free-flow characteristics. Additionally, the usability of haul roads plays a crucial role in your operations, requiring them to be well-designed, constructed, and maintained. Whether they are one-way or two-way, haul roads significantly impact operational safety, haulage costs, and environmental factors.

EARTHMOVING EQUIPMENT OPERATIONS

Figure 99: Example of a 2-way haul road. Erich Ferdinand from Germany, CC BY 2.0, via Wikimedia Commons.

Pre-start inspections, commonly known as walk-around inspections, are typically the initial task undertaken before beginning a shift or daily work. It's crucial to conduct these inspections regularly, especially when operating under adverse conditions. Consulting the manufacturer's manual is essential to ensure that any specific points pertinent to your machine are included in the inspection procedure outlined below. It is your responsibility to familiarize yourself with the components of the haul truck through training or by studying the operation and maintenance manual before conducting a walk-around inspection.

These inspections must adhere to the recommendations provided by the haul truck manufacturer and company policy. Be vigilant for any signs of oil or fuel leakage or the accumulation of flammable materials around high-temperature components like the engine muffler or turbocharger, as these may lead to fire hazards. Any abnormalities should be reported immediately for repair or addressed by contacting your distributor.

The walk-around check involves examining the machine and its undercarriage for loose nuts or bolts, oil, fuel, or coolant leaks, and assessing the condition of work equipment and the hydraulic system. Pay attention to loose wiring, play, and dust accumulation in areas prone to high temperatures. Below is an example procedure extracted from a manufacturer's manual for a specific haul truck model:

1. Inspect dump body, frame, tyres, cylinders, linkage, and hoses for damage, wear, or play.

2. Clean dirt from around the engine, battery, and radiator. Ensure no flammable material is accumulated around high-temperature engine parts.

3. Check for water or oil leakage around the engine.

4. Inspect for oil leakage from the transmission case, differential case, final drive case, hydraulic tank, hoses, and joints. Look for signs of oil leakage on the undercover or dripping on the ground.

5. Check for loose air cleaner mounting bolts.

6. Examine dump body mount rubber for cracks, embedded foreign objects, or loose bolts.

7. Inspect handrails for damage and loose bolts.

8. Check for damage to gauges, lamps, and loose bolts. Ensure no damage to the panel, gauges, or lamps.

9. Clean rearview and under-view mirrors, adjust their angles for proper visibility, and replace damaged mirrors.

10. Assess seat belt and clamps for abnormalities. Replace damaged

parts, including the belt, if any external damage, fraying, or deformation is observed, or after any impact with the machine.

Work environment procedures are conducted prior to each shift, typically led by the shift supervisor, to ensure safe and efficient operations. During these briefings, operators receive important details including truck identity and allocation, the nature and scope of tasks, achievement targets, haul routes and their conditions, site lighting, vehicle defects, and potential hazards. Coordination requirements and any pertinent issues are also addressed to facilitate smooth operations.

Geological knowledge is essential for open-cut mine equipment operators, encompassing terms and features encountered during operations. This includes familiarity with mine site coal seams and their codes, characteristics associated with the seams, and various lithology codes such as sandstone, silstone, overburden, interburden, and coal. Operators should also understand faults, dykes, and weathered coal formations they may encounter.

Geotechnical workplace inspections are crucial for identifying potential hazards, and operators should be vigilant in recognizing and reporting any concerns to the supervisor or mine geologist before commencing work. Highwall conditions may include fracturing, fresh rocks at the base, excessive seepage, overhanging material, joint openings, and noticeable changes in rock structure. Lowwalls may exhibit cracks, slumping, oversteepening, rocks on roads below, and signs of water accumulation or changes in composition. Similarly, dump areas may present hazards such as water accumulation, slumping, fractures, excess reject material, and undercutting, all of which require careful monitoring and reporting to maintain a safe work environment.

Prior to starting each shift, the haul truck operator must conduct a pre-start check to ensure the truck's safety and record the inspection on a check sheet. It's imperative that the operator has received proper training and is familiar with the truck's components, lubrication, and coolant levels before commencing this check to avoid overlooking any crucial items that could result in personal injury or harm to others. The Pre-Start Check section of the manufacturer's manual should be thoroughly understood, as each make and model may have distinct features and requirements.

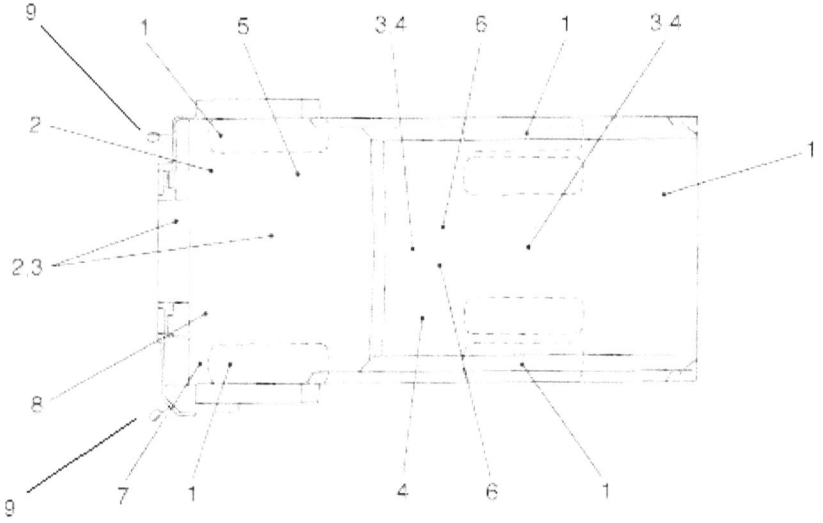

Figure 100: Haul truck check points.

The following procedure outlines the pre-start check for a specific make and model of haul truck:

1. Check Coolant Level: Verify the coolant level visually by removing the radiator cap (if necessary) and ensuring there is no oil in the water or any other abnormalities. Use caution to prevent hot water from spilling out.

2. Check Oil Level in Engine Oil Pan: Confirm the oil level with a dipstick while ensuring the machine is parked on a level surface. Wipe the dipstick clean before reinserting it to check for oil discoloration and ensure it falls within the acceptable range.

3. Check Oil Level in Transmission Case: Assess the transmis-

sion oil level according to the manufacturer's recommendations, adding correct oil if necessary through the oil filler cap.

4. Check Oil Level in Hydraulic Tank: Examine the hydraulic tank oil level on horizontal ground and add correct oil if below the recommended level, taking care to tighten the cap securely.

5. Drain Water, Sediment from Fuel Tank: Loosen the valve at the bottom of the fuel tank to drain water and sediment collected at the tank's base together with the fuel, in adherence to company policies and procedures.

6. Check Fuel Level: Utilize the fuel gauge, dipstick, or sight gauge to check the fuel level, taking precautions to prevent fuel overflow and wiping any spills completely.

7. Inspect Tyres: Examine tyres for irregularities, cuts, bulges, or signs of rubbing against body parts, ensuring dual wheels are matching and equally inflated if applicable.

8. Check Wheel Hub Nuts: Verify that hub nuts are tightened to the specified torque and report any loose nuts to the supervisor if necessary.

9. Tightening Torque: Follow the manufacturer's recommendations for tightening torque.

10. Check Tyre Inflation Pressure, Check for Damage: Assess tyre inflation pressure when tyres are cold, checking for damage and foreign objects embedded in the tyre.

11. Check Engine Air Cleaner Fitter Restriction Indicators: Inspect the air cleaner to ensure the red piston has not appeared in the transparent portion of the dust indicator, cleaning or replacing the element as needed.

12. Drain Water from Air Tank: Open the tank drain valve to drain water from the tank, particularly in cold areas where freezing may occur.

13. Clean dust/mud off tail lights.

14. Wipe down climbing steps/rails, steering wheel, hand levers, pedals, knobs, and other controls to prevent slipping.

15. Clean out the cabin, secure tools into a safe place, and remove unauthorized materials from the cab for disposal.

16. Check warning systems, including lights, reversing signals/alarm, warning horn, and signalling devices.

17. Verify the functionality of the two-way radio communication system.

18. Check for loose fan belts,

19. Check oil, fuel, and air filters.

20. Check for loose panels or fittings.

21. Ensure Personal Protection Equipment readiness, including overalls, safety boots, protective eyewear, ear muffs, gloves, safety hat, and face mask.

Startup procedures may differ depending on the specific truck and site protocols. It's essential to adhere to the established procedures. Carefully enter the cabin and ensure adequate ventilation to avoid exposure to fumes before starting. Prior to starting the engine, ensure familiarity with the manuals, confirm the area around the truck is clear of people and obstructions, and ensure the park brake switch is in the "Apply" position. A customary practice is to sound the horn once before starting, as outlined in site procedures. Starting the engine with the park brake switch released poses a risk of the truck moving once pressure builds up to release the brake. After starting the engine, double-check instrument readiness and equipment functionality, including signalling devices, fuses, windshield wipers, pressure gauges, and control functionality. Adjust and secure the seat belt, test the accelerator pedal, and verify the functionality of the two-way radio. Before moving, alert others by sounding the horn twice, as specified in site procedures.

Emergency procedures are crucial knowledge for haul truck operators to ensure their safety and that of others in case of unexpected events. Familiarity with the location and operation of warning devices on the haul truck is paramount. For instance, if the dump body angle warning light illuminates, indicating a tilt beyond the safety range, immediate action must be taken to lower the dump body and relocate the machine to a stable area. Additionally, understanding the operation of emergency steering and braking systems is essential, as all haul trucks are mandated by law to be equipped with such features.

Some haul trucks may also feature emergency exits, such as a door on the right-hand side of the cabin or a side window that can be opened by following specific procedures. Operators should verify the location of emergency exits in their truck and manuals, seeking assistance from mentors if necessary.

Furthermore, familiarity with site emergency procedures is imperative, typically outlined during the induction process by the company and available with the Safety Officer. These procedures detail actions to be taken in emergencies, including reporting protocols, emergency contact information, the location of emergency equipment such as stop buttons and fire extinguishers, safe assembly areas, and first aid provisions. Understanding the meaning of various signals, signs, and procedures during blasting operations is also essential.

In the event of the machine contacting live power lines, operators must observe strict precautions to mitigate risks. Remaining inside the cabin, warning others to stay clear, and attempting to move the machine away from the power lines without assistance are initial steps. If unable to move, operators should remain inside the cabin and inform the power supply authority to disconnect the power. Jumping from the truck should only be considered if absolutely necessary, with specific precautions to be followed to minimize risks of injury or electrocution. It's critical to avoid contact between the machine and the ground simultaneously and to move away cautiously from the energized area to prevent electric shock. Additionally, operators should be aware of the potential risk of tyre explosions after contact with power lines, necessitating isolation of the machine and appropriate warning signs to minimize hazards.

Operating a Haul Truck

Prioritize the completion of prestart checks and adhere to start-up procedures before operating the truck. Conduct a thorough inspection by walking around the vehicle to ensure the surrounding area, both above and beneath, is free from obstacles, including other vehicles and individuals. Before moving, use the horn as a warning signal. Utilize designated pick-up areas for driver change-outs and maintain effective communication practices for embarking and disembarking trucks. Access and exit the truck using proper techniques, maintaining three-point contact at all times, and refrain from jumping, even from the lowest rung.

Avoid attempting to carry heavy or cumbersome materials onto truck platforms. Ensure the use of seatbelts and harnesses fitted within the vehicle. Adhere to all road regulations, including speed limits, signs, and traffic control systems. Regularly inspect tyre inflation and monitor tyre conditions, as damaged or under-inflated tyres can pose risks of explosions or fires. Verify brake functionality every time the truck is set in motion and adapt driving speed to match road conditions, particularly exercising caution in wet weather.

When navigating downhill slopes, refrain from coasting out of gear. Keep the transmission engaged and utilize the retarder system. Maintain cleanliness within the cabin, as loose items may impede brake or accelerator pedals. Utilize two-way radios for effective communication during overtaking manoeuvres or when entering congested areas, ensuring adherence to radio procedure and protocol. Refrain from using service brakes on downhauls except in emergencies, opting instead for correct gears and the retarder system.

In the event of a load hang-up during tipping, seek assistance from a supervisor. Use "Danger" and "Out of Service" tags when necessary and acknowledge any tags present. Maintain a safe distance of five truck lengths between vehicles traveling in the same direction. Exercise caution near buildings and populated areas, paying attention to the positioning of overhead powerlines and other structures. Never drive with the tray raised, as it may collide with overhead powerlines, posing fatal risks to personnel and causing significant damage.

Exercise caution around other mobile equipment, such as graders, dozers, and water trucks, giving them ample room to manoeuvre. Reduce speed when navigating bends and corners to mitigate risks of rollovers or rock spillage. If encountered, avoid areas with rock spillage and notify supervisors or the grader driver for remediation. Ensure the truck is regularly washed and maintained for visibility during both day and night operations.

Approach dumping areas cautiously, positioning the edge on the driver's side and ensuring visibility. Refrain from dumping over the edge of stockpiles above areas where material has been or is being removed until clearance is confirmed safe. Avoid using the retarder as a parking brake and promptly tag out and report any truck defects.

Additionally, submit reports for all incidents, including near misses, to ensure continuous improvement in safety protocols.

Special precautions must be taken when operating underground to ensure safety and prevent accidents. It is essential to test the brakes before entering the portal and avoid driving down declines using the service brakes. Correct gear selection and the use of a retarder, if available, are crucial for safe navigation. Additionally, before entering the portal, always ensure that the tray has been lowered to prevent any collisions or obstructions.

Excavations should only be entered if they are designed to accommodate the size of your truck, ensuring proper clearance and manoeuvrability. Operating only in areas with adequate ventilation is vital to prevent the buildup of harmful gases and ensure a safe working environment. If a vehicle is emitting excessive black smoke, it should be reported to the supervisor immediately, and the vehicle should be removed from service to address any potential issues.

Vehicles should never be left unattended unless the power has been switched off, and the brakes have been applied to prevent unintended movement. When parking on a slope, it is essential to turn the wheels towards the wall to prevent the vehicle from rolling in the event of a brake failure or other unforeseen circumstances. These precautions are essential for maintaining safety and minimizing the risk of accidents in underground mining operations.

Haul trucks are equipped with a range of safety features aimed at protecting the operator during operations. These safety devices include seat belts, seat interfaces, operator protection bars (ROPS-FOPS), safety props, bars, and pins, safety guards and covers, warning devices, supplementary steering and emergency brakes, as well as warning labels. Seat belts are essential for preventing the operator from falling out of the seat during manoeuvres, and it's imperative for operators to wear them at all times. The seat interface ensures that the machine operates only when the operator's weight is detected. Operator protection bars, including ROPS and FOPS, provide crush protection in the event of a rollover or tipping. Safety bars, props, and pins are utilized to prevent sudden collapses of machinery components during inspections or maintenance tasks. Safety guards and covers must be checked for proper positioning before operation, and warning devices alert operators to potential hazards. Supplementary steering and emergency brakes offer additional control in case of system failure. Safety plates and labels are strategically placed on the machine to highlight potential hazards, and it's crucial for operators to understand and adhere to these safety messages. Regular inspection and maintenance of safety features are essential to ensure their effectiveness in protecting personnel and preventing accidents.

Adhering to safe practices and site-specific safety requirements is essential for haul truck operators to ensure their safety and the safety of others. Each site may have unique safety protocols outlined by the company, which operators must be familiar with and adhere to diligently to prevent potential accidents or injuries. Failure to comply with these safety regulations could lead to personal injuries, fatalities, or costly machinery repairs.

The following list provides examples of safe working practices and serves as a general overview:

- People Safety: Operators must maintain constant vigilance, never assuming that people will stay clear of potential hazards. Avoid distractions while operating the haul truck and remain vigilant of bystanders and other equipment in the vicinity. Do not allow unauthorized individuals to approach the truck's wheels or pinch points, and use warning tags to indicate when servicing or repairing the machine is underway.

- Operator Qualifications and Health: Only qualified operators should operate haul trucks, having undergone proper training, testing, and appointment for the specific machine type. Operating machinery under the influence of alcohol, medication, or other drugs is strictly prohibited due to the risk of impaired judgment and potential accidents.

- Personal Protective Equipment (PPE): Wearing appropriate PPE such as safety footwear, hard hats, gloves, safety glasses, ear protection, respirators, and reflective vests is essential to mitigate injury risks. Loose clothing, jewellery, and long hair should be avoided to prevent entanglement in controls or moving parts.

- Pre-Start Checks and Mounting/Dismounting: Performing pre-start checks on the machine is mandatory, and any faults should be reported to the supervisor promptly. When mounting or dismounting the machine, operators should face the equipment, use provided steps and handholds, and maintain three points of contact to prevent falls or injuries.

- Cabin Safety: Ensure that steps, handholds, walkways, and decks are clear of debris and slippery materials to prevent accidents. Keep the cabin free of loose objects that could become projectiles in the event of an accident.

- Vehicle Operation: Before moving, operators must fit and adjust their seat belts, as wearing them while in motion is mandatory. Conduct thorough checks on brakes, steering, lights, and warning indicators to ensure they are operational and in good condition. Familiarize yourself with emergency brake and supplementary steering operations and conduct regular checks to ensure their functionality. Testing brakes within the first 500 meters of each shift is recommended as per the manufacturer's manual.

- Park-Up Area: Understand the company's policy for exiting the park-up area before proceeding. Ensure that the brake air pressure is within the operating range, the dump body is lowered, the hoist control is in the float position (if applicable), and sound the horn before moving off. Transporting passengers on the haul truck is prohibited unless the truck is specifically designed for carrying passengers or for operator instruction purposes.

While driving on haul roads, it is imperative to adhere to safe practices and comply with site-specific safety regulations. Here are guidelines to ensure safe operation:

On the Road:
- Always obey road signs and warnings, and consider posted speed limits as maximum under ideal conditions, adjusting speed according to road conditions, visibility, and load, as well as personal competency and confidence.

- Drive defensively, remaining vigilant of other plant and equipment in operation.

- Follow company policies regarding travel direction and side of the road.

- Avoid reversing along haul roads unless for road maintenance purposes.

- Refrain from driving haul trucks over unprotected pipes, electrical cables, or demarcated pipeline routes.

- Yield to vehicles as per company policy, giving way to loaded trucks, scrapers, and road maintenance equipment.

- In emergency situations, prioritize safety by allowing the most capable vehicle to stop or manoeuvre, disregarding normal procedures.

- Give way to trucks on main haul roads when turning onto or off them.

- Use headlights in reduced visibility conditions and refrain from overtaking unless the vehicle ahead is stationary and parked to the side.

Following Distance and Manoeuvring:
- Maintain a minimum separation of thirty meters or as directed by company policy when following other haul trucks, increasing the distance with higher speeds.

- Execute U-turns safely and provide adequate time for other vehicles to observe the manoeuvre.

- Keep a safe distance from cliffs, overhangs, and slide areas as directed by company policy.

- Always maintain control of the haul truck and avoid coasting in neutral.

- Select the correct gear range before descending and refrain from changing gears during the downgrade.

At the Face/Bench:
- Maintain a safe distance from cliff edges, overhangs, and slide areas.

- Do not enter or exit the cab while the haul truck is being loaded or dumping.

- Work up and down slopes whenever possible to avoid tipping.

- Maintain visibility by cleaning windows and mirrors regularly, avoiding cleaning while loading or in the pit without wearing a hard hat.

- Ensure safety measures are in place when dumping over a bank, such as providing effective bank stops, spotters, or illumination after dark.

- Avoid traveling with the tray up unless necessary for clearing purposes.

Emergency Procedures:
- Know emergency procedures and comply with them in any emergency situation, prioritizing safety over normal procedures.

- Familiarize yourself with company policies and procedures regarding safe working practices and site-specific safety requirements, seeking assistance from mentors or referring to company documentation if needed.

Remember, it is your responsibility to be aware of and adhere to your company's site-specific safety requirements and emergency procedures. When in doubt, seek assistance to ensure safe operations at all times.

Dumping loads poses significant hazards, particularly the risk of machine rollover, especially when tipping material from an elevated tip head area. Factors that can increase this hazard include incorrect windrow construction, unstable ground, improper operating techniques, and unsafe positioning of other machines and personnel. To mitigate these risks, haul truck operators must adhere to the following guidelines:

- Dump only in stable dump areas with adequately established and maintained tip heads, following instructions on dump locations strictly.

- Ensure sufficient lighting, especially during nighttime operations, by utilizing lighting plants.

- Notify supervisors promptly if any maintenance is required for the dump area.

Approaching the dump area requires specific procedures:

1. Establish radio contact with the dump cleanup machine operator.

2. Approach the tip head at a safe speed in a clockwise direction, keeping the dump on the left side.

3. Dump material from right to left, starting from where the last dump occurred.

4. Maintain a safe distance of approximately 10 meters from the tip head when driving parallel to the dump edge.

5. When reversing to dump, execute a left to right turn (a 'T-turn').

6. Avoid pulling in front of another truck to tip, maintaining a distance of 20 meters or at least two dump truck loads between trucks and dozers.

7. When reaching the dump area, turn the truck to the right until positioned 90 degrees to the tip head, using a wide turning circle to prevent tyre damage.

EARTHMOVING EQUIPMENT OPERATIONS

Figure 101: Approaching the dump area. Jon Lavis from Seaford, CC BY 2.0, via Wikimedia Commons.

Important checkpoints to observe in the dump area include:

- Cracks: Notify supervisors or dozer operators of any cracks and monitor changes in their width throughout the shift.

- Rocks: Remove any rocks from the windrow to prevent tyre damage and windrow instability.

- Slumping: Report any slumping at the tip head immediately to supervisors or dozer operators.

- Wet Material: Notify dozer operators and supervisors promptly if the windrow becomes excessively wet, causing instability.

- Windrow Height and Construction: The windrow should be half the height of the largest truck tyre in use. If there are concerns about windrow height, dump short and inform the dozer operator. The windrow serves as a guide for stopping the truck and indicating the dump edge.

The windrow can sustain damage through bashing, which compacts material in front and dislodges material from the back, or by moving forward before lowering the tray when tipping. These actions must be avoided to maintain windrow integrity.

Figure 102: Dumping a load. Jon Lavis from Seaford, CC BY 2.0 , via Wikimedia Commons.

Reversing towards the tip head:
1. Ensure that the ground is level before proceeding.

2. Position the truck in a straight line and reverse slowly towards the tip head, utilizing side mirrors or a reverse monitor for guidance.

3. Keep the truck as straight as possible during the reversing process.

4. Reverse until the rear tyre gently contacts the windrow. Ensure that the inner tyre makes contact first before straightening up. Avoid using the windrow as a braking mechanism.

5. Apply the park brake and shift to neutral gear.

Dumping a load:
1. Follow the engine acceleration procedure outlined in the training manual for dump truck operations (RPM's).

2. Pull the tip control lever to the raised position and hold until the tray is almost fully raised.

3. Reduce engine speed as the tray nears its maximum height and release the tip control lever.

4. Wait until all the material has cleared the edge of the tray.

5. Move forward approximately half a meter and fully lower the tray. If dumping onto the ground, drive forward slowly to ensure the tray empties before lowering completely.

6. Release the control lever.

7. Select drive (D) and release the park brake.

8. Check for other equipment in the vicinity and move forward at a safe speed.

Note: Prioritize personal safety and, if uncertain, opt to tip the load short rather than risk compromising safety.

Dumping near another truck:

1. Prepare to reverse alongside the other truck following standard procedures.

2. Keep the other truck to your left-hand side.

3. Maintain a minimum distance of two dump truck widths between trucks at all times.

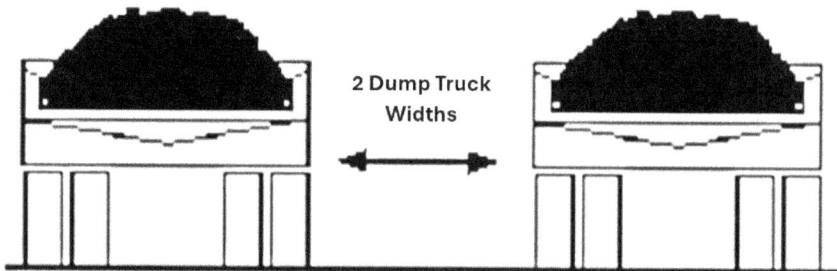

Figure 103: Maintain separation when dumping next to another truck.

To ensure a square and uniform tip head, thereby minimizing the risk of off-side tyres crossing the windrow, truck operators can follow these steps:

1. Begin tipping from the right-hand corner (facing the dump) and continue tipping in the same spot until material no longer spills over the windrow.

2. Once the initial location is full, shift one truck length to the left and repeat the process. Continue moving across until the entire width of the dump area is covered.

3. Repeat the tipping operation, working from right to left.

If repairs are initiated on a portion of the windrow before the entire dump width is covered:
- Leave the last full windrow section as a marker for ongoing tipping.
- Continue tipping to the left of this marker until the entire dump width is covered.

In the event of a rounded or uneven dump:
- Focus tipping efforts on the right and left-hand corners.
- Once the outer sections align with the middle section, resume tipping following the regular sequence.

Stuck Loads: Occasionally, loads may become stuck in the tray due to overloading or incorrect positioning. In such cases:
1. Inform the supervisor of the situation.
2. The supervisor will direct the operator to return "loaded" to the excavator for partial or complete load removal with caution.
3. Re-position or reload according to accepted practice and return to the dump location. Under no circumstances should attempts be made to tip the load by abrupt manoeuvres such as hopping, jerking, or excessive reversing and braking.

Paddock Dumping: Paddock dumping is a method used for flat dumping areas to be levelled by a dozer, aiding in building up a specific area. To execute this procedure effectively:
- Manoeuvre to the advised position.
- Short-tip the load following the regular dumping procedure.
- Dump loads closely together and compact them.

Before commencing operation, it is essential to conduct a thorough inspection of the vehicle to ensure its proper functioning. Additionally, the operator must assume a suitable driving position and fasten the seat belt for personal safety. Adherence to all mine site road and traffic regulations is paramount, along with maintaining vigilance regarding potential hazards. Before initiating any reversing manoeuvres, it is imperative to exercise necessary safety precautions.

Operation: During both forward and reversing manoeuvres, several operational factors must be considered. These include criteria for changing direction, acceleration techniques, braking systems, and proper application of the park brake. Additionally, methods for retardation, monitoring of instruments and gauges, as well as procedures for raising and lowering the body of the truck, must be adhered to.

Downgrade Retarding: Proper management of ground speed to match road conditions, selection of the appropriate gear, and maintenance of steady engine speed are crucial for effective downgrade retarding. Additionally, the use of the service brake to trim speed, upshifting the transmission when necessary, and avoiding coasting in neutral are essential safety measures. Regular monitoring of brake oil temperature and cooling measures during loading are also vital aspects of downgrade retarding.

Loss of Power and Retardation on an Incline or Decline: In the event of engine power loss during navigation on inclines or declines, specific steps must be followed to ensure safety. This includes the application of service brakes to halt the truck, engagement of emergency brakes if required, and steering the truck to a safe location. Proper reporting of the incident to the supervisor and remaining in the truck until the situation is resolved are crucial steps to mitigate risks.

Loss of Steering: If a steering malfunction occurs, the emergency steering system will activate automatically to facilitate safe manoeuvring. The operator must steer the truck to a safe parking position, apply the park brake, and notify the supervisor of the situation. Remaining in the truck until deemed safe to exit is essential for personal safety and adherence to protocol.

Operate the truck defensively and remain vigilant of other plant and equipment in the vicinity. Adhere to company policies regarding direction and side of the road to travel, posted speed limits, and road signs. Additionally, exercise caution around edges, overhangs, and slide areas. Give way to loaded vehicles and adjust driving to suit ground conditions. Maintain a safe following distance with other trucks and ensure control of the truck at all times. Select the correct gear before negotiating a downgrade and utilize the retarder when necessary.

Position the truck under the loading machine according to the directives provided by the loading machine operator. Align the truck with markers on the loading machine to ensure proper positioning for loading. It's essential to remember that the loading machine's reach and bucket positioning are limited, and the operator will expect the truck to be in the correct position for loading.

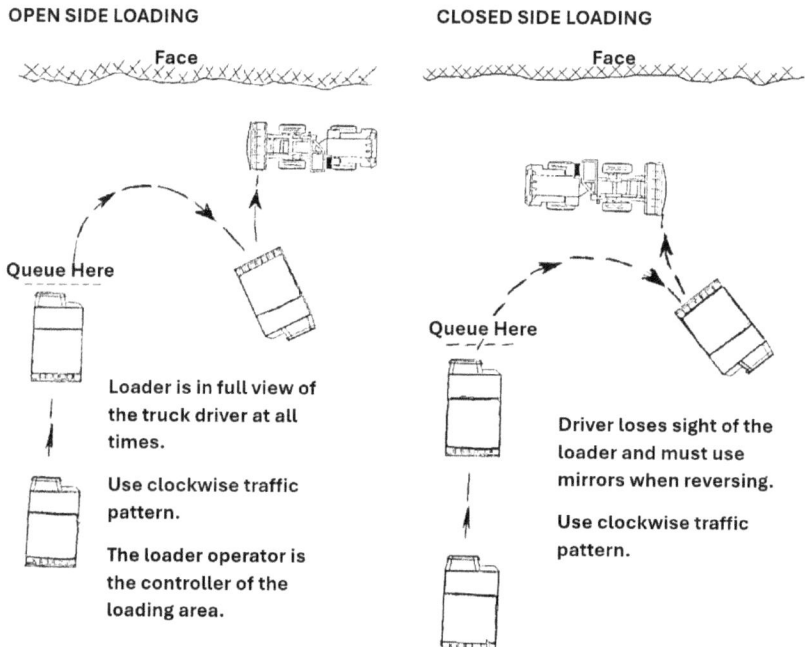

Figure 104: Open and closed side loading.

While the truck is being loaded, it is imperative that you remain in the cabin. Ensure that the loading machine operator distributes the load evenly across the dump body. Uneven load distribution can lead to excessive tyre wear, axle loading issues, and instability during unloading.

EARTHMOVING EQUIPMENT OPERATIONS

Figure 105: Correct loading. Greg Goebel from Loveland CO, USA, CC BY-SA 2.0, via Wikimedia Commons.

Leaving the Loading Area: Before departing from the loading area, carefully inspect the route you intend to take to ensure it is free of any obstructions or other plant and equipment. Exit the area with caution to avoid accidents.

When Loaded: Follow the recommendations outlined in the manufacturer's operation and maintenance manual when moving off after being loaded.

Travelling Loaded: Drive the truck to the dump area, utilizing gears, brakes, differential locks, and retarders (if applicable) as advised in the manufacturer's manual. Adhere to company policies regarding traveling procedures.

Travelling Downhill: When descending downhill with a loaded truck, maintain a safe speed appropriate for the road width, road surface conditions, and other job site factors. Exercise caution and maintain control as the handling characteristics of the loaded truck may differ significantly from when it is unloaded.

Unloading Area: Before unloading, ensure the area is clear of any obstacles or personnel. If a spotter is present, follow their directions to safely navigate the unloading process.

Reversing: Due to limited visibility to the rear of the truck, take every precaution to prevent workmen, plant, and equipment from getting behind the truck while reversing.

Unloading: When unloading, adhere to company policies and procedures. Be mindful of potential danger areas such as obstructions, edges, excavations, and overhead hazards. Operate the dump body according to the manufacturer's instructions. After unloading, lower the dump body as recommended to ensure it rests properly on the frame, with the dump body lever in the float position.

Entering Park-Up Area: Follow company policy when entering and parking the truck in designated areas.

Engine Shut-Down: Shutdown the engine following the manufacturer's recommendations to ensure proper maintenance and safety.

Dismounting from Truck: When disembarking from the truck, use three points of contact to ensure stability and prevent falls.

Checks after Stopping Engine: After stopping the engine, conduct checks around the work equipment, bodywork, and undercarriage to detect any signs of oil, water, or fuel leakage.

Operating articulated dump trucks (ADTs) may seem straightforward, especially with their automatic transmissions resembling those of everyday vehicles. However, to ensure optimal performance and longevity of these robust machines, operators must familiarize themselves with essential functions such as retarders, differential locks, and dump operations, while also understanding their limitations.

The most apparent distinctions between off-road haul trucks and typical vehicles are their size and weight. Loaded ADTs weigh approximately ten times more than personal vehicles and often navigate through undeveloped roads. Operating them safely and efficiently necessitates foresight in engaging features like retarders and differential locks well in advance to control the load effectively.

Using axle or service brakes excessively instead of retarders to slow down the truck can significantly shorten brake life. However, many operators tend to favour service brakes due to their immediate stopping power. Yet, mastering the use of retarders is crucial as they require anticipation and application ahead of the desired slowdown point.

Automatic transmissions in modern trucks are highly efficient, typically requiring only selecting "D" for drive. However, specific conditions may call for manual gear selection to optimize performance, such as steep grades or muddy terrain.

When shifting gears, especially downhill, it's essential to anticipate the need for a different gear before it becomes necessary. This proactive approach helps maintain control and prevents unnecessary wear on the transmission.

Understanding when and how to use differential locks is equally critical. While engaging all differentials may be necessary in challenging terrain, doing so unnecessarily can reduce efficiency and increase wear and tear on the truck.

Managing haul roads is another crucial aspect of ADT operation. While these trucks can navigate less maintained roads, it's essential to maintain diligence in road maintenance to prevent accidents and reduce cycle times.

Returning to the loading zone with an empty truck requires extra caution, as heavy-truck suspensions are tuned for carrying a load. Speed and ground conditions must be carefully monitored to ensure safety.

When unloading, operators must position the truck properly and pay attention to potential hazards such as side slopes and load distribution.

Overloading trucks not only affects fuel efficiency but also compromises safety and stability.

Operators should also be mindful of dumping operations, especially when dealing with sticky materials or dumping downhill. Raising the dump bed slowly and attentively is crucial to prevent accidents and maintain stability.

When operating a dump truck in wet and slippery conditions, it is essential to adhere to the following precautions and requirements:

- Identify causes of skidding and loss of traction.
- Adjust truck speed when approaching corners or descending ramps.
- Reduce speed and drive according to the conditions.
- Familiarize yourself with braking and retardation techniques.
- Understand the characteristics of the vehicle when laden and unladen in wet conditions.

During a series of manoeuvres, familiarize yourself with the following operating procedures: (Note: A water truck may be necessary to simulate wet conditions.)

- Understand the requirements for changing direction.
- Adjust acceleration appropriately.
- Practice braking systems and braking procedures.
- Learn effective retardation techniques. • Monitor instruments and gauges for any indications.

In the event of engine power loss while negotiating an incline or decline, follow this procedure:

- Apply the service brakes to halt the truck.

- Engage the emergency brakes if necessary.

- If feasible, reverse or steer the truck into a safety berm or dump a load on the downhill side for safe parking.

- Apply the park brake and activate hazard lights.

- Report the incident to the supervisor.

If a steering malfunction occurs during operation, the emergency steering system will activate automatically. Follow these steps:

- Steer the truck to a safe parking position.

- Apply the park brake and shut down the truck.

- Isolate the truck as necessary.

- Notify the supervisor promptly.

Retarding the Haul Truck when Navigating a Decline: Before descending a decline, it's crucial to observe the following precautions. First, reduce your speed appropriately. Next, select the correct gear position according to the recommended gear and road speed indicated on the "in cab" Retarding Chart. If the retarding oil temperature exceeds the safe range, indicated by reaching the red zone on the gauge or hitting 100°C, take immediate action. Shift to the next lower gear and, if necessary, briefly engage full braking to decrease speed and facilitate the downshift. Avoid coasting down a decline with the transmission in neutral, as this could lead to loss of control, posing risks of injuries, fatalities, and damage to the truck.

Familiarize yourself with the haul road network at the job site and stay alert to approaching declines. Operate the truck in strict accordance with the truck manufacturer's operation and maintenance manual or company policy to ensure safe navigation of declines.

Always maintain control of your haul truck to prevent accidents and injuries. Stay vigilant and adhere to safety protocols at all times.

Note: Different makes and models of haul trucks may require varying operating techniques for negotiating declines. Refer to your manual for specific instructions.

The braking and retarding procedures outlined below are derived from a Caterpillar 769C off-highway truck operation and maintenance manual.

Braking Operation: For 768C Tractors and 769C Trucks equipped with oil-cooled multiple disc brakes on the rear and dry disc brakes on the front:

- Utilize the brake lever to engage both front and rear brakes by moving it to the left and depressing the brake pedal.

- Move the lever to the right and depress the brake pedal to engage only the rear brake.

- Avoid using the front wheel brakes for retarding on long steep downgrades to prevent overheating and reduce the service life of brake components.

Service Brake: The service brake pedal applies either all four wheel brakes or only the rear brakes based on the front wheel brake switch position.

Retarder and Secondary Brake: The retarder control applies only the rear wheel brakes, regardless of the front wheel brake lever position. The secondary brake control applies all four wheel brakes, regardless of the front wheel brake switch position. Be prepared to use the secondary braking system if the air pressure in the service brake/retarding tank falls to approximately 415 kPa (60 psi).

Parking Brake: Engage the parking brake switch to activate only the rear wheel brakes, regardless of the front wheel brake switch position.

Retarder Operation: When using the service brake pedal for braking or retarding, deactivate the front wheel brake switch to prevent overheating. Apply the retarder lever gradually on slippery roads to prevent rear wheel lockup and potential transmission downshift. Avoid frequent engagement and disengagement of the retarder; make adjustments as necessary to maintain a safe speed during retarding.

Retarding Information and Conditions: Ensure that ground speed is maintained at a level that prevents brake overheating. Maintain engine speed within the green operating range to prevent damage. If the brake oil temperature becomes excessive, stop the machine, run the engine at moderate speed until the oil cools, then proceed at a slower speed in a lower gear.

Downgrade Retarding: Always keep the transmission in gear and avoid coasting downhill in neutral.

Safe Reversing Procedures: Ensure that operational reversing alarms are functional and rear-view mirrors are properly adjusted. Exercise caution when reversing due to limited rear visibility. Stay clear of hazardous or soft ground areas.

Load Spotter: Follow the directions of a load spotter if present, and keep them in view at all times while reversing.

Reversing Area: Ensure the reversing area is clear and prevent anyone from entering the truck's path during reversing manoeuvres. If a spotter is unavailable, designate a safety person to monitor reversing in hazardous or low-visibility areas.

Certain haul trucks are equipped with a dedicated emergency braking system designed to safely halt the vehicle in critical braking situations. The operation of this system typically involves either a manually operated lever or automatic activation triggered by a drop in air pressure below a predetermined threshold, such as 60 psi.

Different truck models may feature varying emergency braking mechanisms, so it's essential to consult your operator's manual for specific instructions. For instance, in some models, when the air pressure in the main tank dips below a certain level, a low air pressure warning alarm is triggered, prompting the operator to engage the emergency braking system to stop the truck.

NOTE: Emergency brake systems are typically reserved for use in the event of a failure in the primary braking system.

During an emergency braking scenario, the truck operator should, if feasible:

- Remain composed and avoid panicking.
- Exert their best effort to maintain control of the truck.
- Alert others by sounding the horn.
- Quickly devise a safe route of escape.
- Steer the truck away from steep embankments.
- Employ a technique known as "pumping" the foot brake pedal if all wheels lock up, allowing the wheels to momentarily turn before locking again for short distances. This aids in braking effectiveness and facilitates steering response.

Emergency braking may be necessary in the following situations:

- Low air pressure in the braking system.
- Evasive action to avoid collisions.
- Adverse road conditions such as slippery surfaces (e.g., clay or snow).
- Loss of control of the truck.

When preparing to receive a load from a loading unit, adhere to the following general site requirements:

- Follow all mine site vehicle and traffic regulations.

- Typically, approach the loading area in a clockwise direction unless instructed otherwise by the loading unit operator or supervisor, or if there is mutual agreement among all parties present.

- If queuing is necessary, park at least one truck length away from the preceding truck and staggered to one side to maintain visibility in the rear-view mirror of other trucks.

- Establish radio contact with the loading unit operator if communication is required.

- Ensure that the monitoring system indicates the truck's arrival at the loading unit.

Receiving a Load:
- Stay inside the truck cabin unless instructed otherwise by the loading unit operator.

- Depart from the loading area promptly upon receiving the signal from the loading unit operator, provided it is safe to do so.

- Monitor the screen to ensure the correct dumping location for material in the truck body.

Loading Position (example):
- Position the truck approximately 20 meters from the loading point in preparation for reversing.

- Reverse the truck to the loading point, either on the loading side or waiting side as applicable (for shovel).

- Avoid driving over any spilled material.

- Stop the truck under the loading unit bucket or as indicated by the operator (loading side) or in the appropriate position (waiting side) for shovel.

- Press the "first bucket" icon when the initial material bucket is placed in the truck body.

Excavator:
- Ensure correct loading operation and sequence.
- Approach the loading unit in a clockwise direction unless instructed otherwise.
- Maintain visual contact with the excavator during topside loading while reversing.
- Keep the safety windrow in view to avoid reversing into the pit.
- For bottom loading at 45°, reverse the truck at a 45° angle to the front track idler. For 900 bottom loading, reverse at a 90° angle to the rear drive sprocket or side of the operator cab, depending on the dig sequence.
- If uncertain about the spotting position, use the bucket teeth as a guide.

Shovel:
- Position the truck as directed for single-sided loading, double-sided loading, loading or waiting side, or shovel modified drive-by loading.
- Halt the truck in the appropriate position.
- Stay in the truck cabin unless instructed otherwise by the loading unit operator.
- Ensure the load monitoring system is operational during load receipt.

- Reverse the truck as the shovel bucket returns to its dig position.

Loader:
- Prepare the truck for reversing to the loading point, ensuring it is not more than 20 meters away.
- Reverse the truck to the loading point.
- Position the truck at a 45-degree angle to the loading face or as instructed by the operator.
- Exercise caution to avoid driving over spillage or sharp rocks.
- Stop the truck under the loading unit bucket or as directed by the operator, especially on the loading side.
- Stay inside the truck cabin unless instructed otherwise by the loading unit operator.
- Verify that the load monitoring system is operational before receiving a load.

When transporting a load, truck operators must comply with mine site regulations and adhere to the manufacturer's specifications. It's essential to consider the following definitions:

Grade: Refers to the vertical rise in the terrain over the horizontal distance, usually expressed as a percentage.

Retard Envelope: The RPM and/or road speed range where the retarder operates most effectively, varying according to truck type and model. Refer to the manufacturer's manual for specific details.

Negotiating a Downgrade: This involves determining the appropriate descent speed from the grade/speed plate, selecting the required descent gear before proceeding downhill, and setting the RSC switch to the "ON" position for mechanical drive trucks.

Overspeed: In the event of an overspeed situation, operators should maintain full retard and apply the service brake with one hard application to slow down. It's crucial not to feather the brake pedal during overspeed to prevent brake overheating.

Requirements for hauling a load from the loading unit to the dump site include:

- Driving according to road, weather, and traffic conditions.

- Observing all mine site speed limits.

- Yielding to other equipment and loaded trucks as necessary.

- Being aware of light vehicles on haul roads/ramps.

- Maintaining a safe distance from the truck ahead and observing its brake/retard lights.

Environmental considerations, such as dust and spills, must also be taken into account:

Dust: Efforts should be made to minimize or eliminate dust during truck operations. Visible and respirable dust should be managed accordingly, and additional dust suppression measures may be required if wheel-generated dust is consistently visible above a certain height.

Spills: All spills should be promptly cleaned up, with major spills or those posing a threat to safety or waterways treated as emergencies. Spills exceeding locally specified limits must be reported to a supervisor.

The operating procedure for hauling a load involves driving within the recommended speed range, observing traffic regulations, and adjusting speed based on road and traffic conditions.

Approaching a downgrade requires attaining the required descent speed before proceeding downhill, using the retarder system to maintain speed, and notifying supervisors if an overspeed situation occurs.

Approaching the dump site and give way or stop signs necessitates following designated procedures to ensure safety and prevent accidents, including maintaining a safe distance between trucks to avoid rear-end collisions.

Dumping at Slurry Ponds and Dams: Dumping at dams/slurry ponds should only occur during daylight hours, with the dump area clearly marked. Material should not be tipped over the edge into the dam/slurry pond; instead, it should be deposited short and then pushed with a bulldozer.

Dumping at Coal Bins MTO: Truck operators should adhere to clockwise travel in the ROM and stockpile area and be mindful of other operations in the vicinity. Before reversing, they must ensure the area is clear of other vehicles and then reverse to the bin, making soft contact with the buffer. Dumping should only occur when ROM control lights are green, and if the allocated bin is full or out of service, dispatch should be contacted for further instructions. The secondary menu on MAPS should be used if tipping at a location other than the allocated ROM bin.

Dumping at Coal Bins MTO refers to the process of unloading material from haul trucks into designated bins at the Run of Mine (ROM) and stockpile area. This includes:

1. Clockwise Travel: Truck operators are instructed to travel in a clockwise direction within the ROM and stockpile area. This direction of travel helps maintain organized movement and prevents collisions or disruptions in operations.

2. Mindful of Other Operations: Operators must be aware of ongoing activities and operations in the surrounding area to avoid interference and ensure safety.

3. Clear Area Before Reversing: Before initiating the reversing manoeuvre to approach the bin, operators must ensure that the

area behind the truck is free of obstacles and other vehicles to prevent accidents.

4. Soft Contact with Buffer: When reversing toward the bin, operators should make gentle contact with the buffer or stopping point to ensure accurate positioning without causing damage to the truck or infrastructure.

5. ROM Control Lights: Dumping should only commence when the ROM control lights indicate green status. This ensures that the bin is ready to receive the load and prevents potential issues with overfilling or equipment malfunction.

6. Dispatch Notification: If the allocated bin is full or unavailable for any reason, operators are responsible for contacting dispatch to receive further instructions. This ensures efficient operations and prevents delays or disruptions.

7. Secondary Menu on MAPS: If the operator needs to dump material at a location other than the designated ROM bin, they should utilize the secondary menu on the Mine Asset Planning System (MAPS) to input the necessary information and ensure proper documentation and tracking of the load.

Operating Tips: Operators should select the appropriate gear for the load and downhill retarding. They should also be familiar with traffic patterns, right-of-way rules, and maintain a safe distance from other equipment. Planning for emergencies is crucial.

Hauling Tips: Safety measures such as not using the retarder for parking, keeping the front brake switch on at all times, and using ARC to maintain a safe speed should be followed.

Dumping Tips: Safety during dumping operations is paramount, including checking for stop berms on high walls and dumping in an organized pattern. Operators should follow directions from dozers or dump bosses and exercise caution during the dumping process.

Stockpile Dumping: Dumping at stockpile sites requires caution to avoid collapse and proper positioning of the truck. Operators must follow company policies and guidelines at all times.

Hopper Dumping: Procedures for dumping into hoppers must be followed strictly, adhering to safety directions and signals.

Dumping Over a Bank: Dumping over a bank necessitates parallel positioning of the rear wheels to prevent tipping. Safety devices such as wheel stops and safety barriers should be used.

Unloading: Unloading techniques vary depending on the site, with safety precautions such as ensuring no persons are close to the machine and avoiding raising the dump body over uneven ground. Operators should be cautious to prevent any part of the load from jamming the gate of the dump body.

Concluding Haul Truck Operations

Park-up procedures for site safety are crucial to ensure the well-being of personnel and equipment. Typically governed by company policies, haul truck operators must familiarize themselves with these regulations and adhere to them consistently. When entering the park-up bay, operators must exercise caution, being mindful of other vehicles in the vicinity and adhering to posted speed limits.

In the absence of speed limits, a safe speed must be maintained to mitigate risks. Trucks should be parked away from entry and exit points, refuelling areas, and fuel/oil sheds, with the dump body lowered unless secured by a safety aid. On slopes, trucks should be angled parked to prevent movement, ensuring the parking brake is applied.

Before leaving the vehicle, engine shutdown should be performed according to the manufacturer's instructions, allowing it to idle and cool gradually. Operators must face the machine when dismounting, using handrails and ladders for stability. Safe shutdown procedures involve selecting a suitable parking area, applying the retarder to slow and stop the truck, shifting to neutral, engaging the parking brake, and allowing the engine to cool gradually.

Overnight parking procedures should be followed, including turning off the engine, removing ignition keys, locking the cabin, and properly dismounting. Before departure, a thorough check around the equipment, bodywork, and undercarriage should be conducted for any signs of leakage. Parking procedures must align with manufacturer recommendations and company policies, emphasizing parking on firm, level ground, avoiding slopes, securely setting the parking brake, lowering the dump body, and removing ignition keys while locking the cabin for added security.

Cleaning a haul truck is important for several reasons:

1. Safety: A clean haul truck reduces the risk of accidents and injuries. Accumulated dirt, debris, and contaminants can obscure visibility, leading to potential hazards during operation. Additionally, cleaning ensures that essential components like lights, mirrors, and controls are visible and functional, enhancing overall safety for operators and workers in the vicinity.

2. Maintenance: Regular cleaning helps to identify potential maintenance issues early. By removing dirt and grime, maintenance personnel can inspect critical components more easily, identifying signs of wear, damage, or leaks. Addressing these issues promptly can prevent costly breakdowns and downtime, ultimately extending the lifespan of the haul truck.

3. Efficiency: A clean haul truck operates more efficiently. Dirt and

debris can accumulate in air filters, cooling systems, and other vital components, hindering performance and fuel efficiency. By keeping these areas clean, the truck can operate at optimal levels, consuming less fuel and reducing operating costs.

4. Compliance: In many industries, regulations and standards govern the cleanliness of vehicles and equipment, particularly in environments where contamination poses risks to health, safety, or the environment. Regular cleaning ensures compliance with these regulations, avoiding potential fines or penalties.

5. Environmental Protection: Cleaning a haul truck helps prevent the spread of contaminants into the environment. Vehicles operating in mining, construction, or industrial sites can pick up substances like soil, chemicals, or pollutants, which may be harmful if dispersed into waterways or ecosystems. Proper cleaning and containment of these substances mitigate environmental impacts.

6. Image and Reputation: The appearance of a haul truck reflects on the company and its professionalism. A clean, well-maintained fleet sends a positive message to customers, stakeholders, and the public, enhancing the company's reputation and credibility.

Overall, regular cleaning of haul trucks is essential for maintaining safety, efficiency, compliance, environmental responsibility, and a positive brand image. A detailed procedure for cleaning an articulated haul truck cabin follows:

New Style Cabin:
- Pay close attention to potential contamination of cabin door rubbers, which are a concern for the department.

- Lift the engine cover, remove rear radiator covers, and check all handrails for open ends or drainage holes.
- Some models allow hydraulic tilting of the cabin for access to the top of the engine block.

Older Style Cabin:
- Similar to the new style, inspect cabin door rubbers for contamination.
- Remove the air-filter pre-cleaner and cabin vents covers.
- Rear non-affixed panels may already be removed for cleaning.

Interior Cleaning:
- Remove rubber floor matting and non-affixed floor pan to access the engine.
- Clean and inspect air-filter cover.
- Internal door voids, door rubbers, and air-conditioning vents may harbor biosecurity risk material and require inspection.

Vent Covers and Pedals:
- Remove the air-vent cover grill and check the internal filter.
- Clean and inspect rubber cabin pedals.

Internal Components:
- Clean behind all internal wall linings and ensure accessibility during inspection.
- Clean and ensure accessibility of joystick control panels and air-conditioning vents.
- Internally clean all storage compartments and behind any wall

panelling.

Special Considerations:
- Depending on the model, the cabin floor pan may be removed for access to the engine block.
- Remove the air-filter pre-cleaner and air-conditioning vent cover for cleaning and inspection.
- Clean all ladder channels and footstep undersides for thorough cleaning.

Engine Housing and Front End:
- Clean fiberglass engine cover and verify cleanliness of insulation foam and internal tubing.
- Clean and inspect the air intake cover.
- Check front drawbar for any hollow channels.

Radiator and Battery:
- Remove non-affixed radiator cover panels for access to radiator and oil cooler fins.
- Clean radiator and oil cooler fins in the presence of the inspecting officer.
- Loosen battery ties for underside cleaning and inspection.

Wheel Arches, Rims, and Tyres:
- Check front wheel arches for open ends or drainage holes.
- Clean channels inside wheel arches and remove protective shrouds if present.
- Check all ledges inside wheel arches for cleanliness.

Articulated Pivot Point:
- Remove contaminated grease from all pivot points and hydraulic hoses.
- Flush drainage holes at the rear of the chassis for cleanliness.

Rear Chassis:
- Lift dump tray for cleaning and inspect plastic conduit for internal cleanliness.
- Remove contaminated grease from the first universal joint and check all ledges for biosecurity risk material.
- Clean box sections at the front of the rear chassis.

Dump Tray:
- Lower dump tray for inspection and flush exhaust openings for cleanliness.
- Thoroughly check the internal 'skin' of the tray for cracks, splits, or evidence of repair.
- Check for any cracks, splits, or evidence of repair on dump tray doors.

General:
- Ensure cleanliness of rear mudguards and the recess where they attach to the tray.
- Check all wiring harnesses and looming for biosecurity risk material.
- Verify cleanliness of internal light fittings.
- Flush all hollow tubing for cleanliness.

Tip Trucks

Tip Trucks play a crucial role in the Earthmoving Industry by facilitating the transportation and disposal of various materials. Transport and disposal expenses often constitute a considerable portion of the costs associated with earthmoving projects. Therefore, seeking expert guidance is imperative to determine the most cost-effective approach for loading, transporting, and disposing of materials.

Figure 106: Mercedes-Benz Arocs heavy-duty tip truck. High Contrast, CC BY 3.0 DE, via Wikimedia Commons.

Typical materials transported by tip trucks encompass clean fill, clay, debris, rocks, bricks, asphalt, mixed fill, and concrete. While certain trucks and drivers are authorized to transport contaminated materials, meticulous management and organization are required for handling such materials.

There are three primary categories of Tip Trucks:

1. Small (Single-drive vehicles with 5-6m^3 capacity) Small Tip Trucks are predominantly utilized in confined spaces with limited material volumes. They are frequently employed in conjunction with earthmoving machinery such as Skidsteer Loaders and small excavators.

2. Medium (Tandem-drive vehicles with 10m^3 capacity) Tandem-drive Tip Trucks represent the most prevalent type. They typically offer better cost efficiency compared to smaller trucks but may face constraints in tight spaces. While not as economical as Truck and Trailers for extensive volume (clean fill) and long-distance transportation, they are versatile and capable of transporting various materials.

3. Large (Tandem-drive vehicles and tipping trailers with 22m^3 capacity) Large Truck and Trailers are primarily deployed for transporting large volumes over long distances. They require ample space for manoeuvring and tipping compared to other truck types.

EARTHMOVING EQUIPMENT OPERATIONS

Figure 107: GMC General medium sized tipper. Frank Denardo from Tucson, AZ, USA, CC BY-SA 2.0, via Wikimedia Commons.

Tipper trucks are a common sight on our roads and find widespread use across various industries. However, the inherent nature of tipper trucks, with their large tilt trays tipping over to discharge tons of material, poses significant risks to those working nearby.

Regrettably, accidents occur, but many can be averted if individuals operating tipper trucks adhere to safety protocols and exercise sound judgment.

Below are some recommendations for safe tipper truck operation:

Owners of tipper trucks must ensure that all vehicles undergo regular maintenance and servicing to uphold their proper functioning. Additionally, they must ensure that drivers possess valid licenses and receive adequate training in operating these heavy-duty vehicles.

Properly filling the tipper truck is crucial before the tipping process begins. Operators should be aware of the truck's maximum capacity and refrain from overloading it. Furthermore, filling the tilt tray evenly contributes significantly to smooth and efficient tipping.

When the tipper truck is loaded to capacity, extra caution is warranted during the journey to the unloading site. Operators should avoid driving at maximum speeds and steer clear of steep inclines and sharp bends whenever feasible. Effective planning ahead of time can help mitigate the risk of accidents en-route to the destination.

Upon entering a drop-off zone, both the driver and their assistant must maintain vigilance for other vehicles and individuals in the area, particularly in adverse weather conditions. This vigilance extends to when they are outside the vehicle, as the presence of multiple trucks operating simultaneously in the same vicinity heightens the risk.

The most hazardous phase of the tipping process occurs when releasing the load. This action results in a significant shift in the truck's weight, posture, and stability as several tons of material are unloaded.

- Park on level ground: Parking the truck on level ground significantly reduces the risk of the entire vehicle tipping when the tilt tray is raised to release the load. Parking on a slope increases the likelihood of a tipping incident when the tray is tilted.

- Tip slowly: Despite any time constraints or urgency, it is imperative to execute the tipping process slowly while maintaining close observation of the truck and tray for potential complications.

- Ensure effective communication: The driver typically operates the tray, while the assistant monitors the truck's positioning and ensures the safety of nearby individuals. The assistant must establish clear communication with the driver to halt the process if necessary. Prearranged signals and warning calls facilitate efficient communication and swift response in emergencies.

- Utilize stabilizers: If the truck is equipped with stabilizers, activate them consistently whenever necessary. Avoid overlooking this step under the assumption that it is time-consuming; a single accident can have severe consequences, endangering lives or causing extensive damage to company equipment.

Other precautions to prevent accidents:
- Attach handrails and/or steps to the truck to facilitate load inspection.
- Use wheel stops if deemed necessary.
- Implement any additional safety measures to mitigate accident risks effectively.

Tipper trucks are vehicles designed to transport loads or goods within a bin or tray, with one side or end capable of being raised to allow the contents to slide or be tipped out.

The unloading process of a tipper truck can be swift, even with a substantial load. However, there exists a risk of the vehicle tipping over entirely during this action. Accidents and hazardous situations frequently arise due to drivers of tipping vehicles neglecting to adhere to safe operating procedures. Such negligence can lead to fatalities or serious injuries for the driver and others involved. Furthermore, in the absence of proper safety practices, the vehicle itself and surrounding property may sustain severe damage in the event of an accident. This document aims to inform industry stakeholders and the wider community about the dangers associated with tipper trucks tipping over.

Several factors exacerbate the risk of tipping over for these vehicles:
- They are commonly utilized in off-road settings, such as construction sites, where the ground may lack levelness or stability.
- During unloading, any lateral slope on the ground can cause the bin to tilt to one side, shifting its centre of gravity closer to the

tipping point. If the unstable ground causes the wheels on one side of the vehicle to sink, this further increases the lateral tilt.

- Certain materials, like wet soil, may not completely slide out of the bin during unloading, leaving residual material at the top that heightens the risk of toppling.

Tipping over poses hazards to nearby individuals, including the driver, and also jeopardizes equipment, making incidents unfortunately common occurrences.

Tip truck operator safe and effective practices include:

- Possess a valid and appropriate license for the truck being operated.

- Adhere to all traffic regulations and laws.

- Ensure that loads are adequately covered and secured when necessary.

- Keep drawbars, tailgates, and side combing rails free of any materials.

- Drive in accordance with road and load conditions at all times.

- Employ correct load tipping procedures consistently.

- Follow all environmental guidelines and legislation during tasks.

- In the event of an environmental incident, make efforts to contain and minimize harm to the environment.

- Utilize the horn solely as a warning device.

- Yield right of way when appropriate to ensure the safety of other road users.

EARTHMOVING EQUIPMENT OPERATIONS

- Maintain a safe following distance as per relevant regulations.

- Leave sufficient space between trucks for safe passing by other road users.

- Reduce truck speeds to minimize dust and noise, especially near private dwellings, road works, and stationary vehicles.

- Refrain from using engine brakes in built-up areas or where signs prohibit.

- Demonstrate calm and courteous behaviour when interacting with other road users and the public.

- Acknowledge acts of courtesy from others.

- Avoid operating trucks while under the influence of drugs or alcohol.

- Refrain from operating trucks while fatigued.

- Promptly report any aspects of operations that may jeopardize safety, the environment, or public welfare to the supervisor.

- Wear appropriate personal protective equipment when necessary.

- Maintain professionalism when using radios, avoiding the use of offensive language.

- Uphold standards of conduct free from discrimination and harassment.

- Reject overloading of trucks.

- Prohibit unauthorized passengers from traveling in the truck.

- Keep trucks clean and tidy.
- Secure all items stored in the cabin adequately.
- Prevent littering.
- Prohibit the transportation of dangerous articles, explosives, or firearms in any truck.
- Prohibit the transportation of animals in any truck or trailer.
- Wear a seatbelt at all times.
- Prohibit smoking in company vehicles.
- Use hands-free devices when using phones, and refrain from phone use during on-site unloading or in quarries loading.
- Follow proper reporting procedures for injuries, incidents, hazards, near misses, and maintenance.
- Ensure completion of Logistics Drivers daily worksheets (DDWS) by every driver.

Tipper trucks transport various commodities, each with differing levels of risk:

- Sand and gravel pose minimal risk as they flow easily, but wet sand may stick to trailer bodies, increasing risk.
- Wet soil typically poses lower risk unless it gets caught at the tipper hoist wells. • Clays and large concrete lumps usually pose lower risk unless they become caught around the hoist well.
- Large or irregularly shaped materials, such as heavy rocks or demolition waste, can pose risks if they get stuck during tipping.
- Dust and certain wet mix products may adhere to trailer bodies,

affecting tipping balance.

- Poor load distribution or imbalance influences road vehicle dynamics.

Constant unloading tasks may lead to monotony, increasing the risk of distraction or inattention. Employing a 'dead man' hoist controller can mitigate this risk by requiring drivers to maintain contact with the controller. Walking floors can also reduce risk by facilitating material discharge without tipping, although they may not be suitable for all applications.

Due to variations in loading procedures and site conditions, it is imperative for drivers to comprehend their duties regarding both the vehicle and the load intended for transportation on public roads. While many sites operate with professionalism, utilizing trained loading personnel and employing weighbridges and washing facilities as needed, others may lack these amenities, placing additional responsibilities on the driver.

Considering the nature of the material being transported and its flow characteristics is essential prior to loading. Certain loads, particularly those with wet, sticky, or solid properties, may exhibit varying movement rates during tipping, posing potential dangers. Unexpected movement of the load at the rear or on one side could lead to vehicle imbalance and contribute to rollover accidents, as well as potential axle overload scenarios.

It is crucial to evenly distribute the load along the length and width of the body while adhering to legal axle weight limits. Failure to achieve proper distribution may result in an unstable vehicle, posing driving hazards and risking axle and tyre overloads, rendering the vehicle illegal. Uneven weight distribution, exacerbated by the high centre of gravity of many tippers, can amplify issues during manoeuvres, braking, and on roads with pronounced camber.

The driver bears responsibility for ensuring compliance with gross plated weight and individual axle weight limits. Proceeding without certainty of legislative compliance is unacceptable. Drivers must be trained to recognize various materials and document individual load weights, as tipper bodies often exceed legal weight capacities.

After loading in off-road conditions, the driver should inspect securing devices, locks, tyres, and low-mounted equipment for damage before departing the site. Employing an appropriate tarping system to contain the load and debris is essential, potentially mandated by local planning regulations.

Addressing concerns about environmental impact and public perception, drivers must remove excess debris and clear rocks/stones from between dual tyres, drawbars, and tailgate tops. Lamp, reflective marker plate, and number plate conditions should be checked before departure, as they may be obscured by mud and grime depending on ground conditions.

Given that most tipper bodies are not waterproof, drivers should allow excess water from wet loads to drain before leaving the site.

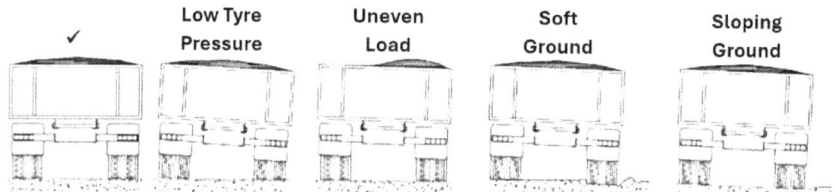

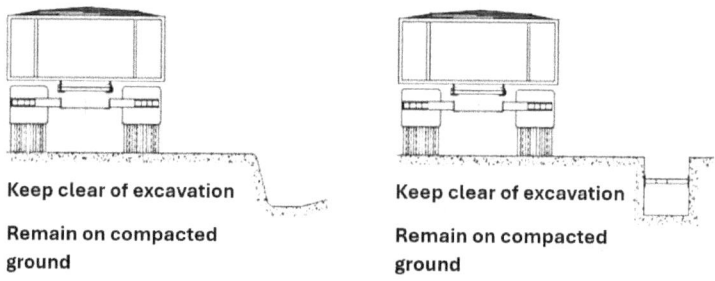

Figure 108: Correct and incorrect positioning and posture.

It falls upon the driver to guarantee that the vehicle does not surpass the gross plated weight or individual axle weights. Consequently, drivers should refrain from proceeding if there are any doubts regarding compliance with legislation. It's worth noting that the density of individual loads can vary significantly, and many tipper bodies have the capacity to accommodate more load than they are legally permitted to carry in terms of weight. Hence, it's imperative that drivers receive training to recognize different types of materials they are expected to transport, and the weight of each load should be known and documented.

Upon loading the vehicle under off-road conditions, the driver should conduct a thorough inspection of all securing devices, locks, tyres, and any low-mounted equipment for damage before departing the site. Additionally, an appropriate tarping system must be utilized and properly secured to retain the load and prevent debris from scattering. It's noteworthy that local planning regulations may mandate the use of tarp systems.

Regrettably, some tipper operators suffer from a negative public image due to the mud and clay residues left on the road by certain operators upon departure from sites. There's a perception that tippers are more prone to causing damage from flying stones and loose materials. Hence, it is incumbent upon the driver to ensure that excess debris is cleared, and any rocks or stones are removed from between dual tyres, drawbars, and tailgate tops.

Before leaving the site, the driver should always inspect the condition of the lamps, reflective marker plates, and number plates, as they may have become obscured by mud and grime depending on ground conditions. Given that most tipper bodies are not watertight, the driver should allow excess water from a wet load to drain from the body prior to departure.

Upon arrival at the site, the driver must adjust the vehicle's speed according to the prevailing conditions. When traveling off the public road, attention should be paid to surface conditions, staying on compacted roadways, avoiding excavations, and being vigilant for overhead cables and other obstructions.

Before unloading the load, it's crucial for the driver to position the vehicle on flat, firm ground. If a slope is unavoidable, it should run from end to end of the vehicle rather than across its width to prevent instability. In the case of an articulated vehicle, such as a truck and trailer, they must be aligned in a straight line to avoid creating another unstable condition.

In many cases, having a rear-facing camera installed in the vehicle provides the operator with a clear view of the area behind the vehicle during reversing or tipping operations. This equipment is now mandated on many sites. Before unloading the load, the driver must ensure that the area where the load will be deposited is clear of personnel and obstructions. The driver should not leave the cab unless wearing suitable Personal Protection Equipment (PPE) and with the parking brake applied.

If the body is equipped with a manual locking system for the tailgate, the driver must ensure that the pressure of the load against the tailgate does not pose a danger to themselves or others. It is essential to prevent anyone from standing adjacent to the vehicle during tipping, as this is a hazardous area. An accident involving a person standing adjacent to a tipper is usually caused by one of three factors, all of which can have fatal consequences.

To maintain control of the load during tipping, the flow rate properties of the material being carried should be considered beforehand. The body should be tipped appropriately to suit the materials being discharged, ensuring a smooth operation and avoiding sudden shocks caused by rapid tipping, lowering, or sudden stops. It's important to ensure that a free-flowing load does not exit with excessive speed and that wet or sticky loads do not create a dangerous situation if they fail to move.

Figure 109: Tipper unloading. Agência de Notícias do Acre, CC BY 2.0 , via Wikimedia Commons.

Drivers should remain in the cab throughout the tipping process, using mirrors to monitor and adjust the rate of discharge. If the driver has any concerns regarding the safety of the tipping process, whether related to ground or site conditions, the load itself, the vehicle and ancillary equipment, or the proximity to people, tipping should be stopped immediately, and the body slowly lowered until the risk is mitigated.

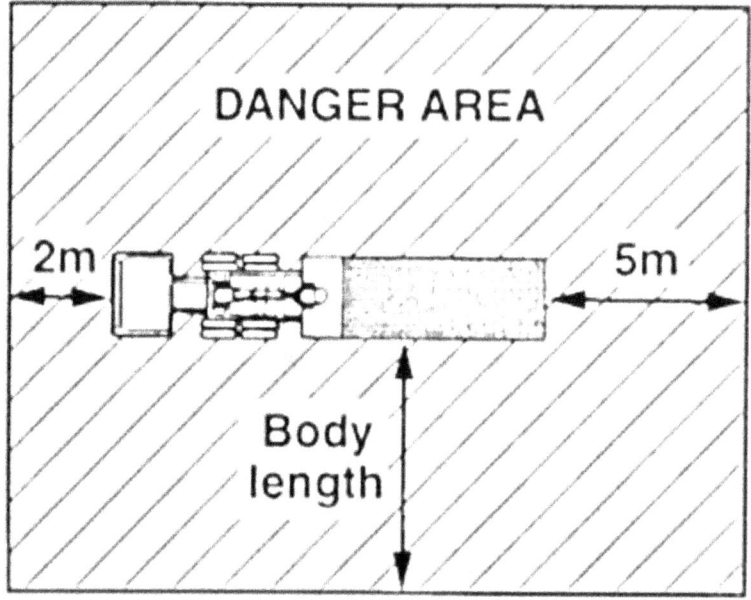

Always ensure that no person. Animal or other equipment is within this area when tipping.

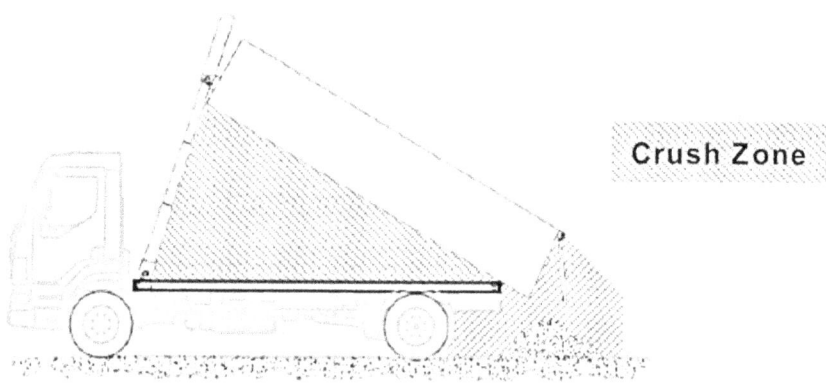

Figure 110: Danger zones around the tipper.

If load discharge is impeded by previously tipped material, it may be acceptable to slowly move the vehicle forward. However, before doing so, the driver must assess whether it is safe to do with the body at its current tipping angle and, if necessary, either partially or fully lower the body before moving.

Chapter Nine

Surfacing Operations

Stabiliser Operations

Soil stabilizers and road recyclers were once similar machines, but they have evolved into highly specialized pieces of road-making equipment, with distinct characteristics. Other terms used to describe them include road profilers, road reclaimers, road millers, road planers, and pavement profilers.

The evolution of in-situ stabilization stemmed from the use of rippers and stabilizers to more advanced "powerful" reclaimers, which allow pulverization and mixing to occur in one or two processes. Reclaimers and stabilizers are designed with a centrally located mixing box.

Figure 111: Bomag MPH125 Stabilizer-Recycler. Bob Adams from Amanzimtoti, South Africa, CC BY-SA 2.0, via Wikimedia Commons.

These purpose-built machines feature special rotors designed to mix materials within the mixing hood. Agricultural equipment, profilers, rotary hoes, and graders are not suitable substitutes for in-situ stabilization, as they often lack effective mixing properties, leading to pavement cracking.

Profilers, whether standard or modified, cannot be utilized for stabilizing pavement materials due to the different rotor designs compared to stabilizers. Profilers typically employ bullet-type teeth and a drum, whereas stabilizers feature wide-shaped teeth on long legs for material mixing.

The outcomes achieved with profilers have been unsatisfactory, resulting in "chunks" of cement aggregate and localized pavement failures.

In contrast, stabilizers equipped with bullet teeth have the capacity to pulverize existing asphalt and pavement materials. However, the long, wide-shaped teeth on stabilizers (refer to Figure 4) are not designed to cut and reclaim compacted materials. Instead, the stabilizer's rotor is specifically intended to mix the binder with pulverized pavement material.

In the 1990s, reclaimers/stabilizers were introduced, marking a significant advancement in road construction machinery. These machines feature rotors with bullet-shaped teeth on long legs, designed to mix pulverized pavement material effectively.

Reclaimers/stabilizers are capable of reclaiming existing pavement materials to a depth of 500 mm, although compacting material beyond 400 mm depth may pose challenges. Modern CMI and Wirtgen machines are now available in both reclaimer and stabilizer configurations.

Different countries often employ varying terminology, making it challenging to distinguish between different machines and the processes they entail.

Soil Stabilizer: A soil stabilizer machine blends existing pavement with lime that has been spread on the surface, with water introduced via a large pipe at the front. It is a construction vehicle equipped with a powered metal drum featuring rows of mixing blades or paddles. These paddles blend soil, a binder agent (typically Portland cement or lime), and water together in the mixing chamber. Generally, soil stabilizers do not cut or mill hard or very thick asphalt or concrete. Modern soil stabilizers have become more powerful and often use carbide tips instead of paddles, making them more akin to road recyclers capable of blending the old road surface into the mixture. Soil stabilizers mix a low-strength concrete and perform a function similar to a concrete mixer but on the ground. Some modern stabilizers use tungsten carbide tips similar to those found on road pavement mills, although to a lesser extent.

Road Pavement Mill: A road pavement mill, such as a Wirtgen road pavement profiler, removes the top surface of the road to facilitate the laying of a new one. This construction vehicle features a powered metal drum with rows of tungsten carbide-tipped teeth designed to cut off the top surface of a paved concrete or asphalt road. With sustainability being a priority, the material extracted by the mill is often recycled into new asphalt. In some instances, the entire road pavement may be removed, typically due to damage requiring replacement. Road pavement mills are highly powerful machines, with some employing engines exceeding 500 hp. They are usually mounted on four crawler tracks, although configurations with three crawler tracks or wheels are also used.

Road Recycler: A road recycler combines elements of both soil stabilization and pavement milling processes. It may involve blending cement or lime and water with the existing pavement, usually thin asphalt. This process typically refers to blending the asphalt road with a binder and base course in a single pass. In a road recycler, the front drum with numerous teeth, similar to those of a pavement mill, is used to remove very hard asphalt or concrete surfaces. The subsequent drums with fewer teeth, arranged in a chevron pattern to reduce motor load, belong to the road recycler. Only a few teeth cut at a time, and this tooth arrangement also facilitates material conveyance to the centre, where it can be easily picked up by a conveyor belt.

Figure 112: Caterpillar RM500 rotary mixer.

A rotating mixer is a type of mixing equipment commonly used in various industries to blend, homogenize, or agitate materials. It consists of a container or drum mounted on an axis, which rotates to mix the contents thoroughly. The rotation of the mixer facilitates the movement of materials inside the container, ensuring uniform blending or mixing.

Here are some common functions and applications of rotating mixers:

1. Mixing: Rotating mixers are primarily used to combine different components or ingredients to create a homogeneous mixture. This is commonly seen in industries such as food processing, pharmaceuticals, chemicals, and cosmetics, where precise mixing is essential for product quality.

2. Blending: They are used to blend materials of different viscosities or densities to achieve a uniform composition. This is particularly useful in the production of various products, including

paints, adhesives, and polymers.

3. Homogenization: Rotating mixers help in breaking down particles and dispersing them evenly throughout a mixture, resulting in a smooth and consistent product. This process is crucial in industries like the pharmaceutical and food industries, where uniformity is critical for product efficacy and quality.

4. Agitation: They provide agitation or stirring action to keep materials suspended and prevent settling. This is important in applications such as chemical reactions, where maintaining a consistent reaction mixture is essential for reaction kinetics and product yield.

Rotating mixers are versatile pieces of equipment used across various industries for mixing, blending, homogenizing, and agitating materials to achieve desired properties or compositions.

A Cold Recycler machine is used in the process of cold recycling, which is a method for rehabilitating or reconstructing existing asphalt pavements. This machine is designed to recycle the existing asphalt pavement by pulverizing it in place, mixing it with new binding agents and additives, and then relaying it as a new pavement layer without the need for heating the material.

The Cold Recycler machine typically performs several key functions:

1. Pulverization: It pulverizes the existing asphalt pavement in place, breaking it down into smaller particles.

2. Mixing: The machine mixes the pulverized asphalt pavement with new binding agents, such as emulsions or foamed bitumen, as well as additives like cement or lime.

3. Homogenization: It ensures that the mixture of the old and new materials is thoroughly blended and homogenized to create a

uniform and stable pavement material.

4. Relaying: Once the recycling process is complete, the Cold Recycler machine lays down the recycled mixture as a new pavement layer, which is then compacted to achieve the desired density and smoothness.

Cold Recycler machines play a crucial role in the cold recycling process, allowing for the efficient and cost-effective rehabilitation of existing asphalt pavements while reducing the need for new materials and minimizing environmental impact.

Figure 113: Cold recycler. Christina Plati, Andreas Loizos, Vasilis Papavasiliou, Antonis Kaltsounis, CC BY 4.0, via Wikimedia Commons.

A soil stabilizer is a construction vehicle designed to blend existing soil with other materials, such as lime, cement, or asphalt emulsion, to improve its strength, durability, and load-bearing capacity. Here's how a soil stabilizer typically works:

1. Preparation: Before soil stabilization begins, the surface to be treated is usually prepared by grading and compacting to remove any loose debris, rocks, or vegetation.

2. Spreading the Binding Agent: The soil stabilizer is equipped with a hopper or tank that holds the binding agent, which is typically lime, cement, or asphalt emulsion. The binding agent is spread evenly over the surface of the soil using a distributor mechanism, such as a conveyor belt or sprayer.

3. Mixing: Once the binding agent is spread, the soil stabilizer incorporates it into the soil using mixing blades or paddles mounted on a rotating drum. As the soil stabilizer moves forward, the mixing action blends the binding agent with the soil, ensuring thorough distribution and uniformity.

4. Moisture Control: In some cases, water may be added to the soil to achieve the desired moisture content for optimal compaction and binding. The soil stabilizer may have a water tank and spray nozzles to control moisture levels during mixing.

5. Compaction: After mixing, the stabilized soil is compacted using rollers or compactors to achieve the desired density and strength. Compaction helps to further blend the soil and binding agent, as well as to improve load-bearing capacity and resistance to water penetration.

6. Curing: Depending on the type of binding agent used, the stabilized soil may require a curing period to allow the binding agent to chemically react and strengthen the soil. Curing times vary depending on factors such as temperature, humidity, and type of binding agent.

Soil stabilizers are essential equipment for improving the engineering properties of soil, making it suitable for various construction applications such as road construction, building foundations, and land reclamation projects. They play a crucial role in enhancing soil stability, durability, and performance, ultimately contributing to the longevity and sustainability of infrastructure projects.

Preparing for soil stabilizer operations involves several key steps to ensure the successful and efficient stabilization of soil for construction purposes. Here's a comprehensive guide on how to prepare for soil stabilizer operations:

1. Site Assessment:

    - Conduct a thorough assessment of the construction site to understand soil conditions, terrain features, and project requirements.

    - Identify any potential hazards, such as underground utilities, unstable slopes, or environmental concerns, that may affect soil stabilization operations.

2. Soil Analysis:

    - Collect soil samples from various locations across the site for laboratory analysis.

    - Analyse soil samples to determine their composition, moisture content, plasticity, bearing capacity, and other relevant properties.

    - Use the soil analysis results to select appropriate stabilizing agents and determine the optimal mixing ratios for achieving desired soil stabilization outcomes.

3. Equipment Inspection and Setup:

EARTHMOVING EQUIPMENT OPERATIONS

- Inspect the soil stabilizer equipment to ensure it is in proper working condition and free from any defects or malfunctions.

- Check all components of the soil stabilizer, including the mixing chamber, blades, conveyors, and control systems, for cleanliness, lubrication, and functionality.

- Set up the soil stabilizer at the construction site, ensuring it is positioned securely and accessible for operation.

4. Stabilizing Agent Preparation:

    - Procure the required stabilizing agents, such as lime, cement, or bitumen emulsion, based on the soil analysis and project specifications.

    - Store stabilizing agents in appropriate containers and ensure they are properly sealed to prevent contamination or moisture absorption.

    - Prepare the stabilizing agents according to manufacturer instructions, including mixing ratios, hydration periods, and temperature requirements.

5. Safety Measures:

    - Implement safety protocols and procedures to ensure the protection of workers, equipment, and the environment during soil stabilizer operations.

    - Provide personal protective equipment (PPE) for all personnel involved in the operation, including safety vests, helmets, gloves, and eye protection.

    - Establish exclusion zones and warning signs to prevent unauthorized access to the work area and minimize the risk of accidents or injuries.

6. Environmental Considerations:

- Develop an environmental management plan to mitigate potential impacts of soil stabilizer operations on surrounding ecosystems, water resources, and air quality.
- Implement erosion control measures, such as silt fences, straw bales, or sediment traps, to prevent soil erosion and sediment runoff from the construction site.
- Comply with regulatory requirements and obtain necessary permits for soil stabilization activities, particularly if working near protected areas or water bodies.

7. Communication and Coordination:

- Coordinate soil stabilizer operations with other construction activities and project stakeholders, including engineers, contractors, inspectors, and environmental agencies.
- Communicate project timelines, goals, and safety guidelines to all personnel involved in the soil stabilization process to ensure effective collaboration and adherence to project objectives.

Operating a soil stabilizer involves several essential steps to ensure effective soil stabilization. Here's a comprehensive guide on how to operate a soil stabilizer:

Pre-Operation Inspection: Conduct a thorough inspection of the soil stabilizer machine to ensure it is in proper working condition. Check all components, including the mixing chamber, blades, hydraulics, engine, and controls, for any signs of damage or malfunction. Verify that all safety features, such as emergency stop buttons and warning lights, are functional. Ensure that all necessary tools and personal protective equipment (PPE) are available.

Site Preparation: Evaluate the soil conditions at the work site to determine the appropriate stabilization method and additives required. Clear the work area of any debris, rocks, or obstacles that may interfere with the operation of the soil stabilizer. Grade the surface to achieve the desired compaction and slope for effective soil stabilization.

Additive Application: Determine the appropriate type and quantity of stabilizing agent (e.g., lime, cement, or bitumen) based on the soil type and project requirements. Load the stabilizing agent into the soil stabilizer's hopper or storage tank. Adjust the application rate and mixing ratio according to the specifications provided by the manufacturer or engineer.

Mixing and Processing: Start the soil stabilizer machine and engage the mixing chamber. Gradually feed the stabilizing agent into the soil as the machine moves forward, ensuring thorough mixing and distribution. Monitor the mixing process and adjust the machine's speed and settings as needed to achieve the desired soil consistency and stabilization.

Compaction and Finishing: Use compaction equipment, such as rollers or compactors, to compact the stabilized soil to the required density. Conduct periodic tests, such as moisture content and compaction tests, to ensure that the stabilized soil meets project specifications. Finish the stabilized surface by grading, shaping, and applying any additional surface treatments, such as sealing or paving.

Post-Operation Inspection and Maintenance: Inspect the stabilized soil surface for uniformity, stability, and adherence to project requirements. Address any areas of concern, such as uneven compaction or insufficient stabilization, through rework or additional treatment. Clean and maintain the soil stabilizer machine according to the manufacturer's guidelines to ensure reliable performance for future operations.

A road pavement mill, also known as a pavement profiler or cold milling machine, is a construction vehicle used to remove the top surface of a paved concrete or asphalt road. Here's how a road pavement mill typically works:

1. Preparation: Before milling begins, the road surface to be removed is typically inspected to assess its condition and determine the extent of milling required. Any obstacles or hazards on the road surface are cleared or marked for avoidance.

2. Positioning: The road pavement mill is positioned at the start of the section to be milled. It is usually mounted on crawler tracks or wheels for mobility and stability during operation. The milling drum, which contains rows of tungsten carbide-tipped teeth, is positioned over the road surface.

3. Milling: The milling drum is lowered onto the road surface, and the machine is engaged to start milling. The rotating drum spins rapidly, and the tungsten carbide teeth bite into the surface of the pavement, cutting and removing the top layer of asphalt or concrete.

4. Material Removal: As the milling drum rotates, the tungsten carbide teeth grind and pulverize the pavement material, breaking it into smaller pieces. These pieces are then conveyed by a conveyor belt or auger system to a collection area or truck for removal from the work site.

5. Depth Control: The depth of milling is controlled by adjusting the depth of the milling drum and the forward speed of the machine. This allows the operator to precisely remove the desired thickness of pavement while avoiding damage to the underlying layers or utilities.

6. Surface Quality: Modern pavement mills often include features for optimizing surface quality, such as automatic leveling systems and multiple milling drum configurations. These features help to ensure a smooth and uniform milled surface that meets project specifications.

7. Recycling: In many cases, the milled pavement material is recycled for use in new asphalt or concrete mixtures. This recycling process reduces waste and conserves natural resources by reusing existing materials in road construction projects.

Road pavement mills play a crucial role in road rehabilitation and construction projects by efficiently removing deteriorated pavement surfaces and preparing the road for new overlays or treatments. They are essential equipment for maintaining and improving the infrastructure of roads and highways.

Preparing for road pavement mill operations involves several important steps to ensure the successful milling of asphalt or concrete surfaces. Here's a comprehensive guide on how to prepare for road pavement mill operations:

1. Site Assessment:

- Conduct a thorough assessment of the road construction site to understand the existing pavement conditions, traffic patterns, and project requirements.
- Identify any obstacles, such as utility lines, signage, or structures, that may interfere with milling operations.

2. Equipment Inspection and Setup:

- Inspect the road pavement milling equipment to ensure it is in proper working condition and free from any defects or malfunctions.

- Check all components of the milling machine, including the cutting drums, conveyor belts, hydraulic systems, and controls, for cleanliness, lubrication, and functionality.

- Set up the milling machine at the work site, ensuring it is positioned securely and accessible for operation.

3. Traffic Control and Safety Measures:

- Establish traffic control measures to ensure the safety of workers and motorists during milling operations.

- Use traffic cones, barricades, and warning signs to redirect traffic away from the work area and create a safe buffer zone around the milling machine.

- Provide flaggers or traffic control personnel to manage traffic flow and communicate with drivers about detours or lane closures.

4. Environmental Protection:

- Implement environmental protection measures to minimize dust, noise, and debris generated during milling operations.

- Use water trucks or dust suppression systems to control airborne dust and maintain air quality in the vicinity of the work site.

- Dispose of milling waste materials properly, following regulations and guidelines for recycling or disposal of asphalt and concrete debris.

5. Material Handling and Logistics:

- Coordinate the delivery of milling materials, such as replacement asphalt or concrete, to the work site in a timely manner.

- Ensure adequate storage space is available for milling equipment, spare parts, and maintenance supplies.

- Plan for the removal and transportation of milled materials off-site for recycling or disposal, if necessary.

6. Operator Training and Communication:

- Provide training to equipment operators on proper milling techniques, safety procedures, and equipment operation.

- Communicate project objectives, timelines, and safety guidelines to all personnel involved in road pavement milling operations.

- Establish clear lines of communication between operators, supervisors, and project managers to address any issues or concerns that may arise during milling activities.

7. Regulatory Compliance:

- Obtain necessary permits and approvals for road pavement milling activities from local authorities or transportation agencies.

- Ensure compliance with regulatory requirements, such as noise ordinances, environmental regulations, and traffic management protocols, throughout the milling process.

Operating a road pavement mill involves several steps to efficiently remove the top surface of paved concrete or asphalt roads. Here's a guide on how to operate a road pavement mill:

1. Pre-Operation Inspection:

- Conduct a thorough inspection of the pavement mill machine to ensure it is in proper working condition.
- Check all components, including the milling drum, cutting teeth, conveyor belts, hydraulic systems, and controls, for any signs of damage or malfunction.
- Verify that all safety features, such as emergency stop buttons and warning lights, are functional.
- Ensure that all necessary tools and personal protective equipment (PPE) are available.

2. Site Preparation:

- Evaluate the condition of the road pavement to determine the appropriate milling depth and width required.
- Clear the work area of any debris, obstacles, or vehicles that may interfere with the milling operation.
- Set up traffic control measures, such as traffic cones, barricades, and warning signs, to redirect traffic away from the work zone.

3. Milling Operation:

- Start the pavement mill machine and engage the milling drum.
- Adjust the milling depth and width settings based on the project specifications and the condition of the pavement.
- Gradually advance the mill machine along the designated milling path, ensuring even and consistent removal of the pavement surface.

- Monitor the milling process closely, adjusting the machine's speed and cutting parameters as needed to achieve the desired milling results.

- Coordinate with ground personnel to manage traffic flow and ensure the safety of workers and motorists in the vicinity of the milling operation.

4. Material Handling:

- Use conveyor belts or other material handling equipment to collect and remove the milled asphalt or concrete debris from the work area.

- Dispose of the milled material properly, following regulations and guidelines for recycling or disposal of pavement debris.

5. Post-Operation Inspection and Maintenance:

- Inspect the milled surface for uniformity, smoothness, and adherence to project specifications.

- Address any areas of concern, such as uneven milling or damage to the underlying pavement layers, through rework or additional treatment.

- Clean and maintain the pavement mill machine according to the manufacturer's guidelines to ensure reliable performance for future operations.

A road recycler is a versatile machine used in road construction and rehabilitation projects. It is primarily used for reclaiming and stabilizing existing pavement materials to create a stable base for new road surfaces. Here's how a road recycler typically works:

1. Preparation: Before the road recycler begins its operation, the existing pavement surface is inspected to assess its condition and suitability for recycling. Any debris, vegetation, or obstacles on the surface are cleared to ensure safe and effective operation.

2. Mixing Chamber: The road recycler is equipped with a mixing chamber where the reclaiming and stabilizing process takes place. This chamber is usually located between the front and rear drums of the machine.

3. Reclaiming: The road recycler's front drum, which contains rows of tungsten carbide-tipped teeth, rotates and cuts into the existing pavement surface. As it moves forward, the teeth break up the pavement material, pulverizing it into smaller particles.

4. Stabilizing: Simultaneously, the recycler adds a binding agent, such as cement, lime, or foamed asphalt, into the mixing chamber. This binding agent helps stabilize the reclaimed pavement material, improving its strength and durability.

5. Mixing: The rotating action of the recycler's drums thoroughly mixes the reclaimed pavement material with the binding agent, ensuring uniform distribution and optimal stabilization. Some road recyclers may also incorporate water into the mixing process to achieve the desired moisture content.

6. Gradation Control: The road recycler may include features for controlling the gradation of the recycled material, ensuring that it meets specifications for particle size distribution and uniformity. This helps optimize the performance and longevity of the recycled base material.

7. Compaction: After mixing and stabilization, the recycled pavement material is compacted using the recycler's rear drum or a

separate compactor attachment. Compaction helps achieve the desired density and stability of the recycled base layer, preparing it for the placement of new pavement surfaces.

8. Surface Preparation: Once the recycled base layer is compacted and stabilized, it is ready for further treatment or overlay with new asphalt or concrete pavement. The road recycler may also include features for shaping and grading the recycled base to meet project requirements.

Road recyclers play a critical role in sustainable road construction practices by reclaiming and reusing existing pavement materials, reducing waste, and conserving natural resources. They offer a cost-effective and environmentally friendly solution for rehabilitating roads and highways while providing a durable and stable base for new pavement surfaces.

Preparing for road recycler operations involves several crucial steps to ensure the efficient and safe recycling of asphalt or concrete surfaces.

Site Assessment: Conduct a thorough assessment of the road construction site to evaluate the existing pavement conditions, traffic patterns, and project requirements. Identify any obstacles, such as utility lines, signage, or structures, that may interfere with recycling operations.

Equipment Inspection and Setup: Inspect the road recycler equipment to ensure it is in optimal working condition and free from any defects or malfunctions. Check all components of the recycler machine, including the mixing chamber, conveyor belts, hydraulic systems, and controls, for cleanliness, lubrication, and functionality. Set up the road recycler at the work site, ensuring it is positioned securely and accessible for operation.

Traffic Control and Safety Measures: Establish traffic control measures to ensure the safety of workers and motorists during recycling operations. Use traffic cones, barricades, and warning signs to redirect traffic away from the work area and create a safe buffer zone around the recycler machine. Provide flaggers or traffic control personnel to manage traffic flow and communicate with drivers about detours or lane closures.

Environmental Protection: Implement environmental protection measures to minimize dust, noise, and debris generated during recycling operations. Use water trucks or dust suppression systems to control airborne dust and maintain air quality in the vicinity of the work site. Dispose of recycled materials properly, following regulations and guidelines for recycling or disposal of asphalt and concrete debris.

Material Handling and Logistics: Coordinate the delivery of recycling materials, such as binders and additives, to the work site in a timely manner. Ensure adequate storage space is available for recycler equipment, spare parts, and maintenance supplies. Plan for the transportation of recycled materials to the appropriate location for reuse or disposal, if necessary.

Operator Training and Communication: Provide training to equipment operators on proper recycling techniques, safety procedures, and equipment operation. Communicate project objectives, timelines, and safety guidelines to all personnel involved in road recycler operations. Establish clear lines of communication between operators, supervisors, and project managers to address any issues or concerns that may arise during recycling activities.

Regulatory Compliance: Obtain necessary permits and approvals for road recycler operations from local authorities or transportation agencies. Ensure compliance with regulatory requirements, such as noise ordinances, environmental regulations, and traffic management protocols, throughout the recycling process.

Roller Compactor Operations

A roller compactor is a machinery utilized to compact materials like soil, sand, and clean fill, typically as part of significant projects. These machines employ static force with hydraulics to compress and reduce the size of soil and other materials. Roller compactors are widely available for hire across the country and are among the most commonly used equipment on construction sites throughout Australia.

Rollers are highly sought-after machines renowned for their compaction abilities and the ability to evenly smooth surface materials. While predominantly used in road construction, they also find applications in agriculture, landfill projects, and compacting concrete, gravel, asphalt, and soil to create a level foundation for precise surface laying. Generally, rollers share common features regardless of type, including a drum (either smooth and static or vibratory), a compaction meter, a water system, tyres, and driver protection.

It's crucial to differentiate between a roller and a flat plate compactor, as both are often labelled as compactors. The latter refers to a wheel-less, walk-behind piece of equipment, roughly the size of a typical lawnmower, commonly used on smaller construction projects.

A roller, whether self-propelled or towed, serves as a vital machine in the construction industry, primarily tasked with compacting various construction materials. It can come in different configurations, such as rubber-tyred, smooth drum, padded drum, or grid (open) face type.

The compaction process employed by a roller typically involves one or more of the following methods:

- Static weight

- Kneading

- Vibration

- Impact

Grid rollers are specifically utilized to break down oversized construction materials. Padded drums, on the other hand, may feature variations like sheepsfoot, padfoot, tamping foot, or wedge foot.

Figure 114: A ride-on roller compactor with vibrating the roller drums for asphalt pavement. Marc-Lautenbacher, CC BY-SA 4.0, via Wikimedia Commons.

Rollers play an important role in constructing solid foundations for various construction projects, ranging from roadworks to agricultural and landfill endeavours. They are adept at compacting concrete, gravel, asphalt, and soil to create a level and sturdy base, facilitating precise surface laying.

Typically, rollers share common features regardless of their type, including a drum—either smooth and static or vibratory—a compaction meter, a water system, tyres, and driver protection. Their ability to enhance the load-bearing capacity of surfaces makes them indispensable in road works, construction, and mining projects, where they prepare soil before concrete or bitumen application and mitigate vehicle risks on mine sites.

There are two main types of rollers based on their operational mechanism: static and dynamic. Vibratory rollers, also known as dynamic rollers, utilize both weight and vibration to compact materials, whereas static rollers rely solely on weight without vibration. Static rollers, equipped with hexpad, sheepsfoot, or tamper-type drum wheels, are suitable for cohesive and clay soils, whereas vibratory rollers are preferred for granular soils like gravel and sand.

Vibratory dynamic rollers employ oscillation, weight, and vibration to increase soil density and strengthen surface load-bearing capacity. They utilize drums to transmit compaction forces generated by vibration-inducing mechanisms, effectively compacting soil, landfill, and other surface materials by removing air voids and increasing density. The combination of static weight and induced vibrations allows dynamic rollers to power through surface materials with frictional or cohesive resistance, ensuring thorough compaction and stable foundations for construction projects.

There are a number of different types of roller. A three-point roller is a static roller that utilizes its mass weight combined with oscillation for surface compaction. These static compaction rollers are commonly employed on granular, semi-cohesive, cohesive, asphalt, and clay soil surfaces, as well as in situations where vibration methods may impede compaction efforts or are unsuitable, such as on bridges.

Multi-tyre rollers, such as the Caterpillar CW34 and CW12, are available in both static and dynamic (vibrating) variants. The dynamic versions, utilizing dynamic kneading, are well-suited for applications on hot mix asphalt, aggregate bases, warm and cold mixes. Static multi-tyred rollers utilize pneumatic tyres, making them ideal for surfacing and sealing endeavours. The static variants are utilized for proof rolling, cement stabilized soils and asphalts, and for the final dressing in road construction. The pneumatic tyres are specially designed for compacting asphalt mixes, soil bases, and sub-bases.

Padfoot rollers (or sheepsfoot rollers), like the Caterpillar CP533E and CP44B, are dynamic compaction machines that employ a unique padded drum wheel and vibrating mechanisms. Their distinguishing feature is the padfoot front drum wheel with a unique padded tread design. These versatile rollers are utilized across a wide range of project types, working effectively on almost all types of semi-cohesive and cohesive soils and clay.

Smooth drum rollers, such as the Caterpillar CB16 and CB8, are well-suited for use on non-cohesive (granular) soils like gravel, sand, and mixed soils. Unlike the rugged bumpy drum of a padfoot roller, a smooth drum roller utilizes a smooth tread on its drum wheel. These common compaction rollers have played a vital role in the construction and upgrading of roadways across Australia.

Landfill compactors, such as the CAT 836K, are typically large machines primarily utilized for landfill and waste compaction on major project sites across Australia. They are unlikely to be found on inner-city house projects.

Pneumatic rollers (generally static multi-tyred rollers), like the Caterpillar CW34, are often employed on cold mix, sub-grade soil, or granular material to increase density and identify weak areas for repair before paving. Additionally, they are used on hot mix asphalt for initial breakdown and intermediate phases to increase density and seal the surface of the mat.

Tandem vibratory rollers (or drum utility rollers) are ride-on open-air compactors, such as the Caterpillar CB1-7, commonly seen on roadwork projects. The standard compaction width of these compactors ranges from 900mm to 2130mm.

Rollers used in civil construction sites encompass various types, each serving specific purposes:

Self-Propelled Pneumatic Tyred Roller: Also referred to as rubber tyred rollers, these rollers are employed to finish freshly sealed asphalt, ensuring a smooth and trafficked surface. They distribute compaction evenly across the tyres and compact the surface by applying pressure from the roller's weight and the rolling action of the tyres.

Figure 115: Ammann AP240 road roller (self-propelled pneumatic tyred roller. Orderinchaos, CC BY 4.0, via Wikimedia Commons.

Self-Propelled Smooth Drum: Vibratory Roller Known as basic rollers, these machines compact surfaces through the weight of the roller and the rolling and vibration of the roller drum.

Figure 116: Self-propelled smooth drum roller. Judgefloro, CC0, via Wikimedia Commons.ription automatically generated

Self-Propelled Padded Drum Vibratory Roller: These rollers are utilized for compaction and pulverization of materials. Equipped with square or rectangular blocks attached to the drum, they enhance the roller's ability to compact and pulverize the ground effectively.

Figure 117: Self-propelled padded drum vibratory roller. James Wagner, U.S. Navy, Public domain, via Wikimedia Commons.

Self-Propelled Double Drum Vibratory Roller: With drums vibrating at varying speeds and frequencies, these rollers achieve greater compaction levels. Operating at half setting results in fast vibration for shallow compaction, while full setting delivers slower vibration for deeper compaction. Vibratory rollers offer an advantage over static rollers as they can achieve higher compaction levels for the same machine weight.

Figure 118: L&T 752 Road Roller, self-propelled double drum roller. Ask27, CC BY-SA 4.0, via Wikimedia Commons.

Self-Propelled Smooth Drum Roller (Including 3 Pointers): Often referred to as static rollers, these machines function similarly to smooth drum rollers by utilizing their weight to compact materials. Compaction is achieved through the roller's weight and the rolling action of the roller drums or wheels.

Compaction rollers, also known as vibratory compactors, serve the purpose of rearranging soil particles to increase density and reduce voids, thereby enhancing the soil's load-bearing capacity. During the process of filling an area to be rolled, the layers of soil beneath the working area are referred to as lifts. The effectiveness of the initial lifts being compacted depends on the composition of the soil materials. Inadequate compaction of these layers may result in settlement cracks in the fill and the surface above it, or any structure supported by the surface.

You may have witnessed a roller in action during road resurfacing projects, where the drum at the front crushes and flattens the surface. The type of roller used varies depending on the specific job requirements, the scale of the project, and the type of soil being compacted. Two common types of rollers are the smooth roller and the padfoot roller.

Smooth Roller: Smooth rollers are frequently employed in road construction to create smooth and level surfaces. They are popular in road construction due to their ability to compress and compact gravel, asphalt, rocks, and sand using a combination of impact, static pressure, and vibration. Smooth rollers are particularly effective in locking together granular soil particles. However, when the soil contains large rocks, the lift thickness should exceed the largest rock size by twelve inches.

There are two types of smooth rollers: the single-drum roller, also known as a steamroller, which features a single steel drum at the front and tyres at the back for movement; and the double-drum roller, which has two steel drums—one at the front and one at the back—providing movement through the action of both drums rather than tyres.

Padfoot Roller: Padfoot rollers, also referred to as tamping foot rollers, are equipped with tapered pads that penetrate and compact the soil to enhance its strength. Like smooth rollers, padfoot rollers apply pressure, vibration, and impact during compaction. However, they also exert manipulative force, ensuring uniform compaction throughout the process. When the pad penetrates the lift surface, it disrupts the bonds between particles, improving compaction effectiveness.

Padfoot rollers feature two types of pad shapes: square pads, effective for smoothing surfaces and compacting semi-cohesive soils with lifts less than six inches thick; and oval pads, suitable for cohesive soils with thicker lifts (six to eighteen inches). Although the oval pad is smaller and less effective at surface sealing compared to the square pad, it applies greater pressure. Padfoot rollers are best suited for compacting soil at greater depths, especially when the soil consists of clay, loam, and/or silt.

A towed roller compactor is a type of compaction equipment that is towed behind a vehicle, typically a tractor or other heavy-duty machinery. It is designed to compact various materials such as soil, gravel, asphalt, or concrete to increase density and reduce voids. Towed roller compactors come in different configurations and types, including grid rollers, pneumatic multi-tyred rollers, padded drum vibratory rollers, and smooth drum vibratory rollers. They are commonly used in construction, road building, landscaping, and other civil engineering projects to prepare the ground for further construction or to improve the stability and durability of surfaces.

Towed Grid Roller: Utilized to break up rocky material while simultaneously compacting it, these rollers are typically towed behind a tractor.

Towed Pneumatic Multi-Tyred Roller: Comprising a series of pneumatic or rubber tyres, this roller kneads and smooths the surface. It compacts the surface by applying pressure with the weight of the roller and the rolling action of the tyres.

Towed Padded Drum Vibratory Roller: Often towed behind another piece of machinery, such as a grader or tractor, this roller serves multiple purposes and helps reduce onsite costs.

Towed Smooth Drum Vibratory Roller: This tow-behind attachment is employed to compact materials using vibration.

Here are the main components of a roller compactor:

1. Drum: The drum is the cylindrical component of the roller compactor that comes in contact with the surface being compacted. It can be either smooth or padded, depending on the type of compaction required. Smooth drums are typically used for compacting non-cohesive materials like gravel and asphalt, while padded drums, also known as padfoot drums, are used for

cohesive soils like clay.

2. Engine: The engine provides the power necessary to drive the roller compactor and operate its hydraulic systems. It is usually located within the body of the machine and can be powered by diesel fuel or gasoline.

3. Hydraulic System: The hydraulic system controls various functions of the roller compactor, such as steering, vibration, and drum movement. It consists of hydraulic pumps, cylinders, hoses, and valves that work together to transmit hydraulic fluid and control the movement of different components.

4. Water System: Many roller compactors are equipped with a water system that sprays water onto the surface being compacted. This helps reduce friction and heat buildup, prevents the material from sticking to the drum, and improves compaction efficiency.

5. Operator's Cab: The operator's cab is where the operator sits and controls the roller compactor. It typically contains the steering wheel, controls for adjusting vibration frequency and amplitude, gauges for monitoring engine performance, and a seat for the operator.

6. Frame and Chassis: The frame and chassis provide the structural support for the roller compactor and house the engine, hydraulic system, and other components. They are usually made of heavy-duty steel to withstand the stresses of compaction operations.

7. Vibratory Mechanism (Optional): Some roller compactors are equipped with a vibratory mechanism that causes the drum to vibrate during compaction. This helps improve compaction

efficiency by reducing the voids in the material and increasing its density.

8. Tyres or Tracks: Depending on the design of the roller compactor, it may be equipped with tyres or tracks for mobility. Tyres are common on smaller, tow-behind compactors, while larger, self-propelled compactors often use tracks for better traction and stability on uneven terrain.

Figure 119: Roller compactor components. Back image - SpielvogelEnglish, CC0, via Wikimedia Commons.

Roller compactor operations involve various hazards that operators and workers must be mindful of to ensure safety on construction sites. Some of the common hazards associated with roller compactor operations include crush injuries, rollovers, struck-by accidents, falls, entanglement, vibration-related injuries, noise exposure, burns and fires, chemical exposure, and overexertion and fatigue.

Crush injuries can occur due to the heavy weight of the roller compactor and the force exerted by its drum, especially if a person becomes trapped underneath or between the machine and another object. Rollovers are another concern, which can result from improper operation, uneven terrain, or excessive speed, particularly with self-propelled roller compactors, posing a significant risk of injury or death.

Workers operating or working near roller compactors may also be at risk of struck-by accidents, where they could be hit by moving parts such as the drum or hydraulic components, leading to injuries ranging from minor bruises to severe trauma. Falls are another hazard, as operators working on or around roller compactors may slip and fall on uneven or slippery surfaces, resulting in fractures, sprains, or head injuries.

Entanglement poses a serious risk, with loose clothing, jewelry, or other items potentially becoming caught in moving parts of the roller compactor, leading to severe injuries or even death. Prolonged exposure to the vibration produced by roller compactors can cause musculoskeletal disorders such as hand-arm vibration syndrome (HAVS) or whole-body vibration syndrome (WBVS), affecting nerves, blood vessels, and joints.

Moreover, roller compactors generate high levels of noise during operation, which can lead to hearing loss or other auditory problems if workers are not adequately protected with hearing protection equipment. Burns and fires are additional hazards, with the engine, hydraulic systems, and other components of roller compactors posing a risk of burns to operators and nearby workers. Fuel leaks or hydraulic fluid leaks can further lead to fires if not promptly addressed.

Chemical exposure is another concern, with workers potentially being exposed to hazardous chemicals such as hydraulic fluids or fuel during roller compactor operations. Inhalation, skin contact, or ingestion of these chemicals can result in health effects ranging from irritation to poisoning. Finally, overexertion and fatigue are risks associated with operating roller compactors, as the physical exertion and concentration required may lead to decreased alertness and an increased risk of accidents.

To mitigate these hazards, employers must provide adequate training, personal protective equipment, and safety protocols for roller compactor operations. Regular maintenance and inspections of equipment, proper communication among workers, and adherence to safety guidelines can also help prevent accidents and injuries on construction sites.

Before initiating the engine, conduct pre-start checks. Walk around the roller and scan for any irregularities or anomalies.

Component Inspection

Structure:

- Assess the overall condition of the roller for signs of wear and tear.

- Look for indications of oil or fluid leakage.

Drums and Wheels:

- Examine the drum surface and condition.

- Verify tyre condition and air pressure to ensure compliance with manufacturer specifications.

Fluids and Lubrication:

- Confirm that engine, transmission, and hydraulic oils, as well as fuel, are at appropriate levels.

- Ensure the coolant level meets specifications.

- Follow manufacturer guidelines for checking transmission fluid.

- Lubricate parts as needed to ensure smooth operation.

Engine:

- Inspect battery condition and security.

- Check electrolyte levels and inspect for damage or wear.

Hydraulic Rams and Hoses:
- Inspect hydraulic rams and pressure hoses for splits, leaks, fractures, bulges, and bent piston rods.

Attachments and Ancillary Equipment:
- Assess the condition and security of attachments.

Decals and Signage:
- Ensure all decals and signage are intact on the machine.

Windows:
- Verify clean windows for optimal visibility from the operator's chair.

Cabin:
- Check seat and safety belt for good condition and cleanliness.

Service History and Logbook:
- Review machine hour meter, manufacturer recommendations, and logbook for service requirements.
- Utilize instruments or computer systems for this information on newer models.

For specific component details, refer to the operator's manual as requirements may vary by brand.

Operational checks are performed after starting the engine.

- Climb to the operator's seat using three points of contact.
- Adjust the seat for comfort and maximum visibility.
- Fasten the safety belt.
- Start the roller following manufacturer instructions.

- Allow the engine to idle for the required duration.

Controls and Functions:
- Ensure all gauges and instruments are functioning correctly without alarms or warnings.
- Test all lights and warning devices for safety.
- Confirm attachment security and functionality.
- Assess the vibratory or compaction system operation.
- Test all movements, including turning and braking, and check the emergency stopping device.
- Test communication devices and any other fitted systems or functions.

After completing operational checks, inspect for external signs of oil or fluid leaks, which may occur during startup due to hose breakage.

In the course of civil construction roller operations, it is essential to:

1. Evaluate the materials involved in the task.
2. Operate the equipment safely within specified technical parameters and limitations.
3. Utilize the equipment only for tasks it is expressly designed for.
4. Maintain continuous vigilance to identify and address potential hazards.

Effective coordination with other personnel is vital during planning and execution to ensure clarity regarding:

- The nature of the work being undertaken.
- Operational details such as methods, timing, and location.

- Assigned responsibilities for each team member.

Clear understanding among all workers about their respective roles and those of their colleagues is paramount before commencing work, facilitating both safety and efficiency.

Collaboration may be necessary with various individuals including:

- Supervisors and management.

- Operators of other machinery and vehicles.

- Traffic control personnel or other onsite workers.

- Team leaders.

- Site safety personnel.

The terrain, prevailing conditions, and gradients on site significantly influence machine operation. Consequently, operators must adapt their techniques to these factors. For instance:

- Adjusting speed appropriately when encountering rough or stony ground.

- Employing specific rolling methods, such as ascending and descending slopes instead of traversing them.

- Navigating ditches cautiously and at an angle to ensure safe passage.

Vigilance is paramount when mounting or dismounting machinery, as improper practices can lead to injuries. Ensure to:

- Clean footwear and hands before climbing.

- Utilize handrails, grab-irons, ladders, or steps for mounting.

- Refrain from using controls as support.

- Never attempt to board a moving machine.
- Maintain three points of contact at all times.
- Ascend and descend ladders in a safe and sensible manner.
- Familiarize yourself with the site's horn signals.

Adherence to fundamental safe operating practices is crucial for the completion of tasks without risk. These include:

- Regular hazard monitoring and communication of dangers to fellow workers.
- Confirming the roller's suitability for ground conditions and tasks at hand.
- Adhering to safe driving speeds relative to prevailing conditions and terrain.
- Ensuring the roller remains within specified tolerances and capacity limits.
- Avoiding areas with holes or soft ground.
- Exercising caution when navigating the high side of trenches to prevent collapses.

Before mounting the machine, conduct a final perimeter check to ensure the absence of obstacles or individuals in the vicinity. Utilize proper mounting techniques, employing three points of contact.

If equipped with a Roll-Over Protective Structure (ROPS), always fasten seat belts before operation. Prior to startup, verify the correct positioning of all controls, including forward/reverse, steering, transmission, and throttle. Ensure the parking brake is engaged before initiating startup. Test all operational and shutdown controls for proper functionality.

Before starting the engine, it's essential to familiarize yourself with the precise starting protocol outlined in your machine's operation manual. Adhere strictly to these instructions to ensure a safe start-up process.

Upon Engine Startup: Conduct a comprehensive check of all gauges to ensure they are displaying accurate readings. Verify that the work area is safe for testing the functionality of controls and attachments. Operate all controls to ensure proper functionality and responsiveness while acquainting yourself with the operational "feel" of the machine. Remain attentive for any abnormal sounds, unusual odours, or visual signs of trouble. Inspect all warning and safety devices and indicators thoroughly. If any safety-related issues are identified, take immediate action by shutting down the machine, rectifying the problem, or informing your supervisor. Do not resume operation until the issue is resolved. Test the operation of service and parking brakes on level ground whenever feasible. Assess the performance of service brakes, including hydrostatic brakes if present, in both forward and reverse operation.

Working on Slopes: When operating on slopes, it's crucial to follow specific precautions: Minimize side hill travel whenever possible to reduce the risk of sliding or tipping. Avoid engine or machine over speeding. Before ascending or descending steep grades, ensure the selection of an appropriate gear for adequate power or engine braking. If the machine features a gearshift, opt for a low gear; for hydrostatic drives, maintain the speed control in the slow travel position, near neutral, avoiding full displacement. Ensure both gear and hydrostatic controls are in their slow travel positions for machines equipped with both. Engage manually operated gear type transmissions fully before ascending grades and refrain from gear changes while on slopes. Maintain a safe distance from overhangs, deep ditches, or holes. Stop the machine with the parking brake engaged if near a tipping point or drop-off. Plan manoeuvres carefully before proceeding. Remain vigilant for potential hazards such as collapsing edges, falling rocks, and slides. Scan for overhead obstacles in addition to hazards at ground level. Exercise caution near obstacles and excessively rugged terrain, navigating around them cautiously. Travel at a slow, steady pace over rough terrain and hillsides, adjusting speed according to working conditions.

Drive to the Work Area: Before compacting any surface, it's necessary to drive the roller to the designated work area:

Ensure the route is clear and travel at a safe speed. Check both shoulders before reversing. Avoid side hill travel whenever possible to minimize the risk of overturning. If descending a slope, proceed directly down the slope rather than across or diagonally to maintain stability. Reduce speed and select an appropriate gear for downhill travel. Opt for a low gear to control the descent during downhill travel, typically the same gear used for uphill climbs. Exercise caution when changing gears during uphill travel, particularly with heavy rollers, to prevent loss of control. If there's insufficient power to climb an incline, reverse down the hill and select the appropriate gear for ascent. Never coast the roller downhill by putting it into neutral.

Roller Techniques: Roller operators play a critical role in achieving optimal results at construction sites by employing various techniques tailored to meet specific design specifications. These techniques cannot simply be learned from a manual; they require on-site practice and guidance from experienced operators or trainers. Some effective techniques include adhering to designated roller patterns accurately, maintaining optimum speeds, identifying potential hard or uneven surfaces, determining the need for attachments, selecting appropriate gears for varying slopes, and ensuring smooth compaction through steady, even speed.

Operate Attachments: Operating within the specified design limits and operational recommendations ensures the safe and effective use of both the roller and its attachments.

Compacting: During the compacting process, it's vital to maintain a safe and acceptable speed, follow an appropriate path of travel, and engage the compacting device as required. Using the correct roller patterns, typically involving 3-6 passes per segment of the work area, is crucial for achieving the desired compaction degrees efficiently. The speed of vibration controlled by the drum controls affects the compaction outcome, with faster vibration resulting in lighter compaction and slower vibration producing heavier compaction.

Figure 120: Roller compacting gravel for temporary lane. OregonDOT, CC BY 2.0, via Wikimedia Commons.

Levelling Procedures: Levelling with the roller involves removing lumps and bumps from the work area to achieve specified gradients. Levelling equipment must be calibrated regularly and checked against site reference points. Levelling information and procedures are typically discussed during task briefings.

Road Works: When using a vibratory roller, it's important to drive slowly against the kerb on uncompacted soil without engaging the vibrator initially. Rolling operations on a road should start from the kerbside and progress in overlapping runs towards the crown. The vibrator should be turned off before stopping the roller to prevent damage to the ground.

Figure 121: Rollers compacting asphalt. Edal Anton Lefterov, CC BY-SA 3.0, via Wikimedia Commons.

Sealing and Finishing the Surface: Sealing and finishing is the final stage of road construction or maintenance, where the roller plays a crucial role in forcing aggregate into liquid asphalt without crushing it. Several passes may be required to complete the surface properly, with the roller driven slowly to achieve the best result. Rolling should cease once the asphalt has hardened to avoid damaging the bond between the aggregate and the asphalt.

Dismount Properly: When dismounting from the machine, ensure it is fully stopped and the engine is shut off. Use the provided steps and handholds for safe dismounting, maintaining three points of contact at all times. Avoid jumping off the machine to prevent injuries.

Before commencing compaction, it's essential to assess the materials at hand to determine the most suitable handling methods. Different materials present varying characteristics; for instance, clay exhibits greater cohesion and resistance to rolling compared to topsoil. Various materials encountered at construction sites may include topsoil, clays, silts, gravel, mud, stone (which may be metamorphic, igneous, or sedimentary), as well as blended or organic materials, and bituminous mixes.

In civil construction, compaction involves compressing materials into a given space to achieve desired stability in the soil. This process entails squeezing out air spaces, voids, and moisture trapped within the materials while pushing more material into the space. Different soil types compact differently; for example, sand may require mixing with other materials before compaction. Clay, on the other hand, requires precise moisture content. Assessing the type of materials, work area, and site grade helps determine the machine's suitability for achieving the required level of compaction. Understanding the desired compaction amount or percentage is crucial, which can be found in site plans, quality assurance plans, or by consulting with supervisors or site quality assurance officers.

Heavy Compaction

Various types of rollers are employed for heavy compaction tasks:
- Smooth Single Drum Vibratory Rollers: Ideal for compacting granular soil, these rollers are versatile and suitable for various construction projects.

- Padfoot Single Drum Vibratory Rollers: Specifically designed for cohesive soils like heavy clays or silt, these rollers play a crucial role in massaging air and water voids out of the material for effective compaction.

- Asphalt Double Drum Vibratory Rollers: Optimized for asphalt compaction, these rollers feature dual amplitude and high vibration frequencies for efficient compaction.

- Asphalt Combination Rollers: Equipped with four rubber tyres at the rear, these rollers are used for asphalt compaction, ensuring a denser and smoother surface texture.

- Pneumatic Rollers: Versatile machines suitable for both asphalt and granular soils, featuring rubber tyres to massage surface stones for denser asphalt.

- Steel Drum Static Rollers: Used in areas where ground vibration is not feasible, these rollers rely on static linear load for efficient compaction.

- Tamping Compactors: Ideal for cohesive and semi-cohesive soils, these machines rely on high operating speed to amplify pressure for effective compaction.

Each type of roller offers unique features and benefits suited to specific compaction requirements, ensuring optimal results on construction sites.

Once operations are completed, ensuring the roller is parked safely is paramount to facilitate easy access and maintain site safety. Safe parking practices encompass several measures:

- Bring the roller to a stop on a flat, level surface within the designated area, ensuring access points remain clear. If parking on a sloping surface is unavoidable, position the roller across the slope, provided no level area is available.

- Park away from overhangs, excavations, access ways, and areas prone to tidal or flood conditions.

- Avoid parking near refuelling sites to ensure access for other machines on-site.

- Engage locks and brakes, and position attachments into the shutdown position, adhering to site-specific safety protocols.

In cases where parking on a public access way is necessary, erect lights, signs, and barricades to warn pedestrians and motorists.

Shutdown procedures involve several steps:

- Allow the engine to cool down before shutting it off, typically equivalent to the warm-up time.

- Monitor temperature and pressure levels during controlled cooldown.

- Conduct a thorough walk-around inspection to identify any signs of damage or faults.

- Secure the vehicle, utilize applicable lockout or isolation devices, and remove keys to prevent unauthorized use.

- Ensure proper stowage of equipment in accordance with site and manufacturer guidelines.

Any issues discovered during shutdown procedures should be documented as per worksite requirements.

Post-operational checks are essential to prepare the roller for the next operator and ensure continued equipment functionality and safety. These checks typically involve inspecting various components, similar to pre-start checks, including:

- Fluid levels.

- Condition of drum or tyres.

- Hydraulics, such as rams, hoses, and connections.

- Structural integrity and attachments for damage or wear.

Performing thorough post-operational checks contributes to equipment longevity and safe working conditions on-site.

Transporting a roller between worksites typically involves the use of a float (trailer), as most rollers are too slow and heavy for road travel. Transport operations must adhere to various regulations and requirements, including:

- Codes of practice
- Traffic management requirements
- Site regulations
- Traffic codes and road rules

When loading the roller onto the transport, caution must be exercised, and the assistance of a spotter is recommended to guide the roller safely up and down the ramps. Once loaded, the roller must be securely locked down to prevent any movement during transport.

If transporting a roller across a public road, strict adherence to traffic rules is imperative.

Figure 122: Transporting a roller by float. Henryk Borawski, CC BY-SA 3.0, via Wikimedia Commons.

Traffic should be stopped to allow the roller to pass without interference, necessitating the implementation of an approved traffic management plan and escort vehicles.

It's important to note that moving a pad foot roller of any kind across a sealed surface can result in significant damage to the road surface.

CHAPTER TEN

Earthmoving in Mining and Civil Construction Work Environments

Mining Environments

In mining operations, various types of earthmoving equipment collaborate in a coordinated manner to extract, transport, and process materials efficiently. Excavators serve as versatile machines for digging and loading materials onto trucks. They often work alongside dump trucks to remove overburden or extract ore from the mine face, while also aiding in creating access roads, leveling terrain, and preparing areas for other equipment.

Dump trucks are indispensable for transporting materials such as overburden, ore, or waste rock from the excavation site to processing or dumping areas. They operate alongside excavators, facilitating the movement of large volumes of material over short to medium distances within the mine site.

Bulldozers play a pivotal role in pushing, spreading, and leveling materials, particularly overburden or waste rock. They are instrumental in clearing vegetation, establishing access roads, and reshaping terrain to facilitate mining operations, often working in conjunction with excavators and dump trucks to optimize material handling processes.

Loaders are utilized for loading materials onto trucks or into processing equipment like crushers and screens. They handle various materials, including ore, overburden, and waste rock, ensuring a steady flow of material throughout the mining operation. Loaders complement excavators and dump trucks in material handling tasks.

Graders are employed to level and grade surfaces such as access roads and mine benches, ensuring smooth and safe operations for other equipment. They maintain proper road gradients, control water runoff, and prepare surfaces for haulage and equipment movement.

Figure 123: Caterpillar 120H grader. CC BY-SA 3.0, via Wikimedia Commons.

Drilling rigs create blast holes for explosives, facilitating ore extraction or overburden removal. They work with loaders, excavators, and haul trucks to optimize the blasting process and maximize material extraction efficiency.

Crushers and screens process mined materials into manageable sizes for further processing or disposal. They often operate in tandem with loaders or conveyor systems, feeding, crushing, and separating materials according to size and composition.

Conveyor systems transport bulk materials over long distances within the mine site or between different processing stages. They enhance material handling efficiency, reduce manual labour requirements, and minimize truck traffic, thereby improving safety and productivity in mining operations.

In conclusion, the collaboration between various earthmoving equipment is crucial for optimizing mining operations, maximizing productivity, and ensuring the efficient extraction and processing of materials while prioritizing safety and environmental sustainability.

Safety protocols for earthmoving equipment in mining typically include a comprehensive set of guidelines and procedures to ensure the safety of workers and the efficient operation of equipment. Some common safety protocols for earthmoving equipment in mining include:

1. Operator Training and Certification: All operators should receive thorough training on the specific equipment they will be operating. Certification or licensing may be required to ensure operators are qualified and competent to operate the machinery safely.

2. Pre-Operation Inspections: Before starting any work, operators must conduct pre-operation inspections to check for any mechanical issues, hydraulic leaks, or other potential hazards. Any problems should be reported and addressed before operating the equipment.

3. Personal Protective Equipment (PPE): Workers must wear appropriate PPE, including hard hats, safety glasses, high-visibility clothing, gloves, and steel-toed boots, to protect themselves from potential hazards on the worksite.

4. Safe Operating Procedures: Clear guidelines should be established for the safe operation of earthmoving equipment, including proper startup and shutdown procedures, safe loading and unloading practices, and protocols for working near other equipment or personnel.

5. Equipment Maintenance: Regular maintenance and servicing of earthmoving equipment are essential to ensure it operates safely and efficiently. This includes routine inspections, lubrication, and repairs as needed.

6. Communication: Effective communication among operators, spotters, supervisors, and other personnel is critical to preventing accidents and coordinating work activities safely.

7. Traffic Management: On larger mine sites, traffic management plans may be necessary to control the movement of earthmoving equipment and other vehicles to minimize the risk of collisions and accidents.

8. Emergency Procedures: Workers should be familiar with emergency procedures, including evacuation routes, first aid protocols, and emergency shutdown procedures for equipment.

9. Environmental Considerations: Operators should be mindful of environmental hazards, such as unstable ground conditions, steep slopes, or bodies of water, and take appropriate precautions to mitigate risks.

10. Risk Assessment and Hazard Identification: Regular risk assessments should be conducted to identify potential hazards associated with earthmoving operations and develop strategies to mitigate these risks.

These safety protocols are essential components of a comprehensive safety management system in mining operations, aimed at ensuring the health and well-being of workers and minimizing the risk of accidents and injuries.

During open cut mining operations, operators will come across various mining-specific terms, including but not limited to:

- Strip: An area of land designated for mining activities.

- Free Dig: Material that can be removed without the need for blasting.

- Shot Face: Material that has been drilled and blasted prior to removal.

- Sleeping Shot: An area prepared for blasting but not yet detonated.

- Misfire: A blast hole that fails to detonate as intended.

- Work Face: The immediate area where mining activities are currently taking place.

- Loading Unit: Any machinery capable of loading trucks, such as a shovel or front-end loader.

- Bench: A level within the pit being mined.

- Bench Height: The distance between the bench floor and the top of the work face.

- Floor: The level to which a loading unit is required to work.

- Toe: The point where the work face or wall meets the floor.

- Wing/Tail: The material extending from the work face of a loading unit into the truck loading area.

- Spillage: Loose material that falls off loaded haul units, often near loading units or on haul road corners.

- Soft Spot: A section of the road surface with poor fill material, such as mud.

- Windrow: Different types include Safety Windrow, Dump Safety Windrow, and Catch Windrow, serving various safety and operational purposes.

- Rehabilitation (Rehab): The restoration of mined areas to their former condition after mining activities cease.

- High Wall: The advancing wall in an open cut operation.

- Low Wall: The wall opposite the High Wall.

- Overburden: Material above the first coal seam.

- Interburden: Layers of material between coal seams.

- Stockpile: Material piled up for loading with equipment like loaders or scrapers.

- Dump: An area designated for waste materials.

- Potholes: Holes that develop in road or dump surfaces due to traffic loads.

- Pegline: A line of pegs used to mark the boundary of dig areas or dumps.

- Fines: Smaller grade material used for finishing or filling potholes.

Surface extraction mining, also known as surface mining, is a method of extracting mineral deposits that are close to the surface of the Earth. This mining technique is commonly used to recover minerals such as coal, copper, iron, gold, diamonds, and various other resources. Surface mining involves removing layers of soil, rock, and other materials that overlay the desired mineral deposits.

There are several methods of surface extraction mining, each suited to different geological and environmental conditions:

- Open-pit mining: This method involves the excavation of a large open pit or quarry to access the mineral deposit. Open-pit mines are typically used for minerals found in large horizontal deposits close to the surface. The process begins with the removal of overburden (the layer of soil and rock covering the mineral deposit) using heavy equipment such as excavators, bulldozers, and haul trucks. Once the overburden is removed, the mineral deposit is extracted using drilling, blasting, and excavation techniques.

Figure 124: Open pitt mining. ПАО «Гайский ГОК»/Rinat Gareev, CC BY-SA 4.0, via Wikimedia Commons.

- Strip mining: Strip mining is similar to open-pit mining but is typically used for minerals that are found in horizontal seams or layers near the surface. In strip mining, the overburden is removed in strips or layers, exposing the mineral deposit. This method is commonly used for coal mining, as coal seams are often found in layers parallel to the surface.

Figure 125: Strip mining operations at the "Navajo mine" of the Utah Construction and Mining Company. Lyntha Scott Eiler, Public domain, via Wikimedia Commons.

- Mountaintop removal mining: This method is used to extract coal deposits that are located beneath the surface of mountain ridges. In mountaintop removal mining, the entire mountaintop is removed using explosives and heavy machinery to access the coal seams below. The overburden and waste rock are then dumped into nearby valleys and streams, leading to significant environmental impact and controversy.

- Quarrying: Quarrying is a type of surface mining used to extract building materials such as limestone, granite, and marble. Quarries are large open pits where rock is extracted for use in construction, landscaping, and other applications. The process involves drilling, blasting, and crushing rock to produce aggregate or dimension stone.

Surface extraction mining has several advantages over underground mining, including lower operating costs, higher productivity, and safer working conditions for miners. However, it can also have significant environmental impacts, including habitat destruction, soil erosion, and water pollution. As a result, surface mining operations are often subject to strict environmental regulations and monitoring to minimize their impact on the surrounding environment.

Open pit mining is a surface mining technique used to extract minerals or other geological materials that are located close to the Earth's surface. This mining method involves the excavation of a large open pit or quarry to access the mineral deposit. Open pit mines are commonly used for minerals such as coal, copper, gold, iron, and various types of aggregates.

Open pit mining operates as follows:

1. Exploration and Planning: The process begins with geological surveys and exploration to identify potential mineral deposits. Geologists analyse the rock formations, conduct surveys, and take samples to determine the size, grade, and quality of the mineral deposit. Once a viable deposit is identified, mining engineers develop a plan for the extraction of the mineral.

2. Site Preparation: Before mining operations begin, the site must be prepared. This may involve clearing vegetation, removing topsoil, and leveling the ground to create a stable working area. Access roads and infrastructure such as offices, workshops, and processing plants may also be constructed.

3. Drilling and Blasting: The next step is to remove the overburden, which is the layer of soil, rock, and other materials that cover the mineral deposit. Drilling rigs are used to drill holes into the rock, and explosives are inserted into the holes. Blasting is then carried out to break up the rock and loosen the overburden,

making it easier to remove.

4. Excavation: Once the overburden has been blasted, it is removed using large earthmoving equipment such as excavators, bulldozers, and haul trucks. Excavators are used to load the overburden onto haul trucks, which transport it to waste dumps or designated areas for storage.

5. Mineral Extraction: After the overburden has been removed, the mineral deposit is exposed and ready for extraction. Depending on the type of mineral and the geological characteristics of the deposit, various extraction methods may be used. This may include drilling, blasting, and excavation techniques to remove the ore or mineral-bearing rock from the pit.

6. Haulage and Transportation: Once the mineral has been extracted, it is loaded onto haul trucks for transportation to processing plants or stockpiles. Haul trucks may carry the mineral directly to processing facilities for further refinement or to stockpiles where it is stored for future use or shipment.

7. Reclamation and Closure: As mining operations progress, areas of the pit that are no longer in use may be reclaimed and rehabilitated. This typically involves reshaping the land, recontouring the pit walls, and revegetating the area to restore it to its natural state. Once mining operations are complete, the pit is closed, and the site may be repurposed for other uses or left in its natural state.

Open pit mining operations require careful planning, coordination, and management to ensure the safe and efficient extraction of minerals while minimizing environmental impacts. These operations often involve large-scale earthmoving equipment, blasting activities, and the management of waste materials, making environmental stewardship and regulatory compliance essential aspects of the mining process.

In contrast, strip mining, also known as surface mining or open-cast mining, is a mining technique used to extract minerals, ores, or coal deposits that are close to the surface. This method involves the removal of layers of soil, rock, and vegetation to expose the mineral deposit, which is then extracted.

the following describes how strip mining operates:

1. Exploration and Planning: The process begins with geological surveys and exploration to identify potential mineral deposits. Geologists analyse the rock formations and conduct surveys to determine the size, grade, and quality of the deposit. Mining engineers then develop a plan for the extraction of the mineral, taking into account factors such as the depth and thickness of the deposit, the type of mineral, and environmental considerations.

2. Site Preparation: Before mining operations begin, the site must be prepared. This may involve clearing vegetation, removing topsoil, and leveling the ground to create a stable working area. Access roads and infrastructure such as offices, workshops, and processing plants may also be constructed.

3. Overburden Removal: Once the site is prepared, the overburden, which is the layer of soil, rock, and other materials that cover the mineral deposit, is removed. This is typically done using large earthmoving equipment such as excavators, bulldozers, and haul trucks. Excavators are used to remove the overburden and load it onto haul trucks, which transport it to waste dumps or designated areas for storage.

4. Mineral Extraction: After the overburden has been removed, the mineral deposit is exposed and ready for extraction. Depending

on the type of mineral and the geological characteristics of the deposit, various extraction methods may be used. This may include drilling, blasting, and excavation techniques to remove the ore or mineral-bearing rock from the surface.

5. Haulage and Transportation: Once the mineral has been extracted, it is loaded onto haul trucks for transportation to processing plants or stockpiles. Haul trucks may carry the mineral directly to processing facilities for further refinement or to stockpiles where it is stored for future use or shipment.

6. Reclamation and Closure: As mining operations progress, areas that are no longer in use may be reclaimed and rehabilitated. This typically involves reshaping the land, recontouring the terrain, and revegetating the area to restore it to its natural state. Once mining operations are complete, the site is closed, and the land may be repurposed for other uses or left in its natural state.

Like open pit mining. strip mining operations require careful planning, coordination, and management to ensure the safe and efficient extraction of minerals while minimizing environmental impacts. These operations often involve large-scale earthmoving equipment, blasting activities, and the management of waste materials, making environmental stewardship and regulatory compliance essential aspects of the mining process.

Traffic management on mine sites involves the planning, organization, and control of vehicular and pedestrian movements to ensure safety, efficiency, and productivity within the mining operation. Here's how traffic management typically works on mine sites:

1. Traffic Planning: Before mining operations begin, a comprehensive traffic management plan is developed to identify potential hazards, establish traffic routes, designate parking areas, and define speed limits. This plan takes into account the layout of

the mine site, the types of vehicles and equipment used, and the movement of personnel.

2. Designated Travel Routes: Clear and well-defined travel routes are established for different types of vehicles and equipment within the mine site. These routes are marked with signage, road markings, and barriers to guide traffic and prevent conflicts between vehicles.

3. Separation of Traffic: To minimize the risk of accidents, traffic is separated into different lanes or areas based on vehicle type, speed, and direction of travel. For example, haul trucks may have separate routes from light vehicles, and pedestrian walkways may be separated from vehicle lanes.

4. Speed Limits: Speed limits are set and enforced to control the speed of vehicles within the mine site and reduce the risk of collisions. These limits take into account the terrain, visibility, road conditions, and the presence of pedestrians and other vehicles.

5. Traffic Control Devices: Various traffic control devices such as signs, signals, barricades, and cones are used to regulate traffic flow, indicate hazards, and provide guidance to drivers. For example, stop signs, yield signs, and traffic lights are installed at intersections to manage right-of-way.

6. Communication Systems: Effective communication systems, such as two-way radios, hand signals, and audible alarms, are used to coordinate traffic movements and convey important information to drivers and operators. This ensures that vehicles and equipment can safely navigate the mine site and avoid collisions.

7. Traffic Monitoring and Surveillance: Mine operators use surveillance cameras, vehicle tracking systems, and personnel stationed at key locations to monitor traffic movements and identify any deviations from the traffic management plan. This allows for quick intervention in the event of an emergency or traffic congestion.

8. Training and Awareness: All personnel, including drivers, operators, and pedestrians, receive training on safe traffic practices and the importance of adhering to traffic rules and regulations. Regular safety briefings and reminders are provided to reinforce safe behaviour and raise awareness of potential hazards.

9. Emergency Response: Protocols are established for responding to traffic incidents, accidents, and emergencies on the mine site. This includes procedures for providing medical assistance, evacuating personnel, securing the area, and documenting the incident for investigation and prevention of future occurrences.

10. Continuous Improvement: Mine operators regularly review and update their traffic management plans based on feedback, observations, and incident reports. This allows them to identify areas for improvement, implement corrective actions, and enhance overall safety and efficiency in traffic management.

The implementation of traffic management on mine sites significantly impacts earthmoving equipment and operations in several ways. Traffic Planning integrates earthmoving equipment operations into the overall traffic management plan, ensuring that their movements align with designated traffic routes and parking areas. This planning prevents congestion and conflicts between different types of vehicles and equipment, optimizing efficiency and safety.

Designated Travel Routes dictate that earthmoving equipment follows clear and well-defined travel routes established within the mine site. These routes accommodate the size and movement patterns of various types of equipment, minimizing the risk of collisions and ensuring smooth operations.

Separation of Traffic segregates earthmoving equipment from other vehicles and pedestrians based on factors such as speed, size, and function. For instance, haul trucks may have separate routes from light vehicles, and designated areas are provided for equipment like excavators and loaders to operate safely without interference.

Speed Limits are enforced for earthmoving equipment to ensure safe operation within the mine site, considering factors such as terrain, visibility, and the presence of pedestrians. This allows equipment operators to maintain control and prevent accidents.

Traffic Control Devices ensure that earthmoving equipment operators adhere to traffic regulations by using signs, signals, and barricades to regulate their movements and navigate the mine site safely. These devices help prevent accidents and guide operators along designated routes and procedures.

Communication Systems enable effective coordination between equipment operators and traffic controllers, ensuring smooth earthmoving operations without conflicts or disruptions. Tools like two-way radios convey important information and instructions to operators, enhancing safety and efficiency.

Traffic Monitoring and Surveillance track earthmoving equipment movements using surveillance cameras and vehicle tracking systems. This allows traffic controllers to identify deviations from the traffic management plan promptly, intervening in emergencies or congestion to minimize disruptions.

Training and Awareness provide equipment operators with training on safe traffic practices and educate them on the importance of adhering to traffic rules and regulations. Regular safety briefings reinforce safe behaviour and raise awareness of potential hazards associated with earthmoving operations.

Emergency Response protocols establish procedures for responding to traffic incidents involving earthmoving equipment, ensuring swift and effective emergency measures. This includes providing medical assistance, evacuating personnel, and securing the area to prevent further accidents or injuries.

Continuous Improvement involves mine operators continuously reviewing and updating their traffic management plans to enhance safety and efficiency in earthmoving operations. Feedback, observations, and incident reports drive corrective actions, promoting a culture of continuous improvement and safety awareness.

Working in an open-cut mine entails facing a challenging and dynamic environment shaped by various factors inherent to mining operations. The typical working conditions within such mines encompass several key aspects:

Topography and Terrain: Open-cut mines are often situated in diverse geographical locations, ranging from flat plains to rugged mountainous regions. The terrain significantly affects accessibility, transportation routes, and the deployment of heavy machinery.

Climate: The climate of the region where the mine is located is pivotal in determining working conditions. Miners may encounter extreme temperatures, ranging from scorching heat to freezing cold, depending on the season and geographic location. Additionally, factors like rainfall, humidity, and wind patterns can influence safety and operational efficiency.

Dust and Particulate Matter: Open-cut mining operations generate a substantial amount of dust and particulate matter, especially during drilling, blasting, and material handling activities. Miners may face exposure to airborne contaminants, posing respiratory health risks if not properly managed through ventilation systems and personal protective equipment (PPE).

Noise and Vibration: Elevated noise levels and ground vibrations from heavy machinery, blasting activities, and transportation vehicles are common within the mine site. Prolonged exposure to such conditions can lead to hearing loss, fatigue, and musculoskeletal disorders among workers.

Safety Hazards: Various safety hazards exist in open-cut mines, including rockfalls, collapses, equipment malfunctions, and vehicular accidents. Strict adherence to safety protocols, proper use of PPE, and regular training are essential to mitigate these risks and prevent accidents.

Work Schedule and Shift Work: Mining operations often run continuously, requiring workers to adhere to shift schedules that may include day, night, and rotating shifts. Long hours and irregular sleep patterns can contribute to fatigue and affect overall well-being.

Remote Locations: Many open-cut mines are situated in remote or isolated areas, posing logistical challenges for transportation, accommodation, medical facilities, and access to amenities for workers and their families.

Environmental Factors: Open-cut mining activities can have significant environmental impacts, such as habitat disruption, soil erosion, water pollution, and landscape alteration. Compliance with environmental regulations and implementation of mitigation measures are necessary to manage these impacts effectively.

Teamwork and Collaboration: Despite the challenges, teamwork and collaboration are crucial in open-cut mines. Effective communication, coordination, and reliance on each other ensure the safe and efficient operation of the mine.

In summary, working in an open-cut mine demands resilience, adaptability, and a strong commitment to safety and environmental stewardship. Miners must navigate diverse working conditions and challenges while striving for operational excellence and sustainable resource extraction practices.

Civil Construction Environment

Earthmoving equipment serves as a cornerstone in civil construction endeavours, fulfilling diverse roles pivotal for infrastructure development.

Site Preparation: Initially, earthmoving equipment is instrumental in clearing construction sites by removing impediments like vegetation, rocks, and debris. Utilizing bulldozers, excavators, and loaders, the terrain is levelled to establish a solid foundation for buildings, roads, bridges, and other structures.

Excavation: Excavators take centre stage in digging trenches, foundations, and basements essential for erecting buildings and laying underground utilities such as pipelines, drainage systems, and sewer lines. Moreover, they facilitate the excavation of channels and reservoirs required for effective water management.

Material Handling: Loaders and excavators are deployed for the efficient handling and transportation of construction materials like soil, gravel, sand, and aggregates across the construction site. They load and unload trucks, manage material stockpiles, and distribute resources to various areas as per construction needs.

Earthwork and Grading: Bulldozers, graders, and scrapers are enlisted for earthmoving and grading tasks, shaping the terrain to meet design specifications. These machines cut and fill soil to establish slopes, embankments, and road surfaces, ensuring proper drainage and structural stability.

Compaction: Compactors and rollers are employed to compact soil, gravel, and asphalt layers to attain the requisite density and stability. They prepare the subgrade for roads, parking lots, and building foundations, enhancing the durability and longevity of pavement layers.

Demolition: Earthmoving equipment, notably excavators and bulldozers, are pivotal in demolition endeavours. They dismantle existing structures, roads, and pavements, crushing concrete and clearing debris to pave the way for new construction projects.

Utility Installation: Excavators play a vital role in trench excavation for laying underground utilities such as water pipes, sewer lines, electrical conduits, and telecommunications cables. By meticulously digging trenches to prescribed dimensions, they minimize disruption to existing infrastructure.

Landscaping and Finishing: Earthmoving equipment finds utility in landscaping and finishing tasks, encompassing grading, leveling, and contouring land to create aesthetically pleasing lawns, parks, and recreational areas. Additionally, they assist in spreading topsoil, planting trees, and installing irrigation systems to enhance site functionality and appeal.

Earthmoving equipment stands as an indispensable asset in civil construction ventures, facilitating the seamless execution of tasks ranging from initial site preparation to final touches. By ensuring efficiency, adherence to quality standards, and consideration for safety and environmental sustainability, these machines play a pivotal role in the timely completion of projects.

As an example of a typical civil construction project, we can consider road construction. To initiate road construction, the foremost requirement is acquiring the appropriate equipment and materials. On a typical road construction site, one can expect to find a variety of machinery including wheel loaders, asphalt mixers, road rollers, excavators, backhoes, skid steers, and compact track loaders.

In terms of road building materials, asphalt and concrete stand out as the primary components. Asphalt, a blend of aggregates and a binding agent, is typically composed of crushed rock, sand, gravel, or recycled material, with bitumen serving as the binder that holds the mixture together. The quality of asphalt hinges on the calibre of aggregates used, with higher-grade materials ensuring the long-term integrity of the road.

Site preparation follows, predominantly involving clearing and excavation tasks. This phase entails the removal of trees, vegetation, and other impediments that may obstruct construction. Equipment such as excavators, mini-excavators, compact track loaders, and similar machinery are commonly employed for earth-moving and land-clearing operations.

Special considerations may arise depending on the location of the road, necessitating measures like enhanced drainage or construction of bridges. Highways traversing mountainous regions might require tunnel excavation or installation of protective structures against natural hazards like mudslides or rockfalls. For such tasks, heavy-duty equipment like articulating dump trucks, wheel loaders, and excavators are indispensable.

Figure 126: Heavy machines for asphalt pavement in Canada. Marc-Lautenbacher, CC BY-SA 4.0, via Wikimedia Commons.

Grading the roadway path is another critical aspect of preparation, involving the removal or addition of soil to ensure an even surface. Proper slope and drainage are essential to prevent issues like potholes, particularly in regions experiencing diverse weather conditions. Equipment such as bulldozers, soil compactors, and wheel loaders are commonly deployed for grading and sloping tasks.

Following site preparation, the first step is laying the sub-base, which provides a stable foundation beneath the asphalt. The sub-base, composed of materials like recycled concrete, granular fill, or crushed aggregates, is compacted to enhance drainage and resistance to temperature-induced swelling and shrinkage. Equipment like Padfoot and sheepsfoot rollers aid in compacting the sub-base, with thickness and density adjusted based on expected load requirements.

Subsequent to the sub-base, the binding layer is applied, typically utilizing bitumen as the primary binding material. Bitumen, renowned for its durability and versatility, serves as the support structure of the road, contributing significantly to its reliability and longevity. Finally, the asphalt installation completes the process, providing a smooth driving surface. Asphalt, easily installed and smoothed out using rollers like tandem or double-drum rollers, offers an aesthetically appealing and durable roadway solution.

As another example, demolition involves the process of dismantling existing structures, roads, or pavements to make room for new construction projects. Earthmoving equipment, particularly excavators and bulldozers, play a crucial role in this endeavour.

Excavators are versatile machines equipped with a hydraulic arm and bucket, capable of precision demolition work. They can reach elevated areas and selectively dismantle sections of buildings or infrastructure. Excavators are often used to tear down walls, remove roofs, and break apart concrete structures.

Figure 127: Building demolition using an excavator. Halibutt, CC BY-SA 3.0, via Wikimedia Commons.

Bulldozers, on the other hand, are powerful machines with a large blade at the front. They are employed to push and clear debris, flatten surfaces, and level the ground after demolition. Bulldozers can efficiently handle heavy materials such as concrete rubble and metal fragments, clearing the site for further construction work.

Together, excavators and bulldozers work in tandem to demolish existing structures, roads, or pavements. They crush concrete, remove debris, and clear the site, preparing it for new construction projects. Their versatility, power, and precision make them indispensable tools in the demolition process, ensuring efficient and safe removal of old infrastructure to make way for modern development.

Earthmoving equipment operators in civil construction navigate a range of working conditions influenced by project specifics, location factors, and the machinery involved. Their typical work environment encompasses the following aspects:

Outdoor Work: Operating predominantly outdoors, operators confront diverse weather conditions, from scorching heat to freezing cold, and endure rain, wind, and other environmental variables that can affect their comfort and safety.

Construction Sites: Tasks unfold on construction sites of varying nature, spanning urban areas with spatial constraints to remote locales characterized by rugged terrains. Sites may feature uneven ground, debris, and rough surfaces, presenting potential hazards amid ongoing civil engineering projects.

Noise and Vibration: The operation of heavy earthmoving equipment emits considerable noise and vibrations, exposing operators to prolonged periods of loud machinery sounds and engine noise. Such conditions pose risks of hearing impairment and fatigue, with vibrations potentially leading to discomfort and musculoskeletal issues.

Safety Measures: Operators adhere strictly to safety protocols aimed at accident prevention and injury mitigation. They outfit themselves with suitable personal protective equipment (PPE), including helmets, gloves, safety boots, and high-visibility attire. Rigorous training ensures equipment operation competence and hazard identification proficiency.

Long Hours: Often required to work extended hours, operators accommodate peak construction demands and project deadlines, which may entail early mornings, late evenings, and weekend shifts. Balancing such schedules can induce fatigue and impact work-life balance.

Physical Demands: The operation of heavy earthmoving equipment demands physical robustness, stamina, and dexterity. Operators engage in tasks that necessitate climbing in and out of equipment cabs, manoeuvring controls, and sustaining repetitive actions over prolonged durations, underscoring the job's physical rigor.

Teamwork and Communication: Integral members of construction teams, operators collaborate closely with peers, supervisors, and project managers. Effective communication and teamwork are paramount for task coordination, safety assurance, and productivity optimization across construction sites.

Environmental Awareness: Operators exhibit keen environmental awareness, particularly when operating equipment in proximity to sensitive areas such as water bodies, wetlands, or residential zones. Compliance with environmental regulations and adherence to best practices are vital for minimizing ecological impacts.

Earthmoving equipment operators in civil construction navigate a dynamic work environment characterized by outdoor exposure, noise, vibration, long hours, physical exertion, and safety priorities. Despite these challenges, their expertise and contributions are indispensable for the successful execution of construction projects, vital for building essential infrastructure and facilities.

Chapter Eleven

Operator Calculations

This chapter outlines a range of calculations useful for earthmoving equipment operators. Earthmoving equipment operators need to perform calculations at various stages of their work to ensure efficiency, accuracy, and safety. Some common scenarios where calculations are necessary include:

1. Material Handling: Operators often need to calculate the volume, weight, and density of materials being moved or transported by their equipment. This helps them determine the appropriate bucket size, load capacity, and distribution of materials to optimize efficiency and prevent overloading.

2. Site Preparation: Before beginning excavation or grading tasks, operators may need to calculate the amount of soil or rock that needs to be removed or added to achieve the desired grades and slopes. This involves measuring distances, depths, and volumes to plan excavation and filling operations accurately.

3. Load Management: When loading trucks or other vehicles with earthmoving equipment, operators must calculate the load weight to ensure it complies with legal weight limits and does

not exceed the vehicle's capacity. Overloading can pose safety risks and result in fines or damage to equipment.

4. Terrain Analysis: Operators may need to assess the terrain's slope, stability, and bearing capacity using calculations to determine the safest and most efficient routes for equipment movement. This helps prevent accidents, minimize soil erosion, and avoid damage to equipment and infrastructure.

5. Safety Precautions: Calculations are also essential for implementing safety measures such as determining safe working distances from excavation edges, assessing the stability of slopes and embankments, and calculating load-bearing capacities of temporary structures like ramps and berms.

6. Fuel Efficiency: Operators may calculate fuel consumption rates based on equipment specifications, operating conditions, and distance travelled to optimize fuel efficiency and reduce operating costs.

Material Density

For bucket loading, before engaging in tasks such as loading, transporting, and stockpiling, it's essential to assess the appropriate bucket size, weight, and capacity for the specific job at hand. Begin by calculating the average density of the material you intend to move, then compare this figure to the loaders' tipping load and lifting capacity to ensure efficient material handling. If dealing with various materials, select the bucket size based on the heaviest material it will handle. Understanding the bucket capacity of each available machine allows supervisors to determine the most suitable equipment for the task at hand. Additionally, consider the physical properties of the material being loaded, as the amount of material carried per machine cycle may not always align with the bucket's rated capacity. This discrepancy, known as the Carry Factor, varies depending on the material type and affects operational efficiency. The table shown as Figure 128 gives typical carry factors for loader buckets (Caterpillar, 2024).

MATERIAL DESCRIPTION	FILL FACTOR
LOOSE MATERIAL	
Mixed Moist Aggregates	95-100%
Uniform Aggregates up to 3mm/1/8"	95-100%
3mm – 9mm/1/8"-3/8"	90-95%
12mm – 20mm/1/2"-3/4"	85-90%
24mm/1" and over	85-90%
BLASTED ROCK	
Well blasted	80-95%
Average Blasted	75-90%
Poorly blasted	60-75%
OTHER	
Rock Dirt Mixtures	100-120%
Moist Loam	100-110%
Soil, Boulders, roots	80-100%
Cemented Materials	85-95%

Figure 128: Typical carry factors for loader buckets.

The basic calculation for loader production is:

Production per hour = Quantity of material the bucket carries per load x Number of bucket loads per hour

Machine Capacity

The material handled by a loader is typically either in a bank state or in a loose stockpile. To convert the excavated material in the bucket to bank cubic meters, you multiply the rated capacity of the bucket by the load factor. To obtain the final machine capacity, this result must then be multiplied by the carry factor, as demonstrated below:

Bank cubic meters per cycle = Rated capacity of the bucket x Load factor x Carry factor

If the material is in a loose state, the machine output can be determined by multiplying the rated bucket capacity by the carry factor:

Loose cubic meters per cycle = Rated capacity of the bucket x Carry factor

Area Calculation

The most frequently encountered area calculations involve rectangles, squares, and circles. *Rectangle*

A rectangle is a flat surface characterized by one side (the length) being longer than the other (the width). To determine the area of a flat, rectangular surface, you multiply the length by the width. Both measurements must be in the same units, typically millimetres or meters. Area is typically expressed in square millimetres (for very small areas) or more commonly in square meters.

For instance, suppose there is a road area measuring 1500 meters in length and 8 meters in width, to be covered with a mixture of gravel, binder, and water. The total area is calculated as follows:

1500 x 8 = 12,000 square meters.

Square

A square represents a particular instance of a rectangular area, where both the length and width are identical. Consequently, the area of a square can be computed as Length x Length, or simply Length squared. For instance, consider a square piece of plywood measuring 1200mm on each side (equivalent to 1.2m). Its area is calculated as follows: 1.2 x 1.2m = 1.44 square meters. To avoid repetitively using the term 'square meters' when expressing an area, either of the following abbreviations can be employed:

- m^2

- sq m.

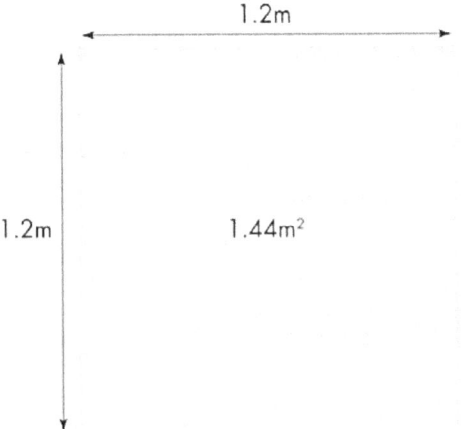

Figure 129: Area of a square.

Circle

The area of a circle is a fundamental calculation often applied in construction endeavours.

A circle is a geometric shape where every point along its outer edge, known as the perimeter, is equidistant from the centre. The measurement across a circle, from one side to the other passing through the centre, is termed the diameter, while the distance from the centre to any point on the perimeter is referred to as the radius. The circumference denotes the total distance around the perimeter of the circle.

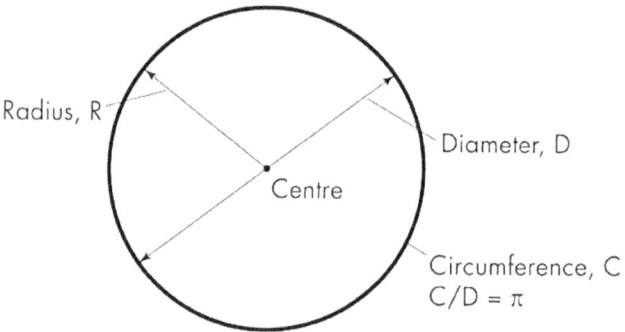

Figure 130: Components of a circle.

In all circles, the relationship between the circumference and the diameter yields a constant value known as Pi (π), represented by the Greek symbol π. Pi is an irrational number, approximately equal to 3.1416 for practical calculations.

To determine the area enclosed by a circle, one of two formulas can be employed:

$$\text{Area} = \pi R^2$$

$$\text{Area} = \frac{\pi D^2}{4}$$

Figure 131: Formulas for calculating the area of a circle.

Calculating Volumes

The term 'volume' refers to the space occupied by a three-dimensional object, whether it's a solid block of concrete or an empty void. In construction work, two primary types of volume calculations are necessary: for rectangular and cubic spaces, and for cylindrical spaces.

Volumes of Rectangular and Cubic Spaces: The volume of a space with rectangular dimensions is determined by multiplying its length, width, and depth. All measurements must be in the same units, typically millimetres or meters. Volume is often expressed in cubic millimetres or cubic centimetres for smaller spaces, or more commonly in cubic meters. A cube, where all sides are equal, represents a special case of a rectangular space. Its volume can be calculated by multiplying the length of one side by itself twice, known as Length cubed. For instance, a cubic block of wood with a side length of 100mm (equal to 0.1m) has a volume of 0.001 cubic meters:

0.1 x 0.1 x 0.1 = 0.001 cubic metres

To simplify, the terms 'cubic meters' can be abbreviated as either 'm^3' or 'cu m'.

Relationship between Fluid and Solid Cubic Measures

In the metric system, commonly used in Australia, two types of cubic measures exist: 'litres' (symbol L) for fluid volumes and cubic meters (etc.) primarily for solids. A litre comprises 1000 millilitres (mL), with each millilitre nearly equivalent to 1 cubic centimetre. As one centimetre constitutes 1/100th of a meter, a cubic meter comprises:

100 x 100 x 100 = 1,000,000 cm^3 (cubic centimetres).

This equates to 1,000,000 millilitres, making one cubic meter equivalent to 1000 litres. Consequently—

1 m³ = 1,000,000/1000 = 1000 litres. However, when dealing with substantial quantities of water or other fluids, either measure can be used interchangeably for convenience. For instance:

- The volume of water dispensed by a road-watering truck may be denoted in kilolitres (thousands of litres) or cubic meters (1kL = 1 m³).

- The water capacity of a reservoir may be expressed in megalitres (millions of litres) or cubic meters (1ML = 1000 m³).

Bulk Density

Measurement Soil bulk density (BD), also referred to as dry bulk density, quantifies the weight of dry soil (M_{solids}) divided by the total soil volume (V_{soil}). This total soil volume encompasses both the volume of solids and the pores, which may contain air (V_{air}), water (V_{water}), or both (refer to figure 1). The average values of air, water, and solid components in soil are readily measurable and provide valuable insights into the physical state of the soil. Soil BD and porosity, representing the number of pore spaces, offer insights into the size, shape, and arrangement of particles and voids, collectively known as soil structure. Both BD and porosity (V_{pores}) serve as indicators of soil's suitability for root growth and its permeability, making them crucial for the soil-plant-atmosphere system. Soil with a low BD (<1.5 g/cm3) is generally preferred as it facilitates optimal movement of air and water through the soil.

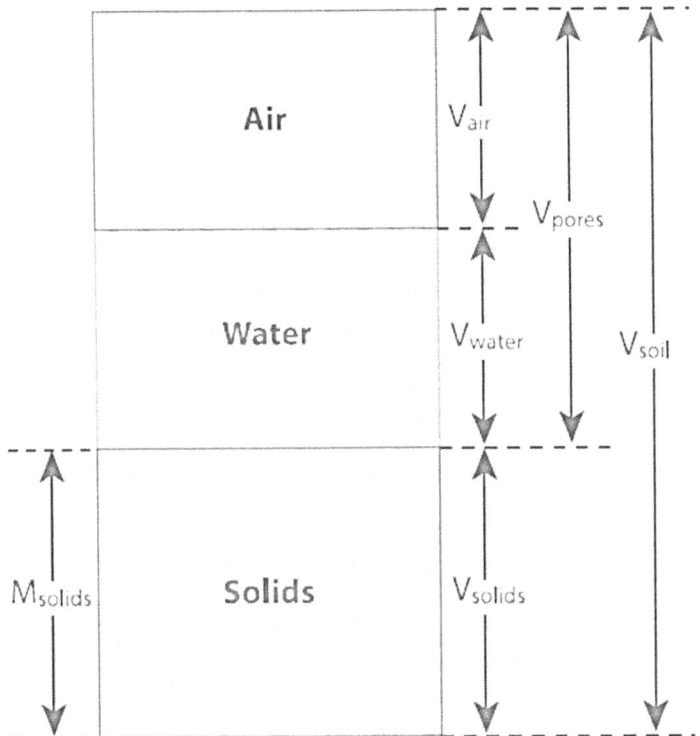

Figure 132: Structural composition of soil, containing soil fraction (Vsolids) and pore space for air (Vair) and water (Vwater).

Understanding soil bulk density (BD) and its implications is essential for earthmoving equipment operators for several reasons. Firstly, BD provides crucial information about soil composition and structure, including the arrangement of particles and pore spaces. This knowledge helps operators assess the suitability of the soil for construction or excavation activities. Additionally, BD influences soil permeability and porosity, which in turn affect how easily air and water can move through the soil. For operators working with heavy machinery like excavators and bulldozers, soil with low BD (<1.5 g/cm3) is preferred as it allows for optimal movement of equipment and minimizes the risk of soil compaction. Understanding BD helps operators make informed decisions about equipment selection, soil management practices, and project planning to ensure efficient and effective earthmoving operations while minimizing environmental impact.

To ensure accuracy and account for variability, it is advisable to conduct multiple measurements of bulk density at the same location over time and at various depths within the soil, such as 10, 30, and 50 cm depths, to assess both surface soil and subsoil conditions. Comparing bulk density between different management practices, such as cultivated versus non-cultivated soil, can also provide valuable insights into how physical soil properties are affected.

The most common method for measuring soil bulk density involves collecting a known volume of soil using a metal ring pressed into the soil (intact core) and then determining the weight after drying. When sampling the soil, it's important to create an undisturbed flat horizontal surface at the desired depth using appropriate tools.

The steel ring is then gently hammered into the soil, and care must be taken to avoid overcompacting the soil. After carefully excavating around the ring and removing it with the soil intact, excess soil is removed, and the sample is sealed in a plastic bag, labelled with the date and location. Common sources of error include soil disruption during sampling, inaccurate trimming, and imprecise measurement of the ring's volume. Calculating soil volume involves measuring the height and diameter of the ring to determine its volume using the formula for the volume of a cylinder.

Dry soil weight is calculated by weighing an ovenproof container, transferring the soil into it, and drying it before weighing again. Bulk density is then calculated by dividing the dry soil weight by the soil volume, typically expressed in megagrams per cubic meter (Mg/m^3), although equivalent units such as grams per cubic centimetre (g/cm^3) and tonnes per cubic meter (t/m^3) are also used.

Quantity of Soil or Rock to be Removed

Before starting excavation or grading tasks, earthmoving equipment operators often need to determine the quantity of soil or rock that must be excavated or added to achieve specific grades and slopes as required by the construction project. This process involves careful calculations and measurements to ensure accurate planning of excavation and filling operations.

For example, let's say a construction project involves building a road with a specified gradient. Before beginning excavation, operators would need to calculate the volume of soil that needs to be removed to achieve the desired road slope. They would measure the length, width, and depth of the excavation area to determine the total volume of soil to be excavated.

Similarly, in a landscaping project, operators may need to calculate the amount of soil or rock needed to fill an area to create a desired slope for drainage purposes. This calculation involves measuring the dimensions of the area to be filled and calculating the volume required to achieve the desired slope.

In both scenarios, accurate calculations are essential to ensure that the excavation or filling operations are carried out efficiently and according to the project specifications. Failure to calculate the correct quantities of soil or rock could result in delays, cost overruns, or improper grading, impacting the overall success of the construction project.

Sample Calculation:

Scenario: Building a Road with a Specified Gradient

Given: Length of the road = 100 meters

Width of the road = 6 meters

Desired road slope = 2% (or 2 meters rise over 100 meters)

Calculation:

1. Determine the volume of soil to be excavated:

- Calculate the difference in elevation between the high and low points of the road:

Rise = Length of the road * Desired road slope
Rise = 100 meters * 2% = 2 meters

- Determine the cross-sectional area of the road:

Cross-sectional area = Length of the road * Width of the road
Cross-sectional area = 100 meters * 6 meters = 600 square meters

- Calculate the volume of soil to be excavated using the cross-sectional area and rise:

Volume of soil = Cross-sectional area * Rise
Volume of soil = 600 square meters * 2 meters = 1200 cubic meters

Result: The earthmoving equipment operators would need to excavate approximately 1200 cubic meters of soil to achieve the desired road slope for the construction project. This calculation ensures that the excavation operation is carried out accurately and according to the project specifications, preventing delays and ensuring the success of the road-building project.

Terrain Analysis

Terrain Analysis involves assessing various aspects of the land to determine its suitability for equipment movement and construction activities. This process includes evaluating factors such as slope, stability, and bearing capacity to identify safe and efficient routes for equipment movement while minimizing risks and potential damage to the environment and infrastructure. Here's how this analysis is typically conducted, along with sample calculations:

1. **Assessing Slope:**

- Slope analysis involves measuring the steepness of the terrain to determine the gradient or incline.

- This can be done using a clinometer or a digital inclinometer, which measures the angle of elevation or depression.

- For example, if the slope angle is measured to be 10 degrees, it indicates that the terrain rises or falls 10 degrees over a horizontal distance.

- Calculations may involve converting slope percentages to degrees or vice versa, depending on the requirements of the project.

2. Evaluating Stability:

- Stability assessment involves determining the stability of the terrain to support equipment and prevent landslides or collapses.

- This may involve conducting soil tests, such as the Proctor compaction test or the Standard Penetration Test (SPT), to assess soil strength and stability.

- Engineers may use empirical formulas or geotechnical software to analyse soil properties and predict stability under different loading conditions.

3. Calculating Bearing Capacity:

- Bearing capacity refers to the maximum load-bearing capacity of the soil without undergoing excessive settlement or failure.

- It is determined based on soil type, density, moisture content, and other factors.

○ One common method for calculating bearing capacity is using the Terzaghi's bearing capacity equation:

$$Q = cN_c + \gamma D_N q + 0.5\gamma B N_\gamma$$

Where:
Q = Ultimate bearing capacity of the soil
c = Cohesion of the soil
N_c, N_q, N_γ = Bearing capacity factors
D = Depth of the footing
γ = Unit weight of the soil
B = Width of the footing

Figure 133: Terzaghi's bearing capacity equation.

Sample Calculation for Bearing Capacity:
Given:
- Cohesion (cc) = 10 kPa

- Depth of the footing (DD) = 2 meters

- Unit weight of the soil (γγ) = 18 kN/m³

- Width of the footing (BB) = 1 meter

Using Terzaghi's bearing capacity equation: Q = cN_c + γD_N_q + 0.5γBN_γ
Q=(10)(5)+(18)(2)(30)+(0.5)(18)(1)(20)
Q=50+1080+180
Q=1310 kN

Result: The ultimate bearing capacity of the soil is 1310 kN. This value helps determine the safe load that the soil can support, guiding equipment movement and construction activities to prevent soil failure or excessive settlement.

By conducting terrain analysis and performing calculations like these, earthmoving equipment operators can make informed decisions to ensure safety, efficiency, and environmental protection during construction operations.

Trench Excavation Depth

Trench excavation depth calculation involves determining the depth to which a trench needs to be dug to meet the requirements of a construction project. This calculation is crucial for ensuring that the trench is deep enough to accommodate utilities, pipelines, or foundations while adhering to safety and engineering standards.

Here's an example of how trench excavation depth calculation works:

Let's consider a construction project that requires the installation of an underground pipeline. The project specifications indicate that the pipeline must be buried at a minimum depth of 5 feet (1.52 meters) to ensure adequate protection and prevent damage.

To calculate the trench excavation depth, we follow these steps:

1. Review Project Specifications: Refer to the project specifications to determine the required minimum depth for the trench excavation.

2. Consider Soil Conditions: Assess the soil conditions at the construction site, including soil type, stability, and any existing underground utilities or structures.

3. Factor in Pipe Size and Depth: Consider the size and diameter of the pipeline that needs to be installed. For example, if the pipeline has a diameter of 12 inches (0.3048 meters), it may require a trench depth that allows for at least 12 inches of cover above the pipeline to protect it from external forces and envi-

ronmental factors.

4. Calculate Total Depth: Add the required minimum depth specified in the project specifications to the additional depth needed to accommodate the pipeline size. For instance, if the project specifies a minimum depth of 5 feet and the pipeline requires 12 inches of cover, the total trench excavation depth would be 5 feet 12 inches (1.52 + 0.3048 = 1.8248 meters).

5. Verify Requirements: Double-check the calculated depth against project specifications and local building codes to ensure compliance with safety and regulatory standards.

Cut and Fill

Cut and fill calculation is a fundamental process in earthmoving operations, where the volume of material to be removed (cut) from one area and placed in another area (fill) is determined to achieve desired grades and slopes for construction projects. This calculation is essential for ensuring that the earthmoving activities are executed efficiently and accurately, minimizing costs and environmental impacts.

Here's an example of how cut and fill calculation works:

Consider a construction project involving the development of a building site on uneven terrain. The goal is to level the site and create a flat surface for construction while maintaining proper drainage and slope requirements.

1. Surveying: Begin by surveying the site to determine the existing elevations and topography. This information is typically obtained using surveying instruments such as total stations or GPS devices.

2. **Establish Design Grades**: Based on the project specifications and engineering design, establish the desired grades and slopes for the site. This includes determining the elevation of the finished surface and any required slopes for drainage.

3. **Calculate Cut and Fill Volumes**: Using the surveyed data, calculate the volume of material to be cut from areas where the existing elevation is higher than the desired finished grade (cut) and the volume of material needed to fill areas where the existing elevation is lower than the desired grade (fill).

   - For example, if the existing elevation at a certain point on the site is 100 meters, and the desired finished grade is 95 meters, the cut volume would be calculated based on the difference between the two elevations.

   - Similarly, if the existing elevation at another point is 90 meters and the desired finished grade is 95 meters, the fill volume would be calculated based on the difference in elevations.

4. **Adjust for Swell and Shrinkage**: Depending on the characteristics of the soil or material being excavated, adjustments may need to be made for swell (increase in volume when excavated) or shrinkage (decrease in volume when placed). These factors are typically determined based on laboratory testing or empirical data.

5. **Verify Calculations**: Double-check the calculated cut and fill volumes to ensure accuracy. This may involve reviewing the calculations with a civil engineer or using specialized software for earthwork estimation.

By accurately calculating cut and fill volumes, earthmoving equipment operators can efficiently manage excavation and filling activities, ensuring that the site is prepared according to the project requirements while minimizing material waste and environmental impacts.

Safety Calculations

Safety calculations in earthmoving operations involve assessing slope stability and bearing capacity to ensure the safe operation of equipment and the protection of personnel and property from potential hazards such as landslides, collapses, or equipment tipping over.

Example Calculation: Slope Stability

1. **Survey the Site**: Use surveying equipment to measure the slope angles and topography of the area where earthmoving activities will take place.

2. **Calculate Slope Stability**: Determine the factor of safety (FOS) for the slope to assess its stability. The factor of safety is the ratio of the forces resisting slope failure to the forces causing slope failure.

    - For example, if the driving force causing slope failure (such as gravity acting on the soil mass) is greater than the resisting forces (such as soil cohesion and friction), the slope may be unstable. A factor of safety less than 1 indicates instability.

    - Calculate the factor of safety using engineering principles and slope stability analysis methods such as the Bishop method, Janbu method, or limit equilibrium analysis.

3. **Mitigate Risks**: Based on the calculated factor of safety, implement appropriate measures to mitigate risks and ensure slope

stability. This may include reinforcing the slope with retaining walls, soil stabilization techniques, or adjusting the slope angle.

Example Calculation: Bearing Capacity

1. **Determine Bearing Capacity Requirements**: Identify the loads that will be exerted on the ground by earthmoving equipment and structures, such as buildings or roads.

2. **Soil Analysis**: Conduct soil testing to determine the soil's bearing capacity, which is the maximum load the soil can support without undergoing excessive settlement or failure.

3. **Calculate Bearing Capacity**: Use empirical formulas or geotechnical engineering principles to calculate the soil's bearing capacity based on its properties such as cohesion, angle of internal friction, and density.

   - For example, the Terzaghi's bearing capacity equation can be used to calculate the ultimate bearing capacity of soil based on its cohesion, effective stress, and bearing area.

4. **Verify Safety**: Ensure that the calculated bearing capacity exceeds the expected loads from the equipment and structures to prevent soil failure or settlement.

By performing safety calculations for slope stability and bearing capacity, earthmoving equipment operators can identify potential hazards, assess risks, and implement appropriate measures to maintain a safe working environment and prevent accidents or damage to property.

Calculating the factor of safety (FOS) is crucial in assessing the stability of slopes in earthmoving operations. Various engineering principles and slope stability analysis methods are employed for this purpose, including the Bishop method, Janbu method, and limit equilibrium analysis.

1. Bishop Method: The Bishop method is a widely used approach for analysing slope stability. It considers the shear strength of the soil and the forces acting on the slope to determine the factor of safety. The method involves dividing the slope into slices and analysing the equilibrium of forces and moments for each slice. By considering factors such as soil properties, slope geometry, and external loads, the Bishop method calculates the factor of safety against slope failure.

2. Janbu Method: The Janbu method is another slope stability analysis technique that evaluates the factor of safety based on soil strength parameters and slope geometry. It involves dividing the slope into vertical slices and analysing the stability of each slice under different loading conditions. The method accounts for factors such as pore water pressure, soil properties, and slope inclination to calculate the factor of safety and assess slope stability.

3. Limit Equilibrium Analysis: Limit equilibrium analysis is a general approach used to analyse the stability of slopes and structures. It assumes that the slope is on the verge of failure and evaluates the equilibrium of forces and moments to determine the factor of safety. Various methods, such as the method of slices, the Swedish slip circle method, and the Spencer method, fall under the category of limit equilibrium analysis. These methods consider factors like soil shear strength, slope geometry, and external loads to calculate the factor of safety and assess slope stability.

These engineering principles and slope stability analysis methods provide systematic approaches for calculating the factor of safety and evaluating slope stability in earthmoving operations. By utilizing these methods, engineers and earthmoving equipment operators can assess the risks associated with slope instability and implement appropriate measures to ensure safety and prevent slope failure.

Here are example calculations for each of the mentioned slope stability analysis methods:

1. Bishop Method:

Suppose we have a slope with the following parameters:
- Slope angle: 30 degrees
- Soil cohesion (c): 10 kN/m^2
- Soil unit weight (γ): 18 kN/m^3
- Horizontal seismic coefficient (Kh): 0.2
- Vertical seismic coefficient (Kv): 0.1

Using the Bishop method, we calculate the factor of safety as follows:
- Determine the critical slip surface and divide the slope into slices.
- Calculate the driving force and resisting force for each slice.
- Sum up the driving forces and resisting forces to find the overall factor of safety.
- For example, if the sum of resisting forces is 120 kN and the sum of driving forces is 100 kN, the factor of safety is 120/100 = 1.2.

Let's consider the same slope parameters as in the Bishop method example. Using the Janbu method:
- Divide the slope into vertical slices and analyse each slice's stability.

- Consider factors such as pore water pressure, soil properties, and slope inclination in the analysis.

- Calculate the factor of safety for each slice and then combine them to determine the overall factor of safety for the slope.

- For instance, if the factor of safety for each slice ranges from 1.1 to 1.3, the overall factor of safety for the slope can be calculated as the minimum of these values, which is 1.1.

For limit equilibrium analysis, let's assume we are using the method of slices for our slope stability assessment:

- Divide the slope into slices and consider the equilibrium of forces and moments for each slice.

- Use soil shear strength parameters, slope geometry, and external loads to calculate the factor of safety for each slice.

- Combine the factors of safety from all slices to determine the overall factor of safety for the slope.

- For example, if the factors of safety for individual slices range from 1.2 to 1.5, the overall factor of safety for the slope can be calculated as the minimum of these values, which is 1.2.

These calculations demonstrate how engineers and earthmoving equipment operators can use different slope stability analysis methods to assess the factor of safety and evaluate slope stability in earthmoving operations.

Production Rate

EARTHMOVING EQUIPMENT OPERATIONS

Production Rate Calculation involves estimating the rate at which material is either removed or placed per unit of time during earthmoving operations. This calculation is crucial for project planning and scheduling to ensure that project deadlines are met efficiently.

To perform a production rate calculation, several factors need to be considered, including the type of material being moved, the capacity of the earthmoving equipment, the distance the material needs to be transported, and the operating conditions at the construction site.

Here's an example of how to calculate the production rate for material removal:

Let's assume we have a project to excavate soil from a construction site using an excavator. The specifications are as follows:

- Excavator bucket capacity: 2 cubic meters
- Travel time for each cycle (including loading and dumping): 10 minutes
- Soil density: 1.5 tons per cubic meter

1. Calculate the theoretical volume of soil excavated per hour:

    - Number of cycles per hour

= 60 minutes per hour / Travel time per cycle
= 60 / 10
= 6 cycles per hour

- Volume of soil excavated per hour

= Excavator bucket capacity * Number of cycles per hour
= 2 cubic meters/bucket * 6 cycles per hour
= 12 cubic meters per hour

1. Calculate the weight of soil excavated per hour:

    - Weight of soil excavated per hour

= Volume of soil excavated per hour * Soil density

= 12 cubic meters/hour * 1.5 tons per cubic meter

= 18 tons per hour

So, the production rate for material removal in this scenario is 18 tons per hour.

Similar calculations can be performed for material placement, taking into account factors such as the capacity of the equipment used for placing material, the distance the material needs to be transported, and the time required for each cycle.

These production rate calculations help project managers and earthmoving equipment operators estimate project timelines, allocate resources efficiently, and ensure that construction projects progress smoothly and meet deadlines.

References

Caterpillar. (2024). *Bucket Fill Factors*. Caterpillar. Retrieved 12/3/2024.

Cumming, M. (2017). Complete Guide To Front End Loader Extensions. *Construction Know-How*.

Custom Truck. (2018). *Operators Manual, Load King, 4000 Gallon Water Tank*.

Glassdoor. (2024). *Haul Truck Operator Salaries in Australia*. Retrieved 12/3/2024.

Goulet, S., & Anderson, L. (2007). *Skid Steer Operator Safety and Development*. Bow Valley College.

Indeed. (2024a). *Backhoe operator salary in United States*. Retrieved 12/3/2024.

Indeed. (2024b). *Excavator operator salary*. Retrieved 12/3/2024.

Lane, K. (2022, 4/3/2024). How to Operate a Skid Steer.

Seek. (2024). *Excavator Operator salary*. Retrieved 12/3/2024.

Seek UK. (2024a). *Backhoe operator salary in United Kingdom*. Retrieved 12/3/2024.

Seek UK. (2024b). *Excavator operator salary in United Kingdom*. Retrieved 12/3/2024.

Symons, R. (1985). *Front End Loader Operation and Maintenance Manual*. Montana Department of Highways.

talent.com. (2024). *Excavator Operator average salary in Canada, 2024*. Retrieved 12/3/2024.

Index

A

Arm, 12–13, 26, 29–30, 64–69, 71–72, 75–76, 81–85, 89, 95–97, 104, 109, 117–118, 122, 127–128, 130, 138, 140–142, 150, 156–158, 160–161, 164–165, 170, 172, 192, 210–211, 216, 218–220, 222–224, 226, 238, 243, 248, 253, 281, 471, 508

Articulated dump truck, 366, 404

Articulated haul truck, 365, 371–373, 419

Asphalt, 158, 214, 423, 439–441, 443–445, 450–453, 455–462, 467–468, 480, 482, 505–508

Attachments, 14, 20–21, 27, 30–31, 37, 39–41, 57–60, 62, 65, 68–69, 71, 76, 79, 81–84, 88–90, 93, 96, 104, 115–119, 121–122, 127–128, 134, 136, 149–151, 154, 157–159, 163, 165, 169–171, 179, 190, 196, 198, 206, 208, 213–214, 216–217, 222–225, 239, 250, 253, 255, 257–259, 277, 377, 473, 477–479, 483–484

Auger, 16, 20, 39, 58, 81, 83, 159–160, 170–171, 217, 223, 225, 258, 450

B

Backhoe, 9, 11, 14–15, 23–24, 128–129, 156–165, 167–170, 172–173, 178–180, 182, 185, 191, 193, 196, 198, 201–203, 205–208, 221, 505, 535

Backhoe loader, 14–15, 157, 163–164, 172, 202

Blade, 15–16, 20, 149, 202, 225, 250, 440, 445, 447–448, 508

Blasting, 235, 385, 488, 490, 492, 494, 496, 498, 502–503

Bobcat, 29, 35

Bridge construction, 221

Bucket, 12–14, 16, 20, 75, 93–96, 103–104, 106–107, 109–111, 113, 117, 119, 122, 127, 130–132, 137–147, 149, 152–153, 156–160, 163–165, 167–173, 178–180, 197–204, 210–212, 216–218, 221, 223, 225–226, 236, 238, 240, 243, 248, 250–253, 255, 258, 262–263, 265–267, 270, 272–274, 357, 401, 411–413, 508, 513, 535

Bucket capacity, 200

Bulldozer, 11, 16, 20, 24, 278–281, 283–286, 291–292, 294–303, 305, 307–310, 313–315, 317, 319–321, 326–327, 415

C

Civil engineering, 11, 107, 221, 468, 509

Compact track loader, 33, 82–83, 505–506

Compaction equipment, 449, 468

Compactor, 9, 171, 217, 330, 445, 449, 457, 459–460, 462, 466, 468–472, 507

Concrete, 32, 57–58, 60, 129, 148, 188, 214, 218, 423, 430, 440–441, 450–453, 455, 457–460, 468, 505–509, 517

Construction equipment, 158, 161

Construction materials, 459–460, 504

Construction projects, 163, 165, 329

Construction site, 11–13, 17, 19, 25–26, 30, 94, 157, 163, 188, 213, 223, 239, 254, 263, 329, 333–335, 337, 345, 375, 427, 446–448, 451, 457, 459, 462, 470, 472, 478, 481–482, 504–505, 509–510, 533

Conveyor, 18, 112, 212, 235, 441, 445, 447, 450, 452, 454–455, 457, 488

Cut and fill, 526

D

Demolition, 12, 27, 58, 60, 82, 158, 162–163, 170–171, 210, 214, 220, 225–226, 430, 505, 508–509

Digging, 11–12, 18–19, 21, 26–27, 31, 33, 58–59, 94, 137, 139–140, 143–145, 147, 156, 158–161, 164–165, 171, 173, 201, 203, 205, 210–211, 213, 215–217, 220–222, 225, 238–239, 242–243, 247, 249–252, 256, 262, 265, 270, 274–275, 486, 504–505

Dozer blade, 16

Drainage, 11, 56–57, 188, 203, 208, 213–214, 229, 235, 420–422, 504, 506–507, 521, 526–527

Drilling, 58, 82, 157–158, 492, 494, 496, 498, 502

Dump truck, 11, 17–18, 269, 366–367, 375–376, 394, 397–398, 404, 406, 486–487, 506

Dumping, 93, 107, 109, 131, 137–138, 141, 144–147, 153, 201, 256, 263, 266, 366, 387, 392–393, 396–399, 406, 411, 415–417, 486, 533

E

Earthmoving, 9–13, 15, 17, 19–25, 27, 29, 31, 33, 35, 37, 39, 41, 43, 45, 47, 49, 51, 53, 55, 57, 59, 61, 63, 65, 67, 69, 71, 73, 75, 77, 79, 81, 83, 85, 87, 89, 91, 95, 97, 99, 101, 103, 105, 107, 109, 111, 113, 115, 117, 119, 121, 123, 125, 127–129, 131, 133, 135, 137, 139, 141, 143, 145, 147, 149, 151, 153, 155, 157, 159, 161, 163, 165, 167, 169, 171, 173, 175, 177, 179, 181, 183, 185, 187, 189, 191, 193, 195, 197, 199, 201, 203, 205, 207, 209, 211, 213, 215, 217, 219–221, 223, 225, 227, 229, 231, 233, 235, 237, 239, 241, 243, 245, 247, 249, 251, 253, 255, 257, 259, 261, 263, 265, 267–269, 271, 273, 275, 277, 279, 281, 283, 285, 287, 289, 291, 293, 295, 297, 299, 301, 303, 305, 307, 309, 311, 313, 315, 317, 319, 321, 323, 325, 327, 331, 333, 335, 337, 339, 341, 343, 345, 347, 349, 351, 353, 355, 357, 359, 361, 365, 367, 369, 371, 373, 375, 377, 379, 381, 383, 385, 387, 389, 391, 393, 395, 397, 399, 401, 403, 405, 407, 409, 411, 413, 415, 417, 419, 421, 423–425, 427, 429, 431, 433, 435, 437, 439, 441, 443, 445, 447, 449, 451, 453, 455, 457, 459, 461, 463, 465, 467, 469,

471, 473, 475, 477, 479, 481, 483, 485–491, 493, 495–505, 507–511, 513, 515, 517, 519–523, 525–529, 531–533

Earthmoving equipment, 9–11, 13, 15, 17, 19–25, 27, 29, 31, 33, 35, 37, 39, 41, 43, 45, 47, 49, 51, 53, 55, 57, 59, 61, 63, 65, 67, 69, 71, 73, 75, 77, 79, 81, 83, 85, 87, 89, 91, 95, 97, 99, 101, 103, 105, 107, 109, 111, 113, 115, 117, 119, 121, 123, 125, 127–129, 131, 133, 135, 137, 139, 141, 143, 145, 147, 149, 151, 153, 155, 157, 159, 161, 163, 165, 167, 169, 171, 173, 175, 177, 179, 181, 183, 185, 187, 189, 191, 193, 195, 197, 199, 201, 203, 205, 207, 209, 211, 213, 215, 217, 219, 221, 223, 225, 227, 229, 231, 233, 235, 237, 239, 241, 243, 245, 247, 249, 251, 253, 255, 257, 259, 261, 263, 265, 267, 269, 271, 273, 275, 277, 279, 281, 283, 285, 287, 289, 291, 293, 295, 297, 299, 301, 303, 305, 307, 309, 311, 313, 315, 317, 319, 321, 323, 325, 327, 331, 333, 335, 337, 339, 341, 343, 345, 347, 349, 351, 353, 355, 357, 359, 361, 365, 367, 369, 371, 373, 375, 377, 379, 381, 383, 385, 387, 389, 391, 393, 395, 397, 399, 401, 403, 405, 407, 409, 411, 413, 415, 417, 419, 421, 423, 425, 427, 429, 431, 433, 435, 437, 439, 441, 443, 445, 447, 449, 451, 453, 455, 457, 459, 461, 463, 465, 467, 469, 471, 473, 475, 477, 479, 481, 483, 485–489, 491, 493, 495–505, 507–511, 513, 515, 517, 519, 521–523, 525, 527, 529, 531–533

Earthwork, 213, 527

Earthworks, 158, 229

Environmental impact, 187–188, 339, 419, 432, 444, 494–496, 498, 503, 520, 526, 528

Equipment maintenance, 22, 377

Erosion control, 448

Excavation, 11–12, 14, 21, 23, 156–158, 160, 162, 164–165, 171–172, 184–186, 201, 203–206, 210, 212–213, 217, 220–221, 228–233, 235, 246–247, 259–260, 263, 267–268, 388, 404, 434, 482, 486, 492, 495–496, 498, 504–506, 525

Excavation depth, 525

Excavation projects, 23, 156, 162, 164

Excavation techniques, 492, 496, 498

Excavator, 9, 11–13, 20, 23–24, 128, 158–160, 162–163, 210–227, 229, 238–243, 247–263, 267–275, 277, 399, 412, 424, 486–488, 492, 496–497, 501, 504–506, 508–509, 535–536
  Excavator attachments, 224, 258
  Excavator operator, 24, 248, 269, 273, 535–536
  Exploration, 495, 497
  Extraction, 212, 488, 492, 495–498, 504

F
  Foundation, 11, 23, 158, 210, 213, 336, 369, 446, 459–461, 504–505, 507, 525
  Front-end loader, 159, 173, 490

G
  Grader, 11, 24, 358, 387, 439, 468, 487, 504
  Grading, 11–12, 15, 21, 26, 30, 58, 104, 140, 142, 213, 378, 445, 449, 457, 504–505, 507, 511, 521

H
  Haul road, 274, 349–350, 378–379, 391–392, 405, 407, 491
  Haul truck, 24, 95, 112, 211, 235, 268, 270, 363–374, 377, 379–382, 385–386, 388–389, 391–393, 404, 407–409, 415, 417–419, 488, 492, 496–499, 501, 535
  Haul truck operator, 377, 381, 385, 389, 393, 417, 535
  Haulage, 378, 487
  Heavy equipment, 93, 156, 167, 249–250, 340, 492
  Heavy machinery, 11, 23, 215, 332, 494, 502–503, 519
  Hydraulic excavator, 218–219
  Hydraulic system, 19, 93, 96, 105, 109–110, 121, 160–161, 167, 192, 215–218, 251, 370, 373, 380, 452, 454, 457, 469, 471

I

Infrastructure, 12, 23–25, 213–214, 416, 446, 451, 495, 497, 504–505, 508–510, 512, 522

L

Landscaping, 11–12, 14, 28, 30–34, 57, 82, 93–94, 103–104, 156, 158, 164–165, 206, 210, 220–221, 223, 225, 229, 468, 494, 505, 521

Loader, 9, 11, 13–17, 23–24, 26–30, 33, 35, 40, 52–53, 57–60, 67, 71, 73, 75–76, 79, 82–83, 90–91, 93–105, 107–114, 119–120, 122–126, 129–134, 136, 138, 140–143, 145–159, 161, 163–164, 169–170, 172–173, 202, 206, 221, 235, 413, 424, 488, 490–491, 501, 504–507, 513–514, 535

Loader arm, 30, 82–83, 96–97, 109

Loader bucket, 131–132, 143, 149, 159, 164, 169, 221, 513

Loader operator, 73, 113, 146

Loading and unloading, 27, 132, 210, 329, 361, 489

Loading ramp, 361

M

Maintenance, 20–22, 27, 34, 47, 70, 78, 89–90, 95, 102, 112–114, 118, 122–123, 130, 135, 151–152, 155, 158, 165–166, 190–191, 209, 227, 237, 277, 335–336, 338, 341–343, 375, 377–379, 389, 391, 394, 400, 403–405, 407–408, 418, 425, 430, 453, 458, 472, 480, 489, 535

Material handling, 32, 58, 99, 103–104, 110, 113, 116, 213, 221, 363, 455, 487–488, 502, 511–512

Material transport, 12, 158

Material transportation, 13

Minerals, 212, 363, 492–493, 495–498

Mining, 11–12, 23–25, 31, 55, 94, 96, 104, 123, 158, 162, 185, 210–213, 220–221, 223, 273, 329–331, 346, 350, 363, 366–368, 371, 377, 388, 419, 460, 486–488, 490–498, 502–503

Mining engineer, 495

Mining industry, 24, 31
Mining operations, 11, 23–25, 94, 185, 211–213, 331, 366, 388, 486–488, 490, 494–498, 502
Mining truck, 346, 367, 377

O
Off-highway truck, 408
Open-pit mining, 493
Operating capacity, 254
Operator comfort, 108
Ore, 365, 486–488, 496–498
Overburden removal, 221, 488

P
Pallet fork, 31, 40, 79, 83, 117
Paving, 158, 163, 449, 462
Pit, 150, 221, 271, 273, 275, 280, 393, 412, 490, 492–496, 498

Q
Quarry, 12, 23, 95, 221, 234, 365, 430, 492, 495
Quarry operations, 12

R
Rehabilitation, 444, 451, 455
Resource extraction, 504
Retaining wall, 259, 529
Road construction, 11, 213–215, 220–221, 330–331, 440, 446, 451, 455, 457, 459, 461, 467, 480, 505
Roadworks, 460
Rock breaking, 16

Roller, 9, 216, 252, 271, 305, 330, 358, 445, 449, 459–474, 476, 478–485, 505, 507–508

S

Safety features, 20–21, 97, 112, 114–115, 121, 131, 167, 215, 369, 388–389, 449, 454

Safety regulations, 21, 152, 227, 329, 376, 389, 391

Scraper, 19, 136–137, 151, 267, 391, 491, 504

Site preparation, 213, 505, 507

Skid loader, 26, 29

Skid steer, 9, 11, 16, 23, 26, 29–42, 49, 57–60, 62–69, 71, 73, 75, 79, 82–85, 87–91, 159, 223, 505, 535

Skid steer, 9, 11, 16, 23, 26, 29–42, 49, 57–60, 62–69, 71, 73, 75, 79, 82–85, 87–91, 159, 223, 505, 535

Skid steer loader, 11, 16, 29–30, 57–60, 67, 73, 79, 82–83, 90, 159

Slope stability, 528

Soil analysis, 446–447, 529

Soil compaction, 33, 101, 171, 331, 356, 358

Soil erosion, 448, 495, 503, 512

Soil stabilization, 441, 445–446, 448–449

Soil testing, 529

Steel structures, 225

Stockpiling, 142, 325, 512

Surface mining, 492, 494–495, 497

Surveying, 229, 526, 528

Sweeper, 151

T

Track system, 102, 223

Traffic management, 489, 498, 500–502

Trencher, 11, 18, 31, 39, 58, 81

Trenching, 12, 14, 26, 158, 160, 164–165, 189, 202–203, 220–221, 267
Trenching, 12, 14, 26, 158, 160, 164–165, 189, 202–203, 220–221, 267
Truck bed, 376
Truck body, 141, 147, 201, 266–267, 411–412
Truck speed, 344, 406, 429
Truck suspension, 405

U
Underground, 23, 53, 78, 112, 115, 193, 195, 203–205, 213–214, 235–236, 244, 246–247, 260, 388, 446, 495, 504–505, 525
Underground mining, 388, 495
Unloading, 27, 132, 210, 329, 342, 361–362, 402, 404–405, 415, 426–428, 430–431, 434–435, 489
Utility installation, 213

V
Versatility, 94, 102, 105–106, 157, 160, 162–163, 171, 212–213, 217, 221, 223, 226, 257, 330, 334–335, 365, 507, 509

W
Wheel loader, 11, 13, 94, 103–104, 107–108, 113–114, 133–134, 152–153, 158, 163

www.ingramcontent.com/pod-product-compliance
Lightning Source LLC
Chambersburg PA
CBHW072142070526
44585CB00015B/984